CHILDREN & YOUNG PEOPLE'S WORKFORCE

Early Learning & Childcare

Penny Tassoni

Kate Beith

Kath Bulman

Sue Griffin

Series Consultant:
Maureen Smith

Part of Pearson

Heinemann is an imprint of Pearson Education Limited, a company incorporated in England and Wales, having its registered office at Edinburgh Gate, Harlow, Essex, CM20 2JE. Registered company number: 872828

www.pearsonschoolsandfecolleges.co.uk
Heinemann is a registered trademark of Pearson Education Limited
Text © Pearson Education Ltd 2010
First published 2010

14 13 12 11 10
10 9 8 7 6 5 4 3 2 1

British Library Cataloguing in Publication Data
A catalogue record for this book is available from the British Library

ISBN 978-0-435-03133-6

Designed by Pearson Education Ltd
Typeset by Phoenix Photosetting
Original illustrations Harriet Stanes
Illustrated by Phoenix Photosetting/Harriet Stanes
Cover design by Woodenark
Cover photo/illustration Image Source/Howard Bartrop
Printed in Italy by Rotolito

Acknowledgements
Pearson Education Ltd would like to thank Claire Dickinson for providing all information and features relating to Functional Skills in this book.

The publisher would also like to thank the following individuals and organisations for permission to reproduce material: BSI Group (The Kitemark, p140); ©Department of Children, Schools and Families (EYFS pack cover, p226 © Crown copyright); the Food Standards Agency (The eatwell plate, p268 ©Crown copyright); Jon Mayled (guidance on dietary requirements, p270; Coeliac UK (gluten free symbol, p.270), The British Toy & Hobby Association (The Lion Mark, p.369).

Video clips first published in *Nurturing Babies and Children under Four* (978-0-435-89984-4), Sally Thomas, Heinemann, 2008 and *Introduction to Child Development DVD* (978-0-435-89982-0), Carolyn Meggitt, Heinemann, 2006

The author and publisher would like to thank the following individuals and organisations for permission to reproduce photographs: p2, p8, p208, p310 ©Pearson Education Ltd/Gareth Boden; p5, p13, p26, p31, p33, p36, p39, p42, p48, p68, p81, p82, p99, p103, p120, p152, p153, p154, p157, p181, p189, p195, p214, p216, p236, p252, p261, p321, p329, p332 ©Pearson Education Ltd/Clark Wiseman; p7 ©Jacky Chapman/Janine Wiedel/Photolibrary/Alamy; p10 ©Creatas; p16 ©Up The Banner/Shutterstock Images; p19 ©Ariel Skelley/Stone/Getty Images; p20, p50, p57, p59, p140, ©Pearson Education Ltd/Tudor Photography; p25 ©Corbis/Jennie Woodcock; p44, p65, p72, ©Jules Selmes/Pearson Education Ltd; p52, p53, p54, p55, p56(l) p56(r), p60, p147, p217, p225, p232, p239, p305, p307, p322, p406, p412 ©Pearson Education Ltd/Jules Selmes; p61 ©ajt/Shutterstock Images; p74 ©Realistic Reflections/Getty Images; p87 ©Rosemarie Gearhart/iStockphoto; p91 ©Picture Partners/Alamy; p100 ©Lisa A Svara/Shutterstock Images; p106 ©Vince Hazat/Photo Alto/Alamy; p109, p131 ©Vstock/Alamy; p115 ©Sean Locke/iStockphoto; p122 ©Ace Stock Ltd/Alamy; p124 ©Cat London/iStockphoto; p129 ©Lemoine/Science Photo Library; p134 ©Shutterstock/Lev Olkha; p135 ©Thomas M Perkins/Shutterstock Images; p137, p277, p282, p.291, p300 ©Kidsunlimited; p141 ©Shutterstock; p145 ©Lorraine Swanson/Shutterstock Images; p148 ©Alamy; p149 ©Paul Doyle/Alamy; p159 ©Eyewire; p160 ©Comstock/Punchstock; p162 ©Picture Partners/Alamy; p166, p168 Image supplied courtesy of DCSF/Kindred Agency:Victor de Jesus/UNP (01274 412222); p171 Image supplied Courtesy of DCSF/Kindred Agency:Jonathan Brady/UNP (01274 412222); p173 ©Denis Felix/Taxi/Getty Images; p183, p248 ©Pearson Education Ltd/Mind Studio; p184 ©Picture Partners/Alamy; p185 ©Photofusion Picture Library/Alamy; p187 ©Patrice Lucenet/Oredia/Retna UK; p190, p194, p210, p219, p256, p281, p312, p327, p338, p363, p374 ©Bananastock/Imagestate; p191 (from top) ©Jules Selmes/Pearson Education Ltd, ©Bananastock/Imagestate, ©JHogan/Shutterstock Images, ©Bananastock/Imagestate; p198, p.199(l) ©Getty Images; p199(r) ©Shutterstock; p200 ©Tim Ridley/Dorling Kindersley; p204 ©JHogan/Shutterstock Images; p204 ©Urban Zone/Alamy; p228 ©Gelpi/Shutterstock; p230 ©Sergey Kolodkin/Shutterstock; p245 ©Losevsky Pavel/Shutterstock Images; p249 ©Caro/Alamy; p262 ©Pearson Education Ltd./Stuart Cox; p266 ©Paul Rapson/Science Photo Library; p269 ©Kumar Sriskandan/Alamy; p273(l) ©Miramiska/Shutterstock Images; p273(r) ©Pearson Education Ltd/Lisa Payne; p283 © Persona Doll Training, 51 Granville Road, London, N12 0JH Tel: 020 8446 7056, personadoll@ukgateway.net; www.persona-doll-training.org; p284 ©Kzenon/Shutterstock Images; p286 ©jabejon/iStockphoto; p290 ©Pearson Education Ltd/Rob Judges; p295 ©MN Studio/Shutterstock Images; p314 ©Digital Vision/Rob Van Petten; p316 ©Monkey Business Images/Shutterstock Images; p324 ©Flashion Studio/Shutterstock Images; p333 © Kokhanchikov/Shutterstock Images; p348 © Eric Audras/PhotoAlto/Corbis; p350 ©dbimages/Alamy; p355 ©Stock Connection Distribution/Alamy; p358 ©Eric Gevaert/Shutterstock Images; p367, p371, p372, p375 ©Harcourt Education Ltd/Gareth Boden; p382, p384 ©Moodboard/Alamy; p382 ©Zurijeta/Shutterstock; p387 ©Will & Deni McIntyre/Science Photo Library; p392 ©Diloute/iStockphoto; p400 ©Bubbles Photolibrary/Alamy; p402 ©Alena Ozerova/Shutterstock Images.

Every effort has been made to contact copyright holders of material reproduced in this book. Any omissions will be rectified in subsequent printings if notice is given to the publishers.

All information relating to the qualification specifications was correct at the time of going to press; units may be subject to minor changes.

Websites
The websites used in this book were correct and up-to-date at the time of publication. It is essential for tutors to preview each website before using it in class so as to ensure that the URL is still accurate, relevant and appropriate. We suggest that tutors bookmark useful websites and consider enabling students to access them through the school/college intranet.

Contents

Introduction

This is an exciting time to be training for work with children and young people. You will be studying for a completely new qualification that has been developed with experts in the field, such as universities and national organisations representing children and young people. An important aspect of the development has been the involvement of employer groups including local government and employer representatives, such as the National Day Nurseries Association, Pre-School Learning Alliance and the National Childminding Association. Through their close involvement employers have been able to state exactly what is best practice in the field they cover and what they expect practitioners to learn in a new qualification for the 21st century.

This book has been written to support the Level 3 Diploma for the Children and Young People's Workforce (Early Learning and Childcare Pathway). The Diploma is based on existing National Occupational Standards and the Common Core of Skills and Knowledge for the Children's Workforce.

Studying the Diploma will help you to develop the high level of professionalism that work with children and young people requires. Although this work is responsible and demanding, it is extremely rewarding and our children and young people deserve a well-trained workforce that is able to work consistently to high standards. During your study you will gain new skills and knowledge that will help you in your everyday life as well as in your professional work with children and young people. Gaining the Diploma will open up a range of career opportunities. It will help you to work in different parts of the children and young people's workforce or to move on to higher-level training if you wish to do so.

The Diploma sets out what is best practice in the workplace as well as supporting government policy. Current government policy is bringing together services for children, young people and their carers in a much more integrated way. Working in partnership helps to safeguard children and young people and give them the very best start in life. The DCSF places positive outcomes for children and young people at the centre of its policy and the Diploma focuses more than previous qualifications on supporting children and young people to achieve the positive outcomes set out in the Every Child Matters agenda, namely:

- be healthy
- stay safe
- enjoy and achieve
- make a positive contribution
- achieve economic well-being.

The five outcomes are for every child and young person, whatever their background or circumstances. Your training will help you to support children and young people who are disadvantaged as well as those who are not.

The introduction of the Diploma has taken place at the same time as all vocational qualifications across all types of work are changing and becoming part of the Qualifications and Credit Framework (QCF). The QCF is a flexible new way of achieving qualifications. It affects the way qualifications are organised but will not make a big difference to the experience you will have of studying and being assessed. By working towards the Diploma you can be sure that you have the most up-to-date preparation for work with children and young people.

How is the Level 3 Diploma different from previous qualifications?

The Diploma brings together three specialist pathways (areas of work) into one qualification:

- Early Learning and Childcare Pathway

- Children and Young People's Social Care Pathway

- Learning, Development and Support Services Pathway (LDSS — mainly level 3 practitioners who work as learning mentors, or support Connexions advisers or educational welfare officers).

In the past there were completely different qualifications for people working in these areas of work. Having one qualification with different pathways assists the government in its aim of creating one children and young people's workforce with a shared identity and shared values and language. This means when you complete the Diploma you are more likely to see yourself as someone who is part of the wider children and young people's workforce. You will understand the specialist language that is used in different parts of the workforce, for example terms like 'assessment' might be used in different ways in a nursery education setting than in a residential childcare setting. Also, as part of the new workforce you will work towards shared principles, for example, always respecting a child or young person's background or valuing the contribution of carers.

Structure of the Level 3 Diploma

The Diploma is made up of QCF units called units of assessment. Although it is important for you to understand the structure of these units and how the qualification is made up, you will be supported by your tutors and assessors to understand what is required. All the information in this section will be explained to you in greater depth when you start your course. As you work your way through this textbook you will be able to understand what is required much more clearly.

Every learner studying for the Diploma will cover the same set of common units but will then specialise in one of the pathways listed on page vi. These specialist pathways will help you to get employment in the specific part of the children and young people's workforce covered by the Pathway.

As you will have studied a common set of units, it also means you will in the future be able to transfer more easily into different areas of work with children and young people. For example, you may start off working in early learning and childcare but then decide you want to work in children and young people's social care. Having the Diploma will help you to do this more easily than at present.

Units of assessment

These units are not the same as the occupational standards that made up NVQs, although they cover similar areas. These are easier to understand than NVQ units and more straightforward to study and assess.

Each unit has a 'level' and a credit value.

Level

The level of the unit is decided by its content. When units are given a level, the following factors are taken into account:

- depth and coverage of the subject matter
- the application of knowledge and understanding, usually in practical situations
- level of responsibility (accountability and autonomy).

Level 3 is broadly equivalent to 'A' level in the QCF. Almost all the units in the Level 3 Diploma are at level 3 as this is the level of the qualification. Some optional units are at level 4. Level 4 is equivalent to study in the first year of a university programme, and these units are for learners who might want to move to higher-level qualifications in the future. No one will be required to study at level 4; it's a matter of personal choice and what is available in local study centres.

Credit

The credit value of the units gives you an idea of the size of the unit and the length of time it will take to achieve. Credit is based on the time taken by an average learner to complete a unit and 1 credit is equivalent to about 10 hours of learning. Not all this learning time is supervised (although some will be) and it includes:

- classes
- tutorials

- practical work

- assessments.

In addition to these, however, learning time includes non-supervised activities such as homework, independent research and work experience.

When you achieve a unit the credit is 'banked' and recorded on your record.

Unit structure

Each unit has a number of learning outcomes and for each of these there are a number of assessment criteria. The learning times for the unit are based on how long it takes a learner to achieve the learning outcomes to the standard outlined in the assessment criteria. All the learning outcomes of the unit have to be assessed.

Here is an example of learning outcomes and assessment criteria.

Learning outcome	Assessment criteria
Understand the expected pattern of development for children and young people from birth to 19 years	1.1 Explain the sequence and rate of each aspect of development from birth to 19 years 1.2 Explain the difference between sequence of development and rate of development and why the difference is important

'Competence' and 'Knowledge and Understanding' Units
Units tend to be divided into units that:

- are about what you know and understand ('knowledge and understanding' units)

- include knowledge, understanding and practical skills which normally have some assessment in the workplace ('competence' units).

For example, the unit about safeguarding is all about knowing how to safeguard and protect children and young people. You need to know about this as you may come across these circumstances in your work — but as a learner you would not normally be able to show skills in this area of work as it would be undertaken by senior staff.

For many units you are required to demonstrate that you 'know and understand' and also that you have the required skills. For example, when providing activities for children's learning you would need to know:

- what activities to provide

- why you provided them

- what the benefits to children would be

- what materials and equipment to use.

You would also need to be able to demonstrate in practice that you can:

- set up activities

- encourage the children to take part

- support the children undertaking activities

- communicate effectively

- use appropriate language

- take opportunities to support and extend the child's learning

- clear away afterwards

- reflect on what the activity achieved and whether it could be improved.

You can build up your qualification by gaining individual units until you have the right number. Your tutors and assessors will help you to understand what is needed every step of the way.

The Level 3 Diploma overview

The Level 3 Diploma is made up of units of assessment which are outlined below. At the time of writing the qualification requires a minimum of 65 credits at level 3 or above.

Table 1: Everyone has to study *all* these units.

Unit title (all level 3)	Credit value	'Knowledge and Understanding' or 'Competence'
Shared Core units (SC)		
Promote communication in children's and young people's settings	3	Competence
Promote equality and inclusion in children's and young people's settings	3	Competence
Engage in personal development in children's and young people's settings	3	Competence
Principles for implementing duty of care in children's and young people's settings	1	Knowledge and Understanding
Children and Young People's Core units (CYP)		
Understand child and young person development	4	Knowledge and Understanding
Promote child and young person development	3	Competence
Understand how to safeguard the well-being of children and young people	3	Knowledge and Understanding
Support children and young people's health and safety	2	Competence
Develop positive relationships with children, young people and others involved in their care	1	Competence
Working together for the benefit of children and young people	2	Competence
Understand how to support positive outcomes for children and young people	3	Knowledge and Understanding
Total credit	**28**	

Table 2: Learners taking the Early Learning and Childcare Pathway have to undertake all these units.

Unit title	Credit value	'Knowledge and Understanding' or 'Competence'
Early Years Mandatory Pathway units (EYMP)		
Context and principles for early years provision	4	Competence
Promote learning and development in the early years	5	Competence
Promote children's welfare and well-being in the early years	6	Competence
Professional practice in early years settings	3	Competence
Support children's speech, language and communication	4	Competence
Total credit	**22**	

To make up the full Level 3 Diploma of 65 credits you will have 15 credits to 'spend' on optional units. There are more than 40 units of different credit sizes in the optional bank of units. Optional units cover many specialist areas such as disability or work with babies. What is available to you will depend on your interest and what is being offered by your centre or training provider.

Levels of literacy, numeracy and ICT

The Diploma will need people with good levels of literacy, numeracy and ICT as this is what employers require. This is to make sure, for example, that you can write accurate reports and are able to support children's learning. Your training provider will be able to advise you about this and the kinds of support available.

Study skills

In terms of the study skills you will use when undertaking the Level 3 Diploma, among other things you will need to know how to:

- read around a subject, understand it and be able to summarise and extract the key points

- use a computer and access the internet for relevant information

- research in journals, books and newspapers

- present information clearly and concisely sometimes using diagrams, graphs and pictures

- write logically and present material clearly in your own words

- reference your findings from books, journals and the internet within your assessment so that the assessor knows you have not simply invented something!

Assessment of the Level 3 Diploma

There are different assessment methods approved for use and these will be decided by your awarding organisation. They decide how to assess your learning based on the learning outcomes and assessment criteria in the unit. The awarding organisations and your assessor or tutor will provide you with help and support throughout the assessment process. Some common assessment methods are outlined below but others may be used as well:

- Knowledge, understanding and skills that are demonstrated through your practice in a work setting and directly observed by your assessor

- Evidence from an expert witness who may be an experienced practitioner who has worked alongside you, or others with suitable backgrounds who can vouch for your practice

- Questions (oral and written) and professional discussion, usually with your assessor, which allows you to discuss what you know

- Assignments and projects of different types including child studies

- Assessment of your work products such as plans, displays, child observations, materials you have made to support children

- Reflection on your practice

- Tests

- Recognised prior learning

It may be possible in some cases for you to decide how to present your evidence for assessment using various methods from this list. This is more likely in a unit that includes knowledge, understanding and skills. Sometimes your awarding organisation will insist on a specific method such as a test or an assignment. Again your tutor or assessor will provide you with help and support to decide the best approach.

Holistic assessment

Assessors of your practical skills will often work with you to assess holistically. This means that assessment may be across more than one unit and observations of your practice may fulfil part of the assessment requirements for several units. This is not always possible but assessors are skilled at making the most of holistic assessment.

It is important for you to become familiar with the requirements of each unit so that you can work with your assessors to decide on holistic assessment opportunities. This will also avoid you duplicating evidence and being assessed more than once for similar learning outcomes that sometimes appear in more than one unit.

Preparing for assessment

You will need to work closely with your assessor to ensure you are ready for assessment. It is important to be well organised and store all your evidence safely. Many people store evidence in folders to protect them. A contents list and cross-referencing system is important so you can easily find pieces of evidence. For example, if you have undertaken a reflective account of your practice that meets the needs of more than one unit, make sure you clearly cross-reference on the document itself and also in a contents list.

It is worthwhile thinking well ahead and planning what you are going to do. You can then prepare properly for the assessment. For example, if you are going to do a cooking activity with children that is to be observed by your assessor, think about what areas of your learning will be covered. It is about supporting children's knowledge and understanding of the world but also about preparing the environment, considering communication and social relationships, using maths, knowing about safety and hygiene, working to setting policies and procedures and probably many more factors as well.

Apply that principle for everything you do in relation to your learning and practical work. Get into the habit of looking for assessment opportunities in your everyday work as well as specific activities.

Apprenticeships

The Diploma will be the main qualification that apprentices will study. In order to complete a full Apprenticeship it is likely that you will also have to study extra courses but these are normally short and lead to other qualifications that will be useful for work with children and young people.

Maureen Smith
Series Consultant

How to use this book

This book contains all the core units you need to complete your Level 3 Diploma (Early Learning and Childcare Pathway) and is divided into four sections:

1. Shared Core units
2. Children and Young People's Core units
3. Early Years Mandatory Pathway units
4. Optional units (includes six of the most popular optional units)

All the chapters are matched closely to the specifications of each unit in the syllabus and follow the unit learning outcomes and assessment criteria – making it easy for you to work through the criteria and be sure you are covering everything you need to know.

Key features of the book

Reflect – provides opportunities for you to reflect on your own skills and performance; asks you to consider different ways of doing things or come up with your own solutions to potential issues.

EYFS in action – activities and suggestions for linking knowledge to the EYFS principles and guidance; designed to bring learning to life and make it relevant to your work with early years children. (For learners working in other frameworks, activities and suggestions will be relevant to your everyday practice with children.)

Over to you – short tasks to enhance your understanding of a piece of information (e.g. internet research or a practical idea you could introduce in your setting).

Case Study – real-life scenarios exploring key issues to broaden your understanding of key topics, demonstrate how theory relates to everyday practice and pose reflective questions.

Best practice checklist – checklists of key points to help you remember the main underpinning knowledge in a unit.

Key terms – important terms defined.

Skills Builder — short activities linked thematically to the unit, specifically designed to develop your professional skills.

Getting Ready for Assessment — an activity to help you generate evidence for assessment of the unit.

Functional Skills — highlights where content in the unit enables you to apply Functional Skills in the broad areas of English, ICT and Maths — matched to the latest (2009) FS Standards at level 2. The tips and explanations show how Functional Skills can be contextualized to work in early years and are of particular benefit to learners on Apprenticeship programmes.

Check Your Knowledge — at the end of each unit, these questions will help you consolidate your understanding and ensure you are ready to move on to the next unit.

Working Life — some core units in the book end with a full-page magazine-inspired feature covering a key issue or topic, with expert guidance relating to problems that may be encountered in your working life. Contains a selection of the following 'mini-features':

- **My Story** — a practitioner's personal account; sometimes inspirational or uplifting, other times sharing a problem

- **Video Corner** — opportunity to view and reflect on a short video clip contained on the **CD-ROM**

- **Ask the Expert** — Questions and answers relating to working practice

- **Viewpoint** — topical issues discussed around the wider aspects of childcare

On the CD-ROM

The free CD-ROM contains the following bonus content:

- Six video clips linked to the 'Video Corner' feature in the Working Life pages — these will support your knowledge and understanding of some of the key topics and give further insight into working life in early years settings

- Key terms — all the key terms found in the book are listed on a pdf document. Save this Glossary on your computer and have it at your fingertips whenever you need to refer to any key terms.

- Links to useful websites — live links that will take you at the click of a mouse to many of the related websites referred to in the book, and to additional sources of useful information that will help you with your assignments or research.

Shared Core Units

SC1 Promote communication

SC2 Promote equality & inclusion

SC3 Engage in personal development

SC4 Principles for implementing duty of care

Promote communication

Communication is an essential part of working with other adults and children in the early years sector. In this unit, you will learn the fundamentals of how to communicate with children and their families and also with colleagues and other adults.

Learning outcomes:

By the end of this unit you will:

1. Understand why effective communication is important in the work setting

2. Be able to meet the communication and language needs, wishes and preferences of individuals

3. Be able to overcome barriers to communication

4. Understand principles and practices relating to confidentiality.

Understand why effective communication is important in the work setting

We are working in a sector that is mainly about relationships and, as relationships and communication skills are closely linked, all practitioners have to be good communicators. This learning outcome looks at the importance of effective communication in work settings.

Reasons why people communicate

There are a variety of reasons why people communicate in work settings. The spider diagram shows some of the key reasons:

Building relationships

When a new parent, child, young person or practitioner joins our setting, the first thing that will happen is some form of communication. This might be a smile, wave or a friendly 'hello'. With this first burst of communication, we are beginning to build a relationship.

Maintaining relationships

When we are working, we may not realise it, but we are in the process of maintaining relationships. Each time we say 'hello' to someone we know or 'goodbye' we are maintaining our relationship with them. The maintenance of relationships accounts for much of our language and communication use although it does not strictly have a professional 'purpose', that is, smiling across at someone, asking if someone had a good holiday.

Gaining and sharing information

We need to gain and share information in work settings not only with children, young people and their families, but with colleagues and other professionals. The information that we gain and share will help us in the way that we work.

Gaining reassurance and acknowledgement

Some of the communication between humans is about gaining and providing reassurance or acknowledgement. With children and young people, we may praise them, give them physical reassurance or acknowledge them by providing eye contact or taking an interest in what they

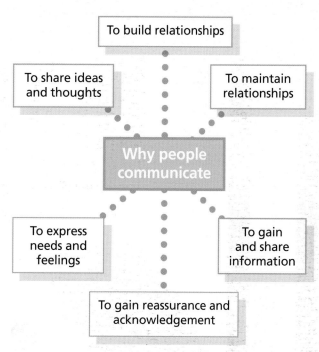

Reasons why people communicate

are doing. In effective work settings, colleagues also reassure and acknowledge each other.

Expressing needs and feelings

As humans we are emotional beings; this means that most of us will need to express our needs and feelings and also be there to allow children and young people to do the same. Children and young people who do not have opportunities to do this can become very frustrated and also isolated.

Sharing ideas and thoughts

Humans are also creative which means that adults, children and young people will have ideas and thoughts that they need to share with others.

Communication affects relationships in the work setting

In order to work effectively with children, young people and their families, and so that we can plan for and meet their needs, it is essential to establish good relationships with a range of people. Relationships and communication skills go hand in hand. Practitioners who have good communication skills are likely to have strong relationships with children, parents and other adults. This is because relationships are influenced by the body language, facial expressions and ways in which others listen and talk to you, that is, the way they communicate (see Unit CYP3.5, section on establishing relationships with children and others).

The spider diagram below shows some of the ways in which professional relationships and communication are pivotal in the early years sector.

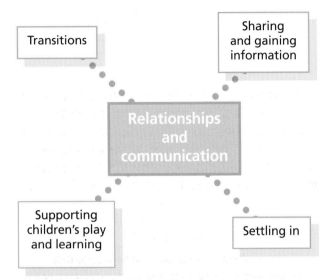

Professional relationships and communication are pivotal in the early years sector

Sharing and gaining information

To work effectively, we will need to gain and share information. This might be routine information about how a child is feeling, what play interests they have or it might be information to do with their long-term health and welfare, such as a referral to a speech and language therapist. The sharing and gaining of information will be a feature of our work with children, parents, colleagues and other adults.

Settling in

Children will find it hard to settle in unless they feel comfortable with us. This means that we need to quickly find ways of communicating with them and building a relationship. Parents, too, will find it hard to leave their children unless they have total confidence and trust in us. This again is about communication and relationships.

Supporting children's play and learning

Children can settle into play and learn more effectively when they are relaxed. This is linked to the quality of relationships that adults have with them. They also will

benefit more from play and learning activities, if adults can communicate effectively and so help them to build vocabulary, develop concepts and express ideas.

Transitions

There will be times when children move between different settings, for example moving from nursery to school. Some children may also move between different settings and carers during a day. These transitions are made easier when the adults involved have a good relationship with each other and also share information effectively.

Effective teams

Many of us will work alongside different colleagues. For teams to work well together, it is essential that our relationships with them are strong and professional. The quality of relationships with our colleagues can be enhanced or threatened by the way that we talk to them, react to their suggestions and the tone of voice that we use. When relationships break down in professional teams, children, young people and their families are likely to receive a less effective service.

Be able to meet the communication and language needs, wishes and preferences of individuals

Everyone has a slightly different style of communicating; it makes each of us unique. This learning outcome looks at the different ways in which children and adults communicate. It also considers some of the skills behind successful communication.

Establishing language needs, wishes and preferences of individuals

Communication is a two-way process. Effective communication requires everyone involved to be able to express their own thoughts and messages and to understand the communication of others. In some ways, our job is to ensure that we find ways of making this happen. Language needs and preferences can be quite wide-ranging. Someone may require an interpreter or signer, or someone else may need communication to take place in a certain way, such as in a quiet environment or at a slower pace.

Adults

When working with adults, we can often ask directly about how to *facilitate* communication or work out for ourselves that a person cannot speak English. It is also important to establish the level of formality required. Not everyone wants to be called by their first name and some people prefer to make appointments with specific times rather than to 'turn up'.

It is also useful to be aware that written communications can be daunting for some people. A home-setting link book is an excellent idea, but will only work if parents are comfortable with reading and writing.

Children

It can be challenging to decide the best way to communicate with children. For example, babies and very

Communication can be challenging

young children will still be developing speech and so talk alone will not work. This is why we use strong facial expressions and gestures and point to things, so that the baby or toddler is more likely to understand what we are saying. We also have to learn to interpret what a baby is trying to communicate when crying or what a toddler is trying to express when pointing to some objects.

Factors to consider when promoting effective communication

There are many factors to consider when communicating with others. The starting point is to consider which communication method to use as it is essential to choose the right style of communication. In many cases, we will use face-to-face interaction, but this is not always the case. Table 1 shows different ways in which we may communicate.

Other factors to consider

Most of our interactions are likely to be face to face. There are some specific factors to consider when using this method.

Environment

To help communication, it is important that we think about location. It is much more difficult to exchange personal information in busy, noisy environments. This means that we need to think about the environment that we provide when communicating. For parents and young people, we may sometimes require a quiet place whereas with toddlers and young children, we may need to create cosy and homely places.

Proximity, orientation and posture

These three factors are very important in setting the style of a face-to-face communication and it is important that you are sensitive to them.

● Proximity is about the distance between you and the person you are communicating with. Babies and children who you have a strong relationship with will benefit from you being very close to them, but this may not be the same for children who do not know you or who are shy. This is because being too close to someone that you do not know is usually thought to be intimidating. As with many aspects of communication, there are cultural differences to be aware of. You need

Table 1: Communication types and uses

Type	Purpose	Comments
Face-to-face interactions	Conversations where both people can respond quickly	Useful for sharing and giving information as it is possible to see another person's reaction. May not always be best for conveying complex information that someone else needs time to consider or see written down e.g. in order to make decisions.
Phone	Conversation when someone is not available to speak face to face.	Can be difficult to interpret the other person's reactions and also hard to assess if they have understood your meaning. Choice of words and tone become very important. Phone conversations do allow for quick responses. In some situations notes should be taken at the time of a call so that a record can be made. If this is appropriate, remember to record the date and time of the call.
Sign language	A language that allows a deaf person to communicate	British sign language is a recognised language and allows someone to communicate fully. If you do not use sign language, you would need to find an interpreter.
Written communications (see also Unit CYP3.6 for tips on how to write reports)		
Letters and memos	Written way of conveying information or sending messages	Useful as it allows the reader to take time and absorb the information. Also likely to be kept. Style and tone has to be thought about so as to avoid misunderstandings.
Emails	Electronic way of sending notes and letters	Useful if a more relaxed style is needed. Be aware that not everyone will have access to a computer or will store/print out emails. This can mean that no records will be automatically kept by the other person.
Reports	A formal way of presenting information	Useful for providing information that has to be structured and 'professional'. Reports need to be accurate and should be dated. Language needs to be formal which may be a barrier for some parents.
Other communication methods		
Makaton	Gestures that support the spoken word. Used to help children and adults who find it hard to understand or process the spoken word	Needs to be used with clear speech and strong facial expression. Most Makaton users, including children, may develop their own variations of the signs, and so getting to know 'their style' can be helpful.
Visual images including pictures and photographs	Visual images can aid understanding	Visual images can help babies and young children to communicate but also understand what we are saying. Signs and cartoons can be useful ways of reminding adults.
Audio/visual recordings	Used so that parents and others can 'see' or 'hear' children in action	Audio/visual recordings can be used to help parents 'see' or 'hear' their children and so provide a way of sharing information with them.

Functional Skills

It is clear from this table that your communication skills are vital. Practising these functional skills means you will be able to develop your ability in each of these different areas of communication.

Why does this matter?

Considering which style of communication will be the most effective is important not only for working with children, but also for working with parents, other professionals and colleagues. You will need to refer to Table 1 when you complete Unit CYP3.6.

Signing with a deaf child

to be observant and notice whether someone tries to move back a little from you or seems to need to be closer.

- Orientation relates to your body's position. If you are directly opposite someone, it sends out different signals from if you are to the side of them. When working with children, you may find that you automatically tend to turn inwards a little so as to create a cosier atmosphere. Being slightly at an angle when communicating with an adult can also be helpful, as it means that either of you can break off eye contact and it allows the communicating style to be less direct.

- Posture is important whether or not you are standing or sitting. The trick for good communication is to think about whether you are giving out 'bored' signals or 'interested' ones. Leaning forward slightly in a chair shows, for example, that you are interested, while leaning backwards may make the other person think that you are bored.

Listening skills

The term 'active listening' is often used to describe the way in which good communicators do not just listen, but think about what they are hearing and also observe closely the body language, gesture and other signals that are sent out by the child or adult. Active listening requires

that you give your full attention to the other person and focus on not just what they are saying but *how* they say it. Active listening is essential when encouraging young children's speech and also when dealing with potentially difficult situations with other adults.

Time

Both adults and children need opportunities to think about how to respond in a conversation and also what they wish to communicate. Allowing sufficient time for this can be vital, particularly when communicating with young children, but also if giving adults information that is complex or unexpected.

Communication methods and styles

Effective face-to-face communication requires significant skill. We have seen already some of the factors that can enhance this. For this assessment criterion, you will need to show that you can communicate in ways that meet individual needs. To do this you will need to consider both verbal and non-verbal communication methods.

Non-verbal communication

This is the umbrella term used to describe all communications that are not oral. We know that non-verbal communication is powerful and is often more important than the language that is used.

Eye contact

Our eyes are powerful tools when we are interacting with someone, and some eye contact is usual when communicating with others. As eye contact is powerful, it is important not to stare or be too intense as this can feel threatening. With babies and young children who do not know you, it can be worth simply gazing across them

Eye contact is a powerful tool, especially with young children

Many hand gestures are not universal across languages

rather than making direct eye contact at first. The level of eye contact can vary from culture to culture and it is important to be sensitive to this.

Touch

Everyone varies in how much touch and physical reassurance they find comfortable. This can be cultural, but it may also be linked to personality, family lifestyle and religion. With babies and young children, touch can be important in making them feel comfortable, but it should be offered, rather than forced on a child; for example, you may put out a hand to see if the child is interested, but then be ready to withdraw it if the child seems unsure or shows in any way that this is not needed. If you are someone who is 'tactile', it will be important not to make the assumption that others will want to be touched. Touch must also be considered in relation to child protection as it must be appropriate. (See also Unit CYP3.3.)

Physical gestures

Gestures are a way of helping our words come to life. Gesturing is particularly important when working with babies, toddlers or anyone who may have a difficulty in understanding the meaning of our words. Most gestures are helpful in communication terms, unless they are used to show aggression such as pointing or jabbing your finger at someone. While hand movements can be used to clarify or help with meaning, it is worth noting that many hand gestures are not universal across languages. A good example of this is the 'o' sign made between thumb and index finger. Many English speakers will see this as a sign that something is good or spot on, but in other languages it is used to convey a zero and so has the opposite meaning! As with other areas of communication, it is important to avoid making assumptions that things have universal meaning.

Body language

Body movements and gestures can reflect our moods. A child who sucks their thumb may be indicating that they are tired or nervous, while an adult who is tapping their fingers on a desk sends outs 'I'm bored' or 'I'm frustrated' signals. Our arm movements are also important. Crossed arms are usually interpreted as meaning that you are unsure or irritated, whereas open body language — hands by the side, for example — may signal that someone is feeling relaxed. Ideally, we should avoid crossing our arms when communicating as it can make the atmosphere tense.

Reading someone's body language is a skill which, of course, becomes easier as you get to know how they react in different situations. This is why we ask parents when their child first joins us to share their knowledge about the way in which their child communicates.

Facial expression

Facial expression is a strong element in communication. People can show a lot of feelings through their faces and a good communicator will not only notice these in other people, but will also be aware of their own. With young children, high levels of facial expression are required so they can interpret what we are saying or to help them maintain interest. With adults, it is important to show through our facial expression that we are interested in them and are thinking about what they are saying or trying to convey.

Smiling is a particularly essential facial expression that conveys warmth, but also a 'peace' message. Smiling when you first meet children and adults is particularly important as first impressions can influence later communication. People who smile are more likely to find that others warm to them and also smile back.

Verbal communication

Vocabulary

Everyone has words and expressions that they can understand and use. With children, young people and also adults who may have English as an additional language, it is essential that we use words and expressions that they can understand. This means not using jargon when talking to parents or modifying our vocabulary to ensure that young children can understand it. With babies, toddlers and children who may have a speech delay, it is important to supplement the spoken word with visual clues by, for example, pointing at the object that we are talking about or using gestures.

Linguistic tone

Tone of voice is stronger than the words that are actually said both in face-to-face interactions as well as those on the phone. Voice tones can say a lot about what someone is really thinking. Interestingly, babies and

children are very sensitive to tone of voice and a baby will become distressed if there are hard or angry tones. Good communicators use warm tones and do this by thinking warm thoughts. Smiling as you talk on the telephone will, for example, give you a warmer tone of voice.

It is also worth noting that the rise and fall of our speech patterns can alter according to the language that is being used. Many English speakers will find that their voice drops down at the end of a sentence, while in other languages it may rise. As tone can help people to understand the meaning of what we say, we need to be aware of this and listen more attentively to those who do not speak English as a first language. We may also need to repeat, slow down or 'recast' sentences when we are speaking so we can check that the other person understands us.

Pitch

Pitch is linked to the tone of our voice although is about how high our voice sounds. Babies and toddlers seem to find it easier to understand us when our pitch is higher, while older children and adults may find a higher pitch voice irritating.

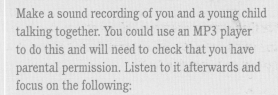

Over to you

Make a sound recording of you and a young child talking together. You could use an MP3 player to do this and will need to check that you have parental permission. Listen to it afterwards and focus on the following:

– your tone of voice

– how much time you allow for the child to respond.

Functional Skills

English: Speaking, listening and communication

By making this recording you will be able to practise your aural skills with children. Remember to think carefully about presenting your information in a clear and concise way so that the child understands and always listen carefully to their response.

Appropriate responses

Good communicators constantly monitor the reactions of others during face-to-face interactions in order to adjust their own body language, facial expression and tone of voice. With young children, we may at times mirror the signals that they give out so that they can see that we are trying to understand them, for example a toddler might giggle and so we might smile and giggle back.

With adults, responding according to what we are observing is equally important. If an adult seems surprised at something in the conversation, we might need to clarify what we have said, while an upset reaction might mean that we should change our tone of voice and consider how best to show empathy. We often do this automatically. Carrying on and ignoring reactions to what we have said — or our style of communication — is not an option!

Be able to overcome barriers to communication

Communication is not always straightforward. Here we look at the reasons for difficulties in communication and focus on ways in which they may be overcome.

The effects of different backgrounds and factors on communication

Communication is about sharing, whether this is a joke or information. Where people have the same shared experiences, they interpret things in similar although not identical ways and this makes communication much easier. This is the essence of why a family member may say a word that will make the rest of the family laugh, but a visitor will remain puzzled. A key point to remember, when thinking about effective communication, is that some people's experiences will be very different from your own on account of their childhood, culture, family background or linguistic knowledge. This means that you cannot take for granted that your viewpoint or style of communication will always be effective. We will consider now some of the factors that affect everyone's communication.

Children's experience depends partly on culture and family background

Culture and family background

Culture and family background affects the way people use the methods of communication that we looked at in the previous learning outcome. For example, eye contact may not be as common in some cultures as in others or may be interpreted differently.

Family background

Family background makes a difference, and every family has their own way of communicating together. Some children, for example, will have heard swearing at home; others may be hearing more than one language. Some children may be in a vibrant and noisy home while others may have a family that is quiet in style. This affects children's communication but later also affects the way that they will communicate as adults.

Personality

Adult and children's personalities can affect the style in which they communicate. Early on, we can often spot children who are more outgoing even when they have not yet developed language. Recognising that personality can affect communication is important as often an adult or child who seems unenthusiastic may simply not enjoy talking in a group or communicating with unfamiliar people.

Confidence and self-esteem

Confidence and self-esteem are key factors in the style and methods in which people communicate. This may be for a variety of reasons, but previous experience plays an important part. For example, a child who was mocked because of something that they wrote incorrectly may become the adult who avoids writing; whereas a child who was listened to carefully may become the adult who is confident to voice an opinion.

Literacy

Reading and writing involve literacy skills. Some people have acquired these to a high level but others may struggle for a variety of reasons. This can be the result of specific learning difficulties or because they are using a language in which they are not yet fluent.

ICT knowledge

Sending and receiving emails, accessing photos and film clips and even having internet phone conversations requires a level of ICT knowledge. As with literacy, people will have different competencies and so may or may not feel comfortable with this media. It is also important to remember that some aspects of ICT may require high levels of literacy skills, such as the ability to read an email or follow written instructions to access websites and so on.

Overcoming barriers to effective communication

Communication is sometimes seen as a cycle with definitive steps. This model can help us to identify some common reasons as to why there may be barriers to communication.

Possible barriers

At each stage of the communication process there are potential pitfalls which will disrupt the smooth flow of communication. Table 2 shows some of these.

| Stage 1: Information: the sender has to decide what needs to be conveyed |

↓

| Stage 2: Encoding: the sender chooses a method of communication e.g. face to face, telephone, facial expression |

↓

| Stage 3: Transfer of information: the message is transmitted e.g. the sender smiles or begins to talk |

↓

| Stage 4: Reception: the recipient receives the message from the sender e.g. the recipient notices that someone is smiling in her direction or listens to what is being said |

↓

| Stage 5: Decoding of information: the recipient now needs to interpret the message e.g. the recipient realises that the sender is sympathetic or the recipient understands the words |

↓

| Stage 6: Feedback: the recipient may show some reaction e.g. smile. Note that the sender will not always see the initial feedback especially if the communication is not face to face |

↓

| Stage 7: Response: the recipient may respond and so the cycle will continue |

Stages of communication

Reflect

Most people in their professional or personal life have experienced communications that have been disrupted because of some of the barriers shown in Table 2.

Reflect on your experience of communication in your professional life. Think about a recent experience when communication has not been straightforward. Identify the possible barriers that contributed to this.

Functional Skills

ICT: Developing, presenting and communicating information

English: Writing

After thinking about the question in the Reflect feature, you could present your findings in a table. Create a table in Word with three columns. The headings could be: 'Recent communication experience'; 'The barriers to communication were…'; and 'I could resolve this in the future by…'. Then you should complete the table with your recent communication experience.

Table 2: Potential barriers to effective communication

Stage	Barriers and difficulties
Information	Sender may have language difficulties and find it hard to express themselves in oral or written forms Sender may not be aware of others' needs
Encoding	Sender may choose an inappropriate method of communication e.g. sending out a formal letter rather than 'having a word' Sender may have difficulty in choosing appropriate words/language or use an inappropriate style or tone Sender may write illegibly Sender may have language difficulties and find it hard to express themselves
Transfer	Background noise may interfere with transfer process Post may go missing Emails may not be received Verbal and written messages sent via children may go astray Verbal messages sent by another adult may be embellished or distorted Voice mail or phone message may not be picked up by recipient
Reception	Hearing difficulties may prevent a recipient of communication from picking up the spoken word Visual impairment may prevent a recipient from picking up facial expressions, gestures or anything that has been written down A recipient may not realise that the communication was intended for them e.g. that a sign on the wall applied to them
Decoding	Recipient may not understand or interpret correctly the message that is being conveyed because of language difficulties, the medium in which it has been sent or the style/tone that has been used Recipient may not have sufficient time/experience to fully understand the message and so may misunderstand its meaning Recipient's past experiences influence the way that they decode and interpret messages e.g. a note from the nursery asking a parent to make an appointment may make the recipient assume that there is a problem based on previous experience Recipient's relationship with the sender will influence the way that messages are decoded e.g. message from someone who is liked may be received differently than from a stranger Recipient may be distressed or distracted and so not absorb all or some of the information
Feedback	Sender may not see feedback and realise that there are any difficulties with the way that they have communicated Recipient may not show much facial expression or be slow to do so Sender may incorrectly interpret the reaction of recipient
Response	Sender may not send back a response because message has not been received or is misunderstood Sender may respond negatively as meaning of communication is not clear or style of communication is inappropriate

Strategies to overcome barriers with communication

We have seen that there are many reasons why communication may be problematic. Below are some strategies that might be used to overcome any barriers to communication (see also the section on extra services/support on page 14).

Time

Make sure that you allow sufficient time when communicating — whether face to face or in phone conversations. Rushed conversations can mean that the recipient does not have enough time to process information or respond. It can also make them feel unimportant. Time will be a key factor when dealing with difficult situations, for example a parent who wishes to make a complaint about the service, or a child is upset.

Speaking clearly

Clear speech is obvious, but can make a significant difference to children and parents who do not have full hearing or who have language needs. It is also important for children and parents to be able to see your face clearly — facial expression is a key factor in communication.

Do not make assumptions

Assumptions can lead to problems. Do not assume, for example, that everyone can read English or finds it easy to write. In the same way, assuming that everyone knows the 'jargon' or the routine of the setting is dangerous. It is also important to be aware that post does go astray, emails do slip out of systems and so, if written methods of communication are used, check that they have arrived. Consider, too, whether the font size or style will help those with visual impairment.

Thinking about the environment can make children feel more secure

Adapting the environment

Creating a good environment can help to communication and break down barriers. Think about how to make an area comfortable, warm and, if necessary, private. Small spaces can make people, especially children, feel more secure.

Clarifying misunderstandings

Misunderstandings can happen too easily because there are many things that can affect the communication process. As misunderstandings can soon escalate, it is essential that they are picked up quickly. Observing people's reactions closely during face-to-face communication is a key way in which misunderstandings can be quickly noticed and then clarified. In the same way, noticing that a person on the phone seems quiet, or their tone of voice has changed abruptly, may also indicate potential difficulties.

Once a misunderstanding becomes apparent there are several things that we could consider.

Modifying or changing our tone/style

Sometimes misunderstandings occur because while the words said or written are in themselves clear, the style of delivery is not working, for example we may say to a parent that their child has settled in, but if our voice does not seem enthusiastic, the parent may not believe us or think that there is a problem.

Changing the medium of communication

If you can detect misunderstandings, it might be that you have to look for an alternative medium of communication. Instead of emailing someone, you might instead suggest a face-to-face conversation at a time suitable to them.

Checking understanding

A good strategy during verbal communication, such as face-to-face exchanges or on the phone, is to check that we have understood what someone has said. The conversation below shows how this might be done:

Child: 'Want that. Me want!'

Practitioner: 'So you want the ball, do you?'

Child: (*Nods*)

With adults, our style might change and we may use phrases such as: 'Can I just check that I understand this...'

Simplifying language

Practitioners also need to know when to simplify their language, especially if they are talking to children or parents who may not have English as a fluent language. We also need to be aware that not everyone has the jargon of our profession. EYFS, EAL and CAF mean nothing to someone who is not working in the sector. Simplifying language is therefore important.

Visual aids

Words alone can sometimes be hard to process. This means that it can be useful, especially when working with children, to point to things or use visual props or pictures alongside speech. We might, for example, show parents a film clip of their child to help them understand what we are saying about their child's progress or difficulty in an area.

Apology

Sometimes, it is important to apologise if there have been misunderstandings. Perhaps you have not used the appropriate tone or style of communication or insufficient time was available. A prompt and sincere apology can diffuse situations and it is also useful to be aware that misunderstandings can affect the long-term relationship that we might have with someone.

Extra support or services to enable individuals to communicate effectively

There will be times when extra support is needed in order to have meaningful communication with a child or an adult or to meet their needs. These include:

- translation and interpreting services
- speech and language services
- advocacy services.

Translation and interpreting services

Many documents will not be accessible if someone who cannot read English is given them. To facilitate written communication, settings may use the services of a **translator**. Translators may also be helpful if parents or others want to show us something that has been written in the language that they are using.

In addition, many settings will also find from time to time that they need the services of a signer or **interpreter** to facilitate spoken communication. Ideally, for sensitive matters, a professional signer or interpreter should be used as they have been trained to translate the message, but not to embellish or distort it. They have also been trained not to voice their opinion or change the nature of what the other person is trying to communicate. It is useful when working with signers or interpreters to find out whether they need any prior information to support their work. It can be helpful, for example, for them to have an explanation of any 'jargon' or to see ahead of time anything that will be read out.

Speech and language services

There may be times when we might need the support of speech and language services such as a speech therapist in order to help us find ways of communicating with children and young people. They may provide suggestions and guidance as to how to use resources such as the **Picture Exchange Communication System (PECS)** or training in visual systems such as **Makaton**.

Key terms

Translation: switching a written text into another written or spoken language

Interpreting: translating a language, while it is being spoken, into another language

Key terms

Picture Exchange Communication System (PECS): a resource that helps children communicate by exchanging pictures with adults

Makaton: a system of signs that help children understand the meaning of words and phrases

Advocacy services

We have a duty under the United Nations Convention on the Rights of the Child to ensure that children can be consulted about matters that are important to them. In order for this to take place, there will be times when advocacy services are used. A child or young person might be assigned an advocate whose task is specifically to reflect their best interest and to relay back to others the feelings and needs of the child or young person. The use of advocates is essential for children or young people who are in local authority care or for children or young people with communication difficulties.

Over to you

Every area will have a range of services and a protocol for contacting them. Find out how you would access the services mentioned above in your area.

Understand principles and practices relating to confidentiality

Confidentiality is about trust. As we want parents, carers, children and other professionals to share information with us, it is essential that we are able to keep it confidential. This learning outcome looks at the principles of keeping information confidential and reasons why occasionally confidentiality may be broken.

What is meant by confidentiality?

Confidentiality is about respecting other people's rights to privacy and keeping safe the information that they have provided. When working with children and young people, there will be times when parents, colleagues or even children themselves will give us information that is not intended to be shared around. Sometimes this information may be of a personal nature or simply not relevant to other people. Information of this kind is called 'confidential' and as professionals we are expected to recognise situations when information is likely to be confidential and to ensure that such information is not passed on to others. As a general rule, you should consider that all information gained during the course of your work is confidential; this means anything that you would not be able to find out as a member of the public is likely to be confidential. In addition, most settings now have a confidentiality policy and you must read and follow it.

Data protection

The importance of confidentiality is taken so seriously that there is legislation in place that covers all information that is stored.

Data Protection Act 1998

The keeping of records, storing of data and passing of information is actually strictly regulated by the Data Protection Act 1998. The Act covers both paper-based and electronic records. The Act is designed to prevent confidential and personal information from being passed on without a person's consent. This Act originally applied only to information that was stored on computers, but it has been updated to include any personal information that is stored, whether on paper or electronically.

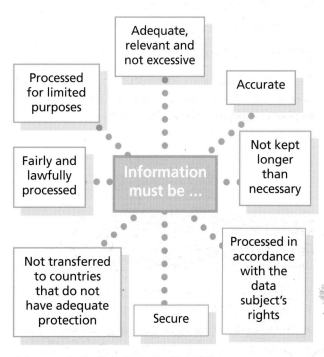

Adherence to the Data Protection Act 1998

Under the Act, organisations that collect and store information must register with the Data Protection Commission. Anyone processing information must also comply with the eight enforceable principles of practice shown on page 15. In terms of working with children and their families, this means that most information that is collected and held in an early years setting will be confidential. It also means that you need to have systems in place to make sure that information is up to date and that access is secure. For further information about the Data Protection Act visit: www.ico.gov.uk

It is vital to create back-up copies of your files

Over to you

- Is your setting registered with the Data Protection Commission?
- What type of personal information does your setting hold with the permission of parents?
- How do you ensure that records are kept up to date, secure and accurate?

Ways to maintain confidentiality in day-to-day communication

Every day you will gain and share a variety of information. Some of this will be orally transmitted and some written. It is important that you think about how you are maintaining the confidentiality of this information.

Paper-based documentation

Observations, children's drawings, and letters from parents are likely to be paper based. Paper-based documentation needs to be stored carefully to avoid being lost, torn, stolen or photocopied by others. It is usual to store paper-based information in separate folders and in a locked cabinet. This works well only if there are lots of key holders and if the keys are not left in the cabinet!

It is also important not to leave paper-based documents lying around for anyone to see. Many settings also prevent staff from taking home any records to avoid their loss or to prevent breach of confidentiality as a person's partner, friends or children could get to see them.

Electronic-based documentation

Increasingly, we are storing photos, film clips as well as emails and electronic profiles on computers, laptops and other devices such as memory sticks or portable hard drives. As with paper-based documentation, it is important to have good security which may include passwords for computers and particular folders. It is also important that passwords are not pasted onto the computers or are so obvious that anyone can have access to them.

Just as paper-based documentation can be accidentally torn, electronic records can be affected by viruses. This means that it is important to back up copies of essential documents and that the computer system is regularly screened. Finally, it is worth remembering that a computer screen may be visible to others and so, if you leave on a computer or other device, you should first close documents that are sensitive.

Why does this matter?

You will need to show for this learning outcome and also for part of Unit CYP3.6 that you have a good understanding of these issues and can demonstrate that you know how to store and maintain records appropriately.

Case study: Contact details are confidential

Erdem's mother wants to invite another mother to a party but cannot find her telephone number. She asks Janice, the nursery assistant, whether she could please just pop into the office and get it for her. Janice can see that this is a genuine request as Erdem's mother does know the other parent's address.

1. What should Janice do?
2. Explain why it is important that confidentiality is upheld.
3. Consider what Janice should say to Erdem's mother.

Maintaining the confidentiality of oral information

Much information that we share and gain orally is likely to be confidential. There are some obvious things that you should do to maintain the confidentiality of this type of information:

- follow the procedures of your setting
- think about whether you are being overheard by others as you are talking
- think about whether you are meant to be sharing the information — if in doubt, don't!
- avoid gossiping.

Tensions between maintaining confidentiality and disclosing concerns

While parents and children have the right to confidentiality, there are occasions when the need to maintain confidentiality might be breached. This could include:

- where there are concerns about a child's welfare, for example abuse
- where a child or young person is suspected of committing abuse
- where a crime has been committed.

Breaching confidentiality is a serious matter, so it is important that you follow the procedures laid down in your setting regarding such situations. Information should be passed quickly and directly to the person in another organisation that has responsibility for dealing with such concerns. In this way partial confidentiality is retained so that other members of staff, parents etc. will not necessarily know anything about the concerns that have been raised.

Why does this matter?

Knowing what to do when there are reasons to breach confidentiality is important. You will need to understand the procedures in your setting so that if a situation arose you would know how to handle this. To whom would you report any concerns? What is the procedure in your setting? Knowing this is a requirement of this learning outcome but also part of CYP3.6.

Handling data according to agreed procedures

Some of our work with children might include collecting official data and statistics. This type of work falls under the remit of the Data Protection Act and so it is essential to carefully follow the requirements of the Act. So many settings will collect data about children's ethnicity, family income and, in schools for example, about children's achievement in the EYFS profile. This data is usually collated in some way and can be sent on to local authorities and government departments. It is essential that data collection is done with the consent of parents and is carried out accurately. As with every aspect of our work with children, data needs to be stored in ways that protect confidentiality.

Best practice checklist: Confidentiality

✓ Do not gossip about children or their families either inside or outside your workplace.

✓ Never give children and families' contact details to others without parental consent, unless requested by the police or social services to do so.

✓ Keep written information in a secure place.

✓ Do not leave notes or observations about children lying about.

✓ Find out about and follow your setting's policy about confidentiality.

Check your knowledge

1. Identify three reasons why people may communicate in the work setting.

2. Explain three factors to consider when promoting effective communication.

3. Explain why eye contact is important when communicating.

4. Why is it important to be aware of linguistic pitch when communicating?

5. Identify three barriers to communication.

6. Describe how misunderstandings can be clarified.

7. Give two examples of extra support that might be used to help communication.

8. Why is maintaining confidentiality essential in the work setting?

9. Describe three ways in which confidentiality can be maintained in the work setting.

10. Explain a circumstance in which confidentiality may be breached.

Promote equality & inclusion

Any form of work with fellow human beings must be underpinned by values which are clearly understood and shared by all practitioners. Promoting equality of opportunity and inclusion upholds the rights of children to fair chances in life, and so is at the heart of work with children and families.

Learning outcomes:

By the end of this unit you will:

1. Understand the importance of diversity, equality and inclusion

2. Be able to work in an inclusive way

3. Be able to promote diversity, equality and inclusion.

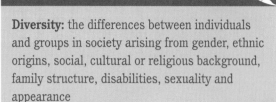

Understand the importance of diversity, equality and inclusion

When children spend time in settings which promote diversity, equality of opportunity and inclusion, they are able to make progress in all areas of development, in an emotionally secure and supportive environment. These principles are such an important aspect of practice in working with children because, without them, children's life chances are jeopardised.

What we mean by diversity, equality and inclusion

Our society is made up of people with a wide range of characteristics and backgrounds. This **diversity** contributes strength to a community, but sadly it is often perceived as a problem. You can help children to see diversity in a positive light.

> **Key term**
>
> **Diversity:** the differences between individuals and groups in society arising from gender, ethnic origins, social, cultural or religious background, family structure, disabilities, sexuality and appearance

The children you work with throughout your career will come from a variety of social and cultural backgrounds and live in families which have a wide range of lifestyles. Exploring the diversity in our society enables you to understand and value the individuality of each child; as the EYFS emphasises, each is 'A Unique Child'.

Seeing each child as an individual will enable you to promote their right to have access to **equality of opportunity** and to be treated with **equal concern** so they are able to progress along the pathway of development and learning.

To promote the positive aspects of diversity and to offer children equal chances in life, all settings for children should work towards **inclusion**.

Each child is a Unique Child

> **Key terms**
>
> **Equality of opportunity:** each individual in society experiences opportunities to achieve and flourish which are as good as the opportunities experienced by other people
>
> **Equal concern:** taking as much care to promote the opportunities and progress of one child as you do for any other child
>
> **Inclusion:** a process of identifying, understanding and breaking down barriers to participation and belonging (definition developed by the Early Childhood Forum – see http://www.ncb.org.uk/dotpdf/open_access_2/earlyyears_inclusion_20080228.pdf)

Effects of discrimination

Significant barriers to inclusion are **discrimination** and prejudice.

Differences between people can become a source of suspicion and antagonism, may lead to divisions and conflict in society, and may give rise to **prejudice**.

Key terms

Discrimination: treating someone less or more favourably than other people, because they or their family are seen as belonging to a particular group in society

Prejudice: a judgement or opinion, often negative, of a person or group, made without careful consideration of accurate relevant information, which may lead to the view that some people are inferior to other human beings, and of less worth and significance

Prejudice can damage self-esteem

Prejudice can result in assumptions such as:

- some people (as defined by their skin colour, gender, impairment, sexuality or appearance) are of less value, or are inferior to, or of less worth or significance than others
- some people (as defined by their skin colour, gender or impairment) are less capable than others
- one culture or religion or social group is superior to another, embodying the 'right' way to live
- if a family is not a two-parent nuclear family, with parents of different genders and the same ethnicity, it is not 'normal'.

Prejudice has harmful effects. When children experience prejudiced attitudes, there is a danger of damage to their self-image, self-esteem and self-confidence. Prejudice leads to discrimination.

Even very young children can experience discrimination as the result of:

- the colour of their skin and other aspects of their ethnicity
- the traditions and way of life of their family, arising from culture and religion
- their disability
- their gender
- their social background — the class or socio-economic group of their family
- the structure or composition of their family.

Many people have to endure prejudice, discrimination and lack of respect as a daily part of life, expressed in many ways such as:

- racism in all its forms, ranging from petty insults to violence
- dismissal of the significance of 'female' roles and qualities, and undervaluing the contribution made to society by women, leading to disparity in pay and fewer opportunities for women to reach the top in work roles (the 'glass ceiling')
- buildings and public transport which disabled people find it difficult to get in to or to move around in
- homophobic abuse.

When children are discriminated against, they are harmed because:

- they are denied the advantages of others so they do not have the chance to fulfil their potential

- they do not progress and experience success in their lives, and the negative effect this has on their self-esteem may dampen their motivation to learn

- they are excluded from certain roles.

All of this means that their potential is lost to society; they are unable to develop their abilities and talents and so be able to make their full contribution to society later in life.

Those who inflict discrimination on others are also harmed. If prejudice leads them to assumptions that some people are of less value than or inferior to others, they develop a distorted and false view of the world.

Prejudice and discrimination are contrary to the values of practice in working with children because they are a denial of children's rights. No child's well-being and learning opportunities should be limited by the negative impact of prejudice and discrimination. This is why it is so important that you base your work on **anti-discriminatory (or anti-bias) practice**, (see Unit EYMP4, page 281).

Key term

Anti-discriminatory (or anti-bias) practice: promoting equality of opportunity by –

- being positive about differences and similarities between people

- identifying and challenging prejudice

- taking positive action to counter discrimination

How inclusion promotes equality and diversity

Discrimination and prejudice interfere with:

- children's rights to have access to equality of opportunity

- promoting the positive aspects of diversity

and they have no place in settings for children. Settings should always aim for inclusion, which promotes both equality and diversity. Inclusion is the opposite of discrimination.

Case study: Vicky, children's centre worker

Vicky and her colleagues set about identifying barriers to inclusion in their children's centre and found that:

- several languages were spoken in the community served by the centre, but the only language to be seen there was English

- although families of various ethnic groups used the centre, those groups were not reflected in the ethnicity of the staff team

- vacancies at the centre were not advertised in the full range of languages used by families in the area, or in places where they were likely to see the information

- disabled family members encountered physical barriers such as stairs

- some parents with restricted literacy skills found it hard to understand the formal, complex English and technical terms used in the information distributed by the setting

- when children or adults spoke in discriminatory ways, they were not challenged.

This hampered the message to families that all were welcome in the centre.

What barriers to inclusion are present in your setting?

Making the languages of the local community visible

Inclusion requires us to appreciate the barriers — real or perceived — to all children and families participating in and benefiting from what a setting has to offer on an equal footing.

Working towards inclusion involves striving to ensure that such barriers are broken down. When we start to remove these barriers and make sure that all children and families can be (and feel themselves to be) part of our settings, we are taking steps to open up equality of opportunity and promote positive attitudes to diversity. We offer each child opportunities to achieve and flourish which are as good as the opportunities experienced by other children, and we ensure that a diverse range of children and families has an opportunity to participate in a setting.

Functional Skills

ICT: Developing, presenting and communicating information

Thinking about inclusion, maybe you could produce a poster on the computer which gives ideas of how to promote inclusion in your setting. Decide who the poster is aimed at (parents and staff; or the children themselves?) and make sure you use appropriate language.

Be able to work in an inclusive way

To work in an inclusive way, your practice must take into account both the legal framework of our state and also the policy framework of your setting. These frameworks should support you in interacting with families in respectful ways.

Laws, guidance and policies

The way we interact with one another in society is regulated by the laws of our land which establish a framework of what is considered to be appropriate or inappropriate behaviour. Laws cannot alone change prejudiced attitudes and assumptions or influence the way people think, but they are important in reducing practical aspects of discrimination. Remember that good inclusive practice goes beyond what the law commands.

Over to you

Find out the significant features of the:

- Race Relations Act 1976, together with Public Order Act of 1986 and Racial and Religious Hatred Act 2006.
- Children Act 1989 and 2004 and Care Standards Act 2000.
- Education Act 1981, together with Education Acts 1993 and 1996, Special Educational Needs and Disability Act 2001, and Disability Discrimination Acts 1995 and 2005.
- Equality Act 2006.

How do these laws apply to your setting and your day-to-day work with children?

The 'letter of the law' often needs interpretation to make it usable in real situations. An example of this is the Code of Practice for Children with Special Educational Needs (SEN Code of Practice) which gives guidance on meeting the learning needs of children with special educational needs.

Over to you

Find out how the SEN Code of Practice applies to your setting and work.

Your setting should have policies that take into account this legislation and guide the way you and your colleagues ensure that equality and inclusion are promoted.

Over to you

Obtain the equality/inclusion/diversity policy for your setting and reflect on how you put it into operation in your work.

EYFS in action

The Statutory Framework indicates the legal responsibility of settings to 'promote equality of opportunity' and 'ensure that every child is included'.

Discuss with colleagues some of the ways you discharge this legal responsibility in your setting.

Functional Skills

English: Speaking, listening and communication

When taking part in a discussion, listen carefully to what has been said so that you can respond in an appropriate way.

Demonstrating respect

It is important that you show by the way you communicate with children and their parents that you value and respect them and their families, however different they are from your own.

Some people will dismiss attempts to use words in a careful and respectful way as 'just being PC', but do not let this distract you from being thoughtful about how language can cause offence. The words we use to express ourselves can affect the concepts, values and attitudes we develop; they mould the way we think and may lead us to distorted or limited opinions. Language both reflects and influences how we think about ourselves and others. It can reinforce the development of stereotyped and prejudiced ideas, or it can help us to think more constructively and treat others respectfully.

Case study: What Vicky did next

Vicky and her colleagues took a critical look at their practice and identified ways they needed to improve.

- None of the staff could speak any of the languages spoken in the local community.
- Admission forms asked for a child's 'Christian name', and families from other religions or none felt that meant they were not welcomed in the setting.

They also identified how important it was to ensure they addressed people correctly – that they get names right because names are an important part of our identity and individuality. They improved their efforts

to check how to pronounce and spell names that they weren't familiar with, especially those from languages other than their own. They stopped anglicising names, realising that it is lacking in respect to use another name just because it seems easier to pronounce.

They also acknowledged that they needed to find out more about the systems used for names and titles in various ethnic and social groups, so they could address family members in ways seen as courteous in the culture to which they belonged.

How can you improve your practice in interacting with families in your setting?

Be able to promote diversity, equality and inclusion

Your daily practice in working which children and families should be inclusive, promoting equality of opportunity and positive attitudes towards diversity. We look at some aspects of this practice in more detail in other units.

You can also play a part in helping others to ensure children's rights to have access to equality of opportunity in an inclusive environment in which diversity is seen in positive ways.

Modelling inclusive practice

Part of your role in promoting inclusion is to help children have positive attitudes towards differences and so reduce the likelihood that they will develop prejudiced views. You can achieve this by:

- extending children's knowledge and understanding both of people who are like themselves and of people who are different from themselves by giving them opportunities to talk about the way they are similar to and different from other people

- helping children see differences in a positive way — as interesting and enriching to all our lives — and develop positive and respectful attitudes towards:

  ○ people from ethnic, cultural and social groups different from their own

  ○ people who live in families different from their own

  ○ disabled people

  ○ people who look or sound different from themselves.

You can do this by discussing differences openly with children, and also providing information and answering their questions. See Unit EYMP4, page 282, where we will look at how you can do this.

Another thread of inclusive practice is to offer children equality of opportunity to participate, develop and learn. This does not mean treating them 'all the same'; we have to acknowledge their diversity and treat children as individuals, with 'equal concern'.

Help children see differences in positive ways

This may require you to treat children differently from one another, according to their stage of development or some other aspect of their individuality. You may have to adapt the way you work with a child according to their individual needs and characteristics, so you ensure they have access to the opportunities which will help them to get the most out of life (see Unit EYMP4, page 281).

Supporting others

In addition to playing your part in contributing to the promotion of the rights of children and families to equality and inclusion, you can and should support the other adults in your setting — parents and colleagues — to work towards that aim.

Parents

> ## Functional Skills
>
> ICT: Developing, presenting and communicating information
>
> To help promote equality in your setting you could use the computer to produce a leaflet for parents. Your leaflet needs to include information on how the setting promotes equality and also pictures that support the information.

Case study: Maz and equal opportunities

When welcoming new parents, Maz spent a little time with a small group, outlining the inclusion and equality policy, which included the pre-school's intent to give girls and boys equal opportunities to participate in the full range of activities. She explained that girls were encouraged in physical play, construction and using technology, and boys were encouraged in creative and imaginative activities and to try out domestic roles in home-play.

One father said: 'I don't want my son to play with dolls or play at cooking and ironing. That's women's work. He should be in with the cars, like a proper boy.' A mother said, 'But we want our daughter to grow up in the culture of our religion to become a mother and homemaker like me, not to get ideas of a career.'

Maz talked to the father about taking a wider view of gender roles in society today and how they may change even further by the time the child have grown up. (She wondered how the child's mother saw 'women's work'!) She wanted to respect other people's religions but she was concerned about limiting children's opportunities – especially for girls. She explained the pre-school's position about giving children choices in life, but she chose her words very carefully and tried to show respect for the families' traditional views.

How do you support parents in developing understanding of promoting equality?

Promoting a wider view of gender roles in society

Colleagues

You may encounter colleagues who have limited understanding of the significance of inclusion and equality, and who have not yet appreciated the need to implement the setting's policies consistently. You may be able to use team meetings to highlight ways of implementing policies that give all children equal chances in life. Remember that confrontational and accusatory approaches are likely to be counterproductive. However, a calm and professional expression of views in constructive ways can help colleagues to develop their understanding and change their practice.

Skills builder

Imagine that a colleague is assuming that the two boys of a black family who are about to join your setting will be a lot of trouble and disruptive. She has formed the opinion that all African–Caribbean parents are harsh disciplinarians and she is adamant that practitioners will 'have to keep on top of them like they're used to at home'. How would you go about convincing her that she shouldn't make pre-judgements about a family, and certainly not make assumptions about children on stereotypical grounds before she's even met them?

Challenging discrimination

We have seen that discrimination and prejudice are contrary to the aims of supporting the development and progress of children, and we must challenge them when we encounter them. Either children or adults may express prejudice or behave in discriminatory ways. If this happens in your setting, you should have strategies to challenge what is said or done.

It is obviously important to support anyone who is the object of discrimination, but you should also try to help the person who is speaking or behaving in a discriminatory way to change their behaviour for the future. This is a demanding aspect of practice, and needs careful thought.

Children

Children are influenced by the adult world around them — at home, in their local community and in the media — and can acquire stereotyped and prejudiced views, at a surprisingly young age. Even the under-fives sometimes behave in discriminatory ways, making hurtful remarks or excluding others from play because of some aspect of their individuality — gender, ethnicity, family background, disability or appearance.

Don't think of name calling such as 'fatty' or 'four eyes' as a minor or unimportant matter, and dismiss it as merely teasing. When it is repeated and done with

intent to hurt, it becomes bullying or harassment. Some adults play down what they see as 'just toughening children up for the real world' and don't intervene. But we should question why a child should be expected to endure comments that undermine their self-image and self-esteem and be ready to support them in facing such torment.

Skills builder

Think how you would respond in situations like these:

A 3-year-old white girl says she won't hold hands with an African-Caribbean boy. She says his hands are dirty and he should wash them properly.

A 4-year-old girl is playing with the dolls, cuddling them and putting them to bed. But she won't let the boys anywhere near 'because boys don't play with dolls'.

Some of the children seize the patka of a Sikh boy and throw it around the room, chanting 'J wears a hankie on his head'.

Best practice checklist: Countering discrimination

When you encounter discrimination:

- ✓ never ignore or excuse one child's bullying or discriminatory behaviour towards another child, any more than you would ignore or excuse them if they inflicted physical pain on that child

- ✓ don't feel that you will make things worse by drawing attention to what has been said and done – if you do not respond, you give the impression that you condone the behaviour

- ✓ intervene immediately, pointing out to the child who has behaved in a bullying or discriminatory way that what was said or done is hurtful and that the behaviour cannot be accepted (using words like 'unfair' or 'cruel'), but don't suggest that they will be punished

- ✓ if necessary, point out anything that is untrue and give correct information and new vocabulary to guide what they say in future

- ✓ help the child to learn from the situation, to see the consequences of their actions, and to understand why their behaviour is regarded as inappropriate (ask 'how would *you* feel?') and should not be repeated in future

- ✓ don't leave the child with the feeling that you dislike them personally for what they have said or done – make it clear that what you won't tolerate is what they have said or how they have behaved

- ✓ support the child who is the object of the discrimination, reassuring them and helping to maintain their self-esteem.

Adults

Responding to children's expressions of prejudice or discriminatory behaviour takes patience and a consistent approach, but responding to the comments and behaviour of adults can be very daunting, and requires strength and, at times, even courage.

Functional Skills

English: Speaking, listening and communication

You could use these situations as discussion starters in your groups. Remember to plan your discussion before starting so that you can respond in an appropriate way.

Always intervene to stop discriminatory behaviour

Best practice checklist: Challenging adults

If it becomes necessary to challenge adults – whether parents or colleagues – use a similar approach as with children:

✓ challenge the remark, politely but firmly

✓ choose your time and place – you may not want to speak strongly in front of children, but you should act as soon as you can

✓ remain as calm as you can but make it clear that you find the remark or behaviour offensive or inappropriate

✓ remember that if you let the incident pass, you are contributing to the person feeling that it is acceptable to speak or behave in that way

✓ offer support to the person who has been the object of the remark or excluding behaviour

✓ offer accurate information if the person's comments or actions seem to arise from being unaware of the implications of what they are saying or doing so they have the option of behaving differently in future.

Skills builder

Think how you would respond in situations like these:

You overhear a parent referring to the disabled children in your setting as 'the spazzes' and 'the crips'.

One of your colleagues becomes vociferous in a staff meeting about two children who are being fostered by a gay couple who hope to adopt them, saying how disgraceful it is. The worker uses some very aggressive and quite unpleasant language, talking about gay men as if they were all promiscuous and paedophiles, asserting that it will ruin the children's future and it was irresponsible of social services to place them with the couple.

Be prepared to challenge the prejudices of adults

Getting ready for assessment

Write a reflective account of your practice in promoting equality and inclusiveness.

Start by writing descriptions of examples of what you do in your regular daily work with parents and children that is aimed at improving equality and inclusiveness. Describe what you do and how you do it.

Identify:

- some features of your practice that represent positive action to
  - offer children equality of opportunity
  - break down barriers to inclusion
- why you think these approaches are successful.

Also identify:

- circumstances where you are less successful in
  - improving children's access to equality of opportunity
  - overcoming barriers to inclusion
- the reasons for this.

Ask a colleague who is familiar with your usual work practice to give you feedback on this aspect of your practice. Ask for examples of when they observe you taking action to

- offer children equality of opportunity
- break down barriers to inclusion.

Ask if they can describe how your practice has been successful and when it has not achieved what you were aiming for.

Look back at what you have written and think about the feedback you have been given.

Pinpoint the areas of practice that:

- are your strengths – what you are doing consistently well
- you need to develop and improve.

Identify the characteristics of your practice that result in greater equality of opportunity for children and inclusion, and those that are less effective.

Describe how you intend to develop and improve your practice – the strategies you can use to extend your knowledge and skills.

Check your knowledge

1. What do we mean by diversity?

2. Describe two examples of assumptions that might be made about people on prejudiced grounds.

3. Why is discrimination harmful to children?

4. Give three examples of how disabled people can be enabled to move around freely in public spaces and have access to facilities independently.

5. What body was set up by the Equality Act 2006? Name five of the areas of equality legislation it is responsible for.

6. Give two reasons why we should be careful about the way we use language in the context of inclusion and diversity.

7. Describe three aspects of how you would respond to discriminatory behaviour by a child.

8. Describe two aspects of your approach to discriminatory behaviour by an adult that are different from those listed in question 7.

Engage in personal development

Working with children is rarely dull. You have to meet children's individual needs, work closely with parents and deliver a service that is closely monitored. In order to meet the high expectations that are part of the job, effective practitioners need to constantly reflect and evaluate on their skills and knowledge. This unit looks at ways in which you might do this.

Learning outcomes:

By the end of this unit you will:

1. Understand what is required for competence in the learner's own work role within the sector

2. Be able to reflect on practice

3. Be able to evaluate own performance

4. Be able to agree a personal development plan

5. Be able to reflect on how learning opportunities contribute to personal development.

Understand what is required for competence in the learner's own work role within the sector

In order to plan properly to gain this qualification, and so you can be an effective practitioner, it is essential to understand fully the requirements of your work role. This learning outcome asks you to consider the duties and responsibilities, as well as the attitudes and skills, that are needed in the job role and whether or not you currently have them or hope to attain them.

Analysing your duties and responsibilities

Employment roles in the early years sector can vary enormously. This qualification will give you the fundamentals required to practise effectively, but it is worth noting that each job role will have its own demands. This means that you need to focus on the skills and attitudes required for *your* job role. A good starting point is therefore to look at either your own job description or, if you are not yet in employment, a sample one which you might obtain from your placement setting.

Skills builder

Below are four statements from a job description. For each statement, consider what knowledge, skills or personal attributes will be important.

- Planning and preparing play and learning activities to meet all aspects of children's development and in line with the Early Years Foundation Stage
- Observing children and keeping appropriate records
- Keeping and monitoring accident, incident and risk assessment records
- Liaising with parents

Job descriptions often outline the tasks that are required and from this you can begin to consider what skills and knowledge are needed to effectively complete them. For example a job description might state that you are required to carry out observations on children. This in turn requires that you have learnt about observation methods and also have a good knowledge of child development (see Unit CYP3.1, page 49) and the early years curriculum (see Unit EYMP2).

Functional Skills

Looking at the statements from the job description, it is clear how Functional Skills will become part of your working life. For example:

- Planning and preparing play and learning activities to meet all aspects of children's development and in line with the Early Years Foundation Stage – your ICT skills will help you to create planning documents

- Observing children and keeping appropriate records – your written English skills will help you to write up child observations and keep records up to date

- Keeping and monitoring accident, incident and risk assessment records – your written English will be used to fill out the forms and your Maths skills will help you to calculate the risks involved

- Liaising with parents – your oral English skills will be essential when liaising with the parents or carers.

Evaluating work role expectations in relation to relevant standards

The early years sector is well regulated and all practitioners, and the settings they work in, must comply with the various standards that in many cases have been set down in law, such as the Childcare Act 2006 and the Health and Safety at Work Act 1974. Most settings ensure that they meet the standards by having a range of policies and procedures that all staff must observe. This means that you need to be aware of the policies in your

Planning for children to be outside is a requirement of the EYFS

year on year, children and their families will arrive with different needs, expectations and interests. Staff too will be developing as they update their knowledge and skills. This means that effective settings rarely do the same thing year in and year out. They talk to parents, other service users and colleagues and focus their energies on improving how they are working. The process of reflective practice, both for individual staff members and the setting, is essential in this. Practitioners must think about which areas, whether they are linked to routine, curricula or policies, are working well and which ones need tweaking or even overhauling. In addition, the national standards and frameworks may also change and this in turn will impact on how a setting should be run.

In order to reflect on your practice, you need to be ready to question what you do and to think about it rather than simply doing it. It can be helpful to begin by considering different areas of your job role and to look at them one by one. This may mean carefully observing the reactions of children and others to help you think about your effectiveness. In situations where you feel you are doing well, consider what skills, knowledge or practice are helping you achieve that success. Where you feel

setting and understand how they link to your work role. A good example of this is the way a practitioner working in a nursery will plan for children to have time out of doors. This is not just good practice, but a requirement of the Early Years Foundation Stage (EYFS).

In addition to national standards that have been drawn up, some organisations also have their own ethos, philosophy or mission, for example a community pre-school, a Montessori nursery or a centre working with refugee children. Practitioners working in such settings will find that their work role will again be influenced by the overall aims of the organisation.

Be able to reflect on practice

The term 'reflective practice' is used to describe the way in which professionals continually evaluate their own work and consider ways of improving what they are doing. For this learning outcome, you will need to show that you understand the importance of doing this and also that you are able to reflect accurately on your practice.

The importance of reflective practice in improving the quality of service

Settings that work well and are effective are usually dynamic and changing environments. This is because,

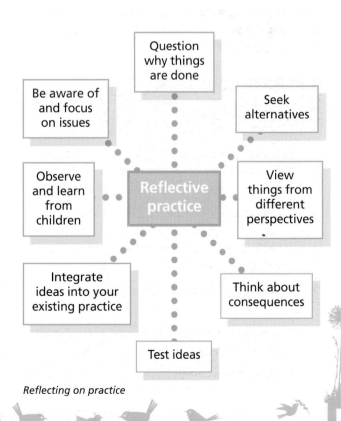

Reflecting on practice

that you have weaknesses, think about what you need to do in order to improve. Generally, most weaknesses are down to lack of experience or knowledge. Viewed in these terms, you can then develop a new personal development plan (see the next learning outcome) or adapt your existing one.

The ways in which you might approach reflecting on your practice are set out in the diagram on page 33. The principle behind them all is to keep an open mind.

Question why things are done

Try out new practices or visit settings that work in contrasting ways.

Synthesise ideas

Be ready to look at ideas and then adapt them to work in your setting.

Observe and learn from children

Observe the reactions of children closely. They are the main service user and so learn about what they want to do and how they react in different situations.

Be aware of and focus on issues

Most settings have small ongoing issues such as where to store buggies, or a staff rota that is not quite working.

Focusing on these rather than accepting them as 'just are' problems can help the smooth running of the setting.

How value systems and experiences can affect your work practice

There are few areas in childcare and education where only one single approach is right. To be able to evaluate your performance means thinking about other possibilities and approaches, even when they are unfamiliar. In order to be able to do this we need to become aware of the value systems and experiences that have shaped our work practice. The ways in which we were cared for and educated as children can have an effect, for example on the way in which we deal with children's behaviour, meal times or settling in. Similarly, if you have worked only in one type of setting, your experiences to date have only allowed you to see one way of working with children and so you may not be either aware of or comfortable with other approaches. This means that it is always good for us to visit other settings and to talk to other practitioners so that we can extend our 'vision' of how to work with children and avoid being narrow-minded.

Getting ready for assessment

Children need a good range of resources and activities in order for them to enjoy playing and learning. Reflecting on how well an activity has worked for individuals and groups of children can help you to plan for the future. Using the questions below, write a reflective account of an activity that you have carried out with children which demonstrates that you can reflect on your practice.

- Did most children appear to be engaged and interested in the activity?
- Can you identify what it was that helped children to be interested? (Perhaps, for example, the activity was sensory and children were active.)
- Were children encouraged to take control and be active during the activity?

- How much input from you was needed?
- Why was this input needed?
- How did you encourage children to be active in their play and learning?
- Was this learning planned or spontaneous?
- How could this learning be reinforced or built upon?
- What did individual children gain from the activity?
- What was your role in helping children to learn?
- What further resources could have been used?
- What were the limitations of this activity?
- How could these limitations be addressed?

Case study: Bea's Ofsted inspection

Bea has been a pre-school leader for twenty years. The pre-school has an excellent reputation and strong community links. She began at the pre-school as a parent helper and over time has gained the qualifications necessary to lead and manage the setting. She has never worked in another setting or visited another pre-school.

Recently, new members of staff have been making suggestions as to how to organise the play and activities differently. Last month, an early years advisor also talked about the need to change the routines in order to meet the EYFS framework, in particular the way that snack time is organised. Bea is adamant that there is no need for any changes. She feels that the routines that were established over thirty years ago have stood the test of time. With regard to snack time, she is convinced that it is good for children to have to wait their turn – even if this is for fifteen minutes – as this was how she was brought up. Yesterday, Ofsted carried out an inspection. The inspector was critical of many aspects of the provision, including snack time, and has made suggestions about how the setting can make improvements. Bea is furious and believes that the inspector is wrong.

1. How are Bea's value systems and experiences influencing her work?

2. Why might it be helpful for Bea to visit other pre-schools?

3. Why is it important to reflect on your own value systems and experiences?

Be able to evaluate own performance

Once you have analysed the demands and expectations of your job role, the next step is to consider what you can already do and which areas you may further need to develop. This learning outcome looks at how you might evaluate your own performance and how you might use feedback to inform you.

Evaluate your knowledge and performance

It is important to think about what you can do already and which areas you need to develop further. To do this you can ask for feedback from colleagues, advisers, assessors or your line manager. You also need to find ways of evaluating yourself. The skills analysis table (Table 1, page 37) will help you begin this process.

Responding to feedback

One of the ways in which we can evaluate our current state of knowledge and performance is by asking others for feedback. This is important because it can be hard to be objective about your own performance; also you may lack the skill or knowledge to be aware of what else you should be doing or other ways in which you might work. Feedback may come from a variety of sources, including parents and colleagues as well as early years advisers and line managers. For this qualification, you may also be given feedback from a tutor or an assessor.

Feedback works best if you trust the people it comes from and if they feel that they can give you an honest view. It is a skill in itself to be able to listen to feedback carefully without becoming defensive. It is often easy to begin to defend the reasons why you do things, but the key is to remember that the focus is on improving performance.

Be able to agree a personal development plan

This learning outcome requires you to identify areas of knowledge, skills or professional practice that need further development and draw up a personal development plan with the support of a tutor or mentor. (A personal development plan is a document in which you set out your priorities for development, how you are intending to address them and the timescale for doing so, along with a way of reviewing and monitoring them.)

Sources of support that will help you to develop the plan

It is always helpful to have some support when drawing up a development plan. Another person involved from

It is important to be open to suggestions from other staff about how to organise long-standing routines

the outset can help you determine some priorities for your plan and give you feedback and may also motivate you. If you are an employee, you may ask your line manager to support you. This can sometimes be carried out as part of an appraisal process during which you will gain feedback from your line manager, and will also tease out areas for further development. Other sources of support may include your tutor or assessor (if you are working towards a qualification with a training provider), a colleague who has experience of your job role or an appointment mentor who can give you advice. It is also helpful to look for sources of support that can assist you with the practicalities of implementing your plan, such as careers guidance, admissions tutor or training co-ordinator.

Over to you

Identify some sources of support that you might use in the planning of your professional development. You might consider:

- carers
- advocates (who work on behalf of the child and represent the child's interests)
- supervisor, line manager or employer
- other professionals.

Why is it important to gain support from a range of sources?

Review your learning needs, interests and development opportunities

Before you can create a plan, you need to analyse your current skills. People often possess more skills than they realise. While some skills are job specific and can be used only in certain situations, such as feeding a baby, others are more transferable, such as being able to use a computer. It can therefore be helpful to rate your skills so that you know which ones should be prioritised.

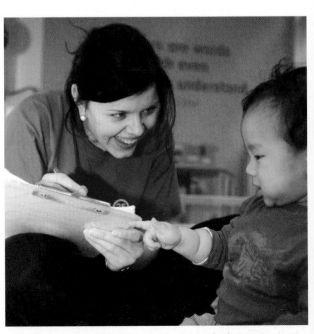

Recording observations for a personal development plan

Below is a table that will help you to begin this process. The first two rows have been filled in as an example. Note that it is not a comprehensive list of skills, as the child care and education sector is a wide area. The table looks mainly at transferable skills across the sector. You will need to add in the skills required by your current job role that you analysed as part of the first learning outcome in this chapter.

The table is divided into five columns. Column one shows some of the key competencies that are useful in the child care and education sector. Column two is where you give yourself a rating: 1 would mean that you need to work on this area, while 5 would mean that you feel you are very competent. Column three is where you provide evidence of having used this skill. Column four is where you indicate how much you enjoy using this skill. You should also think about what this means for your future career. Column five is for writing down how you might develop this skill if you decide to focus on it. This is a column that you might need to leave until later on, so that you can talk it through with the person who is supporting you.

Table 1: Skills analysis

Competency (skill, knowledge or experience)	Self-rating (1=low, 5=high)	Evidence	Enjoyment of using this competency (1=low, 5=high) and implication	How can I develop this?
Knowledge and experience of working with children of different ages, with different needs and in different settings	3	Worked in a nursery for 3 years with children aged 3–5 years. Worked as a midday supervisor for 1 year with children aged 5–11 years. Now working in day care with children 3–4 years	5: I enjoy working with children who have particular needs. I definitely want to work with children for most of the day. I will not be interested in becoming a manager	Learn more about children's learning and behaviour. Have responsibility for a child with particular needs
Observation, planning and record keeping	1	I fill in activity sheets and checklists, but am not responsible for the planning	3: I quite enjoy this and will need it for other jobs	Ask Sandie to show me how she does it. Ask if I can do more training days
Building positive relationships with parents				
Knowledge of the curriculum/ framework				
Working in partnership with parents				
People and leadership skills				
Managing a budget				
Information technology skills				
Writing skills (e.g. letters, reports, newsletters)				
Health and safety				
Knowledge of legislation affecting the sector				
Multi-agency working				

Functional Skills

ICT: Developing, presenting and communicating information; and Using ICT

By completing this table in Word you can refer back to it in the future in order to reflect on your skills. Remember it is very important to save this document somewhere on your computer where you will be able to find it and also with an appropriate name. Maybe you could create a new folder and then any electronic feedback you receive could be saved to the same place.

Prioritising your learning needs

Once you have reviewed your learning needs, you must then prioritise what you should tackle first. A good starting point is to think about your current job. What should you do to develop and become more competent in your role?

You also have to try to think ahead. Are you likely to want to stay in the same role or are you interested in moving on? Remember that moving on does not necessarily mean taking on more responsibility, but can mean simply working with a different age group or in a different setting. If you are not sure what job opportunities are available in the sector, look at some of the vacancies that are advertised locally and also in the specialist press. This will also give you an idea of the type of skills that are involved. Focus on what you want to achieve rather than on any limitations, such as your age or family circumstances. Usually it is possible to find a balance between these limitations and what you want to do.

Agreeing a personal development plan

Once you have considered the areas in which development might take place, you should think about how to achieve your objectives. Common approaches include training, asking to take on responsibility or **shadowing** a colleague. This should include a timescale for the achievement of your objectives, which might affect how you prioritise them. For example a college course may enrol students only once a year, and so while waiting to enrol you might begin work on another area of personal development that you have identified.

Key term

Shadowing: following another practitioner in order to understand his or her way of working

Large areas of development can be broken into smaller ones. This will have a bearing on the timescale. Setting yourself realistic goals is essential, as it will help to ensure that your plan works. The term 'SMART' is often used when setting goals. The aim of SMART goals or targets is to help people focus clearly on what they want to achieve and to avoid unrealistic objectives.

There are no set formats for a personal development plan, but any plan should show when and how you intend to implement it. You should show how you intend to check your progress. It is also a good idea to record

Specific
Try to make sure in your planning that you have thought clearly about what you need to learn, experience or develop.

Measurable
Consider how you will know whether you have achieved this part of your plan. You may, for example, need a qualification or certificate or want others to recognise that you have become more skilled.

Timescale
Thinking about how long each part of the plan will take is essential. Many people need a start and an end time to help them work effectively. Working out a realistic timescale will help you to remain motivated.

S = Specific M = Measurable A = Achievable
R = Realistic T = Timescale

Achievable
When thinking about your plan, make sure that it is possible to complete each target. This will include thinking about how you will organise it and whether it will meet your needs.

Realistic
There is always a danger of being over-enthusiastic and over-optimistic at the start of any project. Think about how you normally cope and check that your plan will meet your needs and the way in which you learn and work.

Your goals should be SMART

what the objectives are for each part of your plan. An example of a format for a personal development plan is given in Table 2; it may give you some starting points for your own, although be ready to adapt it so that it suits you.

Table 2: Example format for a personal development plan

Area	Why?	How?	By when?	Update
Working with children with particular needs	To gain a qualification	Local college	September 2011	

Discussing your plan with others

It is helpful to discuss your plan with other people, such as your employer, tutor or assessor. They may be able to offer support and advice. An employer might, for example, be ready to pay for some training or have other suggestions about how you might gain experience or knowledge. In some cases your personal development plan may be used as part of the staff review and appraisal process. A tutor or assessor may know of a suitable qualification that will meet your needs. As a result of such input be ready to revise your plan.

Functional Skills

English: Speaking, listening and communicating

ICT: Developing, presenting and communicating information

Holding a one-to-one discussion with your tutor, employer or assessor is a different kind of discussion from one that you may have practised in other units. This is a very focused discussion and it centres mainly around you. You could help to prepare for this by emailing your plan to them via an attachment so that he or she could read through it before your meeting.

It is helpful to discuss your plan with other people

Be able to reflect on how learning opportunities contribute to personal development

For this learning outcome, you should have begun your personal development plan as you need to consider how the learning that you have undertaken has affected your practice.

How to review learning activities

There are many different ways in which you might go about implementing your personal development plan so as to gain knowledge, experience or further skills. Table 3 below provides you with some suggestions. When you have tried out different learning activities, it is important to think about how you can implement the learning that you have gained. It is also important to think about which type of learning you have found the most useful, for example some people like home study while others prefer to learn by being taught or tutored.

Table 3: .Types of learning activities

Courses, conferences and workshops	Many practitioners attend training that does not lead to qualifications. Much of this type of training lasts only a few hours. But it is valuable, as it can give you a taster or update your knowledge if you already have a qualification. A good example of this is training that focuses on one area of a curriculum or child protection training. This type of training is also useful because you can meet other practitioners in your area.
Observing the way other professionals work (shadowing)	It will help you to reflect on the way in which you work if you are able to see how other people handle situations, plan activities and relate to children. This can be done in your own setting, but it is also useful to watch others in similar jobs who work in a different setting. Watching other people in this way is sometimes known as 'shadowing'; it can help you see things from a different perspective.
Full-time and part-time courses leading to a qualification	While short bursts of training can be very motivating and interesting, they may not be sufficient in themselves. Full-time and part-time courses can lead to a whole qualification or accreditation of a single unit.
Meeting other professionals	Many early years teams organise 'cluster groups' in which practitioners from the local area are able to meet. Meeting other professionals in this way can help you to explore different ideas and so to reflect on your practice. Sometimes other people will tell you about how they have brought in a new system or piece of equipment and their experiences can help you to explore your own ideas.
Internet, articles and books	Articles and books can provide you with new information and ideas. Magazines and professional journals can make you aware of new developments within the sector and so it is a good idea to find the time to look through them. Books can offer new ideas and activities and help you to reflect on practice. The Internet can also be used, but it is important to be sure that the source is reliable, up to date and accurate.
Training materials	Some learning can be undertaken using specially prepared training materials e.g. DVDs, recorded programmes. As with all self-study, it is important to be motivated, but also to supplement it with professional discussion.

Evaluate the effectiveness of learning opportunities

Once you have completed some professional development, such as training, it is important to consider how you can integrate your new information so that it is reflected in your practice. This may mean looking again at the welfare requirements and the early years curriculum that you are working with and thinking about how you need to change your practice. If you are leading a team, or have responsibility for specific areas of a curriculum, it may mean devising an action plan or sharing your information with colleagues. In some cases, small adjustments to the way you work or plan activities might be required, such as changing the layout, while in others it can mean a significant overhaul of policies and procedures. A good example of this is child protection, where, over the past ten years, there have been significant changes to the procedures adopted in settings.

Over to you

Think about a training course that you have recently attended.

How did you use the information to improve your practice?

Recording progress

It is a good idea to keep a record of the training that you have undertaken. If you are taking a qualification, you will be able to track your progress using the Individual Learning Record. This will show the number of credits that you have obtained. For short courses, such as those provided by local authorities, it is a good idea to keep a file which contains notes and handouts as well as certificates of attendance. Your record of training is important when you apply for jobs, as it shows how you have kept up to date and extended your professional knowledge. Remember to keep any certificates safe so that you can find them easily. It is now common practice for employers to ask to see the original of any qualifications. In addition, you should try to gain written feedback on your work once you have undertaken some learning activities. You may therefore be able to show progress in this way.

It is a good idea to keep a record of the training that you have undertaken

Check your knowledge

1. Briefly outline the responsibilities and duties that you undertake in order to fulfil your job role.

2. Explain why practitioners should reflect on their practice.

3. Give two reasons why it may be hard to reflect on practice.

4. Why is it helpful to have feedback when reflecting on practice?

5. What is a personal development plan?

6. Explain the process of drawing up a development plan.

7. Why is it important to identify priorities when agreeing a plan?

8. Identify three different learning opportunities.

9. Why is it important to review practice as a result of attending training or other learning opportunities?

10. Explain why a record of progress towards achieving the personal development plan should be kept.

Principles for implementing duty of care

Children, especially young children, are vulnerable because they have not yet developed the physical and cognitive capacity to care for themselves, so they need protection and care from the adults around them. All practitioners who work with children have a duty of care towards them. However, at times this duty may seem to be at odds with the rights of children and their families, and you need to understand how to resolve such dilemmas.

Learning outcomes:

By the end of this unit you will:

1. Understand how duty of care contributes to safe practice

2. Know how to address conflicts or dilemmas that may arise between an individual's rights and the duty of care

3. Know how to respond to complaints.

Understand how duty of care contributes to safe practice

Duty of care is a key concept in working with other human beings.

What we mean by duty of care

When human beings interact with one another, each has a **duty of care** towards the others.

> ### Key term
>
> **Duty of care:** a requirement to exercise a 'reasonable' degree of attention and caution to avoid negligence which would lead to harm to other people

Work with children brings a significant duty of care, and the younger and more vulnerable the child, the greater the duty of care. Your vigilance and attention keeps young children safe as they develop:

- the ability to foresee and cope with potential dangers
- more robust immune systems
- empathy – understanding that their actions may hurt or upset others
- communication skills to be able to talk about the harm others may be doing them.

How duty of care safeguards children

Babies and the under-threes are almost entirely dependent on adults to care for them in ways that protect them from harm – whether physical or psychological. In your work with young children, you safeguard children in various ways such as:

- carrying out risk assessment in your setting and taking precautions to avoid potential hazards which might

lead to harm to the children – either through accidents or spreading infection

- setting clear expectations and boundaries for children's behaviour, and using strategies to discourage behaviour which may harm or distress others, according to the stage of development of each child
- observing children and assessing their development, being alert to any indications that their progress is not as broadly expected for children of their age, so that relevant action can be taken in partnership with parents and other professionals
- understanding the ways children may be abused by others, being aware of the signs that a child may be experiencing such harm, and following appropriate procedures if abuse is suspected.

> ### Reflect
>
> Over a period of two weeks, think about your daily practice and note a range of examples of actions that you take to exercise your duty of care for the children you work with. In what ways are your actions safeguarding or protecting the children?

Know how to address conflicts or dilemmas that may arise between an individual's rights and the duty of care

While duty of care is so important in work with children, there are times when this principle seems to conflict with another principle, that of respecting the rights of children and families. A balanced approach has to be taken in deciding which has the greater priority in certain circumstances.

Individuals' rights and responsibilities

Children have rights, such as those set out in the UN Convention on the Rights of the Child.

Parents' rights are modified by their responsibilities towards their children. The Children Act 1989 made clear that it is the welfare of the child that is paramount, and the law often gives priority to children's rights, overriding those of parents.

People who work with children must acknowledge parents' responsibilities and be wary of usurping the role of parents. You play a temporary part in the lives of the children you work with but their parents have the central and life-long role.

When you exercise a duty of care, you have to be sensitive to ways in which intervening in the lives of children and families could bring you into conflict with their rights and responsibilities. You must always balance your duty and desire to keep children safe with avoiding situations where you intrude into their lives in ways that infringe their rights or the responsibilities of their parents.

Risk taking

The duty of care could conflict with children's rights to have experiences which facilitate their development and learning. An element of challenge and risk taking in children's play is essential in enabling children to learn how to predict and avoid dangerous situations.

If practitioners become over-zealous about predicting possible hazards when children engage in play, and seek to 'wrap them in cotton wool', they are carrying their duty of care too far.

Confidentiality

Another area of potential dilemma concerns the rights of children and parents to the privacy of their home and family life. Settings must ensure that sensitive information about them is kept confidential, only sharing information with the knowledge and permission of parents. However, children's welfare must always be paramount in your professional practice. This conflict becomes most apparent in the context of safeguarding children from abuse, particularly if a family member is suspected of being the perpetrator of the abuse. There are times when information must be shared with other appropriate professionals in the interests of the welfare of the child – sometimes without the consent of parents being sought first.

Balancing duty of care with rights and responsibilities

Diligent exercise of duty of care must be balanced with children's rights and parents' responsibilities.

Risk taking

Sometimes rights may take precedence over duty of care. Practitioners should discharge their duty of care in ways that support children's rights to acquire life skills through learning how to cope with risky situations.

Risk taking is part of healthy development

Skills builder

With a colleague, identify:

- ways that you make sure that children are kept safe while engaged in activities that might involve risk
- activities that you think have too great a risk element in relation to potential learning opportunities.

number of skills the children might learn and ways their creative play could be extended.

1. Who do you think they should turn to for support in taking this venture forwards?
2. Where might they find advice on managing risks effectively?

Confidentiality

In other situations, duty of care may prevail over rights. Your duty of care to protect children from abuse must be balanced with families' rights to have their private information treated confidentially.

Confidentiality

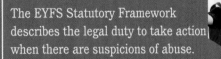

EYFS in action

The EYFS Statutory Framework describes the legal duty to take action when there are suspicions of abuse.

What are the procedures for this action in your setting? Who would you seek advice and support from about how to act if you had suspicions that a child was being abused?

Over to you

Obtain a copy of the confidentiality policy of your setting. How does it contribute to maintaining children's and families' rights in the context of protecting children from abuse?

Know how to respond to complaints

Inevitably when a potentially difficult dilemma, such as that of balancing duty of care and individual rights, is concerned, practitioners will sometimes find themselves in a position where parents feel that the duty of care for their children has not been given sufficient priority, or the children's rights have been wrongly perceived.

Support and advice

Making judgements which balance duty of care and the rights of children and families may present professional dilemmas, and sometimes you will have to seek support and advice.

Risk taking

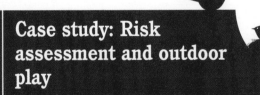

Case study: Risk assessment and outdoor play

Jess and her colleagues wanted to extend the range of outdoor activities in the nursery and decided that they would like to make woodworking tools such as hammers and saws available. They identified a

Responding to complaints

Complaints should never be ignored. Parents have responsibilities to ensure their children's welfare and to complain if they feel that a setting is not exercising sufficient duty of care.

Complaints procedures

As with many aspects of a setting's practice, complaints should be handled in ways which are guided by a pre-planned procedure, to ensure that families' rights are properly supported while also protecting practitioners by providing them with appropriate guidance.

Case study: A mother's concern

Jess and her colleagues consulted the appropriate people and made careful preparations for the introduction of the new equipment. However, when one mother heard about the idea, she was appalled and threatened to take her child away from 'such a dangerous place'.

How would you have responded to this comment?

EYFS in action

The Statutory Framework requires settings to have a written complaints procedure. Obtain a copy of the procedure for your setting. If a complaint arose as the result of the way a child protection issue was handled, what would the procedure require?

Check your knowledge

1. Explain what is meant by 'duty of care'.

2. Give three examples of how practitioners safeguard young children by exercising their duty of care.

3. Why is it important not to take duty of care to the point where children are protected from all elements of risk in their play?

4. Children and parents have a right to privacy in their home and family life, and normally settings must uphold this right by ensuring that sensitive information about families is kept confidential, only sharing information with the knowledge and permission of parents. Under what circumstances might a duty of care outweigh this right?

5. Why should a setting have a complaints procedure?

Getting ready for assessment

Write a reflective account of your practice in exercising a duty of care.

Start by writing descriptions of examples of what you do in your regular daily work with parents and children that is aimed at fulfilling this duty. Describe what you do and how you do it.

Identify:

- some features of your practice that have safeguarded children
- why you think you have been successful in discharging your duty of care.

Also identify:

- circumstances where you are less successful in ensuring duty of care
- the reasons for this.

Ask a colleague who is familiar with your usual work practice to give you feedback on this aspect of your practice. Ask for examples of when they observe you taking action to balance the need for care with the rights of children and families. Ask if they can describe how your practice has been successful and when it has not achieved what you were aiming for.

Look back at what you have written and think about the feedback you have been given.

Pinpoint the areas of practice that:

- are your strengths – what you are doing consistently well
- you need to develop and improve.

Identify the characteristics of your practice that result in a good balance between duty of care and families' rights, and those that are less effective.

Describe how you intend to develop and improve your practice – the strategies you can use to extend your knowledge and skills.

Children & Young People's Core Units

CYP3.1 Understand child & young person development

CYP3.2 Promote child & young person development

CYP3.3 Understand how to safeguard the well-being of children & young people

CYP3.4 Support children & young people's health & safety

CYP3.5 Develop positive relationships with children, young people & others involved in their care

CYP3.6 Working together for the benefit of children & young people

CYP3.7 Understand how to support positive outcomes for children & young people

CYP3.1

Understand child & young person development

While all children are unique and special in their own ways, it is helpful for practitioners to have some feel of what children are likely to be able to do at different ages. In this unit, we explore children and young people's development, factors that might affect it and also what we might do if we have concerns about a child's development.

As child development is fundamental to many aspects of working with children and young people, you will find that this unit will act as reference for other units within the qualification that you are taking.

Learning outcomes:

By the end of this unit you will:

1. Understand the expected pattern of development for children and young people from birth to 19 years

2. Understand the factors that influence children and young people's development and how these affect practice

3. Understand how to monitor children and young people's development and interventions that should take place if this is not following the expected pattern

4. Understand the importance of early intervention to support the speech, language and communication needs of children and young people

5. Understand the potential effects of transitions on children and young people's development.

Understand the expected pattern of development for children and young people from birth to 19 years

Children and young people do follow a pattern of development. Knowing what you can expect to see at different ages and stages will help you to support children's development and to identify those children who may need additional support, either within your setting or from other professionals. This learning outcome requires you to have a good knowledge of children and young people's development.

Aspects of development

Before looking at children and young people's development, it is important to understand its meaning. The term 'development' refers not to the physical growth of children and young people, but to the skills and knowledge that they are developing. Obviously, the two are interconnected as growth impacts enormously on children and young people's development, so neural growth (increase in the number and complexity of neural connections) affects the way that children and young people are able to think. It is usual when looking at child development to divide it into the following areas.

- *Physical development*. This area of development is about learning how to master physical movements. It is usually subdivided into fine motor skills (such as tying shoe laces), gross motor movements (such as throwing a ball) and locomotive movements (such as balancing and walking). Physical development allows children to gain independence.

- *Cognitive development*. This area of development is also known as intellectual development. It is a huge area, as it encompasses the way in which the brain processes information. Being able to remember someone's name or being able to distinguish between two different colours are examples of cognitive skills. Imagination is also a cognitive skill. Cognitive development is strongly linked to communication and language development.

- *Communication*. This area of development is about learning to communicate with other people and understanding their communications. Talking, reading and writing and also use of gestures are all examples of skills that most children learn. Communication and language development are linked to cognitive development because more sophisticated communication involves thinking about what others are trying to convey as well as thinking about what you are trying to express.

- *Social and emotional development*. This area of development is about relationships and also about understanding oneself. Being able to feel sorry for someone, knowing what behaviour is acceptable and having the ability to control your emotions are examples of skills that children learn. This area is closely tied to cognitive and language development.

- *Moral development*. This is a sub-set of social and emotional development with strong links to cognitive development. The development of morality is about the decisions that children and young people take, the principles that they adopt and their behaviour towards others.

Development is holistic

It makes sense to separate out areas of development, but it is essential to understand that they do not work 'separately'. They are co-dependent so a child who does not have the physical skills to sit up, turn pages or the language to decode the text, will not be able to sit and read a book. This co-dependency means that while you may find it helpful to focus on one area of a child's development, you must always remember that children are 'whole' people.

Over to you

Make a list of the skills and aspects of development involved in the following:

- playing football in a team
- dressing up and playing in the home corner with other children
- taking part in a cooking activity with other children.

Sequence and rates of development

When working with children and young people, it is useful to have an idea of typical development for their age. Outlined in this section are some expected patterns of development for children and young people. These need to be seen as 'pictures' that represent the general population of children and young people, because an individual child's rate of development can vary as we will see below.

Babies at birth

Most babies are born around the fortieth week of pregnancy. Babies who are born more than three weeks early are described as premature. Premature babies are likely to need a little more time to reach the same levels of development as a baby who is born at around 40 weeks.

Babies are born with many reflexes, which are actions they perform without thinking. Many reflexes are linked to survival. Examples of reflexes include:

- *Swallowing and sucking reflexes*. These ensure that the baby can feed and swallow milk.

- *Rooting reflex*. The baby will move its head to look for a nipple or teat if its cheek or mouth is touched. This helps the baby to find milk.

- *Grasp reflex*. Babies will automatically put their fingers around an object that has touched the palm of their hand.

- *Startle reflex*. When babies hear a sudden sound or see a sudden bright light, they will react by moving their arms outwards and clenching their fists.

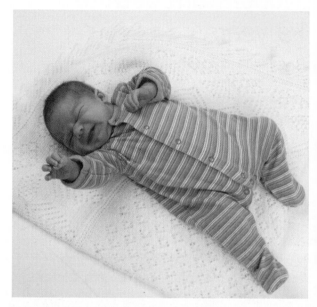

The startle reflex

- *Walking and standing reflex*. When babies are held upright with their feet on a firm surface, they usually make stepping movements.

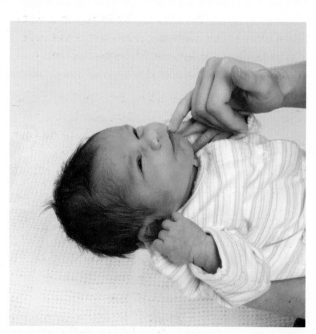

The rooting reflex

The walking and standing reflex

Examples of what you might observe	
Physical	Reflexes – see above
Cognitive	Babies who recognise the smell and sound of their mother's voice
Communication	Babies crying when hungry, tired or distressed
Social, emotional and behavioural	Close contact between primary carer and baby, especially when feeding

Babies at 1 month

In their first month of life babies change a lot. Babies at 1 month have usually started to settle into a pattern. They sleep quite a lot of the time, but will gradually start to spend longer periods awake. They cry to communicate their needs, and their parents may be starting to understand the different types of cries. Babies are also learning about their parents or carers: they may stop crying when they hear their soothing voices; they also try hard to focus on the face of whoever is holding them (they can focus at a distance of 20–25 cm).

Examples of what you might observe	
Physical	Babies looking less curled up and startle less
Cognitive	Babies stop crying because they hear a familiar voice
Communication	Babies coo when contented (from around 5 or 6 weeks)
Social, emotional and behavioural	Fleeting smiles when asleep (smiles of contentment begin from 5 or 6 weeks)

Fleeting smiles when asleep

Babies at 3 months

Babies at 3 months have grown in height and weight. Some babies have learnt the difference between day and night and are able to sleep through the night. They are likely to cry less and most parents are getting better at knowing what their cries mean. They are also starting to sleep a little less and are far more alert. They may smile quite often and show that they know the sound of their parents' voices and movements.

Examples of what you might observe	
Physical	Babies lift and turn their heads
Cognitive	Babies start to notice mobiles and other objects around them
Communication	Babies smile back when they see a smiling face
Social, emotional and behavioural	Enjoyment of bath time

Babies at 6 months

Babies at 6 months have learnt many skills. They are very alert and turn their heads to see what is happening. They enjoy playing and show it by smiling and squealing with delight. They can now reach out and grab a toy and move it from one hand to another. They are able to focus in on an object and explore it if it seems interesting. Babies also start to show that they understand a little of what is being said to them, and they try to communicate.

They usually enjoy their food and are beginning to try to feed themselves by grabbing a spoon (this can be quite messy). Many babies will also be getting their first teeth, which can be painful for them.

Babies of this age are also getting stronger. They can sit up with support in a high chair and are able to roll over from their backs to their fronts. Babies at 6 months have usually settled into a routine and will have periods in the day when they nap and others when they are keen to play and to be held.

Examples of what you might observe	
Physical	Babies who look like they are parachuting as they lift both their hands and feet up in the air and balance on their fronts
Cognitive	Toys and objects being explored in the mouth as well as with fingers

Communication	Arms lifting up to show a carer that they want to be picked up
Social, emotional and behavioural	Smiles of delight when they are playing with their primary carers

Examples of what you might observe	
Physical	Using fingers to feed
Cognitive	Exploring objects using hands and mouth
Communication	Tuneful strings of babbling
Social, emotional and behavioural	Trying to stay near their parent or carer

Babies at 9 months

Babies' physical development is now very noticeable. Many babies will be crawling or finding other ways of being mobile. They are also able to sit up without any support. These new movements mean that babies can explore more. They also spend a lot of time sitting and playing. As well as large movements, babies are picking up objects, handling them and becoming more skilled at touching things, although objects still get popped into the mouth.

Babies' language is also developing: babbling has become more tuneful and longer strings of sounds are put together. Babies are learning what some key words mean. They may start to get excited when they hear words such as 'drink' or 'dinner'. Babies are starting to show who they enjoy being with. From around 8 months, they start to cry when they are left with a stranger and will actively try to be with their parents or main carers.

Babies are also likely to have made a leap in their cognitive development. This is sometimes referred to as object permanence. At around 8 or 9 months most babies will understand that objects and people do not disappear but continue to exist when they are out of sight. This is an important breakthrough and is one explanation why babies at around this time begin to protest when their familiar carer leaves the room. Up until this point, babies have not been troubled if people and things 'disappear', but now they know that their carer is still around and are desperate to be with them again.

Babies at 1 year

The first birthday of a child is for many families a special event and a cause for celebration. Babies have developed a lot and are now mobile and may be on the verge of walking. They may try to stand up by holding onto furniture and some babies are already walking by holding onto things ('cruising'). Good adult supervision is essential. Babies are now able to crawl very quickly and have eyesight that is just as developed as that of adults. As well as being mobile, babies are also becoming quite skilled at using their hands. Objects are touched, moved and organised. They enjoy putting things into containers and taking them out again or dropping things and looking to see what happens to them. A strong feature of their play is the way in which they enjoy doing something over and over again. They may keep taking their hat off or pulling off their socks.

At 1 year, babies are able to sit up and feed themselves using their fingers. Most also know what they do and do not like. Food that they enjoy is eaten, while other foods may be thrown on the floor.

Finding ways of being mobile

Babies enjoy doing something over and over again

Babies are now able to understand more of what is happening around them. They not only notice what other people are doing but also understand more and more of what is being said. Long strings of babbling are still the way in which babies try to communicate, but hidden in the babbling are the beginnings of first words. These are usually noticed by parents and carers from around 13 months.

Examples of what you might observe	
Physical	Standing up and holding onto furniture
Cognitive	Recognising the routines of the day (e.g. becoming excited when they hear the bath water or have a bib put on)
Communication	Fingers pointing at objects to draw an adult's attention to them
Social, emotional and behavioural	Need to stay near their parents and carers and anxiety if strangers approach or handle them

Children at 18 months

The word 'toddler' is used for children who have begun to walk. It is a delightful term, as the child walks with a side-to-side movement. At 18 months children have literally begun to find their feet. They start to move quickly and enjoy the freedom this gives them. They are also keen to play with adults and are often fascinated by other children. They notice what older brothers and sisters are doing as well as children of their own age.

Around this age toddlers start to want some independence. They have learnt that they are separate from their parents and are starting to develop as individuals. They cry and protest if they want something and do not get it.

Children's language skills are also still developing. Most children will be able to use several words and will understand a lot of what adults are saying. This does not mean, however, that they can understand the need to share, wait and be cooperative. Many parents say that, at this age, their children start to develop minds of their own.

Toddlers can be quite restless and change moods quickly. This can be tiring for parents and carers. Toddlers also become distressed when they are left with unfamiliar people, and need a familiar adult if not with their parents or carers.

Examples of what you might observe	
Physical	Sitting and pushing off with legs on sit-and-ride toys
Cognitive	Enjoyment of pop-up and posting toys
Communication	Less babbling and more recognisable words
Social, emotional and behavioural	Interest in other children Signs of temper and frustration

Children at 2 years

By the age of 2 years, children are very much showing their individuality. They know what they want to do, touch and hold. They can now move confidently and are enjoying walking and being able to pick up things and play with them. They like to do things for themselves and are keen to do more and get frustrated when they are not able to. This is sometimes because adults realise that what they want is dangerous and

Playing on sit-and-ride toys

at other times because their skill does not match what they want to do. Their frustration can lead to temper tantrums and emotional outbursts. This is often a way of communicating how they are feeling and is why this period is sometimes known as the 'terrible twos'.

Toddlers do get frustrated and angry, but they are also emotional in other ways. They smile, laugh and squeal with enjoyment. They notice other children and enjoy being near them, even though they may not actively play together. Favourite games are played over and over again. Children are also starting to enjoy pretend play. They may take an empty cup and pretend to drink from it or give a teddy a hug; 2-year-olds are often starting to chat aloud and to point out objects and name them.

Some 2-year-olds are starting to be ready to move out of nappies (although some children may not be physically ready until they are about 3 years old).

Signs of temper and frustration

Examples of what you might observe	
Physical	Running and climbing
Cognitive	Playing with building bricks and doing simple jigsaw puzzles
Communication	A vocabulary of around 200 words
Social, emotional and behavioural	Parallel play — (playing next to rather than with other children) Anger and frustration if they cannot do what they want to do

Children at 2½

Children at 2½ years are still keen to be independent. They may find it hard to wait and to understand why they cannot always have what they see or do what they want. Their language is really starting to develop. Some are putting two words together to express their ideas and others are even starting to use sentences. Good supervision is still needed, as children's developing physical skills combined with their determination can mean that they go to extremes to get hold of an object. Moving chairs to climb up or standing on tables to reach up high is fairly common.

Children are also starting to play more with other children of their own age, although some of their time will be spent simply playing alongside others. Pretend play and play with small world toys become popular, as do tricycles, slides and climbing frames. They are still keen to have plenty of adult attention and will enjoy snuggling

up for a cuddle, as well as spending time helping an adult. Separating from parents remains difficult unless children really know who they will be with.

This is often the period in which toilet training starts in earnest, and, if children are ready, they can be out of nappies within a few days.

Examples of what you might observe	
Physical	Pedalling a tricycle or pushing it along with the feet
Cognitive	Pretend play with farm animals, teddies or in the home corner
Communication	Two-word compounds such as 'daddy-gone' or 'drink-no'
Social, emotional and behavioural	Playing alongside other children and copying their actions Temper tantrums if they are frustrated
Moral	No understanding of wrong and right, but understanding of the word 'no'

Pedalling a tricycle

Interest in other children and some cooperative play

Children at 3 years

Most children at 3 years old are making a huge developmental leap. This is linked to their use of language: suddenly, instead of showing that they are not happy, they can say so, and temper tantrums start to decrease. Children begin to understand more about what is happening and to understand the needs of others. From this point onwards most children are able to play with other children, and the sharing of toys and equipment becomes less difficult. Other children start to become important in their lives. In consequence they may look forward to going to pre-school or nursery each day. Children are also happier at being separated from their parents, as they can now understand that their parents will return; they are more able to talk to the staff looking after them.

Examples of what you might observe	
Physical	Walking upstairs on alternate feet
Cognitive	Interest in mark-making, painting and books
Communication	Speech that is easily understood
Social, emotional and behavioural	Interest in other children and some cooperative play
Moral	No understanding of wrong and right, but can follow simple rules most of the time

Children at 4 years

By 4 years old, most children have made huge steps forward in their development. They will be fairly fluent in their speech and should be easily understandable to adults who do not know them. There will still be the odd grammatical mistake and interesting pronunciation

TO40423

of a word, but by and large they will have mastered the spoken language. Most children's behaviour will be cooperative but this is dependent on their getting plenty of praise and recognition from adults.

Most 4-year-olds also enjoy being with other children and will be starting to plan their play and have definite ideas of what they want to do. They are also learning to be independent. They can generally dress and feed themselves and can organise their play if they are given the opportunity. They enjoy being with responsive adults, especially when they are being given responsibility and encouragement.

Most children will be attending some pre-school provision, such as a playgroup, nursery or crèche. This is important for them as they generally enjoy the company of other children and are beginning to develop friendships. They will also be learning – often without realising it, as activities will be planned for them. Depending on where they live, many children during this year will be starting school. For some children, this is a difficult transition, as they have to adapt to being part of a much larger group.

Examples of what you might observe	
Physical	Skilful use of the hands to carry out activities such as threading, pouring and using scissors
Cognitive	Concentration when an activity has caught their interest
Communication	Children asking questions and enjoying talking
Social, emotional and behavioural	Cooperative play between children along with the odd squabble and argument Children responding well to adult praise and recognition
Moral	Children who are thoughtful at times towards others, but who do things mainly for adult approval

Children at 5–6 years

In these years, changes in physical development are much less rapid. Instead, children gain in confidence and coordination. This is true also for other skills, such as their spoken language and ability to socialise. A good example of this is the way that, at around this time, children begin to enjoy hearing and making jokes.

At around 5 years, most children have begun formal education. This can be a difficult transition period for some children, especially if they are not interested in learning to read and write. For those children who are ready, learning to read and write can prove exciting and they enjoy the intellectual challenge of a classroom. As well as school, some children will also be starting activities such as swimming, dance or music. The ways

Pretend play that models adult life

Enjoyment of jokes

in which children play also begin to change. Children of this age are keen to work out the rules of different situations and enjoy playing games with rules.

Friends are important to children of this age. Many children will start to have established friendships and preferences. Staying for tea or even overnight is quite common and helps children to learn about other families, although of course children still rely on their parents to meet many of their emotional needs.

Examples of what you might observe	
Physical	Ability to kick and control a ball More legible handwriting and increased fine manipulative movements
Cognitive	Ability to count and do simple calculations
Communication	Beginning to decode some familiar words
Social, emotional and behavioural	Some friendship preferences
Moral	Keen to understand and use rules

Children at 7–9 years

Children's development in this period is more gradual than before. By now children are generally well co-ordinated, both in small and large movements. As a result of improved coordination, children often gain in confidence. Children continue to grow in height, but the main changes are in the way they think and reason. This can be seen in the way they play: their games and play become more organised, and they make up as well as follow rules. The way in which children think and reason also shows itself as they start to be able to solve simple problems and enjoy practical situations in which they have to work things out for themselves. Most children are also cooperative and enjoy being given responsibility. They respond well when adults give clear explanations for rules and when their behaviour is acknowledged and praised.

In these years, reading and writing become easier, although there will be variations in the speed at which children become competent and confident in this respect. Children also become more physically skilled. This physical ability means they are more able to do things more quickly, confidently and accurately. Doing up a coat, for example, is now an easy task, as is cutting out with scissors or drawing a simple picture. Friendships are becoming increasingly important. Many children will have groups of close friends and some will have 'best friends'. The lack or temporary absence of a friend starts to become an issue. Children may want to attend a club only if they know a friend is also likely to be there.

As most children are at school, life in the classroom and playground is a major influence on them. This is also a period in which children start to compare themselves with others. In some ways this is part of the thinking process, as they carry on working out what they are like. They may notice which children are the fastest runners, best readers or quickest at finishing tasks. This can start to affect their confidence and even enthusiasm.

Cooperative play

Examples of what you might observe	
Physical	Drawing and writing are neater; cutting out is more accurate
Cognitive	Reading books silently
Communication	Telling jokes and enjoying chatting Verbal arguments, persuasion and negotiation
Social, emotional and behavioural	Stable friendships Clear differences in the play activities that interest boys and girls
Moral	Children who tell others the rules and are keen to point out when rules have been broken

Children at 9–11 years

In some ways this period in most children's lives can be summed up as the 'calm before the storm'. Most children are fairly confident and have mastered many skills, and they will often have decided what they are good at. They can now read, write, draw and use some logic. They are often skilled communicators and enjoy having friends. This is a time when many children feel quite settled, although from the age of 9 onwards the first signs of impending **puberty** will show in girls. Breasts are likely to 'bud', and at around 10 or 11 years girls will begin to grow rapidly in height too. Some girls may even start menstruating before the age of 11 years, particularly when their weight to height ratio is high.

Detailed and representational pictures, which children enjoy drawing

Key term

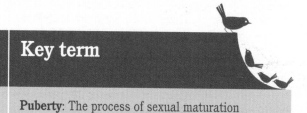

Puberty: The process of sexual maturation

Examples of what you might observe	
Physical	Greater coordination and speed when carrying out both fine and large movements
Cognitive	Problem solving (e.g. how to play cooperatively, use materials fairly)
Communication	Stories and writing that show imagination as well as being legible and reasonably grammatical
Social, emotional and behavioural	Stable relationships with friends Enthusiasm when given areas of responsibility
Moral	Awareness of consequences of behaviour and increased thoughtfulness

Young people at 11–13 years

This period in children's lives marks the start of their growing independence. While parents remain important, children begin to show signs of wanting to grow up. They may, for example, now ask to walk home or get buses home by themselves. Some children also begin to question rules at home and may try to push the boundaries. Young people's relationships with others of the same age become increasingly important. This can

put a lot of pressure on children, as their friends may have very different ideas to their parents. This period also sees other pressures on them. They are likely to be changing to another school for the next stage in their education. Quite often the new school will be larger and the curriculum more formal. They may have a series of teachers during the day, rather than just one or two.

This period also marks physical changes for young people as their bodies begin to prepare for adulthood. Girls' puberty usually begins at around 11 years, while boys may not start until they are 13 or 14 years old. The physical changes can cause embarrassment and anxiety and so create further pressure. Girls who feel that they are developing too quickly or not quickly enough can lose self-esteem.

Examples of what you might observe	
Physical	Growth and changes to their bodies
Cognitive	Understanding of more abstract concepts Reasoning and problem solving
Communication	Good reading and writing skills Negotiating and persuading adults and peers
Social, emotional and behavioural	Strong attachments to friends Anxiety about coping with the pressures of school Exploration of boundaries in relationships e.g. arguments with parents
Moral	Understanding for the need of rules in society

Relationships with others of the same age become increasingly important

Young people from 13–19 years

In this period, young people move closer to and reach adulthood. Physically, by around the age of 15 or 16, girls will have finished becoming women. For most boys, puberty will start at around the age of 14 and is likely to take about three years to complete.

Pressure in school is likely to increase as most young people prepare for examinations and may be starting to think about their futures. During these years, some young people will begin to 'drop out' of education. They may show avoidance behaviours such as truanting, messing around in class and bullying.

From 2009, children entering secondary school are required to stay in education until they are 18. They will then need to decide whether to leave education and find a job or go on to higher education. Some will have developed skills that are equal to those of adults (such as the ability to use computers). For young people who decide to leave school to go into employment, a job or college, this is a significant stage in their lives as they will be leaving a familiar environment and must adapt to new codes, relationships and expectations.

Being with friends is likely to be more important than being with family at this stage of life. Young people who do not have a group of friends are likely to feel they are missing out and may become anxious. Some may experience bullying if they are not part of a group. This can have a detrimental effect on their self-esteem and, in extreme cases, can result in suicide attempts, to draw attention to their unhappiness. For those who carry out the bullying,

the outcomes are not good either as they may learn that this is a way of gaining respect from others.

This is a time when young people are also trying to explore their own identity. They may have tastes in music, clothes and activities that are different from those of their parents. This may cause clashes as young people try to develop their own personality and create their own space. They may test the boundaries at home and sometimes at school. As the transition to adulthood is not complete, young people will also at times revert to 'child-like' comments, activities and games.

Somewhere during this period, many young people will experience their first romantic relationship. For some this may result in a sexual relationship, although sexual intercourse below the age of 16 is illegal.

Examples of what you might observe	
Physical	Occasional poor spatial awareness as a result of the body shape changing quickly – particularly common in boys
Cognitive	High level of skills (e.g. using computers)
Communication	Use of phones and technology to communicate with friends
Social, emotional and behavioural	Confidence and enjoyment when with friends Behaviour linked to low self-esteem (e.g. smoking, misuse of substances, early promiscuity)
Moral	Understanding about right and wrong and consequences of actions Interest in moral issues

Confidence and enjoyment when with friends

Creating a personal space can be problematic

The difference between sequence of development and rate of development

Some aspects of development follow a definite sequence. This is particularly true when it comes to physical development: for example, babies have to learn to lift their heads before they can sit; toddlers have to walk before they can run. It is also the case in other areas such as communication as, for example, a baby recognises words before producing them. While these sequences of development are typical in all children, what can change between individual children is the speed or rate at which they develop. This means some babies will sit unsupported at 7 months, while others may take a couple of months longer.

It is also interesting, when looking at an individual child's development, to note the way that they may have different rates of development in different areas; for example a baby at 13 months may not be walking, but may already be saying a few words, an 8-year-old may be a strong swimmer, but find reading difficult.

The importance of sequence and rates of development

It is important when working with individual children and young people to note both the sequence and the rate of their development in each of the different areas. Sequence is needed in order to plan effectively for them, but looking at rate of development is also essential to check whether their rate of development is atypical and needs further investigation or support (see below).

Understand the factors that influence children and young people's development and how these affect practice

What makes children so different even when they are the same age? This is an important question and one that has not yet been fully answered. We do know, however, that children's development is shaped both by intrinsic or personal factors, such as their health, but also external factors such as their family environment and their access to educational provision. This means that while a child may be born with the potential to be a great artist, this potential is unlikely to be realised unless the child has the chance to paint and draw and is encouraged by adults.

Personal factors

There are a range of factors that will affect children and young people's development. This is an interesting area and one that increasingly is being informed by **genetics**.

> ### Key term
>
> **Genetics**: the unique biological code that each person inherits

Influences before and at birth

Children's development starts from the moment they are conceived. Genetic information is packaged together from the egg and the sperm. The child's hair, for example, will be decided genetically, as will, to an extent, the child's height (although this will also be affected by the child's later environment and diet). It increasingly seems that genetics may play a part in causing addiction, depression and issues to do with self-esteem, by pre-disposing us in some way. This means that our genetic code does not absolutely govern what we will do or become, but certain environmental factors will trigger the genes to affect us.

As well as the genetic information that is put together at the moment of conception, a baby's development can be affected during pregnancy. The baby can be harmed if the mother smokes or uses drugs or alcohol at this time. Infections that the mother picks up, such as rubella, can create difficulties for the developing baby. Maternal anxiety and stress, as well as diet, also seem to influence development.

Children's development can also be influenced by when they are born and what happens during the birth. A few babies are born too early and this can play a part in their later development. This is one reason why premature babies' progress is measured according to the date they were due to be born rather than their actual birth date.

Birth itself can be tricky for a few babies. A baby may not breathe straight away or may be injured during the birth. Lack of oxygen (anoxia) can affect brain function and can result in learning difficulties.

Health status

Health is determined both by genetic make-up and by factors such as diet, environment and stress. In some cases children are born with a condition that will automatically affect them, such as a blood disorder. Other children may have a predisposition towards certain diseases but do not develop them unless particular circumstances trigger them. A good example of this is

asthma, a condition that affects breathing and is currently on the increase. Children who live in areas where the air quality is poor, who live in damp conditions or whose parents smoke are more likely to develop asthma.

Ill health can affect many aspects of children's development. They may not feel like playing or their condition may restrict what they can do. Children may find it harder to make friends because they miss playgroup sessions or cannot physically join in. As a practitioner, you should look for ways to ensure that children with a medical condition miss out on as little as possible.

Disability, sensory impairment and learning difficulties

Earlier in this unit we have seen that each area of development is co-dependent on others; for example an 8-year-old making a sandwich is using cognitive skills to sequence its making as well as physical skills. This co-dependency can mean that a child who has specific difficulties may be disadvantaged in other areas

Using an inhaler to relieve asthma

Case study: Michael's new school

Michael was born without sight. He has just changed school and now attends a primary school where a special needs assistant supports him. In the playground some of the children want to play with a ball. In his last school, he could not join in and so did not have many opportunities to be physically active. In this new school, the playground lines are raised slightly and there are balls that have bells in them. His special needs assistant is also at hand and she encourages him to join in.

1. Why might Michael's social development also be affected if he cannot join in with other children's play?

2. Explain how Michael's special needs assistant is making a difference to his overall development.

3. Why is it important to support children who have a disability or learning need in all areas of their development?

of development. Sometimes disadvantage may not be inevitable if the child is properly supported, as the case study on page 61 shows.

External factors

We have seen that there are many intrinsic or personal factors linked to a child or young person's development, but this is not the whole story. What happens to a child after they have been born also plays a part. These are sometimes called environmental or external factors.

Poverty and deprivation

Poverty affects children and their families in a variety of ways. Poverty in the UK is categorised as relative rather than absolute, meaning that children are not starving, but the effects of growing up in poverty are still very marked, as the spider diagram below shows.

Diet

Children's growth, behaviour and development can be affected by their diet. A balanced diet will help children to remain healthy as well as to grow. Families on low incomes may buy cheaper foods, often processed foods with high levels of salt, fat and sugar, which have lower nutritional value.

The effects of growing up in poverty are still very marked

Housing

Families on lower incomes may live in poorer quality housing and may not have sufficient money to heat them adequately. Damp, crowded housing is more likely to affect children's health and opportunities to play freely.

Education

Children from low-income households are less likely to do well academically because they may not attend the best schools and they may not have equal access to educational tools and resources such as books or the Internet.

Play and leisure opportunities

Stimulation is important for children's cognitive and other areas of development. Play is one of the ways in which this takes place, but it also happens as children get older through leisure opportunities such as swimming, playing an instrument or joining a club or organisation (such as Brownies or Cubs etc.). Children from low-income families may not have transport or the financial resources to access play and leisure opportunities.

Aspirations and expectations

Being poor not only affects the physical conditions in which people live, but also their outlook. Parents can become depressed and children and young people can develop a feeling that their lives cannot be changed. This in turn can lead to a lack of motivation which will have an important effect on all areas of development.

Family environment and background

Children's development is influenced by their family environment. Parents in particular are extremely important in children's lives and this is why policies in early years settings are designed to work in partnership with them. Most parents do a very good job of nurturing and providing for their children. They provide them with a reasonable diet, care for them and provide opportunities for play and socialisation. Parents may also support their children as they go through school by being actively involved in homework or taking an interest in what the child does. This has a significant impact on children's development, especially in the areas of cognitive and social and emotional development.

Unfortunately, however, some parents are not able to cope so well. This can affect the way their children develop. Depression, drug-taking and alcoholism are examples of conditions that might contribute to parents' inability to fulfil their parenting role easily. While parents may neglect babies and younger children, older children may find themselves taking on a caring role within the family. It is not unknown for children aged as young as 5 years to dress and feed younger siblings.

Family circumstances

Most families suffer stress from time to time (for example as a result of a family member becoming ill or unemployed or because of the need to move house). Some stresses are temporary, but others are more permanent, such as coping with a long-term illness or disability. In some cases, a family may separate as one parent leaves, or a lone parent may settle with a new partner. These types of stresses on families can affect children and young people's development. A child may start to become anxious, a young person may no longer be motivated to work at school or may drop out of education and develop antisocial behaviour.

Personal choices

As children develop into young people, they are usually given more independence and autonomy. This means that they are often in situations where they can make their own decisions, such as whether or not to smoke, drink or have sex. The choices that young people make can have an effect on their development. This is particularly true, it seems, in terms of drug use. Cannabis, for example, can interfere with the healthy growth of the brain in the teenage years. Young people may also make choices about what to eat and this again can affect their physical and possibly their cognitive development; for example it would seem that not having breakfast can adversely affect concentration.

Looked-after children

There are many reasons why children may be in the care of the local authority, including family breakdown, inadequate parenting, youth offending and disability.

Some children may be in residential care or living with foster families or may have **care status**.

Key term

Care status: where children deemed to be in need are the responsibility of the local authority because a care order has been granted by the courts.

Statistically, children and young people who live with their parents but are the responsibility of local authorities have less favourable outcomes. There are many reasons for this, but a key factor is the lack of a stable, warm and consistent environment in which children and young people can make strong attachments. The need for children and young people to have a strong and enduring attachment with a primary carer seems to make a difference in terms of children's academic development, as well as their social and emotional development.

Education

Quality education can enhance children's overall development considerably. Most education is received in schools, but it is important to recognise that children and young people also learn at home, by taking part in groups such as churches or mosques and through specific activities such as singing in choirs. Good education stimulates children's cognitive development, allowing them to learn to read, write, problem solve and reason. Education can also help children to socialise, develop moral codes and learn to be organised. In good schools, children and young people may have access to wider learning possibilities such as sports, technology and languages. Children and young people who feel engaged in their education are likely to have their development enhanced but, unfortunately, this is not always the case. Some children and young people find education an alienating experience and one that lowers their self-esteem. This in turn means that they cannot benefit from the opportunities on offer.

Children and young people who feel engaged in their education are likely to have their development enhanced

Theories of development and frameworks to support development

While we can see that there is a range of factors that affect children's development, the education and care they receive will also affect them.

Theories of development

Theories of development are important as they can influence practice and also help us to understand children's behaviour, reactions and ways of learning. In this section we consider approaches to how children learn and also behave. We also look at theories of attachment as these are needed to understand the effects of transition, which we consider later in the chapter. Table 1 outlines some of the main approaches and theories that are commonly used to explain children's development.

Table 1: Common theories of development

Approaches to cognitive development	Outline	Theorists
Constructivist	Constructivist theories look at the way in which children seem to be able to make sense of their world as a result of their experiences and how they are active learners	Jean Piaget Lev Vygotsky
Behaviourist	Behaviourist theories look at the way in which children repeat actions in response to stimuli and reinforcements	John B. Watson Ivan Pavlov B.F Skinner
Social Learning	Social Learning theorists look at the way children can learn through imitation	Albert Bandura
Approaches to Social and Emotional Development	**Outline**	**Theorist**
Psychoanalytical	Personality and actions are determined by the unconscious mind which develops in childhood	Sigmund Freud
Humanist	Motivation and personality are linked to our basic needs being met	Abraham Maslow
Attachment theory	Social and emotional development are linked to babies and young children having strong bonds or attachment with their primary carers	John Bowlby

Piaget's theory of cognitive development

Jean Piaget (1896–1980) was a zoologist who became interested in children's cognitive development as a result of working on intelligence tests. He noticed that children consistently gave similar 'wrong' answers to some

Assimilation. The child constructs a theory (schema).

↓

Equilibrium. The child's experiences to date seem to fit the schema (everything balances).

↓

Disequilibrium. An experience occurs that casts doubt on the effectiveness of the schema. (Things don't add up any more!)

↓

Accommodation. The child changes the original schema to fit the new piece of experience or information.

Stages of learning in Piaget's theory

Piaget's theory says that children construct or build up their thoughts according to their experiences

ours. Piaget also suggested that, as children develop, so does their thinking. He grouped children's cognitive development into four broad stages. Table 2 outlines these four stages.

questions and began to consider why this was. Piaget used his own children to make detailed observations and gradually developed a theory that has been very influential.

Piaget's theory of learning is sometimes referred to as a 'constructivist approach' because he suggested that children *constructed* or built up their thoughts according to their experiences of the world around them. Piaget used the term 'schema' to refer to a child's conclusions or thoughts. He felt that learning was an ongoing process, with children needing to adapt (hence Piaget's term 'adaption') their original ideas if a new piece of information seemed to contradict their conclusions. For example, a group of toddlers may come to believe that milk is served in blue beakers, because their experience of having milk is linked with it being served in a blue beaker. If one day they are given juice in the blue beaker instead of milk, they will need to reconsider the theory and thus come to the conclusion that milk and other drinks come in blue beakers. Piaget used specific vocabulary to describe the process of children learning in this way.

Piaget's belief that children develop schemas based on their direct experiences can help us to understand why young children's thinking is sometimes different from

Table 2: Piaget's four broad stages of cognitive development

Stage	Approximate age	Features
Sensori-motor	0–2 years	Development of object permanence
		Child begins to use symbols (e.g. language)
Pre-operational	2–7 years	Child uses symbols in play and thought
		Egocentrism
		Centration
		Animism
		Inability to conserve
Concrete operational	7–11 years	Ability to conserve
		Children begin to solve mental problems using practical supports such as counters and objects
Formal operational	11–15 years	Young people can think about situations that they have not experienced
		They can juggle with ideas in their minds

Links to practice

Piaget's work has meant that early years settings and schools have attempted to provide more hands-on and relevant tasks for children and young people. His work is often thought to have influenced 'child-centred' teaching in which the teachers start by working out the needs of children and plan activities accordingly. Piaget's work has influenced approaches to managing children's behaviour as he also looked at the development of children's morality again from a child's rather than an adult's perspective.

Over to you

Piaget linked children's moral development to their cognitive development. Try out the following question on children of different ages. Note their different responses.

Jimmy was helping his mother to wash up. He dropped ten plates. They all broke. Another child, Noah, did not like his dinner. He threw his plate on the floor and it broke.

Who was the naughty child?

(Piaget suggested that younger children would not consider the intentions of the child – only the result of the actions.)

Functional Skills

Maths: Interpreting and Analysing

You could record the different responses from children in the form of a table. You could then calculate the percentage of the results that favoured Jimmy over Noah and this could then be converted into a fraction.

Vygotsky's theory of cognitive development

While Piaget's work is well known, another theorist, Lev Vygotsky (1896–1934) has proved influential and his work has been especially adopted in the early years frameworks of England and Scotland. Vygotsky believed that children's social environment and experiences are very important. He considered that children were born to be sociable and that by being with their parents, and then with their friends, they acquired skills and concepts. Vygotsky saw children as 'apprentices', learning and gaining understanding through being with others (a process termed 'scaffolding').

Vygotsky also suggested that maturation was an important element in children's development and that carers needed to extend children's learning so that they could use their emerging skills and concepts. He used the term 'zone of proximal development' to define this idea, although we might think of this as 'potential'.

Links to practice

Vygotsky's work has been influential. He suggested that people working with children need to extend and challenge their thoughts so that their zone of proximal development can emerge. He stressed the importance of social interaction and the need for adults to work alongside children, and he also felt that children could guide and develop each other's potential. This has meant that children and young people are often encouraged to do tasks together. It is interesting to note that although Vygotsky saw that direct teaching was important, he also stressed the importance of children being active in their learning.

Reflect

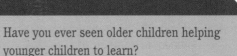

Have you ever seen older children helping younger children to learn?

Do you encourage this in your setting?

Functional Skills

English: Writing

You could write a diary account of a time when you have seen older children helping younger children to learn. Take care with your punctuation, spelling, grammar, sentence structure and paragraphs.

Behaviourist approaches to learning

The behaviourist approach suggests that learning is influenced by rewards, punishments and environmental factors. The term 'conditioning' is often used by behaviourists. It means that you learn to act in a certain way because past experiences have taught you to do or not to do something. You may know this as 'learning by association' (for example, not touching a flame after once being burned by a candle).

Two types of conditioning are well documented: classical conditioning and operant conditioning.

Classical conditioning

The idea of conditioning was born out of research into dogs' digestive systems. Ivan Pavlov (1849–1936) was a physiologist who, while studying dogs, noticed that they always started to salivate before food was put down for them. He came to the conclusion that the dogs were anticipating the food and were salivating because they had learnt to associate the arrival of food with other things, such as the sound of footsteps and the sight of buckets. To show this more clearly he devised an experiment in which he fed dogs while a bell was sounded. Normally dogs do not salivate when hearing bells, but the dogs began to associate the bell with food and would salivate simply on hearing it.

Pavlov also looked at what would happen if the bell repeatedly rang and no food was offered to the dogs. He found that gradually the conditioned response (dogs salivating) became weaker until finally the dogs did not react to the bell. The term used by behaviourists when this happens is 'extinction'.

John B. Watson (1878–1958), took up Pavlov's work and demonstrated that children and adults could be classically conditioned. In a famous experiment, which would now be considered unethical, he created a phobia of rats in a small boy, known as Little Albert.

Reflect

Can you detect a regular pattern of behaviour among babies and young children at meal times? For example a baby who always bangs their highchair tray when they know it is meal time.

Links to practice

Although classical conditioning is not used with children or young people as part of practice, it is useful to understand, especially in relation to children or young people's phobias such as going to the toilet in a strange place, fear of needles etc.

Operant conditioning

The essence of the operant conditioning theory is that learning is based on the type of consequence or reinforcement that follows an initial behaviour. B. F. Skinner (1904–90) is recognised as being a key figure in developing the behaviourist approach to learning theory and, in particular, for developing the theory of operant conditioning.

Skinner suggested that most humans and animals learn through exploring the environment and then drawing conclusions based on the consequences of their behaviour. This means that people tend to be active in the learning process – unlike in the theory of classical conditioning.

Skinner divided the consequences of actions into three groups:

- *Positive reinforcers* are likely to make people repeat behaviour when they get something they desire (for example, they may buy a new food product after having tried and liked a free sample). Skinner suggested that using positive reinforcement was the most effective way of encouraging new learning. Positive reinforcers for children include gaining adults' attention, praise, stickers, sweets and treats.

- *Negative reinforcers* are likely to make people repeat behaviour as well, but the difference is that the behaviour is repeated to stop something happening. Children going down a slide might learn to use their hands to slow them down if they are feeling unhappy about the speed.

- *Punishers* are likely to stop people from repeating behaviour. For example, they may learn to stay away from an electric fence after receiving a shock.

Frequency and timing of reinforcement

Skinner looked at the effect on behaviour of giving positive reinforcers at different intervals. How long would behaviour be shown – without a positive reward – before extinction took place? Interestingly, he found that unpredictable reinforcement works better than continual reinforcement. This would seem to work because it

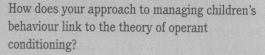

teaches learners not to expect a reward or reinforcement every time — hence they keep on showing the behaviour just in case a reinforcement is given.

Children need frequent positive reinforcement as this helps them to learn wanted behaviour. Giving children praise or stickers unexpectedly will help them to carry on showing wanted behaviour until such time that it becomes learned and, in some way, becomes automatic behaviour.

Timing

Immediate positive reinforcements are the most effective because the behaviour is then more strongly linked to the reinforcement. Delaying positive reinforcement, for example saying to children that they can have a sticker at the end of the week, weakens the effect of the reinforcement.

Unexpected positive reinforcers

Skinner found during his experiments that it was often hard to predict what would act as a primary reinforcer and that it was sometimes only *after* the event that this became clear. An example of this is when children sometimes deliberately behave badly in order to attract their carer's attention. If they manage to attract attention, they are more likely to show the behaviour again, although they might be in trouble. Gaining the carer's attention in this case is the positive reinforcer, even if they are scolded.

Links to practice

Most professionals working with children and young people use operant conditioning in some form or other, even if they do not know it as such! It is usual, for example, to praise children and young people, give them treats, certificates or other rewards if they do well.

Skinner suggested that using positive reinforcement encourages new learning

Reflect

How does your approach to managing children's behaviour link to the theory of operant conditioning?

Do you praise children soon after seeing wanted behaviour?

Have you noticed how some children act in ways to gain adult attention?

Why does this matter?

The classical conditioning theory and operant conditioning theory are used as tools to support children's positive behaviour. You may need to re-visit these sections when you complete Unit EYMP1.

Social learning theory

Social learning theory is another behaviourist approach. The key figure among social learning theorists is Albert Bandura (born 1925). Social learning theorists accept the principles of conditioning but suggest that another type of learning is also taking place: learning by watching others.

Observational learning

Social learning theorists suggest that people also learn by observing others. This is sometimes referred to as 'observational learning'. It is an interesting theory and many early years workers will have seen children copy each other's or an adult's behaviour. One of the features of observational learning is that it is spontaneous — children will naturally learn by imitating rather than being shown or taught. Observational learning can also occur without any reinforcement, which is an important difference from conditioning. Since the early days of the theory, some refinements have been made as researchers have been interested to understand why children and young people are able to copy some things, but not others. Cognition seems to be important in this, with the child needing to be able to notice the activity and also be able to remember it accurately. Interestingly, in view of the cognitive aspects, Bandura has revised the name of his theory to reflect this, calling it now 'social cognitive theory'.

Links to practice

Children and young people will learn a lot of social behaviours by observing the way that those around them act. This means that most settings will encourage staff to act as good role models for children and young people by, for example, speaking to them courteously and showing healthy behaviours such as not smoking.

> ### Why does this matter?
> The social learning theory is used in part to help us promote children's positive behaviour. You may like to re-visit this section when you complete Unit EYMP1.

Personality

It is fascinating to see babies quickly develop their own characteristics and personalities. Theories of personality are interesting. One of the most influential is that of Sigmund Freud (1856–1939). He is particularly famous for his psychosexual theory of development, which is often used to explain unconscious thoughts and actions. His work shaped counselling and therapeutic work, although has now been superseded by other methods.

Freud's structure of personality

Freud suggested that there were three parts that made up our personality: the 'id', the 'ego' and the 'superego'. Not all of these parts are present at birth but develop with the child.

- *The id.* This is the instinctive part of the personality. It is governed by the drives and needs of the body, such as hunger or finding pleasure. The id does not consider how meeting desires and wants will affect others and so is often thought of as the selfish and passionate component. Freud suggested that babies had only the id when they were born; hence a baby will cry and cry until it gets fed, regardless of how tired the carer is or whether there are other children that also need feeding. Getting the desire or need met is known as 'gratification'.

- *The ego.* The ego has a planning role. It works out how to meet the id's needs and desires in the best way. The ego develops from the id in the first few months. Babies might learn that by smiling in some situations

they are more likely to get their needs met, while in others it is better to cry. In some situations the ego may make the id wait for its demands to be met. For example, children may learn that if they snatch a cake from a tray they might have it taken away from them, but by waiting to be offered they will eventually get it. The term 'deferred gratification' is used when this happens. The ego is often thought of as being the common sense part of our personalities.

- *The superego.* The superego develops later in childhood. It tries to control the ego. It comprises two elements: the conscience and the ego-ideal. The conscience will punish the ego if it misbehaves. This is the source of guilt. The ego-ideal will reward the ego if it shows good behaviour. This is the source of pride and confidence.

Links to practice

Freud's work has been criticised as it has not stood up to scientific scrutiny. However, his observations into the link between our unconscious actions and our mind are still seen as useful. It is worth reading about defence mechanisms, for example, the way that children and young people may put a hand over their mouth if they are lying, as if to stop the words from coming out.

Maslow's theory of motivation and personality

In the 1940s Abraham Maslow (1908–70) looked at people's motivation. He came to the conclusion that people had certain fundamental needs which had to be met before they could begin to fulfil their potential or 'self-actualisation.' If the basic needs were not met, they

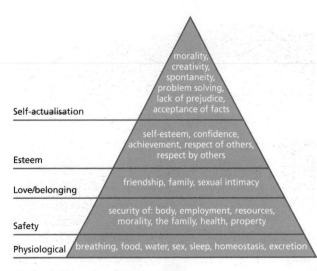

Maslow's Hierarchy of Needs

Self-actualisation — morality, creativity, spontaneity, problem solving, lack of prejudice, acceptance of facts

Esteem — self-esteem, confidence, achievement, respect of others, respect by others

Love/belonging — friendship, family, sexual intimacy

Safety — security of: body, employment, resources, morality, the family, health, property

Physiological — breathing, food, water, sex, sleep, homeostasis, excretion would create a deficiency in the person. His basic needs or 'deficiency needs' are hierarchical, but all have to be met before a person can achieve self-actualisation.

Links to practice

It is recognised when working with children and young people that their needs for warmth, food and shelter must be met, along with psychological needs such as love and promoting of self-esteem. This means that, in practice, professionals need to think about the environment that they are creating for children as well as forming strong relationships with them.

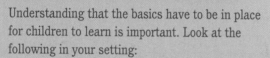

Reflect

Understanding that the basics have to be in place for children to learn is important. Look at the following in your setting:

- temperature of the indoor space at different times of the day
- snack and meal times
- amount of time children spend with their key person.

Are each of these meeting children's needs?

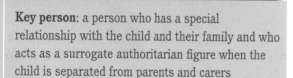

Key term

Key person: a person who has a special relationship with the child and their family and who acts as a surrogate authoritarian figure when the child is separated from parents and carers

Attachment

The term 'attachment' is widely used by psychologists studying children's early relationships. An attachment can be thought of as a unique emotional tie between a child and another person, usually an adult. Research has repeatedly shown that the quality of these ties or attachments will shape a child's ability to form other relationships later in life. Psychologists have also studied the effects on children when attachments are not made in infancy or when they have been broken (for example through separation).

A key theorist in relation to attachment theory is John Bowlby (1907–90). In the 1950s he identified that children and young people's mental health and behaviour could be linked to separation from a child's primary carer. He also identified that young children can show separation anxiety if their primary carer is not there for them. Further work on attachment has shown that the effects of separation can be reduced if an alternative strong attachment is made available for children.

There seems to be a general pattern to the way children develop attachments.

Table 3: The stages of attachment

Age	Stage	Features
6 weeks to 3 months		Babies begin to be attracted to human faces and voices. First smiles begin at around 6 weeks.
3 months to 7/8 months	Indiscriminate attachments	Babies are learning to distinguish between faces and show obvious pleasure when they recognise familiar faces. They are happy to be handled by strangers, preferring to be in human company rather than left alone (hence the term indiscriminate attachments).
7/8 months	Specific attachments	At around 7 or 8 months, babies begin to miss key people in their lives and show signs of distress, for example crying when they leave the room. Most babies seem to develop one particularly strong attachment, often to the mother. Babies show a wariness of strangers even when in the presence of their 'key people'. This wariness may quickly develop into fear if the stranger makes some form of direct contact with the baby, for example by touching them.

Table 3: The stages of attachment (continued)

Age	Stage	Features
From 8 months	Multiple attachments	After making specific attachments, babies then go on to form multiple attachments. This is an important part of their socialisation process.

Links to practice

Attachment theories have shaped practice in day-to-day child care and education but also social care practice. In pre-schools, young children are provided with a key person; an adult who will develop a strong bond with the child to act as a substitute attachment. In social care practice, children and young people are kept with their families or put in long-term foster care wherever possible rather than being taken into local authority residential homes.

Why does this matter?

Attachment theory is at the heart of understanding how to support children when they separate from their parents and also how to help them settle in to new environments. You will need to re-visit this section to support your knowledge in relation to Units CYP3.2 and EYMP1.

Frameworks to support development

We have seen that there are many theorists who can help us in our work with children. Over the past few years, different theories and ways of working with children have been combined and used to provide frameworks for children's care and education. A good example of this is the Early Years Foundation Stage. This framework contains elements of Vygotsky's theories, as there is a focus on adults working closely with children and observing and planning for their development. It also has elements of Piaget's theory as children are meant to be given opportunities to play and explore independently.

Social pedagogy

We have seen that theories of development and ways of working with children and young people can be brought together to create frameworks for care and education.

Reflect

Think about the framework that you are using with children and young people. Can you trace any components back to theories?

This holistic way and thoughtful way of working is known as social pedagogy. The aim of social pedagogy is to find ways of working with children and young people which will improve their life chances and social outcomes.

Understand how to monitor children and young people's development and interventions that should take place if this is not following the expected pattern

We have seen the sequence and rates of development associated with different ages of children and young people, but not all children will match them. This is sometimes a matter of concern and so will be investigated to check that are there no underlying reasons for this. This learning outcome looks at how this monitoring might take place and the type of support for children and young people that is available.

Monitoring and assessing children

Children and young people are likely to be monitored and assessed at many different points in their lives and by different services; for example the health service will check a newborn, while schools may administer a range of tests. In terms of children's early development, monitoring and assessment is crucial as it has been seen that early intervention can make a significant difference to a child's overall outcomes; for example a child who is not fully hearing will find it harder to learn language unless support is given early on.

Methods of assessing development

There are many ways in which children and young people's development is considered. In Unit 3.2 we will look in more detail about methods that you might use in the workplace; in this unit we consider general methods. When looking at methods of monitoring and assessing development, it is important to note that the most effective way to check a child's developmental progress is to use a range of sources and different methods. This provides a fuller 'picture' of the child or young person.

Assessment frameworks

In education, there are specific frameworks against which children's development is measured — particularly in terms of academic performance. Good examples of this are the Early Years Foundation Stage Profile or, for children with learning difficulties, the P-scales.

There are many different ways in which observations can be conducted

measurements and tests carried out by educational psychologists, such as reasoning tests. In addition, many children in schools will be assessed using Cognitive Aptitude Tests. Standardised tests are useful as they help professionals to see how a child is doing in relation

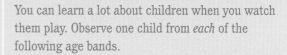

Over to you

What type of assessment frameworks are used in your setting?

How is the information used?

Observation

Observation literally means watching children. There are many different ways in which observations can be conducted. Some observations require that the observer does not interact with children, while in others, the observer acts as a participant. In early years settings, observations play a key part in assessing children's development and are linked closely to planning for groups of children (see Unit 3.2 for specific methods of observation).

Standard measurements

There are some standardised assessment methods which are used by a variety of different professionals. These include auditory assessments, health assessments — including height, weight and head circumference

Over to you

You can learn a lot about children when you watch them play. Observe one child from *each* of the following age bands.

- 1–3 years
- 4–8 years
- 9–11 years.

Look for a situation where the child is playing around other children. Try to observe the following:

- hand movements
- coordination
- cooperation and interest in other children
- communication and language skills
- concentration.

Write a report based on your three observations, comparing the development of the three children.

to a large population of same-age children. This can mean that a child who appears to be 'just average' when compared to their peers in a setting, may when assessed against standardised measurements be 'above' average.

Information from parents, carers and others

It is recognised in the early years sector that monitoring and assessing children should be carried out by a wide range of people who are involved with the child. This is because they will see the child in a variety of different situations. It is also useful to involve children, where appropriate, as they may also have a different perspective. A 6-year-old, when asked what they would most like to be able to do, might suggest something that is important to them, but which has been overlooked by the adults. Children aged 4 years, when shown a film clip of their play, might talk about what they tried to do and may comment about what they would like to do next. Interestingly, parents are often able to spot a developmental difference in their child earlier than some professionals. This might be because they spend longer with their child or because they are simply more attuned to their child.

Why children and young people's development may not follow the expected pattern

At the start of this unit, we looked at influences on children's development. For most children, it will be these influences that are the reason behind their not following the expected developmental pattern for their age. The spider diagram shows these and some additional reasons. Occasionally there are children for whom, despite investigation, no specific reasons can be found.

Disability

A disability may prevent a child from developing in one or more areas. Early support might minimise the effect of the disability by, for example, organising specific equipment for the child.

Emotional reasons

A significant element in children's overall development seems to be how settled and emotionally attached they are. Children or young people who are depressed or lacking in confidence may not be motivated to try out new skills.

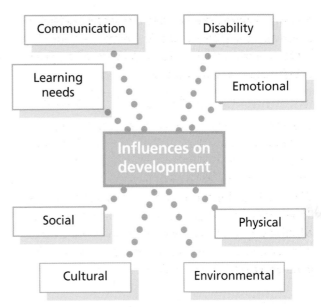

Why children and young people's development may not follow the expected pattern

Physical reasons

Some children's developmental pattern is affected by their genetic code. This may mean they are slow to develop in many areas for no specific reason. Children's development can also be slowed down by difficulties in physical growth.

Environmental reasons

We saw earlier in the chapter that external influences such as where a child grows up, their family structure and the type of educational setting they attend may all contribute to – or adversely affect – their development.

Cultural reasons

The way families bring up their children can vary enormously. This in turn can affect children's development. In some families there are very significant differences in the ways that they bring up boys and girls. This can in extreme cases mean that a child's development is adversely affected. Families will also have different ideas as to what they consider to be important in terms of giving children freedom and independence. This will affect children and young people's development.

Social reasons

Family structure and lifestyle seem to affect development. Although there is no 'perfect' family, children whose parents have separated are more likely to have negative 'blips' in their development – as do children who are born into poverty. Some families may accord less importance to some activities that are developmentally favourable, such as playing outdoors, going to the library or talking together as a family, and this may also affect a child's development.

Learning needs

There are many reasons why children may have specific learning needs. They include damage to specific chromosomes, disease and difficulties at birth. Learning needs may be specific, such as a difficulty in learning to read, or more generalised difficulties that affect children's overall cognition.

Communication skills

Children's communication levels can have a huge impact on other areas of their development. Children whose communication levels are low may become frustrated easily and show aggressive behaviour; they may find it hard to concentrate in activities that require listening and processing of information. As communication is also linked to literacy skills, children with low levels of communication may find it harder to learn to read and write.

How differences may be recognised

Recognising that a child's development is not typical for their age has to be done carefully and sensitively. In some cases, specific assessments will pinpoint that a child has, for example, a hearing loss or a sight problem. In other cases, it will be those caring for the children, including parents, who will notice that a child seems to respond differently or slower than other children of the same age. Routine observations may also help practitioners to see how a child is progressing, as most early years settings will compare a child's stage of development with the previous record. In some cases, it will be the child who will say something that may help staff to realise that there is a concern, such as suspected abuse.

How disability may affect development

In the last fifty years, there has been a huge shift in thinking when it comes to the care and education of disabled children and young people. In the past, the medical model of disability (see also Unit 3.7) meant that opportunities for learning and development were often denied to children and young people with disabilities. Today, a different approach is taken so that most settings

look for ways of increasing learning and development opportunities for these children. Having said this, some disabilities can affect a child's overall development as aspects of development are interlinked; for example, a child's behaviour may be affected by their language.

Stereotyping and low expectations

When children and young people have development that does not match the expected pattern, there is a danger of stereotyping and this can lead to low expectations. For example, a child with specific learning needs might be expected to do poorly in all subjects at school, not just those affected by the learning need. If adults working with children have low expectations for them, this can be harmful as they can in turn lower children's own expectations of their capabilities. This means that, while it is important to recognise the extent of a child's difficulty, the focus of our work with children should be to consider ways of overcoming it.

Technology can support children and young people's development in many different ways

Different types of intervention

Once children are identified as not following the expected pattern, a range of agencies may become involved. In some cases, professionals from different services will work together, in what is known as a multi-agency approach. In some instances, the focus will be to work with the family as a whole, particularly if the reason for the delay is cultural or social. Table 4 shows some of the different professionals who may work to support children and young people's development.

Assistive technology

There are now many different ways in which children and young people's development can be supported using technology. Children and young people with fine motor skills delay may, for example, use voice-activated computer programmes to assist with writing, while children and young people with mobility difficulties may use the latest generation of wheelchairs. Choosing the right type of assistive technology is likely to be the responsibility of physiotherapists, speech and language therapists and also professionals working to support sensory impairment.

Table 4: Professionals involved in interventions with children

Professional	Role
SENCO	A person in an education setting who has responsibility for organising identification and support for children with special education needs.
Social worker	Employed by local authority or voluntary organisation to support vulnerable children and young people and their families. Vulnerable children may include those with disabilities as well as those on protection registers.
Speech and language therapist	A professional who supports children and young people who have difficulties in communication. Speech and language therapists also provide training for professionals working with children.
Educational psychologist	A professional who supports children who have difficulties with behaviour or learning. Will identify difficulties and also provide programmes of support for teachers, early years practitioners and others to follow.
Psychiatrist	A medically trained doctor who has specialised in mental health. May diagnose and support children and young people with mental health problems including depression. Will work alongside counsellors, play therapists and also psychiatric nurses.
Physiotherapist	Professional who has been trained to maximise the body's movement and skill level. A physiotherapist may help a child who has difficulty controlling their movements e.g. a child with cerebral palsy.
Nurse specialist	Increasingly, the health service is using specialist nurses to support and give advice to children and their families about managing chronic medical conditions. Some nurse teams are also involved in measuring and assessing children's development.
Additional learning support teams	Most education services will provide a range of services within and out of schools that will help children who may have specific educational needs. These may include specialist teaching assistants, home tutors as well as advisers who visit settings to support and train staff.
Youth justice teams	Children and young people who show antisocial behaviour will work with staff from the youth justice team. This may include probation officers in conjunction with social workers.

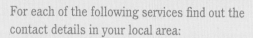

Over to you

For each of the following services find out the contact details in your local area:

- Speech and language therapy
- Physiotherapy
- Educational psychologist
- Additional learning support team.

Functional Skills

ICT: Finding and selecting information

English: Writing

You could use the Internet to search for the contact details of your local agencies and then produce an information leaflet containing all the relevant details. Remember that this will be an information leaflet and it will need to be clear, concise and organised in a way that makes sense to the reader. Take care with your spellings, punctuation and grammar.

Understand the importance of early intervention to support the speech, language and communication needs of children and young people

Speech, language and communication are so fundamental to children's outcomes that you will be looking at this in more detail in Unit EYMP5. (You may wish to read pages 291–307 alongside this section.) The language and communication skills of children and young people play an enormous role in their development, particularly in relation to the development of their cognitive, social and emotional skills. This learning outcome requires you to understand the importance of early intervention to support speech and language and also how it may be supported.

The importance of early identification of speech, language and communication delays and disorders

Language is at the heart of cognitive and social development. Language allows you to think, to control your behaviour and process new information. Without a way of using language, communication can be limited and so children can feel isolated and frustrated. They may find it hard to control their behaviour and play with other children. Language is also linked to the development of literacy. This means that children who have poor speech find it hard to understand the link between sounds and letter shapes and so reading can be delayed. Writing can also be affected as you need 'words' in order to write.

In addition to speech, some children may have difficulties with communication. They may find it hard to 'connect' with others and/or find it hard to process complex sentences.

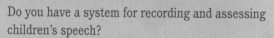

Reflect

Do you have a system for recording and assessing children's speech?

Is sufficient time spent with individual children to assess speech?

Do you regularly consider whether all children are hearing and seeing?

Do staff focus on reasons why children may be showing withdrawn or antisocial behaviour?

Are staff aware of the expected speech and language patterns for the ages of children who they are working with?

Early identification is important

Young children's brains are still developing as they grow. This means that early identification can change the potential impact of any difficulty if early support is provided. In addition, finding ways to help children communicate is important for their emotional well-being as children who have language and communication difficulties can quickly become isolated and withdrawn or develop antisocial behaviours.

How multi-agency teams work together to support speech, language and communication

Once parents and those involved with the child have identified that a child needs additional support, a multi-agency approach may be used. The parent visits their health visitor or GP who will then make an appropriate referral. This may initially be to rule out hearing or visual impairments. In other cases, the GP may refer directly to the speech and language service, although in some areas settings can do this or there may be 'drop in' sessions for parents. For some children, an assessment by an educational psychologist will be required – especially if communication difficulties are linked to other learning difficulties. Once it is established what type of support a child requires, a collaborative approach is required in order that all professionals, the parents and the setting work together.

Play and activities to support the development of speech, language and communication

Children do not learn language and communication in a vacuum. They learn by being with adults and other children and particularly while they are having fun. Play and activities that interest children are usually used to support the development of speech and language, because they are motivating; for example, saying a nursery rhyme that encourages speech movements will be more engaging for a child than simply having to repeat the movements in isolation. The spider diagram below shows play types and activities that are often seen as useful when supporting a child who has speech, language or communication difficulties.

Case study: Jamie's speech development

Jamie is just over 3 years old. The staff at the pre-school are concerned about his speech development as, although Jamie makes eye contact and points to objects, his speech is unclear. He often has tantrums, becomes frustrated with other children and finds it hard to play with others. His hearing has been tested, but it has been agreed with his mother that a referral to a speech and language service would be beneficial. The speech and language therapist has come today into the setting to observe Jamie and also to give some initial advice to the staff and his parents.

1. How much language would you expect a 3-year-old child to have?

2. How might his behaviour be linked to his speech delay?

3. Why is it important the speech and language therapist and the setting work closely together?

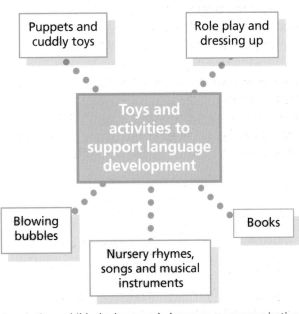

Supporting a child who has speech, language or communication difficulties

Puppets and cuddly toys

These can be used to motivate a child to talk or vocalise. Puppets with mouths can be used to encourage a child to make specific movements.

Role play and dressing up

Children from the age of three onwards tend to enjoy imaginative play. Adults can take on roles and play alongside children.

Nursery rhymes, songs and musical instruments

Nursery rhymes, songs and using musical instruments can help children to listen and take turns, but also to sing and communicate. Some nursery rhymes can help children to practise particular speech sounds.

Books

Books can help to increase vocabulary and can help children to learn the meanings of words. Some books can help children to participate, for example a book that makes musical sounds when a picture is pressed. Books can also be made specifically to meet a child's interests and so encourage the child to point or vocalise.

Blowing bubbles and other activities

Blowing bubbles is an example of an activity that might be used to encourage children to point or show interest in what they are seeing. Sometimes children will be encouraged to blow bubbles in order to make specific sounds.

Understand the potential effects of transitions on children and young people's development

The word transition is used to describe changes that may affect children or young people. It is commonly used to describe events such as a child moving school or starting with a childminder, but this learning outcome also looks at physical changes such as puberty. In this learning outcome, we consider the types of transitions that children and young people may experience and the importance of adult relationships with children.

Types of transitions

Children and young people benefit from stability. The old adage that 'children are adaptable' seems not to be accurate as even 6-month-old babies can be quite put out sleeping in an unfamiliar cot! There are, however, times in children and young people's lives when transitions are inevitable. Table 5 gives examples of the transitions that children and young people may experience.

Effects of transition on children

Children and young people may be affected by the transitions they make. Sometimes the effects are short

Table 5: Transitions that may affect children and young people

Type of transition	Examples
Changes to family structure	New baby, parents separating, new step-parents, new step-siblings, grandparents or other family members coming to live
Moving home	Change of home, change of location e.g. county, country
Illness and bereavement	Illness or bereavement of a family member or friend
Being with a new/ additional primary carer	Starting with a childminder, starting at a pre-school, moving into foster care, moving into adoptive care
Moving setting	Changing school, changing from pre-school/nursery to school, changing group/class, changing youth group, leaving care
Admission into institution	Admission into hospital, youth offenders' institution, boarding school, children's home
Changes to body	Changes to body image caused by, for example, puberty, scarring, accident, chronic illness

term and temporary, but it is important that adults working with children and young people monitor them as in some cases extra support might be needed. The spider diagram below shows the many ways in which children and young people may show distress.

The importance of positive relationships during transition

We can see in the spider diagram below the possible effects that transitions can have on some children and young people. However it can help considerably if the child or young person has at least one strong relationship with someone who is supporting them during the transition process. In early years settings, when children are first settling in, children will of course have their

Case study: Ayse starts school

Ayse is 4 years old and has just started school. She has not attended pre-school or nursery and so this is the first time that she has left her mother. At first she seemed to be settling in, but the reception teacher has noticed that she is particularly tearful and clingy. At home, her mother has found that she has started to wet the bed and is eating less.

1. What transition has Ayse made?

2. How are her behaviours linked to the transition?

3. Why is it important that they are identified?

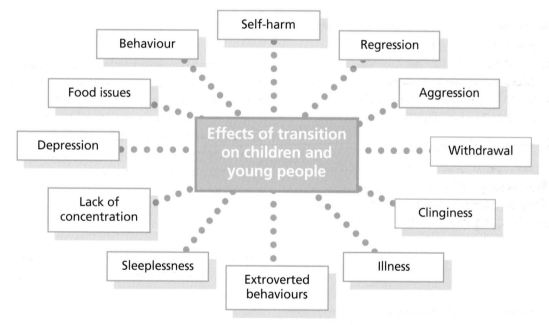

Regression: showing behaviours of younger children e.g. bedwetting, sucking thumb, talking like a younger child.

Aggression: frustrated outbursts, unreasonable behaviours, temper tantrums.

Withdrawal: quiet, solitary behaviours, unwilling to join in with others or new activities.

Clinginess: unwilling to leave the sight of a carer or familiar adult. Requires more physical reassurance than before.

Illness: genuine and psychosomatic – complaints of stomach pains, cold sores, increased number of colds and viruses.

Extroverted behaviours: unusually cheerful, outgoing, boisterous and attention seeking.

Sleeplessness: difficulty in falling asleep, nightmares, waking in the night, tears at bedtime.

Lack of concentration: difficulty in concentrating, lack of motivation, easily distracted.

Depression: sadness, tearfulness, also other signs such as sleeplessness, lack of appetite.

Food issues: refusal to eat, fussy eating, overeating and eating disorders.

Behaviour: uncooperative behaviour, antisocial behaviour, slamming doors, shouting, swearing.

Self-harm: cutting, drinking alcohol, taking drugs, risky behaviour e.g. bets and dares on train tracks.

Ways in which children and young people may show distress

parents but, as we have seen on page 79, the effects of separation anxiety are such that they will also need a relationship within the setting. This will take the form of a key person who will have a positive relationship with the child. The key person approach is also being used in other settings, particularly in social care and the health service. Children who are admitted into hospital may, for example, have one nurse who takes special care of them.

The idea behind the key person is that children have one person who they can go to with whom they feel secure. This person should have a warm relationship with the child and be able to reassure, as well as listening and validating the child's experience. A key person will also notice and monitor the reactions of the child to their new situation. This can provide warning in cases where the effects of transition are not temporary.

EYFS in action

The EYFS has, as one of its statutory requirements, the need for each child to be assigned a key person. The statutory guidance explains what the nature of this relationship is.

How effective do you think the key person system in your setting is in meeting the statutory guidance?

What changes do you feel might be necessary?

Getting ready for assessment

Write a leaflet for new practitioners about transition and young children. The leaflet should contain the following information:

- Attachment theory
- Types of transition that children may encounter
- Effects of transition on children's development
- How positive relationships can support children during transition

Check your knowledge

1. Explain the difference between sequence of development and rate of development.
2. Identify three personal factors that might affect a child's development.
3. Outline three external factors that might influence a child's development.
4. Explain how Piaget's theory of cognitive development links to current practice.
5. Explain how operant conditioning is used to guide children's behaviour.
6. Briefly describe two reasons why children's development may not follow the expected pattern.
7. Describe two interventions that may support a child who is not following expected development.
8. Explain the importance of early identification and support for children with speech, language and communication delay.
9. How might play be used to support the development of speech and language?
10. Describe three types of transition that may occur in the lives of young children.
11. Outline the possible short-term effects of transition on children.

Promote child & young person development

It is not enough just to know about children and young people's development. Practitioners have to be able to use this knowledge to inform their practice. This unit looks at ways in which we can assess the developmental needs of children and young people and how, through our work, we can promote their development.

Learning outcomes:

By the end of this unit you will:

1. Be able to assess the development needs of children or young people and prepare a development plan

2. Be able to promote the development of children or young people

3. Be able to support the provision of environments and services that promote the development of children or young people

4. Understand how working practices can impact on the development of children and young people

5. Be able to support children and young people's positive behaviour

6. Be able to support children and young people experiencing transitions.

Be able to assess the development needs of children or young people and prepare a development plan

In order to work effectively with children and young people, we must be able to assess their development and then plan to support them. This learning outcome requires you to demonstrate that you can assess a child and produce a plan accordingly. This unit links to Unit EYMP2 where we look in detail at how to use observation methods in early years settings. It may therefore be helpful to read pages 234–37 alongside this section, if you are new to observing young children.

Factors that need to be taken into account when assessing development

Assessing children and young people has to be done sensitively and accurately. There are therefore a number of factors that have to be considered.

Confidentiality

Before you can carry out an observation on a child, it is usual to gain permission from parents or those responsible for the child. Most parents are happy for their children to be observed, although they probably will not want other parents – or people who have no involvement with their child – reading the reports. This means that you must not leave notepads or records lying where others might find them. You should store observations carefully and make sure, when you discuss a child, that you are only doing so with colleagues and other professionals who have a right to know.

If you have to show evidence of observation and assessments, for example as part of completing this unit, it is important to protect a child's identity by using an alternative name or using terms such as 'child A'.

Children's wishes and feelings

Children have rights and there will be times when it will not be appropriate to observe/assess children; for example if a child is upset we may ask if they would like to leave an assessment until another day. It is also important to remember that the way we write about children in observations and records must be respectful. A good tip is to ask yourself if you would like a child in your family to be written about in the language used.

Ethnic, linguistic and cultural background

It is important that we can assess children's development reliably. Sometimes the behaviours, skills and interests that children show are dependent on their ethnic, cultural or linguistic background. For example, a child who does not take part in the story of the three little pigs may not feel comfortable because she associates pigs with being unclean; but an observer may interpret this as the child not being interested in drama. Bearing in mind children's linguistic background is particularly important as the child may not show a certain skill because the words used to describe what they need to do are unfamiliar.

Disability or specific requirements

Some children and young people may have disabilities or particular needs which have to be taken into consideration when observations/assessments are carried out. In schools it is usually accepted, for example, that children with dyslexia need additional time in order to sit tests, while in a nursery, a child may need an adult

Statements based on observations of a child's development must be accurate

to remember to give just one instruction at a time. Not understanding the nature of a child's disability or specific requirements can lead a practitioner to underestimate children's abilities.

Reliability of information

There is no point in assessing development unless we can do so fairly accurately. Statements made about children and young people that are inaccurate can actually harm children's development, especially if they lead to adults underestimating a child's potential. This means we have to consider the reliability of information that we gather and also the limitations of any observation methods that are used.

Avoiding bias

It is difficult but important at all stages of observing and assessing children and young people to be completely objective. Two people recording the same activity may produce different observations — for example, one person may decide that a smile is important and record it, while another person may decide otherwise. It can be especially difficult for practitioners who have a strong relationship with a child or young person to be objective (see case study below) but it is still important if a child's development is to be properly assessed. This is why, in some settings, different colleagues also observe children as they may notice other elements about the child.

Case study: Harry's profile

Harry is 4 years old. He has been with his childminder, Polly, since he was a baby. She enjoys looking after him and cares for him well. Harry is starting school and Polly is completing a profile on him. The profile asks whether he can count five objects reliably. Polly knows that quite often she needs to help Harry or correct him when he is counting, but she still ticks a box that says he can do it, arguing to herself that he can *nearly* do it.

1. Suggest a reason why Polly found it hard to make an accurate recording.

2. Why is it important to be objective when recording?

Open and closed recording methods

Some recording methods can also make it easier for observers to show bias. These are usually the more 'open' methods that allow observers to select which information to focus on, for example the sticky note method where observers write down anything that they see of importance on a sticky note. The danger is that an observer may subconsciously not pay attention to a behaviour or skill that a child is showing; for example a practitioner who believes that boys are not good at social skills may not notice that a group of boys are actually taking it in turns to jump over a puddle.

Closed methods, such as checklists, are less likely to produce biased results as the observer is primed to look out just for certain pieces of information, for example 'can stand on one leg for 20 seconds'.

Mixing methods

Ideally, the way to avoid bias is to use a range of methods and also to take into consideration the observations and thoughts of others — including parents and colleagues.

Assess a child or young person's development

There are many ways to assess the developmental needs of a child or young person. A good starting point is to consider what information is required and how the information will be used. In this unit, you will need to show that you can produce a development plan for a child or young person. This should be a holistic plan that encompasses several areas of development and so you will need to use methods that will help you gain information about each of the following areas:

- physical
- communication

- intellectual/cognitive

- social, emotional and behavioural, as well as moral where appropriate.

You should also look for some methods that will indicate a child's interests as, when you eventually draw up a developmental plan, it will include ideas for activities and these are likely to be more successful if they are based on the children's interests and strengths.

Observations

One of the key ways in which we collect information about children and young people is by observing them as they play. This information can tell us about their development and interests, and also their interactions with friends and adults and their levels of concentration.

Table 1 has some suggestions as to how you might collect this information. To ensure that the information that you collect is reliable and free of bias, it would be useful to use several methods.

Table 1: Ways of recording information

Method	Purpose
Free description (also known as narrative description and written record)	To record the behaviour of a child over a very short period of time, often less than five minutes. The observer notes down what he or she is seeing, which gives a portrait of a child's activity during this time. Some settings also use a sticky note system where they jot down something they have seen. This is a good method for looking at several areas of development.
Checklists and tick charts	These are used to assess children's stages of development. This is one of the methods used by health visitors during routine check-ups. Specific activities are looked for, either during a structured assessment (i.e. where children are asked to do activities) or by observing children over a period of time. You could look out for a series of checklists which cover each of the areas of development.
Time sample	This method is used to look at children's activity over a predetermined length of time, for example a morning. A child might be observed at regular intervals during the recording, say every 10 minutes, and the observation is recorded on a prepared sheet. You could use this method as a way of observing several areas of development at once.
Event sample	Often used to look closely at one aspect of a child's development or behaviour, such as how frequently the child sucks their thumb, or shows aggression towards other children. Every time a child shows the type of behaviour or activity, it is recorded on a prepared sheet. This could also be used to look at how often a child talks to other children or staff.
Target child	Used to record one child's activity over a long period without any gaps in the recording process. Several codes or signs are used during the observation to allow the observer to maintain the recording. A prepared sheet is used to help the observer. This method would give you information about several areas of development.
Standardised tests	These are often used with older children to consider their skills in literacy, mathematics or overall cognitive development. For standardised tests to be useful, the practitioner needs to know how to use them and also how to interpret their results.
Filming, photographs	Watching children in action can be useful, but it is essential that permission is obtained both from the child, or their parents, and from other children who may come into shot. This method will provide you with information about several areas of development and you will also be able to play it several times to pick up on things that you may otherwise have missed if you were carrying out a paper recording.
Sound recordings	An MP3 player or other recording device can be useful to record children's speech and language development. A series of recordings can help to establish whether children are making progress.
Information from parents and colleagues	Parents and colleagues see children in different situations and so may have a different view of a child's development. Information from parents can be gained from questionnaires, face-to-face structured interviews or informal chats. Some practitioners also encourage parents to observe their children at home using a recording method such as videoing.

Assessing the child or young person

Ideally, you should observe children not only using a range of methods but also in a range of situations as everyone behaves differently according to where they are and whom they are with. Young children may also be affected by tiredness and lack of interest as well external factors such as the weather. Once you have collected information from your observations, begin by considering how reliable they are and how much importance you will accord them. Then you can start to draw some conclusions. You can do this by focusing on each area of development in turn. Look at what you have observed and then refer to the patterns of expected development to consider whether the child has any specific need or, if not, what their likely next step would be. In some settings, this process is done every few weeks and a summative report is then shared with parents.

Evaluating the selection of the methods

It is important that we are able to justify the methods we have used to assess children and young people. We also need to understand the limitations of methods. Parents, colleagues and other professionals may want to know how we have arrived at our conclusions about children and so it is important to be able to explain and evaluate the methods that we have selected. In this unit, you will need to be able to show that you can assess children's development, but also explain the reasons behind your selection of methods. Table 2 shows some of the advantages and limitations of some common methods of assessing children.

With the free description method, the observer can be unobtrusive and record children without them being aware

> ## Functional Skills
>
> English: Reading
>
> Over time you could collect a range of different blank forms that are currently being used in settings that you have visited. Summarise how effective you feel the different documents are in relation to assessing children.

Table 2: Advantages and limitations of assessment methods

Method	Advantages and limitations
Free description (also known as narrative description and written record)	For: Observer can be unobtrusive and record children without them being aware For: Flexible method allowing observers to carry out frequent observations Against: The open method of this recording can mean that it is easy for observers to show bias Against: Observers may find it hard to record everything that a child does or says
Checklists and tick charts	For: Observer is clearly focused on developmental skills to be observed and so less danger of bias Against: Observer may not record children's attitudes and dispositions towards activities or how they socialise Against: Observer may alter children's performance if they know that they are being observed or 'checked'
Time sample	For: Observer can see what a child is doing over a period of a morning or a session For: Observer can pick up on many different areas of development, but also attitudes, friendships and confidence Against: Interesting or significant behaviours might fall out of the sample time Against: Open method of recording may allow for observer bias
Event sample	For: Observer is focusing on the frequency of one type of behaviour Against: This type of record does not necessarily explain why the child shows the type of behaviour

Table 2: Advantages and limitations of assessment methods (continued)

Method	Advantages and limitations
Target child	For: This method helps the observer gain an overall picture of what a child is doing Against: Observer may not choose a period of time in which the child is showing their usual behaviours
Standardised tests	For: Closed method of recording means that observer bias is less Against: Children may recognise that they are being tested and so may not perform to usual levels Against: Children may be 'rehearsed' and may show better performance as a result
Filming	For: Visual nature with sound means that more information can be gained Against: Open method of recording means that observer chooses what to film and when to film — the selection may not be typical of the child Against: Children may be aware that they are being record and this may change their usual play and behaviours
Sound recordings	For: Intonation and speech patterns of children can be accurately recorded Against: Observer chooses when and what to record Against: Children may be aware that they are being recorded
Information from parents and colleagues	For: Parents and colleagues may see children involved in other activities or situations Against: Parents and colleagues may show observer bias

Developing a plan to meet the development needs of a child or young person

Once children and young people's needs have been assessed, the next step is to develop a plan that will support them. In most settings, the drawing up of the plan is done with parents and children or young people themselves. This is important as children and young people are key stakeholders. Involving children and young people in planning will take different forms according to their age and, of course, level of maturity. In some cases, children will give us suggestions as to activities that they enjoy while young people may set their own targets and have strong ideas as to how they might go about achieving them.

Most plans include the following elements.

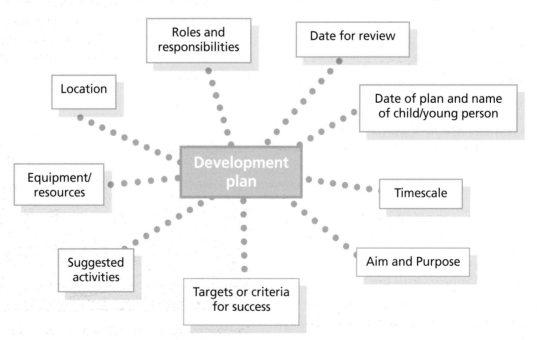

Elements to consider when drawing up a development plan

Date of plan and name of child/young person

This is important for record keeping and to prevent the wrong plan from being followed.

Timescale

A decision has to be made as to how long the plan is to last. Some plans may last for three weeks, others for three months.

Aim and purpose

For a plan to work, it is essential that everyone involved understands the aim and the purpose of the plan.

Targets or criteria for success

Targets and/or criteria for success help us to focus on exactly what needs doing and are also the way in which we can tell that it has been achieved.

Suggested activities

Plans usually suggest actions that need to be taken. In the case of children, this is often about activities that children will be offered. Activities must take into consideration the interests of children and young people.

Equipment/resources

For some developmental needs, particular resources or equipment are needed and so these may be listed on the plan.

Location

Some plans are drawn up so that they can be followed in a number of settings, for example home, childminder and nursery.

Roles and responsibilities

To make a plan work, it is important that everyone knows who is responsible for implementing its different elements.

Date for review

Plans need to be reviewed and, if needed, modified.

Be able to promote the development of children or young people

In order to promote children and young people's development, many settings produce plans to help them decide how best to work with individuals or groups of children. For this learning outcome, you need to show that you can implement a development plan and evaluate it. You must also show that you can work with children and young people in ways which meet their needs and interests.

Implementing the development plan

A plan is of no use unless attempts are made to follow it. This means that settings have to find ways of implementing plans that they have made for children. In some settings, such as in a baby room, this is quite straightforward as each key person will follow the plans that have been drawn up for their key children. In other settings, children's individual plans need to be incorporated into the overall planning, for example in a reception class. This may mean that while all children will have access to the play opportunities provided, some of the opportunities are targeted at specific children.

Reception age children's individual plans need to be incorporated into the overall planning

Roles and responsibilities

We have seen that plans are often drawn up in consultation with others, and that particular roles and responsibilities are also identified as part of the plan. For plans to work well, it is important that you implement the plan according to your agreed role. This may mean, for example, spending ten minutes every day sharing a book with a child or being responsible for playing with children in a role play area.

Development is holistic

It can be very easy for adults working with children to focus only on their 'needs'. This 'deficit' model of working can prevent us from recognising children's overall strengths and interests. Working effectively with children means finding activities and opportunities which help a child to develop and which are also enjoyable. This means that we may need to observe children and consider what they can already do and what they enjoy doing and weave this into our plan. For example a child who loves climbing may enjoy hunting for her name card that is attached to the top of a climbing frame.

Evaluate and revise the development plan

It is often not until we actually use a plan that we begin to see how well it works and whether it is fulfilling its objectives. Plans should be routinely monitored and added to or adapted, as the needs of children are reviewed and their progress is considered. This means that plans should be seen as work in progress rather than completed documents that cannot be changed. In some cases, we may see that a child has a preference or a dislike for an activity or that an activity or idea is not really effective. Changing or adapting plans must be done in consultation with those who have overall responsibility for the child as they may wish to make some assessments of the child beforehand. It is also important to ask for feedback from the child or young person concerned when reviewing the development plan.

Why does this matter?

Planning for individual children's development and learning is a key requirement for the Early Years Foundation Stage although plans for the children in the EYFS will also be linked to the six areas of learning. This is looked at in Unit EYMP2.

Person-centred and inclusive approach

Any plans that involve supporting an individual should be focused on their needs and interests and wherever

Best practice checklist: Reviewing a development plan

✓ Is the child benefiting from the plan?

✓ Is the child enjoying suggested activities?

✓ Are the activities supporting the child's development?

✓ Are there any unforeseen benefits from any of the activities?

✓ Are there any difficulties or limitations?

✓ Do the targets seem realistic?

✓ Does the timescale of the plan need altering?

✓ Are there any other activities, resources or pieces of equipment that need to be used?

Case study: Robert's hand preference

Jen has noticed that Robert, who is 3 years old, has not established a hand preference. She plans a series of activities that will strengthen hand preference. These activities are two-handed activities in which one hand acts as a stabliser while the other hand is active. She has noticed that Robert enjoys playing with water and helping out. She asks Robert and a couple of other children if they would like to wash up the beakers at snack time. The activity is a great success. Robert holds cups in one hand while wiping them with a sponge and water with the other. He asks if he can do this again tomorrow.

1. How are Robert's interests incorporated into this activity?

2. How is this an inclusive activity?

3. What other activities might also be planned?

possible we should involve them in the planning process. This is what is meant by being 'person centred'. When working in the early years sector, this term is replaced, of course, by the term 'child centred'. Child-centred planning takes into consideration what is best for the child, as well as how it might engage and involve the child. It is also important, when planning, that we do not segregate a child from others, but consider ways in which either other children can become involved in the activity too, or ways in which an activity might be adapted so that the area of development that needs support can be incorporated. The case study below shows how one practitioner did this.

We have to work with children in ways that make them feel valued, and this includes listening to them

Listening and communicating in ways that encourage children and young people to feel valued

As part of planning for children's development, we have to work with them in ways that make them feel valued. This is important as otherwise children will simply not be responsive to activities and play opportunities that we have planned. The importance of and ways of communicating with children and valuing them is looked at in Unit CYP3.5. You will need to read pages 155–63 and consider how this applies to the way that you implement plans.

Active participation

Children and young people should be involved in decisions that affect them and this is actually a right under the United Nations Convention on the Rights of the Child (see Unit SC2). In terms of promoting children's development this means looking for ways of involving them in the choice of activities that we provide to support their development and also encouraging them to set their own priorities for learning and development. This is important as when we involve children and young people, they are more likely to make significant progress. For early years settings, involving children means encouraging them to get out activities, toys and resources for their child-initiated play and consulting them about the type of adult-led activity that they would like to participate in. Working with older children and young people means taking into account their feelings and views and also asking them to set their own targets and helping them to achieve these. The case study below shows how beneficial involving children and young people in their own learning can be.

Case study: Involving children in learning to spell

Mark is 10 years old and in year 5 at school. Each Friday, his class has a spelling test consisting of 15 words. At the start of the term, Mark tried to learn them but found them very difficult. He did not do well in the tests and for the last few weeks he has no longer bothered to get them out at home. This week, his class teacher has asked the children to look at their written work and select their own spellings based on words that they find difficult. Mark decides to choose words that he often gets wrong, but also choose one that he knows will be difficult to learn. He and the other children are quite excited because they have never had a choice of what to learn before. On the day of the test, the teacher puts the children into pairs and tells them to test each other. Mark gets all of his words right. He also enjoys testing his friend. The teacher looks at the children's spelling afterwards. She notices that many of the children who usually have low scores have done particularly well. She decides to keep using this approach.

1. Why did Mark learn his spellings this week?
2. What did Mark learn about himself this week?
3. How can helping children to set their own goals promote their learning and development?

Be able to support the provision of environments and services that promote the development of children and young people

The physical and emotional environment that we create for children has a huge impact on their development. This learning outcome requires you to understand the features of an environment that will support children's development. This links also to Unit EYMP1 and you may need to revisit this section when undertaking that unit.

The features of an environment or service that promote the development of children and young people

Planning an environment for children or young people requires a significant amount of thought. The term 'environment' is more than just the furniture or the activities. It relates to the entire running and ethos of the setting. The spider diagram below looks at the features that you need to consider as part of this learning outcome. Beneath the spider diagram is a brief explanation of how they link to an early years setting.

Stimulating and attractive

Young children learn through using their senses. This means that environments for them need to be interesting and visually attractive. The word 'stimulating' also refers to the types of activities and play opportunities that are provided. Examples of what you might use are considered in Unit EYMP2.

Well planned and organised

Working with children requires great organisational abilities. Babies need to be fed when they are hungry, toddlers get restless and older children need opportunities to explore. Every child will have their own needs, interests and personality. To accommodate this,

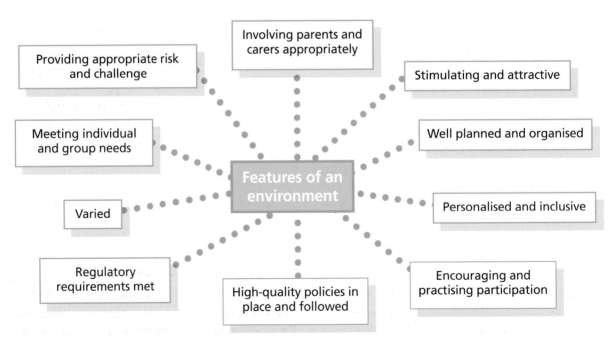

Planning an environment for children or young people requires a significant amount of thought.

early years settings have to plan effectively and everyone within the setting needs to be organised.

Personalised and inclusive

The EYFS requires early years settings to personalise the activities and play opportunities for children in ways that are inclusive. This means thinking not only about what is available for children, but also how things can be made accessible for children.

Encouraging and practising participation

Early years settings need to be welcoming places where everyone feels that they are valued and that they belong. While every early years setting will have its 'core' group of users, it is important that, within the core group, parents, children and people new to the setting feel they are not being excluded. Encouraging participation is also about shaping children's attitudes. Settings which encourage participation look for ways of helping children to learn about valuing others. (See also Unit SC1 Promote equality, diversity and inclusion.)

Regulatory requirements met

All settings must meet the requirement of legislation. This will include compliance with the statutory framework of the EYFS, health and safety legislation and also other legislation involving the safeguarding of children and the protection of children's rights.

High-quality policies in place and followed

The need for policies and procedures follows on from the need of settings to follow legislative requirements. Policies must also be reviewed, updated and evaluated to check for effectiveness.

Varied

All early years settings should think about what they are doing for children so as to vary the provision and maintain children's interest. Settings can become 'sluggish' if they do not think about how to vary what they are doing.

Meeting individual and group needs

As part of the requirement to personalise children's learning and development opportunities, EYFS settings need to show how to meet individual and group needs. The case study on Robert's hand preference above was a good example of how this looks in practice.

Providing appropriate risk and challenge

Over the past few years, there has been a change towards our understanding of how best to keep children safe. A few years ago, it was almost desirable to eliminate risk from children's lives. Now it is recognised that this is not helpful and that in order to keep safe, children actually need to experience situations in which they are learning to evaluate risk for themselves. This means that outdoors children may be encouraged to climb trees, with supervision, or to jump off a low wall.

Children need to learn to evaluate risk for themselves

Involving parents and carers appropriately

Working with parents is a key part of the work of early years setting. It is recognised that parents play a pivotal role in their children's development and so careful thought is given to the ways in which we interact with parents and make settings welcoming.

Organising your own work environment to promote the development of children

We have seen that the environment that you create or are a part of is very important for children's development. For this learning outcome, you will need to reflect on how your work setting supports children's development. The way in which your work environment is organised will vary according to the service that you provide.

Personal and external factors

The way that you organise your environment will depend on many factors including your personal taste, philosophy and experiences to date. This means that some people always find ways of bringing plants and photographs into the physical environment while others include music. In addition, the working environment is also affected by external factors such as the building, location, policies and the type and timing of services that are being offered.

Providing specific activities

In some settings your brief will be very specific, for example if you are an early years pre-school you provide opportunities for play and learning and may also visit children's homes as part of your settling-in policy.

Providing services

Whatever your setting, you will be providing a service to children, young people and/or their families. Many settings look for ways of enhancing their provision by providing additional services such as family learning in pre-schools or career signposting for parents who wish to return to work but need additional support.

Measuring outcomes

Showing that your work environment is making a difference to children and their families is important as it affects funding and the viability of your service. Outcomes are measured in a range of different ways, but may include parent satisfaction surveys, statistics based, for example, on children's progress in their learning and development.

Communicating effectively, showing empathy and understanding

In Unit SC1 we looked at the importance of communication in relation to working with children, young people and their families. This is a major part of delivering services and so must be considered when organising the environment. Space and time will be required to allow children, young people and parents to communicate with us.

Supporting participation and involving parents and carers

Services must respond to the needs of those using them. This means that effective settings look for ways of supporting participation by helping parents and carers by, for example, having drop-in sessions at convenient times for parents. Many settings also involve parents according to the type of service that they offer; so a nursery may invite parents to be part of a steering group and the **portage** team will involve parents when setting goals and targets for their child.

Supporting children and young people's rights

The way that we organise services must take into account the rights of children and young people. This will show itself in the policies and procedures that are put in place as well as the way that children and young people are involved in decisions that affect them; for example a school may have a school council so that children can be consulted and a nursery may ask children to choose the play activities that are to be put out.

Below are some typical ways in which early years settings work to create a good learning and development environment for young children.

Functional Skills

ICT: Developing, presenting and communicating information

Using a suitable software package on the computer (such as Microsoft Publisher/Word), produce an information leaflet about your setting. This should explain the services that the setting offers, how they are organised and how their impact is measured.

Over to you

Analyse the services that your setting provides as part of its remit.

How are these organised?

How is their impact measured?

Key term

Portage: a system of supporting children with additional needs that is carried out in children's homes by 'portage workers' who involve parents in the process

The way that we lay out play opportunities and resources can influence children's development

Play areas – indoor and outdoors

It is a requirement of the EYFS for children to spend time in and out of doors. Many settings will create different areas so that children can play in a variety of ways (see Reflect box below).

Opportunities to work closely with parents

An essential part of working in the early years sector is to work with parents closely. It is good practice in settings for parents to be involved in the observation and planning of their children and also to contribute to their records.

Adult-directed activities

As well as opportunities for child-initiated play, early years settings should provide high-quality adult-directed activities such as cooking, sharing stories and playing board games. Adult-directed activities are useful as they draw children's attention to concepts and help to build language.

Functional Skills

ICT: Developing, presenting and communicating information

Maths: Interpreting

Using a suitable software package on the computer (such as Word) you could create an information booklet about how each of these play opportunities support children's development. You should include in your booklet text, pictures and graphs of the most popular play opportunities in your setting.

Observation and planning to meet children's individual needs

A statutory requirement of the EYFS is that children's developmental and play needs have to be met. This has to be achieved by observing children and then planning for them (see also Unit EYMP2).

Reflect

The way that we lay out play opportunities and resources can influence children's development. Children will need varied opportunities that are appropriate to their age and stage of development. Look below and reflect on how many of these opportunities your setting provides:

- dough
- mark making
- digging
- sand and water
- role play/dressing up
- wheeled toys i.e. sit and rides, tricycles, scooters
- construction toys
- resources for climbing and jumping
- small world play
- sensory play.

For each of these areas, think about how they support children's development, for example role play helps fine motor skills and language development.

Understand how working practices can impact on the development of children and young people

The care and education that children and young people receive can make a difference to their overall development. This learning outcome asks you to consider how you work in ways to support children's development and also the role of other services in supporting development.

> **Link**
>
> This learning outcome links to units 3.6 and 3.7 where each of the assessment criteria below are dealt with fully. It is therefore recommended that you read pages 167–84 in Unit 3.6 and pages 191–98 in Unit 3.7.

Effects of your own working practices on children and young people's development

One of the main reasons why adults enjoy working with children and young people is because they feel that, through their work, they may be able to make a difference. For this assessment criterion, you need to consider how through your work you can positively affect children's development. You should also consider whether relationships between staff, their attitudes and values allow the child's needs to come first. This requires you to be a reflective practitioner and to consider how effectively you plan and work with children. There are therefore clear links between Unit SC3 Personal development earlier and Unit CYP3.7.

The checklist is to help you reflect on the effectiveness of a session in terms of supporting children's development. This should help you when considering ways in which you support children's development.

Best practice checklist: Supporting children's development

- ✓ Were the adults in the setting aware of the development needs of the children?
- ✓ What systems do you use to ensure that everyone gets the information that they need to work effectively with individual children?
- ✓ Are activities specifically planned to support every child's development?
- ✓ Was there a balance of activities to engage children's interests?
- ✓ What was the balance between child-initiated and adult-initiated activities?
- ✓ Does the balance of activities cover each of the aspects of learning in the curriculum but also build on each of the developmental areas?
- ✓ Do adults have sufficient time to work with individual or small groups of children?
- ✓ Were there any children who were not engaged or participative during part or all of the session?

Institutions, agencies and services

Today there is an understanding that outcomes for children and young people, including their development, can be improved when a multi-agency approach is taken. This means that many other services will be involved in working with children in ways that will support their development. This is looked at in more depth in Unit CYP3.6 which primarily deals with multi-agency working. You should also refer back to Table 4 in Unit EYP3.1, which shows the different services that might be involved in supporting children's development.

Case study: Sophie's speech delay

Sophie is 2 years old. She attends a drop-in toddler group held at a children's centre. Sophie's mother is concerned that, although Sophie is happy and settled, she is not yet talking and her physical development is slow. She mentions her concerns to the supervisor of the group and the centre's health visitor comes and watches Sophie. She makes some suggestions as to how Sophie's mother might stimulate her at home, but also refers Sophie to a paediatrician. The paediatrician confirms that Sophie's development is atypical and, as well as conducting some medical tests, refers her to the speech and language therapist. Sophie's mother is pleased as she knows that her concerns about Sophie's development are being taken seriously. Six months later, Sophie has made some progress and, as well as attending drop-in centres, a portage worker visits the family each week to work on specific elements of her development.

1. Why is it important for Sophie's development that she has access to other services and agencies?

2. What would happen if a multi-agency approach was not taken?

3. How would a child like Sophie receive support in your local area?

Functional Skills

ICT: Finding and selecting information

English: Writing

Focusing on question 3 in the case study, use the Internet to search for agencies in your area which would be able to support Sophie. You should present your findings in Word using a logical, clear and concise style.

Children's behaviour is always a hot topic

Be able to support children and young people's positive behaviour

Children's behaviour is and always has been a hot topic. Over the years, there have been many different ideas about how best to manage behaviour. Today the focus is on supporting children to show positive behaviour and we are encouraged to be sensitive to children's needs and development when working with them.

Expectations

It is essential to have realistic expectations of what most children can achieve at given ages/stages. This allows us to set clear boundaries fairly. Table 3 outlines the expectations for children and young people.

Table 3: Stages of development and behaviour goals

Age	Stage of development	Goals for behaviour	Role of adult
1–2 years	• Actively explores environment	• To play alongside other children (parallel play)	**Good supervision**, as children of this age do not understand the dangers around them.
	• Imitates adults in simple tasks	• To carry out simple instructions such as 'Please find your coat'	**Distraction**, to stop unwanted behaviour, as children often forget what they were doing. For example, if a child wants another child's toy, offer them a different toy instead.
	• Repeats actions that gain attention		**Praise**, so that children understand how to get an adult's attention in positive ways and to help develop self-esteem.
	• Alternates between clinging and independence		**Calm and patience**, as children of this age are often persistent and may, for example, keep going back to something that is potentially dangerous.
	• Has understanding that toys and other objects may belong to others		**A good role model**, as children are learning behaviour by imitating those around them.
2–3 years	• Wants to be independent but does not always have the skills	• To wait for needs to be met, for example at meal times	**Good supervision and anticipation** — the keys to working with this age range. Children are trying to be independent, but lack some of the physical and cognitive skills they need. This can make them frustrated and angry. Adults need to anticipate possible sources of frustration and support children, either by offering help or by distracting them. For example, a child who is trying to put on a coat may need an adult to make a game of it so that the child does not become frustrated. Where possible, adults should try to provide as many opportunities as possible for children to be independent.
	• Becomes frustrated easily and has tantrums	• To share toy or food with one other child, with adult help	**Calm and patience**, as children who are frustrated can trigger negative feelings in adults. This has the potential to inflame a situation. It is a good idea to allow plenty of time for children to complete day-to-day tasks. Children of this age often forget and need reminding about boundaries and goals.
	• Is jealous of attention shown to other children	• To play alongside other children	**Praise and encouragement**, to enable children to learn what behaviour adults are expecting of them. Some unwanted behaviour that is not dangerous should be ignored so that children do not repeat it in the hope of gaining adult attention. Adults should also provide plenty of love and attention if children have had a tantrum as some children can be frightened by the force of their own emotions.
	• Has no understanding of the need to wait	• To sit and share a story for five minutes	**Consistency**, as children are trying to work out the limits on their behaviour.
	• Finds sharing difficult	• To say 'please' and 'thank you' if reminded	**A good role model**, as children model their behaviour on others. This is especially important at this age as they act out their experiences through play.
	• Is active and restless	• To follow simple instructions, with help, such as 'Wash your hands'	

Table 3: Stages of development and behaviour goals (continued)

Age	Stage of development	Goals for behaviour	Role of adult
3–4 years	• Follows simple rules by imitating other children; for example, collects apron before painting	• To follow rules in games (e.g. lotto) when helped by adult	**Praise and encouragement**, to build children's confidence and make them more likely to show desirable behaviour.
	• Is able to communicate wishes	• To say 'please' and 'thank you', often without reminder	**Explanation** of rules, as children are now more likely to remember and understand them.
	• Enjoys activities such as painting	• To take turns and share equipment	**Patience**, as children will still need reminders about the boundaries and goals for behaviour.
	• Enjoys being with other children	• To follow instructions of adults (e.g. 'Let Simon have a turn') most of the time	**Good supervision**, as although children are able to do many things for themselves, they are still unaware of the dangers around them. Most of the time children will be able to play well together, but squabbles will break out.
	• Can play cooperatively	• To help tidy away	**A good role model**, to help children learn the social skills they will need to resolve arguments and express their feelings.
	• Enjoys helping adults		
4–5 years	• Plays with other children without help from adults	• To consider other people's feelings	**Providing activities and tasks** that are stimulating and allow children to develop confidence. Children of this age are keen to help adults and enjoy being busy. Tasks such as setting the table or fetching things allow children to feel independent.
	• Is able to communicate feelings and wishes	• To comfort playmates in distress	**Praise and encouragement**, so that children feel good about themselves. This is important because children are often starting school at this time. They need to feel that they are able to be 'good'.
	• Understands the needs for rules	• To say 'please' and 'thank you' without reminder	**Explanation**, to help children to remember and understand the need for rules or decisions.
	• Can wait for needs to be met	• To ask playmates for permission to use their toys. To tidy up after activities	**A good role model** to help children to learn social skills, as they are copying what they see.
5–6 years	• Is developing strong friendships	• To apologise to others	**Praise and encouragement**, as children become more aware of others and compare themselves critically. Praise also prevents children from looking for other ways of gaining attention.
	• Will argue and question decisions	• To listen to others	**Explanation** so that children can understand the reasons for rules and decisions. Children should also be made to consider the effects of their actions on others.
	• Copies behaviour of older children (e.g. swearing and spitting)	• To follow instructions	**Set and enforce clear boundaries**, to counter children's tendency to argue back as they become older.

Table 3: Stages of development and behaviour goals (continued)

Age	Stage of development	Goals for behaviour	Role of adult
From 6–8 years	• Understands the needs for rules and plays games that have rules	• To work independently and quietly in school settings	**Being a good role model** is still important as children are trying to understand more about the adults they are with. Speech and actions are modelled increasingly on adults whom children admire.
	• Understands the difference between right and wrong	• To be helpful and thoughtful	**Encourage children to take responsibility for their actions** by asking them what the boundaries or limits on their behaviour should be.
	• Has many self-help skills such as getting dressed, wiping up spills	• To take responsibility for actions	**Provide activities and responsibilities** to help children to 'mature' as they learn more about their capabilities. Small responsibilities help children to become independent and give them confidence (e.g. they may be asked to tidy areas of a setting or pour out drinks for other children).
From 8 years onwards	• After this age behaviours are more closely linked to cognitive development and continue to be linked to social context	• To take responsibility for their actions and to understand the consequences	**Give increasing levels of responsibility,** and work in ways that allow children and young people to set their own boundaries

Encouraging positive behaviour

Practice has moved on considerably in terms of children's behaviour over the past few years. It was commonplace for adults to see children whose behaviour was challenging as being the problem. Today, as part of the thinking on behaviour, the focus is turned away from the child and onto the adults. The emphasis is on thinking about the workers' responses and considering whether these are the most effective. To reflect on your own responses often means observing children carefully. Children's behaviour is closely related to their needs. As part of reflecting on this area of work, it is important to think about how you are meeting the child's particular needs. In addition, you should also consider some of the other approaches to supporting children's positive behaviour that are described below.

Best practice checklist: Supporting children's positive behaviour

✓ How often do you smile or acknowledge the child positively?

✓ How much time do you spend listening to and talking to the child?

✓ What type of activities does the child most enjoy?

✓ How do you use these activities to help the child learn?

✓ To whom does the child respond well?

✓ How does this person react and work with the child?

✓ In what type of situations is the child likely to show unwanted behaviour?

✓ How do you work to avoid these situations?

✓ How do you encourage the child to take responsibility for his or her own behaviour?

✓ Is the child showing unwanted behaviour in response to being bored, frustrated or anxious?

✓ Are you reacting or taking a proactive approach to preventing unwanted behaviour?

✓ How do you react to situations when the child shows unwanted behaviour?

✓ Does this reaction make a long-term difference to the child's behaviour?

Different approaches to supporting positive behaviour

There are many different strategies and approaches when it comes to supporting children's behaviour. Most practitioners find that they will need to draw on several of these.

Least restrictive principle

One approach to supporting children's positive behaviour is to consider the ethos in the setting. Is it a setting with many petty rules that restrict and confine children or is it a setting that aims to give children responsibility and some freedom? This is important as children who are in very authoritarian settings tend not to develop a sense of responsibility for their actions.

Reinforcing positive behaviour

Reinforcing positive behaviour is about sending signals and rewards to children and young people so that they become inclined to repeat behaviours that are appropriate. This approach is well known and links to the behaviourist theory that we considered in Unit 3.1 known as operant conditioning. This theory forms the basis of some specific behavioural management programmes. The theory suggests that certain types of behaviour are repeated if they are rewarded in some way. For example, a child who says 'Thank you' and is praised for doing so will be more likely to show this behaviour again. Rewards are referred to as *positive reinforcements*. Types of behaviour that are not rewarded or that are punished in some way are less likely to be repeated.

Children and young people are more influenced by positive reinforcements than by punishments. Where rewards are used, good behaviour is seen over the long term, even when no further rewards are given. Where punishments are used, good behaviour may be shown, but once the threat of punishments has been lifted the behaviour is more likely to return.

Positive reinforcers are anything that acts as a reward. Common ones used by adults with young children are praise, stickers, extra attention and small rewards.

The timing of positive reinforcers is extremely important — where a reward happens quickly after the behaviour, there is a chance of the behaviour being repeated. Surprisingly, if children are rewarded only occasionally, or the positive reinforcement is not automatic but occasional, the behaviour is more likely to persist than if the reward is consistently given. It is almost as if they come to an understanding that sometimes they will get a reward and sometimes not, although it is always worth trying just in case a reward follows. So children do not need to be praised or positively reinforced for every single action in order that they continue doing it.

Positive behaviour can be reinforced

Best practice checklist: Positive reinforcement

✓ Give positive reinforcement when children show desired behaviour (e.g. praise when they are sharing equipment).

✓ Praise or give some other form of positive reinforcement while the children are showing the behaviour, or immediately afterwards, so that they associate a reward with their behaviour.

✓ Make sure children understand why they are being rewarded (e.g. 'Here is a special sticker because I saw how kind you were being to Junaid').

✓ Do not be reticent with praise – frequent praise simply helps children to keep on showing wanted behaviour.

✓ Choose rewards carefully so that children do not simply show behaviour to gain a large reward (so it would be inappropriate to give a child a whole chocolate bar because he or she said 'Thank you').

Identify reasons for inappropriate behaviour, and think about the response

Modelling

Children learn some of their behaviour from others, especially those around them. This is the basis of the Social Learning theory, which we looked at first in Unit 3.1. The implications of this theory mean that anyone who works with children will need to be a good role model, which includes being polite, showing consideration for others and waiting with patience. The theory also suggests that adults need to evaluate television and computer programmes likely to be viewed by children.

Positive culture

The expectations adults have about children, and their attitudes towards them, will influence their behaviour. For example, where an adult believes that a child is 'difficult', the child is more likely to behave in this way, whereas an adult who is positive about a child will probably find that the child shows appropriate behaviour. It seems that children can sense the level of behaviour expected from them and will meet these expectations. This is why a positive culture is important when supporting children's behaviour.

Looking for reasons for inappropriate behaviour and adapting responses

It is important to consider whether there are any background difficulties that might be at the heart of a child's behaviour. Understanding the needs of children, and thinking about what might be influencing their behaviour, is at the heart of helping to promote positive behaviour. Some factors, such as feeling unwell, might be short-lived, but others such as the formation of a new family unit might be longer term. It is also important to think about whether any changes of behaviour might be linked to the child being the subject of abuse (see Unit 3.3) Once we have identified reasons why children may be showing inappropriate behaviour, it is important to think about our responses. It may mean that we will have to adapt our own responses so as not to inflame a situation, for example a child who is hungry and tired will not be able to reason properly and so, instead of giving long explanations, we might instead simply focus on dealing with the underlying cause of the behaviour. Table 4 looks at some common reasons for inappropriate behaviour.

Table 4: Causes of inappropriate behaviour

Cause	Possible effects on behaviour
Hungry	Irritable, unreasonable, temper tantrums, poor concentration
Feeling poorly	Withdrawn, irritable, poor concentration
Overheated, hot	Irritable, quarrelsome, poor concentration
Moving home	Clingy, unreasonable, poor concentration
Change to family unit, e.g. separation of parents, arrival of step-parent	Clingy, irritable, jealous, temper tantrums, aggression, withdrawn, attention-seeking
Long-term medical condition	Poor concentration, irritable, clingy, tired condition, withdrawn, anxious, attention-seeking
Birth of sibling	Clingy, attention-seeking, aggressive, demanding
Parents struggling with boundary setting	Clingy, attention-seeking, aggressive, demanding
Moving setting	Clingy, withdrawn, attention-seeking
Learning difficulties/special needs	See text below

Speech, language and communication difficulties

Children's behaviour is linked to their language acquisition. Children who have difficulties expressing their needs or who are not using a language fluently often find it harder to manage their behaviour. This means that we may observe behaviours that are linked to frustration, especially tantrums, anger outbursts and aggressive acts such as biting. By looking at ways of improving communication, or by being good at predicting the child's needs, we can help children's behaviour. This might mean introducing pictures, or systems such as Makaton, to support communication. Advice can usually be gained from your local speech and language team on which methods to use with individual children.

Attention deficit

Some children have naturally low levels of arousal. This means that they have difficulties in concentrating because, in order to concentrate, you need to have sustained arousal levels. Where children have low levels of arousal or 'attention deficit', they are likely to show erratic and restless behaviours. These behaviours are easily misinterpreted as the child being uncooperative or disruptive, especially during quiet activities such as story time. While working with children who have attention deficit is challenging, it is important to find ways of keeping and retaining their interest. Sadly, children's learning is affected by attention deficit, as they are often not settled enough to learn. The following tips can be useful when working with these children.

- Provide plenty of sensory activities.

- Keep to strict routines and structures.

- Avoid situations in which the child is kept waiting.

- Make sure that activities are open-ended so that the child can leave them if their concentration wanes.

- Provide frequent feedback to the child, including incentives such as stickers.

- Use visual cues and props rather than 'telling' the child.

Individual behaviour planning

Where an individual child is showing inappropriate behaviours, it is usual that a plan or system to manage the child's behaviour is drawn up. This should be done with parents and, where appropriate, the child or young person.

Phased stages

The starting point should be to consider what exactly needs to be achieved. If there are several issues that need tackling, it is often better to prioritise them, rather than attempting to tackle them all at once. This means that a plan may have phased stages.

It is essential that expectations are in line with the child's ability to meet them and that ways of reducing the effect of the underlying issues are also examined. Many children who show unwelcome behaviour, for example, do not use language to help them express themselves or to reflect on their actions. For these children, the behaviour management programme must also link to language activities so that the underlying difficulty with language can be addressed.

Behaviour management programmes work well when they are written clearly and goals or targets are identified. These have to be both realistic and focused. It is also important to set out a timescale and a date to review progress; this might be a week or a fortnight ahead at first. Once parents and practitioners begin to take an agreed approach, progress can sometimes be quite swift. It is also important for everyone to stay in close contact so that any difficulties, relapses and, of course, successes can be shared.

Following management plans

It is important that everyone in the setting is working together to follow agreed plans with children as well as following the setting's behaviour policy. This is because children need consistency and can find it hard to cope when different approaches are being taken with them.

De-escalate and diversion

Young children are exploratory, impulsive and are easily led by the context in which they find themselves. Very little of their unwanted behaviour is premeditated. This means that sometimes we can simply find ways of diverting them and thus not escalating unwanted behaviour. This strategy is important – especially with young children – as it keeps the atmosphere in the setting positive rather than negative. The case study shows an example of how this might be achieved.

Containment

Containment is about preventing children from getting themselves further into trouble or – in the case of some young people – from committing further offences. In some cases, children and young people know in some way that they are out of control and look towards the adult to help them stop what they are doing. For a young child, containment may mean staying close by and not putting the child back into a situation that they were not coping with.

Case study: Aaron's attention-seeking behaviour

Aaron is 3 years old. His mother has recently had a baby, and at home and at nursery Aaron is showing that he is unsettled. He has been clingy with both his key worker and his mother, but is also showing some attention-seeking behaviour. His mother feels that she is constantly saying 'no' to him at home because of his behaviour, and staff at the nursery are also finding him demanding. The key worker and Aaron's mother decide to take a joint approach. They agree that Aaron does need more attention, but that it should be given only when he is showing wanted behaviours. They agree not to focus on his inappropriate behaviours, but to praise and spend time with Aaron when he is showing positive behaviours. As Aaron is keen on animals, they have decided to use a small finger puppet as a little incentive and also a distraction. The plan is for the finger puppet to come out when Aaron is showing more cooperative behaviours and also to distract him in situations in which he is likely to be less compliant. Aaron loves the finger puppet and is delighted with the extra attention.

1. Why is it important for staff and parents to think about the causes of unwanted behaviour?

2. Why is it important for staff and parents to draw up a plan together?

3. How does Aaron benefit from the staff and his mother working together?

Case study: Diversion tactics

Casey, a nursery manager, notices that two boys are slamming the door on the playhouse outdoors and that their play is becoming increasingly boisterous and aggressive. She goes over to the boys and asks if they would like to make a pirates' cave. They are very excited by this and go with her to the storage room. Together they choose boxes and fabric and start to make plans about where the pirates' cave should go. Casey asks if they can manage alone and reminds them that they must consider other children and let them help as well. A few minutes later, Casey smiles as she sees that five children are now involved in making the pirates' cave in the outdoor area.

1. Were the boys' actions premeditated?

2. How did Casey distract them?

3. Why was this a useful approach?

Boundary setting and negotiation

Imagine driving a car and not knowing the rules of the road. Working them out would not be easy, and while doing so you would be likely to get into trouble. Imagine also that every time you got into the car, the rules had changed. For young children, learning about behaviour is also about understanding boundaries and what is expected of them. They need to know that boundary setting is not arbitrary and prone to random change. It is good practice to involve children in setting boundaries as soon as they are old enough. With older children, this can be quite revealing, as they sometimes explain how they are feeling. Working with older children to draw up a contract of behaviour can be very successful. It allows children to recognise and take responsibility for their behaviour. With younger children, you may simply explain what the new boundaries and consequences are for their behaviour. They should also know that when they show positive behaviour they will gain attention, praise and perhaps small tokens or rewards, if appropriate.

Helping children to reflect on their own behaviour

It is useful for children to become aware of and responsible for their own behaviour. This, of course, has to be linked to their level of development. We can help children to reflect on their own behaviour by asking them questions such as: 'Are you enjoying playing with Josh? Why do you think that you are playing so well?'

This might help children to focus on skills that they are showing, such as sharing or listening to each other. It can be useful to focus on the positive behaviour that children are showing, rather than focusing on unwanted behaviour as it is more likely to help children think about what they need to do in the future.

Reflection on and management of own behaviour

As well as looking at children's reactions and behaviour, it is also important to consider our own. Firstly, we must make sure that we are calm in situations — especially when children are overwrought. Being calm helps to avoid escalation and also helps the child to feel safe. In addition, we have to consider our expectations of children. Are they really fair and age/appropriate? Finally, we also have to consider whether we might actually be contributing to a child's behaviour or positively reinforcing it in the way in which we are dealing with it; for example a child who is attention-seeking and showing unwanted behaviour may actually be showing more of this behaviour because we are reacting and giving attention.

Anti-bullying strategies

Young children's social skills are still developing, which means that we should use this time to ensure that they

Focusing on positive behaviour is more likely to help children think about what they need to do in the future

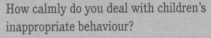

Reflect

How calmly do you deal with children's inappropriate behaviour?

Do you sometimes provide attention when children are showing unwanted behaviour linked to attention-seeking?

Do you explain boundaries and consequences to children?

Are you a good role model in terms of showing children how to be calm, fair and respectful of others?

If you find that one strategy of managing children's behaviour is not working, do you consider alternatives?

learn how to play and learn alongside each other. We can do this by praising children when they are thoughtful and cooperative, and modelling behaviours ourselves that teach children to be accepting of others. It is also important in the early years to intervene quickly when children are trying to exclude others or dominate them. This can help children to learn what is appropriate behaviour. With older children and young people, it is usual that more explicit anti-bullying measures are put into place. Circle time, discussions about playing nicely and using training materials from organisations that specialise in supporting children can help to prevent bullying. It is also important that settings working with children and young people have a robust anti-bullying policy and that bullying as an issue is taken seriously by all staff.

Over to you

There is plenty of discussion and resources available about anti-bullying strategies. Visit two of the following websites to gain up-to-date information:

www.bullying.co.uk

www.kidscape.co.uk

www.nspcc.org.uk

Functional Skills

ICT: Finding and selecting information

Accessing and using these websites will help to develop your ICT skills.

Time out

The idea of time out is not to punish children, but simply to allow them to calm down and step back from the problem. Time out should not be used with very young children as they can simply feel rejected and will not have the skills to reflect and calm down. But older children particularly benefit from time out, especially if a sympathetic adult can talk about why they need to calm down. Children should not be made to feel that they

are being rejected, but rather that you are helping them to avoid conflict or temptation. Used properly, time out should be a supportive strategy for children. However, long periods of time out for a child are tantamount to exclusion and should not be used.

Physical intervention

At one time it was considered acceptable to use physical punishment as a way of controlling and disciplining children. This is no longer the case, and children's rights are protected by law. The message is very clear to those who care for children: physical punishment is not an option; it is an offence.

There are very few occasions when it is acceptable to use physical restraint on children. The main reasons would be if:

- children are in danger of harming themselves
- children are in danger of harming others.

If restraint is needed, it must be kept to the minimum and must not be used as a way of disciplining or controlling children. You should also protect yourself from allegations of abusing children by keeping up to date with guidance, recording the incident and, if possible, ensuring that another adult is present. Physical restraints such as reins and harnesses should be used only to keep young children safe (for example when walking near busy roads), and in no circumstances should children be punished by being harnessed.

Challenging inappropriate behaviour

In addition to the approaches above, there are some simple strategies that can be used on a day-to day-basis when working with children.

Through eye contact/facial expression

Sometimes a simple look will warn children that they are over-stepping the boundary and this will be enough to remind them that their behaviour is not appropriate. Eye contact may need to be held with a child, accompanied by an expression of disapproval. Once the child starts to show appropriate behaviour, you should make sure that immediate praise is given. This strategy is particularly useful if you are working with a group and you do not want to disrupt the activity.

Say a determined 'No!'

Most children respond to this expression and understand its meaning. For this to work, it is important that you use it sparingly. It is also important that children understand 'no means no', and you do not allow children to continue with inappropriate behaviour. This strategy is particularly effective if combined with facial expression and is useful in situations in which children must be prevented from doing something potentially dangerous.

Explain the consequences of children's actions

It is good practice to make children aware of the consequences of their actions. They may not realise that throwing sand can lead to pain for a child who gets it in the eye. It is also worth explaining to older children what will happen if they continue to show unwelcome behaviour – this sets clear boundaries for them; for example, 'If you carry on kicking the ball towards the road, I will have to take it away in case it hits a car'. Once you have suggested that there will be a sanction, it is essential that you are prepared to carry it out. Do not threaten sanctions that you cannot justify or carry out, otherwise children will not believe you another time.

Removal of equipment

Taking away equipment should be a final measure, but may be necessary if children have either been threatened with this sanction or are putting themselves or others in danger; for example by tying a rope around a child's neck to play horses. This type of activity may be so exciting that even if you warn children about the dangers,

they will still be tempted to carry on. If you remove equipment, it is a good idea to give children something else to do so that they do not go from one inappropriate situation into another.

Why does this matter?

Supporting children's behaviour is an important part of working with children effectively. This is why it is also considered in Unit EYMP1. This means that you will be re-visiting this section when working on that unit.

Be able to support children and young people experiencing transitions

There will be times in all children and young people's lives when they will have to face changes. Some of these changes will be expected and planned for, such as moving to a primary school, while others might be sudden and potentially traumatic for a child such as the sudden death of a sibling or the illness of a parent. This learning outcome requires you to demonstrate that you understand how to support children who face or are going through transitions. This section must be read alongside pages 78–80 in Unit CYP3.1 where the different types of transitions have already been identified.

Supporting children and young people experiencing different types of transitions

In Table 5 of Unit CYP3.1 we looked at the many different transitions that children and young people might experience. We saw that the most important part of supporting children with changes is that they should be able to rely on someone with whom they have a positive relationship. This is therefore the starting point in supporting children and young people. In addition, this person needs to have a strong relationship with parents, family members and, where appropriate, other

Getting ready for assessment

Write a reflective account that demonstrates how you can encourage positive behaviour with the children who you work with.

Your account should include the following:

- the context in which you supported positive behaviour i.e. age of children, what was happening at the time
- the strategies that you used to support positive behaviour
- a rationale for the strategies that you used
- an evaluation of how you used the strategies.

professionals so that the information which may affect or is affecting the child can be shared; for example that court proceedings about abuse are due to start or when a new baby in the family is due.

Ways of supporting children

Children can be supported in some of the following ways.

Explaining to children what is likely to happen

Children and young people are more likely to make a successful transition if they understand what is going to happen. The timing and depth of this explanation is crucial. For young children, who do not have a strong sense of time, it is important not to overwhelm them too far in advance with too much information and detail and so we may choose to feed information little by little. Where children have developing language, or difficulty in processing language, we can prepare children by using photographs and pictures.

Taking our cues from children

Throughout any transition it is important to take our cues from children. Some children may appear not to be interested, while older children may want to change the subject. How much information to give, and how much explanation is required, should therefore be governed by the cues given by children.

Allowing time for information to be processed

Children and young people may sometimes show delayed reactions to what has been proposed or said. It is important to expect this and to realise that a child who is quiet at the time may have questions or react to what has been said later on.

Being truthful and answering questions

Children and young people need to trust us. This means that if they ask a question, it is best to be truthful. In some situations, children will ask one question and then later on another. This allows them to come to terms with what is happening in their own time.

Listening to and acknowledging children's feelings

Adults generally want to see children happy and it can be easy to fall into the trap of avoiding listening to and acknowledging children's feelings. Listening to children means taking on board what they are feeling — even if this is resentment, disappointment or anger. It is not helpful for the child to be told things such as 'don't

Case study: Preparing for death

The nursery's rabbit has been sick for a few days. The vet treating it has said that it might die. Lyle, a 4 year old, comes and sits next to Jamie, a nursery assistant. Lyle asks if the rabbit is getting better and Jamie replies that the rabbit is still poorly. There is a pause. Lyle asks whether the rabbit will ever get better. Jamie replies that he does not think so. A few minutes later, Lyle asks if the rabbit might die and adds that his grandfather is dead. Jamie tells Lyle that the rabbit might die, but that the vet has given some medicine. Lyle nods and goes over to the mark making table. Later in the afternoon, he shows Jamie a get well card that he has made. He also says that if the rabbit does die, it will be all right because it can sleep with his grandad.

1. Why might young children need time to take in information?
2. Why was it important for Jamie to allow Lyle to ask questions?
3. Why is it important not always to tell young children everything at once?

Children may need reassurance

say that' or 'you don't mean that'. Learning to listen to children and acknowledging their feelings means we can help children because they feel that they are being taken seriously and can be helped to confront these feelings.

Reassuring children

Children may need reassurance when going through a transition. They may find it helpful to know that what they are feeling is normal or that other children have gone through similar experiences and have coped. Through listening to children, and allowing them to express their fears and anxieties, we can also help to reassure them.

Structured opportunities to explore the effects of transitions

There are many ways of helping children to explore the effects of transitions in their lives. The spider diagram below outlines some of them. The age/stage of the child will be important in their selection as too will advice from others including play therapists, bereavement counsellors, parents and voluntary organisations.

Play activities

Some types of play activities can help children come to terms with the way that they are feeling or allow them to 'open' up and talk to us. Commonly used play activities include water, sand and dough, along with role play opportunities.

Books and stories

Books and stories can help children to explore a transition in a safe way. Books need to be chosen carefully so that they accurately reflect what a child might experience; for example a book in which a child's parents reunite would not be helpful for a child whose parents are divorcing.

Circle time

Circle time is a forum for older children and young people which can allow them to talk about how they are feeling. This is best used when groups of children or older people are all facing the same challenge.

Visits

When children are changing settings or carer, a series of structured visits can be helpful so that children are gradually introduced to the new environment and person.

Resource packs

Many voluntary organisations and government departments produce resource packs which are designed for parents or other adults to use with children. These should be checked carefully first to be sure that they are age/stage and context appropriate.

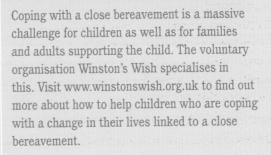

Over to you

Coping with a close bereavement is a massive challenge for children as well as for families and adults supporting the child. The voluntary organisation Winston's Wish specialises in this. Visit www.winstonswish.org.uk to find out more about how to help children who are coping with a change in their lives linked to a close bereavement.

Structured opportunities to explore the effects of transitions

Structured opportunities to explore the effects of transitions

Functional Skills

ICT: Finding and selecting information

English: Reading and writing

This task will help to develop your ICT skills. You could present the information that you find in the form of a fact sheet and also include information from other sources.

Check your knowledge

1. Outline four factors that need to be taken into account when assessing children's development.

2. Identify one method of assessing children's needs.

3. Why is it important to assess children using a variety of methods?

4. Outline the benefits of drawing up a development plan for a child.

5. Identify who may be involved in the drawing up of a plan for a child.

6. Describe three features of a service that is organised to promote the development of children.

7. Explain four reasons why children may show inappropriate behaviour.

8. Outline three strategies that might be used to help children show wanted behaviour.

9. Describe how a practitioner may support a child who is experiencing a transition.

10. Describe a structured opportunity that might support a child who is experiencing a transition.

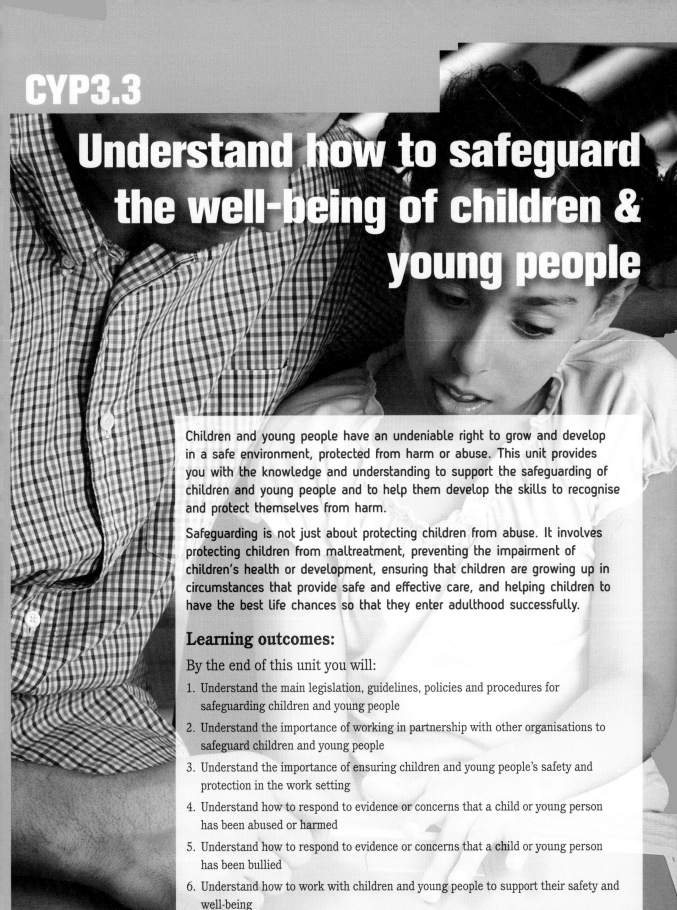

CYP3.3

Understand how to safeguard the well-being of children & young people

Children and young people have an undeniable right to grow and develop in a safe environment, protected from harm or abuse. This unit provides you with the knowledge and understanding to support the safeguarding of children and young people and to help them develop the skills to recognise and protect themselves from harm.

Safeguarding is not just about protecting children from abuse. It involves protecting children from maltreatment, preventing the impairment of children's health or development, ensuring that children are growing up in circumstances that provide safe and effective care, and helping children to have the best life chances so that they enter adulthood successfully.

Learning outcomes:

By the end of this unit you will:

1. Understand the main legislation, guidelines, policies and procedures for safeguarding children and young people

2. Understand the importance of working in partnership with other organisations to safeguard children and young people

3. Understand the importance of ensuring children and young people's safety and protection in the work setting

4. Understand how to respond to evidence or concerns that a child or young person has been abused or harmed

5. Understand how to respond to evidence or concerns that a child or young person has been bullied

6. Understand how to work with children and young people to support their safety and well-being

7. Understand the importance of e-safety for children and young people.

Understand the main legislation, guidelines, policies and procedures for safeguarding children and young people

Legislation, guidelines, policies and procedures that affect the safeguarding of children and young people

Polices and procedures for **safeguarding** and **child protection** in England and Wales are the result of the *Children Act 1989* and in Northern Ireland of the *Children (Northern Ireland) Order 1995*. The *Children Act 2004* introduced further changes to the way the child protection system is structured and organised in England and Wales.

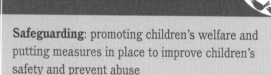

> **Key terms**
>
> **Safeguarding**: promoting children's welfare and putting measures in place to improve children's safety and prevent abuse
>
> **Child protection**: part of the safeguarding process where it is necessary to take action when there is a reasonable belief that a child is at risk of significant harm

Children Act 1989 (England and Wales)/Children (Northern Ireland) Order 1995

These Acts aimed to simplify the laws that protected children and young people in the respective UK countries. They were seen as a serious shake up of children's rights and protection and made it clear to all who worked with children what their duties were and how they should work together in the event of allegations of **child abuse**. England and Wales produced separate documents –

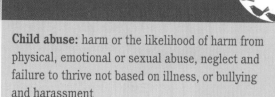

> **Key term**
>
> **Child abuse:** harm or the likelihood of harm from physical, emotional or sexual abuse, neglect and failure to thrive not based on illness, or bullying and harassment

Working Together to Safeguard Children (1999) – which emphasised the responsibilities of professionals towards children who are at risk of harm.

Children Act 2004

By 2003 it was clear that services for children were still not working together to identify and protect vulnerable children in our society. This was highlighted by the tragic death of Victoria Climbié at the hands of her carers, resulting in an independent inquiry into her death. The Laming Report in 2003, in common with other inquiries into child deaths over the years, criticised the approach to protecting children in our society. The Laming Report resulted in a green paper, *Every Child Matters*, which in turn led to the Children Act 2004 in England and similar bills and Acts in all four countries in the UK.

The main features of the Act included:

- the integration of children's services and the introduction of children's directors with responsibility for local authority education and children's social services

- lead councillors for children's services with political responsibility for local child welfare

- the establishment of Local Safeguarding Children's Boards (LSCB) with statutory powers to ensure that social services, the NHS, education services, the police and other services work together to protect vulnerable children

- a new Common Assessment Framework to assist agencies in identifying welfare needs

- revised arrangements for sharing information.

Working Together to Safeguard Children 2006

The 2006 revised version of this document provides an update on safeguarding and a national framework to help agencies work individually and together to safeguard and promote the welfare of children. It also reflects changes to safeguarding practice in recent years, especially in the light of the Laming and Bichard Inquiries (see page 114).

Legislation and policy vary between the UK nations. Four very useful websites containing information on child policy developments within the four nations of the UK are as follows:

- Scotland – www.childpolicyinfo.childreninscotland.org.uk
- England – www.cpinfo.org.uk
- Northern Ireland – www.ci-ni.org.uk
- Wales – www.childreninwales.org.uk

The DCSF website on Every Child Matters has a number of links to very useful additional information on safeguarding requirements. Go to www.dcsf.gov.uk/everychildmatters/safeguardingandsocialcare/

The Vetting & Barring Scheme

The Scheme was introduced in October 2009 with the aim of preventing unsuitable people from working with children and vulnerable adults. From July 2010 and phased in over a five-year period, anyone working or volunteering with children or vulnerable adults will be required to register with the Independent Safeguarding Authority (ISA). The ISA will make decisions to prevent unsuitable people from working with children and vulnerable adults, using a range of information from different sources, including the Criminal Records Bureau (CRB). The CRB will process applications for ISA-registration and continuously monitor individuals against any new information, while continuing to provide employers with access to an individual's full criminal record and other information to help them make informed recruitment decisions.

Enhanced

Page 1 of 2

Applicant Personal Details	
	Number: 000000000
Surname: SMITH	**Date of Issue:** 05 May 2010
Forename(s): JANE ALISON	**Employment Details**
Other names: n/a	Position applied for: NURSERY SUPERVISOR
Date of Birth: 25 OCTOBER 1955	Name of Employer: DAFFODIL NURSERY SCHOOL
Place of Birth: BARNET HERTFORDSHIRE	
Gender: FEMALE	**Countersignatory Details**
ISA Reg No.:	Registered Person/Body: ATLANTIC DATA LTD
	Countersignatory: CHRISTINE JONES

Police Records of Convictions, Cautions, Reprimands and Warnings
NONE RECORDED

Information from the list held under Section 142 of the Education Act 2002
NONE RECORDED

ISA Children's Barred List information
NONE RECORDED

ISA Vulnerable Adults' Barred List Information
NOT REQUESTED

Other relevant information disclosed at the Chief Police Officer(s) discretion
NONE RECORDED

This document is an Enhanced Criminal Records Certificate within the meaning of sections 113B and 116 of the Police Act 1997;

Continued on page 2

Example of completed CRB documentation

Functional Skills

English: Reading

By researching and reading around this subject you will be able to expand your knowledge of how to write for a different purpose.

Over to you

Visit the ISA website (www.isa-gov.org.uk/) and the Criminal Records Bureau website (www.crb.homeoffice.gov.uk) to find out more about how the Vetting & Barring Scheme works.

Reflect

How is your local area responding to the need for joint working to protect children?

Find out about the roles and responsibility of your local safeguarding board.

Ask the manager of your setting if they think that services work together more effectively now than they used to do. If so, how?

Reflect

In the Ofsted TellUs (2007) survey, 95% of children said they felt very or quite safe at home and 85% did so when going to, and in, school. This drops to 74% who felt very or quite safe around their local area and 68% on local transport.

Why do you think that fewer children feel safe in their local area or on local transport than at home or at school?

DCSF (Department for Children Schools and Families) – overall responsibility for safeguarding and child protection in England

Issue statutory and non-statutory guidance to local authorities

Local authorities – use guidance to produce procedures for services and practitioners

Services use as basis for their policies and procedures

The lines of responsibility to ensure children are protected

Child protection within the wider concept of safeguarding children and young people

Safeguarding is about much more than just protecting children from direct abuse. Any service that works with children and young people has a wider role than simply protecting them from neglect and abuse. The Staying Safe action plan recognises a number of important aspects in the wider view of safeguarding including:

- keeping children safe from accidents
- crime and bullying
- forced marriages
- missing children
- actively promoting their welfare in a healthy and safe environment.

How national and local guidelines, policies and procedures for safeguarding affect day-to-day work with children and young people

It is very important that anyone working with children should be able to recognise if a child is at risk of harm or in need because of their vulnerability. The earlier this is recognised, the better the outcome for the child involved.

Clear lines of responsibility exist to ensure children are protected. Look at this diagram:

A similar system exists in Northern Ireland, where it is the responsibility of the Department of Health, Social Services and Public Safety to issue guidance to the four local health and social services boards. The National Assembly for Wales has recently started producing some guidance of its own for local authorities within Wales.

All the guidelines are intended to make sure that all the services and agencies involved with children and young people work together to improve safeguarding.

Childcare practice

Any childcare setting should have clear policies and procedures that cover all aspects of safeguarding. This should include policies and procedures for:

- health and safety (see Unit 3.4)
- child protection
- contact with children and performing personal care – see page 120 for more details
- outings
- visitors to the setting.

Risk assessment

Risk assessments should be carried out to make sure that there are no safeguarding threats to the children in a setting.

The list of requirements in the Best practice checklist on page 113 forms the basis of the risk assessments. Premises need risk assessing — for example are there entrances to the building that an unauthorised person could use? Could a child leave the building without anyone noticing?

For more detailed information about risk assessments, see Unit 3.4.

Best practice checklist: Requirements for settings to keep children safe

All settings working with children and young people must have the following:

✓ a policy for the protection of children under age 18 that is reviewed annually

✓ arrangements to liaise with the Local Safeguarding Children Board

✓ a duty to inform the Independent Safeguarding Authority of any individual (paid employee, volunteer or other) who poses a threat to children

✓ appropriate training on safeguarding for all staff, governors and volunteers, which is regularly updated

✓ training for all staff, governors and volunteers working with children under age 18 to recognise signs of abuse, and how to respond to disclosures from children

✓ a named senior member of staff in charge of safeguarding arrangements who has been trained to the appropriate level

✓ effective risk assessment of the provision to check that the safeguarding policy and plans work

✓ arrangements for checks (including CRB) on all staff who have regular, unsupervised access to children up to age 18, and where appropriate for governors and volunteers

✓ a single, central record of all checks on provider staff*

✓ contact details for a parent or carer for all children under 18.

* Governors and volunteers require clearance if they have frequent or intensive contact with the children.

Reflect

Can you think of anything else that should be risk assessed in relation to safeguarding?

Inquiries and serious case reviews and sharing the findings to inform practice

All too often children die or are seriously injured because of abuse or avoidable accidents. Society has a duty to protect children and young people: we have a network of professional organisations supported by legislation, polices and procedures to do this. When the policies and procedures do not work, society fails in this duty and it is vital that the causes of failure are known and dealt with.

Serious case reviews are called by the Local Safeguarding Children's Board when a child dies and abuse or neglect are known or suspected to be a factor in the death. They involve the local authority children's service and the police, as well as health, education and other agencies as needed.

Each service involved conducts an individual management review of its practices to identify any changes that should be made. The LSCB also commissions an overview report from an independent person, which analyses the findings of the individual management reports and makes recommendations. Local authorities are required to notify Ofsted of all incidents involving children that are grave enough that they may lead to a serious case review, including where a child has died or suffered significant harm as a result of abuse or neglect, or where concerns are raised about professional practice or have attracted national media attention.

Lessons learned from serious case reviews usually include the importance of:

● sharing information and communication

● keeping an accurate timeline of events

● clear planning and roles

● overcoming the problems of hard-to-reach families

- good assessment of the child's situation
- early recognition of children in need of protection by mainstream services such as schools or health services
- partnership working with agencies that parents may be receiving services from — for example mental health services.

A **public inquiry** is sometimes held after a serious incident. Members of the public and different organisations may give evidence and also listen to oral evidence given by others. The findings of the inquiry are produced as a written report, given first to the government and soon after published to the public. The report usually makes recommendations to improve the management of public organisations in the future.

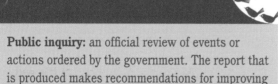

Key term

Public inquiry: an official review of events or actions ordered by the government. The report that is produced makes recommendations for improving practice

Laming Inquiry

Lord Laming produced a landmark report in 2003 following a public inquiry into the death of Victoria Climbié. She died in February 2000 of malnutrition and hypothermia, having suffered horrific abuse at the hands of her great-aunt and the aunt's boyfriend. Lord Laming's public inquiry found a series of missed chances for the authorities to save her life. A lack of communication between social workers, nurses, doctors and police officers allowed her great-aunt and her lover to torture the little girl to death. Many professionals involved in the case admitted that their workloads were too big while pay and morale were low, and that they did not communicate with one another. The inquiry made a number of key recommendations for improvements to services that led to the Children Act 2004.

A further inquiry into the death of 'Baby P' resulted in the 2009 report which identified that child protection has not been given the priority it deserved. The report made 58 recommendations for how to bring about a 'step change' in protecting children from harm.

Bichard Inquiry

This inquiry resulted from the murders of two young girls in Suffolk by a school caretaker, who was known as a danger to children by one police authority. The information had not been identified when he had a CRB check in Suffolk. It led, among other things, to the formation of the Independent Safeguarding Authority.

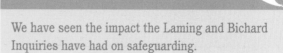

Over to you

We have seen the impact the Laming and Bichard Inquiries have had on safeguarding.

Look up the Laming Inquiry on the Internet to see the full recommendations of the report.

The *Every Child Matters* website has links to the Laming and Bichard Inquiries and the review of the death of Baby P to start with. See if you can find the 'official' reports on government websites.

Why do you think Lord Laming had to carry out another review?

Functional Skills

English: Reading

Reading through the official reports on the government websites, and summarising the main points of the articles, will help you to develop your reading skills.

Complying with legislation that covers data protection, information handling and sharing

The Data Protection Act 1998 covers personal information about individuals which is held by organisations. Any business holds a huge amount of information about its staff, the people it does business with and possible customers. They have to keep information in a safe way that ensures other people do not get hold of it.

Over to You

Find out what information is held on children in your setting and how it is kept accurate, up to date and safe.

Settings that work with children and young people have the same responsibilities: except that the information they hold is about young people and children who are vulnerable because of their age.

The Data Protection Act places responsibilities on organisations holding personal information to:

- use it only as needed
- keep it secure
- make sure it's accurate
- keep it up to date.

On behalf of children, adults and parents have the right under the Data Protection Act to have information corrected if it is wrong. They also have the right to claim compensation through the courts if an organisation breaches the Act and causes them damage and distress.

The Data Protection Act and the Privacy and Electronic Communications Regulations also give people the right to stop personal information being used for any sort of direct marketing, such as unwanted junk mail, sales calls, or email and text messages. This means that in most cases organisations should ask before they use personal information to send marketing messages.

'Every full double-decker school bus at the end of the day is likely to be taking home around seven seriously unhappy children'

Understand the importance of working in partnership with other organisations to safeguard children and young people

The importance of safeguarding children and young people

Far too many children and young people suffer abuse or neglect at the hands of their parents or carers. Research shows the scale of this, and reports of children dying as a result of abuse or accidents are all too often in the news. The statistics for the amount of abuse in the UK are worrying to say the least.

> 'Every full double-decker school bus at the end of the day is likely to be taking home around 7 seriously unhappy children. Most of the lower deck would at some time during their childhood have been going home to serious worries. Approximately 10 children may be going home to a 'double-shift' of cleaning, laundry, shopping and preparing meals, and 2 or 3 will be in fear of violence between their parents while they were out, or of what might happen that evening.'
>
> *Cawson et al. (2000) Child maltreatment in the United Kingdom: a study of the prevalence of child abuse and neglect.*

In 2000 the NSPCC published the results of a national survey of 3,000 young people aged 18–24 about their experience of a wide range of issues (Cawson, 2000) and found that:

- 7% had been physically abused by a carer
- 6% had suffered emotional and psychological maltreatment as children
- 6% had been seriously physically neglected
- 4% had been sexually abused

- 80% of physically abused children have also known domestic violence
- a significant number of children face repeated serious and multiple forms of abuse at the hands of parents or carers
- abuse is more common in families with drug or alcohol abuse problems.

At the end of March 2003 there were 25,700 children on child protection registers in England. The most commonly recorded risk was for neglect (39%), followed by physical abuse (19%) and emotional abuse (17%) (source: Department of Health, 2003)

By 2006 this figure had risen in England to 26,400. For Northern Ireland the figure was 1,639; for Wales 2,163 and Scotland 2,288.

As you can see the number of children suffering abuse is steadily increasing. Some say that the increase is due to better awareness of abuse but whatever the reason it is clear that it is crucial we continue to raise our efforts to safeguard children. Some children are more at risk than others. Studies into the prevalence of maltreatment among children with disabilities have found that these children are over three times more likely to experience abuse and neglect than non-disabled children. (Kennedy (1989); Westcott (1993) cited in National Working Group on Child Protection and Disability (2003)).

The importance of a child- or young person-centred approach

Every Child Matters sends out a very strong message to society and adults who care for children of the importance of each and every child. A key feature of Every Child Matters is that each child is a unique individual who needs support from adults to achieve the best possible outcomes as they grow and develop. The aim of Every Child Matters is to give all children the support they need to:

- be healthy
- stay safe
- enjoy and achieve
- make a positive contribution
- achieve economic well-being.

Every Child Matters aims to have a national framework to support the joining up of services so that every child can achieve the five Every Child Matters outcomes.

Reflect

In the past, services for children sometimes gave more consideration to the service and staff rather than the children being cared for. Ask your grandparents or anyone over 50 if they have any memory of being in hospital as a child; you will hear stories of restricted or no visiting, no toys or play – it was very different from today's children's wards which are very child centred.

All services aimed at children or young people are based around individuals — planning to meet their needs, rather than for a whole group.

The Children's Plan is a ten-year strategy by the government to make England a good place for children and young people to grow up. It places children and families at the heart of policy on the basis that children and young people spend only one-fifth of their childhood at school. Because young people learn best with family support, the Children's Plan covers all areas of children's lives.

Over to you

Find out how Every Child Matters has changed practice in your setting. Ask staff who have worked in early years for a number of years.

Ensuring the voice of the child or young person is heard

The United Nations Convention on the Rights of the Child (Article 13) states that all children should have the opportunity to have their voice heard — on plans for activities, what is happening in their lives and anything else they want to make comment on (see page 189). Some children do not find this easy; think about children with barriers to communication. Events in a child's life can sometimes affect their ability to express themselves.

Over to you

Think about the children in your setting – do any of them struggle to let people know their thoughts and feelings? What are the reasons for this? How can you help them to have their voice heard?

Partnership working and safeguarding

Safeguarding and promoting the welfare of children depends on effective partnership working between agencies and professionals. Each has a different role and area of expertise. Vulnerable children need coordinated help from health, education, children's social care, and the voluntary sector and other agencies, often including justice services.

The importance of partnership working runs through every aspect of safeguarding from government legislation to local working.

The key elements of Every Child Matters: Change for Children are all focused on partnership working at all levels including:

1. The duty to cooperate to promote the well-being of children and young people
2. The duty to make arrangements to safeguard and promote the welfare of children and young people
3. The development of statutory Local Safeguarding Children Boards (LSCBs)
4. The appointment of local directors of children's services to coordinate local government services
5. The National Service Framework for Children, Young People and Maternity Services bringing together all child-related health services
6. The Five Outcomes Framework
7. The development of an integrated inspection framework including education, care and health inspections
8. The appointment of a Children's Commissioner
9. The development of a Common Assessment Framework to ensure all agencies contribute to an assessment of a child's needs
10. Workforce reform to help develop skills and ensure staffing levels.

In every inquiry and serious case review the main reasons identified for the failure of care tend to be linked to lack of communication and information sharing between some or all of the major agencies. Every child or young person and their family are known to at least two of these settings or agencies, and often those who have fallen through the net are known to many more of them.

Anyone who has contact with a child or young person and has concerns about their welfare has a responsibility to pass that concern to the most appropriate agency. 'Working Together to Safeguard Children' (DCSF 2006) clearly sets out how individuals and organisations should work together to safeguard and promote the welfare of children and young people.

Key features of effective working

The following points are key in enabling effective partnership working to take place:

- a lead person who is responsible for coordinating actions and who acts as the main point of contact for children where more than one practitioner is involved

Safeguarding and promoting the welfare of children depends on effective partnership working between agencies and professionals

- effective sharing of relevant information between agencies and practitioners.

Roles and responsibilities of different organisations

When a child or young person has been abused or harmed the first line response will be at the point of the allegation or discovery. This may be in many settings, for example at school, in a medical setting or by a child contacting a helpline such as ChildLine.

As you have already seen all children are known to a number of different organisations – all of which are involved in any safeguarding issues affecting that child.

- *Social services* have statutory responsibilities to provide support to vulnerable children and families in need. This may be after a death or when families are finding every day life difficult. Most social workers are employed by social services.

- *Health visitors* have a responsibility for the health of babies and young children under five. They provide support and guidance to the parents of young children and carry out assessments of a child's development.

- *General Practitioners* (GPs) work in the community – usually from health centres – and are the gateway to other health services. GPs are often the first people to identify possible abuse when a child attends surgery.

- *Probation services* support people convicted of some offences to be rehabilitated into the community. They have a key role in monitoring people convicted of offences against children and should ensure they do not pose a threat to local children.

- *Police* are involved in the criminal proceedings that may result from safeguarding issues.

- As all children and young people should be in education or training between the ages of 5 and 18 years, *schools* and training organisations are key to identifying and supporting children when they are in need of help. All staff working with children and young people should be trained in safeguarding and child protection.

- *Child psychology services* will often be needed to support children who have experienced abuse or harm.

Case study: Alarm bells

Neighbours of the family who had just moved in to number 20 felt sorry for Jake, the little boy. He looked about 3 years old and wasn't seen out very often but, when he was, his mum was always shouting at him and dragging him by the arm. But they weren't too surprised; they had already heard too many arguments she was having with her latest boyfriend. The police had been round a few times in response to complaints about the noise. Staff at the nursery Jake used to attend didn't question where he had gone when he stopped coming and, in fact, one or two of the staff were pleased they didn't have to stay behind anymore when his mum forgot to collect him on time. His GP was very busy and no one had taken much notice of three letters from different accident and emergency departments in the past year. The health visitor went to see Jake for a routine check at his old address, but neighbours there said the family had moved out and didn't know where they had gone.

1. What are the causes for concern for Jake's welfare?

2. How should partnerships be working to safeguard Jake?

Over to you

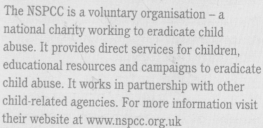

The NSPCC is a voluntary organisation – a national charity working to eradicate child abuse. It provides direct services for children, educational resources and campaigns to eradicate child abuse. It works in partnership with other child-related agencies. For more information visit their website at www.nspcc.org.uk

How is the NSPCC involved with safeguarding? How does this differ from the statutory organisation in the list above?

Case study: John the health visitor

John is a health visitor in a rural area. He is based in a GP surgery and is part of a health visiting team. As a health visitor he supports about 600 families. He carries out checks to ensure babies are safe and developing as they should. John also runs child health clinics for families to attend. These are often the first place for families to go if they are concerned about their child. John works closely with the midwives, who hand over care for families.

As well as being part of the health visiting team, John is part of a much wider multi-agency service, funded by the Children's Trust and aimed at improved community access to a broader range of services.

The service has lots of input from other workers including school nurses, children's centre staff, volunteers, local youth clubs and youth workers, health outreach workers, social services, housing services, the police and a youth offending team (YOT). The service is based in a GP surgery on a social housing estate with many socially excluded groups. The service offers a whole variety of different services, such as encouraging play between parents and children, tackling issues faced by reconstituted families, and providing outreach work with young teenage mums.

1. What do you think John might do if a child from one of his families is abused?
2. How would being part of the multi-agency service help him to be more effective?

Understand the importance of ensuring children and young people's safety and protection in the work setting

Ensuring children and young people are protected from harm within the work setting

Parents leave children in your care with an expectation that they can trust you and your colleagues to keep their children from harm. It is difficult for many parents to leave their children in an education or care setting and go to work; they need to be fully confident that their children are in safe, supportive hands with people who will help their development. Failing to meet this is a gross breach of your professional values.

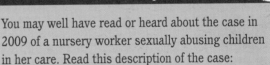

Case study: Sexual abuse in a nursery

You may well have read or heard about the case in 2009 of a nursery worker sexually abusing children in her care. Read this description of the case:

A nursery worker admitted sexually assaulting children in her care, taking more than 100 images of her victims and sharing the pictures with two other paedophiles she had met on the Internet. Families who sent their toddlers to Little Ted's Nursery do not know if their children were abused because their faces were not shown in the images. Police admit they may never firmly identify any of the victims.

1. How do you think that the worker avoided being caught earlier?
2. How do you think the parents might feel?
3. What effect do you think this could have on the children involved?
4. How could they be supported?

Policies and procedures to protect children and young people and adults who work with them

As well as having policies to ensure that only suitable people work in their setting, managers need to promote very clear practices and ways of working to protect both the children and adults they work with. It is too easy for actions to be misunderstood – particularly physical contact.

Everyone in a setting has a responsibility to work hard to promote the welfare of the children in their care. Well-run settings have a set of clear policies and procedures that support safe working – to the benefit of staff and children. Some of these are detailed below.

Working in an open and transparent way

The layout and arrangements of buildings and rooms can be important. Think about a nursery for example that has open-plan rooms: this ensures that no member of staff is totally alone and out of view with a child. Sharing plans and talking about different ways of working also helps to make sure that staff work in the most appropriate ways.

Listening to children and young people

You learn a lot about children by listening to them and sometimes you may hear things that concern you. Whenever possible avoid agreeing to keep something a secret. Always tell a child if you feel you need to share information – especially if you feel a safeguarding issue is involved. It is important that you record and report any concern you have about a child's welfare; make sure you know who to go to in your setting.

Power and positions of trust

If you are involved in the care of children or young people, you are working in a position of trust. You have authority over the children and parents have placed their trust in you to look after them; this brings responsibilities. People who wish to occupy positions of trust with children, young people and vulnerable adults have to have enhanced CRB checks.

Propriety and behaviour

Children and young people tend to respect and look up to people in positions of trust. You must think carefully about your own behaviour and the example you set to children and young people in your care.

Physical contact

All settings should have a clear policy on how to manage physical contact with children. Young children need physical contact; if they have fallen over, a cuddle

Open-plan rooms ensure that no member of staff is totally alone and out of view with a child

Case study: Saturday night out

While they were supervising the after-school club, Jess and Laura were talking about the fun they had had on their night out on Saturday. Both of them had drunk far too much and Jess had been sick in the taxi on the way home. She still felt ill at work on Monday morning but it had been such a good night...

The next morning both girls were puzzled that Mrs Singh the manager wanted to see them. She was very unhappy about the conversation she had overheard the girls having in front of the children.

1. Why should Mrs Singh be unhappy?

2. Why should Jess and Laura not have had that conversation in front of the children?

can help them to recover and get back to playing. However, too much physical contact can be easily misunderstood. A number of people working with children have lost their jobs and reputations through inappropriate contact. Make sure you are familiar with what is acceptable.

In the same way, you should check out the procedures for performing intimate personal care for children. Taking a child to the toilet, changing a nappy or helping a child change out of soiled clothes are all normal everyday tasks; but never do any of these in a room with the door closed or out of sight of other members of staff. Remembering this protects not only the child but yourself as well.

Photographs and video recordings

Photographing or videoing activities in any setting are great ways to let parents see what their children have been doing. Events may often be reported in the local paper. However it is important that some basic rules are followed:

● photos and videos are not available to anyone other than parents and carers

● always make sure that parents have given permission for photos to be taken

● check your policy on parents taking photos or videos.

Over to you

Check out the policies and procedures in your own setting that protect both the children or young people and staff.

Do you understand them?

How often are they updated and how are staff informed about this?

Reporting concerns about poor practice

Whistle blowing

At some stage in your work with children you may be faced with the problem of what to do about someone whose practice is unacceptable. You must *not* ignore poor practice – no matter who it is being carried out by. It can be very difficult to report someone you work with – or even your manager. If in doubt, just think about the effect of the poor practice or behaviour on the children in your care.

How to whistle blow:

● think about exactly what is worrying you and why

● approach your supervisor, manager or safeguarding named person

● tell someone about your concerns as soon as you feel you can

● put your concerns in writing, outlining the background and history, giving names, dates and places where you can

● make sure something happens.

Note that some organisations have confidential whistle blowing phone lines.

Whistle blowing does take courage: there is the risk of being bullied or harassed as a result. But anyone who

Case study: Kuldeep's concerns

Kuldeep was a part-time nursery worker at Little Gems nursery. She was very worried about the attention paid to health and safety by the deputy manager – especially about not checking the identity of adults other than parents who collected children. On one occasion Kuldeep was very concerned when someone claiming to be the child's aunt collected Sam, aged 4. Sam was not happy about going with her and was crying. Kuldeep reported the incident to the manager, who was very annoyed with the deputy for not making the checks. After the incident the deputy would not speak to Kuldeep and was very unpleasant. Two weeks after she reported the incident the manager said they were cutting back on staff and Kuldeep lost her job. An employment tribunal found that this was due to her disclosure and awarded her compensation.

What do you think you would have done in Kuldeep's position?

whistle blows has the right to protection from the person they have raised concerns about. Your manager should provide you with support. If you lose your job or suffer as a result of a whistle blowing incident the UK Public Interest Disclosure Act (1998) offers legal protection.

Explain how practitioners can take steps to protect themselves

The best way to protect yourself from accusations or suspicion of abuse or inappropriate behaviour is simple.

- Always make sure that you fully understand the policies and procedures about working on site, off site or performing intimate tasks for children.
- Follow the policies and procedures at all times.
- Avoid being alone in a closed room with a child.
- If in doubt check with your manager.

Off-site visits need careful thought and planning

Case study: Care needed

William had worked as a classroom assistant for three years in a primary school. After the latest safeguarding training he was always very careful not to be alone with individual children. One day a supply teacher asked him to take the more confident readers, one at a time, into another room to listen to them read. William didn't think this was a good idea, but the teacher said William wouldn't be able to hear them properly in the main classroom.

1. What should William do?

2. Why might William be concerned at the teacher's suggestion?

Off-site visits

These need careful thought to make sure that everyone gets the most out of them and also so that the children are safe and avoid any incidents or accidents. See Unit CYP3.4 for more information on the health and safety aspects of off-site visits.

Understand how to respond to evidence or concerns that a child or young person has been abused or harmed

Signs, symptoms, indicators and behaviours that may cause concern

It is important that you are aware of the indications of child abuse. However, not every sign means a child is being abused. Have you cared for children who always appear a bit grubby and maybe smell a little, but seem to be happy and loved by parents? Some physical signs, such as darkened areas, can be birthmarks and not bruising; for example, some infants of Asian or African heritage can have a dark bluish area on their lower back or buttocks, sometimes known as a Mongolian blue spot.

Sometimes the first signs that you observe are not physical but a change in behaviour. It is important that you record your concerns and monitor any unexplained changes in a child's behaviour. Sometimes a child may be experiencing more than one type of abuse.

Physical abuse

Physical abuse is when a child is physically hurt or injured. Hitting, kicking, beating with objects, throwing and shaking are all physical abuse, and can cause pain, cuts, bruising, broken bones and sometimes even death.

Signs and symptoms of physical abuse can include:

- unexplained recurrent injuries or burns
- wearing heavy clothes to cover injuries, even in hot weather
- refusal to undress for PE or games at school
- bald patches of hair
- repeated running away from home
- fear of medical examination
- aggression towards self and others
- fear of physical contact; shrinking back if approached or touched.

Many signs of physical abuse can be confused with genuine accidental injuries, but they are often not in the

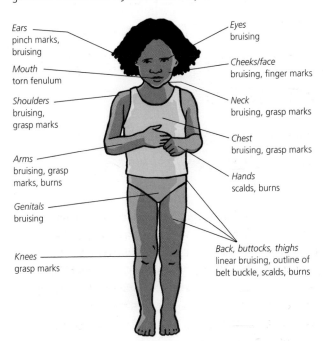

Usual position of injuries in cases of child abuse

Ears
pinch marks,
bruising

Mouth
torn fenulum

Shoulders
bruising,
grasp marks

Arms
bruising, grasp
marks, burns

Genitals
bruising

Knees
grasp marks

Eyes
bruising

Cheeks/face
bruising, finger marks

Neck
bruising, grasp marks

Chest
bruising, grasp marks

Hands
scalds, burns

Back, buttocks, thighs
linear bruising, outline of
belt buckle, scalds, burns

Case study: Concern for Leanne

Leanne, aged 6, has been away from school for two days; a note from her mum said that she had been unwell. Tanisha is helping the class to get ready for PE in the hall and Leanne is reluctant to take her blouse off. When she does, Tanisha notices that her back and upper arms are covered in deep purple bruising. When she gently asks how they happened, Leanne says she fell off a swing in the park.

1. What should Tanisha do immediately?
2. What should Tanisha not do?
3. What actions should be taken by the school?

places or distributed as you would expect. Sometimes the explanation does not fit the injury, or you may see the outline of a belt buckle or cigarette burn. Suspicion should be aroused if the parents have not sought medical advice soon after the injury occurred.

Emotional abuse

Emotional abuse occurs when children are not given love, approval or acceptance. They may be constantly criticised, blamed, sworn and shouted at, told that other people are better than they are. Emotional abuse also involves withholding love and affection. It is often linked with neglect (see below).

Signs and symptoms of emotional abuse can include:

- delayed development
- sudden speech problems such as stammering
- low self-esteem ('I'm stupid, ugly, worthless')
- fear of any new situation
- neurotic behaviour (continual rocking, hair twisting, self-mutilation)
- extremes of withdrawal or aggression.

Neglect

Neglect, which can result in failure to thrive, is when parents or others looking after children do not provide them with proper food, warmth, shelter, clothing, care and protection.

Case study: Sam and Jess

Sam is 6 years old and his older sister, Jess, is 11. Their mum and dad both have drinking problems. Sometimes there is nothing to eat in the house. Jess is often left alone to look after her brother. The school they both go to has noticed that they are always tired and appear very thin. Their clothes are often dirty and Sam is sometimes in the same clothes for a few days. One day when Jess comes to collect Sam from the classroom to go home, Sam bursts into tears and says he does not want to go home.

1. What do you think Sam's teacher should do?
2. What do you think should already have happened?
3. What structure should be in place in the school to deal with this incident?

Signs and symptoms of neglect can include:

- constant hunger
- poor personal hygiene
- constant tiredness
- poor state of clothing
- unusual thinness or lack of normal body weight
- untreated medical problems
- no social relationships
- stealing food
- destructive tendencies.

Sexual abuse

Sexual abuse is when a child is forced or persuaded into sexual acts or situations by others. Children may be encouraged to look at pornography, be harassed by sexual suggestions or comments, be touched sexually or forced to have sex.

Signs and symptoms of sexual abuse can include:

- sexual knowledge or behaviour that is inappropriate to the child's age
- medical problems such as chronic itching, pain in the genitals, venereal disease

- depression, self-mutilation, suicide attempts, running away, overdoses or anorexia
- personality changes, such as becoming insecure or clinging
- regressing to younger behaviour patterns, such as thumb-sucking or bringing out discarded cuddly toys
- sudden loss of appetite or compulsive eating
- being isolated or withdrawn
- inability to concentrate
- lack of trust or fear of someone they know well, such as not wanting to be alone with a babysitter or childminder
- starting to wet or soil again, day or night
- becoming worried about clothing being removed
- drawing sexually explicit pictures
- trying to be 'ultra-good' or perfect; overreacting to criticism.

Actions to take if a child or young person alleges harm or abuse

All settings that have contact with children and young people must have clear policies and procedures to follow in all cases of abuse. Staff must have training in these and there should be a clear line of responsibility within the organisation for dealing with the situation.

All settings that have contact with children and young people must have clear policies in cases of abuse

Disclosure of abuse by a child can occur at any time, and it can be a shock to hear details. The way an allegation is received can be very important in the outcome to a child, even many years later. There have been many examples in the past of children not being believed at the time they declared their experience – often resulting in serious problems later in life.

Key term

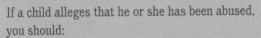

Disclosure of abuse: when a child tells or implies to you that he or she has been abused

Best practice checklist: Disclosure of abuse

If a child alleges that he or she has been abused, you should:

✓ Listen to what the child says carefully and attentively.

✓ Try not to display shock or disbelief and do not ask direct or leading questions.

✓ Communicate at the child's own pace and without undue pressure.

✓ Accept what is being said.

✓ Stress that it is right to tell.

✓ Reassure and support the child.

✓ Never promise to keep a child's allegation a secret.

✓ Do not criticise the perpetrator – the child may well still love him or her.

✓ Promptly follow the procedures for your setting.

Functional Skills

ICT: Developing, presenting and communicating information

Look again at the checklist for disclosure of abuse, then, using your ICT skills, you could try to organise this information in a different way; for example you could create a spider diagram or a flow chart.

Over to you

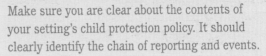

Make sure you are clear about the contents of your setting's child protection policy. It should clearly identify the chain of reporting and events.

If you feel in need of more information, then the NSPCC, BASPCAN, ChildLine or Kidscape have good sections aimed at professionals:

- ChildLine www.childline.org.uk
  - provides telephone support and guidance to children being abused (also a good source of information for child professionals).

- Kidscape www.kidscape.org.uk
  - a registered charity committed to keeping children safe from harm and abuse.

- Bullying Online www.bullying.co.uk
  - offers advice on bullying

- BASPCAN (British Association for the Study and Prevention of Child Abuse and Neglect) www.baspcan.org.uk

The rights of children, young people and their families

Children and their parents or carers have important rights even in cases of suspected abuse. It can be difficult to understand this, especially where the circumstances are distressing. Older children often have a clear idea of what needs to be done to ensure their safety and well-being. Most children feel loyal towards those who care for them even when they have been responsible for the abuse, and have difficulty saying anything against them. In situations where harm or abuse is suspected or alleged, it is important to remember the following guidelines.

- Children and young people should receive help so they can express themselves fully, understand what is happening and the decisions that have to be made.

- A child or young person has a right not to be subjected to repeated medical examinations or questioning following any allegation of abuse, whether of a physical or sexual nature.

- Family members normally have the right to know what is being said about them and to contribute to important decisions about their lives and those of their children.

- Children should be kept fully informed of processes involving them, should be consulted sensitively and decisions about their future should take account of their views.

Understand how to respond to evidence or concerns that a child or young person has been bullied

Types of bullying and the potential effects

Bullying and the fear of bullying are major worries for many children and young people.

The Children's Rights Director has surveyed children's views on bullying. In his survey in 2008, 41% of children thought bullying was getting 'a lot worse' while 23% thought it was getting 'a bit worse'. Electronic bullying increasingly worries children; this includes sending threatening mobile texts, messages and emails and posting unpleasant comments and pictures on social websites. This form of bullying had been experienced by 40% of children surveyed. Children who said they had been bullied felt depressed, unhappy and sometimes suicidal and had low self-esteem. More than half of children (57%) thought that adult intervention had helped to stop the bullying, but 24% thought it had made no difference and 19% said it had made it worse.

Types of bullying

The victims of bullying are usually different in some way from the bully; the differences may be as simple as a different physical characteristic or being seen as a swot. Bullying can be specific, for example, homophobic or gender based, racist or related to special educational needs and disabilities. Whatever the basis for the bullying it can take one or more of the following forms:

- physical (pushing, kicking, hitting, pinching and other forms of violence or threats)

- verbal (name-calling, insults, sarcasm, spreading rumours, persistent teasing)

- emotional – including not speaking to and excluding someone, tormenting, ridicule, humiliation

- cyber-bullying (the use of Information and Communications Technology particularly mobile phones and the Internet, deliberately to upset someone else).

Bullying can be carried out by one person against another, or by groups of people 'ganging up' on a person. Bullying is not always delivered as a personal, face-to-face attack, but can also be delivered through technology, such as mobile phones and the Internet, for example through social networking sites (known as cyber-bullying).

Case study: Bullying and harassment

Lee, aged 13, eventually contacted a telephone support service after years of being bullied at school. He had often had things stolen from him, especially his mobile phone or trainers. The two boys who were bullying him had started it at primary school by calling him names and following him home. More recently he had been receiving nasty text messages on his mobile. Lee had started to play truant to avoid meeting the bullies. The telephone counsellor explained to Lee that it was his right not to be bullied and encouraged him to ask a friend to go with him to talk to the head of their year.

1. Why do you think it took so long for Lee to tell someone?

2. How do you think this made Lee feel about himself?

3. What do you think you could have done if you were working at Lee's school?

4. What should the school do now that this has come to light?

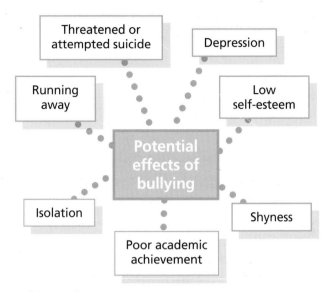

Bullying can have many consequences

Policies and procedures in response to concerns or evidence of bullying

All schools are required by law to have anti-bullying policies in place but these vary in how they are worded and the subsequent actions that need to be taken. Schools must also have policies to encourage good behaviour and respect for others on the part of pupils.

The Department for Children, Schools and Families (DCSF) is clear that no form of bullying should be tolerated. Bullying should be taken very seriously; it is not a normal part of growing up and it can ruin lives. The DCSF provides support for schools to develop anti-bullying policies, and procedures to tackle bullying through practical-guidance documents and advisers.

The current anti-bullying guidance for schools: *Safe to Learn: embedding anti-bullying work in schools* was launched in September 2007.

Over to you

Visit www.teachernet.gov.uk for more information on *Safe to Learn* and find out how organisations can help to reduce bullying.

www.bullying.co.uk also has lots of practical ideas for children and parents as well as schools.

Supporting a child or young person when bullying is suspected or alleged

When dealing with someone who is being bullied it is important to remember that they will be very upset although they may not show it on the outside. If they have plucked up the courage to talk to you then they need to know you will take the problem seriously.

In the case of an older child, it is a good idea to ask them to write down exactly what happened and who was there so that you can speak to other people. The more information you have, the better you will be able to deal with the problem and the faster you can sort out exactly what happened.

Reassure the victim that you will be back in touch with them as soon as you have completed your investigation and that if there are any more problems in the meantime they must let you know immediately.

Supporting the family

Parents can find it very hard to know how to help their child if they are being bullied. Some parents will have to cope with the news that it is their child who is a bully. You need to know how to support parents in both these cases.

Best practice checklist: Supporting a victim

✓ talk to them out of earshot of other children

✓ listen to the child or young person

✓ believe what they tell you

✓ reassure them that you will take the complaint seriously

✓ write down exactly what happened and who was there

✓ do not promise to keep it a secret

✓ tell them you will help them by telling someone in authority

✓ explain how you will investigate the complaint

✓ be back in touch with them as soon as you have news.

Listen to parents; let them explain how they are feeling. Direct them to useful information so that they can start to think how to support their child.

Look on the Internet for some good sites on bullying; for example:

- Bullying UK
- ChildLine
- NSPCC.

Understand how to work with children and young people to support their safety and well-being

Supporting children and young people's self-confidence and self-esteem

Children and young people who are:

- assertive
- self-confident
- self-aware
- and have high self-esteem

are less likely to be vulnerable to abuse.

In order to feel safe and protected, children need to feel good about themselves. A child who has high self-esteem will do better in many aspects of development. Self-esteem can be supported by:

- giving lots of praise and encouragement
- encouraging independence and choice, with many opportunities to try things out
- teaching children how to be assertive (which means having their own needs met but still respecting those of others)
- encouraging cooperation, respect and tolerance between children, and giving a positive example yourself.

Supporting resilience in children and young people

Resilience is the ability to deal with the ups and downs of life, and is based on self-esteem. The more resilient a child is, the better they will deal with life as they grow and develop into adulthood.

Many factors can positively affect a child's resilience:

- secure early attachments
- confidence of being loved by family and friends
- good sense of self-identity
- ability to act independently
- confidence to try new things.

Reflect

Can you think of children you work with who cannot tick all the factors on the list?

How do they cope with disappointment or failure?

What do you do to support them when that happens?

These are the children who need more support from you and other workers to improve their resilience. Start to think how your organisation could support children who need help in building their self-esteem.

Strategies to help children protect themselves

What do we mean by 'safe'? What is acceptable behaviour and what is not? Childcare settings — together with agencies such as the NSPCC, ChildLine and Kidscape — are very important in educating children about looking after themselves. The important thing for all children to remember is that they should never feel uncomfortable about someone they are with or something being done to them.

Children and young people need support to be able to keep themselves safe. You can help by:

- teaching them effectively about the dangers posed by some adults and how to minimise them, including the dangers arising from some aspects of electronic media

- teaching them effectively about how to behave in activities which present higher than normal safety risks (for example in outdoor pursuits and in workshops) and about road safety

- teaching them effectively about the dangers involved in substance abuse

- providing them with effective sex and relationship education, including sexual health risks, and supplementing this with impartial and confidential advice and guidance.

It is important to be available to talk with children about any concerns they may have. If they are upset by a reported case of abuse, be as reassuring as possible. These cases are very rare, even though this may be hard to believe when they are constantly in the media. Stress that almost all children lead safe and happy lives and only a very few adults want to hurt children in any way.

Using correct anatomical language, at a level appropriate to the child, is important when you are talking about bodies. However, you also need to be aware of the many different terms used by people for a part of the body such as the genitalia or functions such as passing urine.

Simple, age-appropriate sessions, linked to other activities, on how the human body works help children to understand what their bodies can do and raise awareness of what is normal and what is not. Delivery as part of the normal activities of the setting — the curriculum in schools for example — 'normalises' sessions rather than making them seem unusual. Indeed, sessions on 'body maintenance' should be an integral part of children's education, not just to warn them of the dangers of misuse.

The Keepsafe Code produced by Kidscape is an effective way of getting across the message about personal safety to young children. Older children need more detailed information such as:

- lessons on normal sexual function, related to adult behaviour (relevant to your setting's policy)

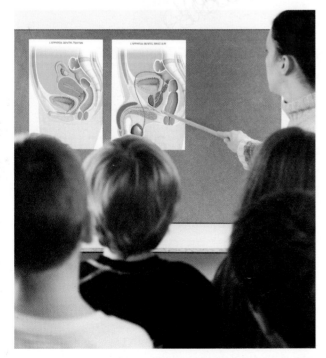

Simple, age-appropriate sessions help children to understand what their bodies can do

Skills builder

Look at the Keepsafe Code from Kidscape. The Keepsafe Code www.kidscape.org.uk/childrenteens/keepsafe.shtml

Try to adapt the Keepsafe Code for children of the age you work with, particularly if you have children who have communication difficulties.

Could you put it into a picture format with titles?

Can you think how you could get the children to practise actions for the Code?

What else might you need to do with the children so that they understand about hugs and touching that they are not comfortable with?

Functional Skills

ICT: Developing, presenting and communicating information

You could adapt the Keepsafe Code into pictures on the computer and then use it in your setting. Remember that this is for children so think about using appropriate images and words.

- information about misuse of their bodies, through smoking, alcohol and illegal drugs

- the risks of HIV and other sexually transmitted infections such as chlamydia, herpes or gonorrhoea, through sexual and drug misuse.

Help from other organisations

Organisations such as Kidscape, ChildLine and the NSPCC can help with information and guidance on these topics. It is important to use them properly and be sure that information is accurate and used to best effect. Ask your local health contact for suggestions.

The citizenship programme in schools offers a useful opportunity for children to look at safety, not only on a general basis but also in terms of their personal safety.

Best practice checklist: Helping children to be safe

- ✓ Explain to children how to keep themselves safe.
- ✓ Encourage them to share worries about abuse with their friends.
- ✓ Encourage them to tell a trusted adult.
- ✓ Make sure they know that being abused is never their fault and that abuse is never right.
- ✓ Promote services such as Childline or the NSPCC Child Protection Helpline to older children.

Functional Skills

ICT: Developing, presenting and communicating information

English: Writing

You could produce a 'Helping Children to be Safe' booklet suitable for school-aged children. You could include all the information you obtain from the checklist. Remember to use accurate spelling, grammar and punctuation throughout your booklet.

Empowering children and young people to make positive and informed choices

Children and young people need to be empowered to keep themselves safe. Children will always push boundaries and take risks – that is how we all learn. Your role is to manage those risks without taking away their independence.

Think about how you help a child to learn a new skill – such as crossing the road. First you cross holding their hand, telling them about looking both ways and thinking about the traffic. When you feel they understand the dangers you cross without holding onto them, gradually moving to letting them cross alone with supervision. Finally, when they are empowered, and can make their own choices, they are able to cross alone and without supervision. In addition to your support, a number of other community safety factors support them: safe crossing places, careful drivers and speed limits.

Over to you

Now think of another example of how you empower children and young people in everyday situations.

Understand the importance of e-safety for children and young people

The risks and possible consequences of being online and of using a mobile phone

'By 2012 every household in Britain should have access to broadband' (*Prime Minister Gordon Brown, January 2009*).

This is an admirable ambition, with huge benefits for everyone – especially in relation to research and learning. But it is also fraught with dangers as the Internet and mobile network also offer possibilities for the abuse of children and young people.

Most children and young people have access to the Internet and the use of a mobile phone. Both offer benefits to children but equally can expose them to threats to their safety and well-being.

The Internet, mobile phones and video games pose a number of risks to children and young people — including cyber-bullying, access to unsuitable sites, exposure to commercial sites and danger from adults seeking to exploit children. The independent Byron Review (2008) reported on the risks to children from exposure to potentially harmful or inappropriate material on the Internet and in video games and issued guidance on how they should be protected.

Supporting a child using technology helps to keep them safe online

Over to you

Look at these two documents – the Byron Review (both the summary for professional and parents and the report for children) and guidance by the Plymouth safeguarding board on cybersafety:

hwww.dcsf.gov.uk/byronreview/

www.plymouth.gov.uk/safeguarding_children_in_cyber_world.pdf

Can you think of ways you could use some of the recommendations at work?

Find out if your LSCB has produced any guidance.

Reducing the risk

Short of banning all access to the Internet and mobile phones it is not possible to eliminate the risks to children and young people. No one can make the Internet completely safe and people are constantly inventing new ways of misusing it. But it is possible to build children's resilience to the material to which they may be exposed, so that they have the confidence and skills to use the Internet more safely.

The Byron Review identified three key objectives to protect children:

- reduce availability

- restrict access

- increase resilience to harmful and inappropriate material online.

There are a number of measures available that start to meet some of these objectives including:

- parental controls that allow Internet sites with unsuitable material to be limited

- blocks on use — such sites can be blocked out through content controls

- improving the knowledge, skills and understanding around e-safety of children, parents and other responsible adults.

The last point is one that schools and other educational settings can be involved in.

Ways in which you can help to improve children's knowledge and skills include:

- making them aware of the dangers

- helping them to develop the skills to recognise danger

- supporting them in dealing with situations they are not happy with.

Combined with a sensible approach, such as making sure that children do not spend time on the computer unsupervised or for too long a period of time – these tools can make using the Internet a useful and enjoyable experience.

Education of parents and carers is also important. Many parents and carers are less skilled at using the Internet than their children are and may not be aware of the dangers or how to control access to certain material.

Skills builder

You can help with educating parents. Using the information from the Byron Review – especially the report for children – design a booklet and/or poster aimed at informing parents of the dangers of mobile phones and the Internet and the actions they need to take to protect their children when using the Internet.

Functional Skills

ICT: Developing, presenting and communicating information

English: Writing

Producing this booklet/poster will support your ICT and writing skills. Remember that this time it is for parents so think carefully about the layout and the language that you use and make sure you use accurate spelling, punctuation and grammar.

Getting ready for assessment

No one working with children and young people wants to have to be in the situation of supporting children who have had their rights violated as a result of abuse or some other safeguarding issue. However, being alert to the issues and knowing how to respond is probably one of the most essential skills you need as a worker in this field.

Much of this unit is based on the relevant legislation, policies and procedures. It is important that you have an understanding of the current policies and where they have come from and your role in supporting children who need it.

Look again at the outcomes for this unit:

- The main legislation, guidelines, policies and procedures for safeguarding children and young people
- How to work in partnership with other organisations to safeguard children and young people

- How to respond to evidence or concerns that a child or young person has been abused or harmed
- How to respond to evidence or concerns that a child or young person has been bullied
- How to work with children and young people to support their safety and well-being
- The importance of e-safety for children and young people

Go back and look at each section. Complete the activities and then see if you could explain your understanding to someone.

Above all, remember that if you are faced with a difficult situation and if in any doubt, always refer to your supervisor or manager. Never try to deal with a safeguarding issue yourself.

Check your knowledge

1. Explain the role of the Independent Safeguarding Authority.

2. What led to the Laming public inquiry?

3. When is a serious case review held?

4. Name five different professionals or organisations that a child is likely to be in contact with.

5. What are the main behaviours that suggest possible child abuse?

6. What is neglect?

7. Explain the concept of resilience.

8. Name four different types of bullying.

9. What should you do if a child tells you they are being bullied?

10. What is the Byron Review?

My Story

Hi, I'm Jaz and I've been working in an out-of-school club for the last year. The kids who come are really cool – a lot of them have their own computers and mobile phones and are always comparing games and equipment.

We had a really bad time a few months ago. Sam – one of the boys in my group – was really upset. He had been having some really strange messages on his computer messaging system, from someone wanting to meet him. He thought he had been talking online to someone of his own age, but got scared when he asked to meet him – and asked him not to tell anyone about it.

It was great that Sam came and told me, then I was able to tell my supervisor and we thought about what to do to help Sam – and the rest of the club.

Janet, my supervisor, told Sam's parents straight away and rang the police. Luckily they were able to track the man who had been trying to meet up with Sam. But what was good about it was that we could then spend some time working with the children to teach them how to stay safe when using their computers and phones. I found lots of really useful stuff on the Internet and ideas to help everyone understand what to do to stay safe.

Ask The Expert ...

Q I am really looking forward to working with children and young people, but this unit worries me. It feels as though I will have to be constantly looking out to make sure that children I work with are not at risk. How can I enjoy my work when I have to be constantly worrying about keeping the children safe?

A Relax – don't let your concern spoil you enjoyment! The most important point is to be aware of the risks and dangers and your role in protecting children and young people. Once you are clear about this – and what to do with any serious concerns about a child's welfare – you then put it all into perspective and focus on supporting children with their learning and development.

Video Corner

▶ **Clip 1: Social & Emotional Development**

Play this video clip on your CD-ROM and then answer the questions below.

You have just watched children on the edge of independence, yet very vulnerable to abuse and harm.

1. **What types of abuse from external sources are children of this age vulnerable to?**

2. **How would you recognise if a child was being bullied or subjected to abuse?**

CYP3.4

Support children & young people's health & safety

Children are full of energy and curiosity about their environment. When they are excited about a new experience, or see something they want to do, children may not think about any possible risks or dangers.

Every year more than 300 children aged under 15 years die in the UK from an accidental injury. Accidents are the greatest cause of death and a major cause of disability and ill-health, with over 100,000 children being admitted to hospital and over 2 million having to visit accident and emergency departments each year. In terms of the number of potentially healthy life-years lost, children's accidents outrank all other causes.

You need to be able to recognise the challenges to the safety and well-being of children and young people you work with, and help to minimise the risks, without taking away from the excitement of their activities. This unit covers the knowledge, understanding and skills required to support children and young people's health and safety. It requires you to demonstrate competence in recognising hazards and undertaking formal risk assessments in your work setting.

Learning outcomes:

By the end of this unit you will:

1. Understand how to plan and provide environments and services that support children and young people's health and safety

2. Be able to recognise and manage risks to health, safety and security in a work setting or off-site visits

3. Be able to support children and young people to assess and manage risk for themselves

4. Understand appropriate responses to accidents, incidents, emergencies and illness in work settings and off-site visits.

Understand how to plan and provide environments and services that support children and young people's health and safety

Factors to consider when planning healthy and safe environments and services

There are a number of important principles to think about when you are planning for healthy and safe environments or activities with children and young people. Most of these are common sense — just remember: everyone is an individual and may have particular needs. If you are clear about the following points it will soon become second nature to include safety in your planning.

- Every child is an individual — with different needs depending on their age and abilities. You must think about this when planning activities, for example when they involve physical play, or if more consideration must be given to the needs of a child who has just become mobile than to an older child, when planning room layouts.

- Some children have specific needs such as sensory impairments; for example think about the challenges to a child with limited hearing understanding explanations about safety.

- The different needs of families and carers must be considered.

- Always be clear about why you are using the environment in question, the activities a child encounters and what sorts of services are offered.

- The **duty of care** of a setting to children, parents and carers is a legal obligation. You should always have the child's safety and welfare uppermost in your mind when planning.

- The desired outcomes for the children and young people are the starting point. Most activities with children and young people should have clear aims and objectives that are based around the required outcomes linked to their age; for example the EYFS for children under 5 years of age.

- Lines of responsibility and accountability: everyone employed in a setting has a responsibility for the health and safety of children and staff, but there should be clear reporting responsibilities.

Key term

Duty of care: a requirement to exercise a 'reasonable' degree of attention and caution to avoid negligence which would lead to harm to other people

Over to you

Go back to Unit 3.1 and look at the section on stages of development. Think about the risks to a child's health and safety at different stages of development. What are the differences in risks for a child of 18–24 months compared to a 10-year-old?

Case study: Risks for Tom

Tom, aged 2½ years, is tall for his age. He is also extremely curious and has just discovered that he can now reach the door handles at home and feel the pattern on them. He goes to a childminder who lives in an old house with a cellar and a front door that opens on to a busy main road. Tom is very independent and when he is out and about does not always like to have his hand held.

1. Can you think of any risks to Tom's health and safety?

2. Why do you think these are risks to Tom?

3. What steps should his parents and carers take to protect him?

Monitor and maintain health and safety and encourage safe working

Any setting should have clear polices and procedures about all aspects of health and safety. All rooms and equipment used by children and young people should have regular checks to ensure that everything is working well and is safe. Some of these checks are required by law; for example electrical equipment must be checked by a qualified electrician every year.

All rooms and equipment used by children and young people should have regular checks

Managers should make sure that health and safety checks are carried out as required. In the case of an accident, failure to check equipment could have serious implications.

Nurseries, schools, summer play schemes – almost every setting where children and young people are supported – have visitors on most days. (Can you think of the range of visitors in your setting?)

Anyone running a place of work, entertainment, shopping and so on must be sure that anyone who works there or visits, for whatever purpose, is not exposed to hazards that could injure them or cause illness.

It is also important that visitors follow safety guidelines to protect children or young people in the setting as well.

Obviously people who work there will be given instructions on health and safety. But how can a manager of, say, a day care setting make sure that

parents and carers or work people, such as a plumber coming to mend the dishwasher, also know about health and safety requirements?

The information they need depends on several factors:

- how long they are at the setting
- which areas of the building they have access to
- their role and responsibilities
- contact with the children or young people at the setting.

Best practice checklist: Health and safety checks

Every person working with children is responsible for their safety. It is important that the environment children are working in is regularly checked, both before and during activities. Some of the things to think about are listed below.

✓ Does any of the equipment have broken parts or sharp edges?

✓ Are large pieces of equipment and toys arranged to allow safe use by all children?

✓ Are the outside play areas free of broken glass, syringes and other dangerous litter?

✓ Are the toilet and washing facilities clean and supplied with toilet paper and soap?

✓ Are all locks, catches and so on that stop children leaving the building alone working?

✓ Are any dangerous items or substances (e.g. knives or bleach and other chemicals) accessible to children?

✓ Are there clear procedures for dealing with spillages of urine, faeces, blood and vomit and are the facilities available to deal with them?

✓ Are there clear procedures for dealing with visitors to the setting?

✓ Do the alarms work and are visitor books and badges in place?

✓ Are all areas for the preparation of food and drink clean and is suitable equipment available?

Someone who is coming to the setting for a half hour meeting with the head or manager needs only very basic information – mainly to protect themselves in case of a fire.

A plumber who is mending the heating system and who needs to move around the building needs briefing on personal safety, but also on the importance of always having a member of staff around when there are children in the area.

Functional Skills

ICT: Developing, presenting and communicating information

You could create a poster on the computer for the staff using the information in the 'Best practice checklist'. Your poster could include key areas that staff should check regularly in order to maintain a safe environment for the children.

Reflect

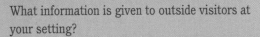

What information is given to outside visitors at your setting?

What are parents and carers told about health and safety?

What sort of information is displayed around the building to inform people?

Can you think of health and safety information you have been given when visiting anywhere?

Over to you

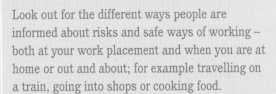

Look out for the different ways people are informed about risks and safe ways of working – both at your work placement and when you are at home or out and about; for example travelling on a train, going into shops or cooking food.

Which do you think are the most effective ways of informing people? Which do you take most notice of?

Sources of guidance for planning healthy and safe environments and services

Your setting should have copies of the latest legislation and guidance as well as their own polices and procedures.

The Internet is a very good source of information, with sites that are specific to children and young people. Look at these websites to start your research:

● Health and Safety Executive: www.hse.gov.uk/

● Child Accident Prevention Trust: www.capt.org.uk/

● Department for Schools and Families: www.dcsf.gov.uk

● Department for Education in Northern Ireland: www.deni.gov.uk

● England and Wales – www.standards.dcsf.gov.uk/eyfs/site/requirements/ index.htm

● Scotland – www.scotland.gov.uk/Publications/2005/04/12103332/33329

Functional Skills

ICT: Finding and selecting information

Tip: the Internet is an excellent source of information but always make sure that you are aware of any copyright restraints that exist on the use of some information.

Implementing health and safety legislation policies and procedures

As an early years worker you have a responsibility for the safety of the children and young people in your care – parents trust you to look after their children. There are a number of legal and regulatory requirements that help to protect children and adults in any setting.

The most important legislation for all countries in the UK is the Statutory Framework for the Early Years Foundation Stage. Since 2008 this sits alongside health and safety legislation and covers every aspect of the welfare of children in all early years settings including:

- safeguarding
- suitable people
- suitable premises and equipment
- organisation
- documentation.

EYFS in action

Look at the Statutory Framework to identify the parts that relate to health and safety.

Are there any differences between them and the requirements of health and safety legislation?

The Statutory Framework is the responsibility of the relevant education services in each of the UK countries. These are the Department for Children, School and Families (DCSF) in England, the Scottish Executive Education Department (SEED), the Department for Training and Education (DfTE) in Wales, and the Department of Education (DENI) in Northern Ireland. The Standards are monitored by the inspectorates: Ofsted in England, HMIe in Scotland, ESTYN in Wales and the ETI in Northern Ireland. Make sure that you are aware of the requirements in your country.

There are differences in the exact application of health and safety legislation in each of the countries in the United Kingdom. It is important that you familiarise yourself with the framework in your own country. You should certainly be aware of the following:

- Health and Safety at Work Act 1974
- product safety marking
- Motor Vehicles (Wearing of Seat Belts) (Amendment) Regulations 2006
- Control of Substances Hazardous to Health (COSHH) Regulations 2002
- Reporting of Injuries, Diseases and Dangerous Occurrences Regulations (RIDDOR) 1995
- Childcare Act 2006 — this sets out the statutory framework for assessment of settings, including health and safety in the Early Years Foundation Stage (EYFS) in force from September 2008 in England and Wales

- Regulation of Care (Scotland) Act 2001 and the appropriate National Care Standards
- Smoking Ban — UK-wide in indoor public places from 1 July 2007. (EYFS includes a legal requirement to ensure children are always in a smoke-free environment)
- Food hygiene legislation 2006 (European directives).

Health and Safety at Work Act 1974

All employment settings are covered by the Health and Safety at Work Act 1974 for Great Britain. This Act gives the overall responsibility for health and safety to the employer but also gives duties to employees, so everyone in a setting has some responsibility for the health and safety of anyone who is there.

The Act requires that:

- buildings should be well maintained and designed with the safety of the users in mind
- the general environment should be clean and safe
- equipment must be used and stored safely
- working practices must promote the health and safety of children.

As an employee you should be aware of the written statement of safety policy that is required in your setting. The Act also provides for your protection as an employee.

- The workplace should be safe and not pose a risk to employees' health.
- Safe systems of working should be in place.
- Articles and substances should be stored and used safely.
- Adequate welfare facilities should be available.
- Appropriate information, training and supervision should be made for the health and safety of employees.
- Any protective clothing needed should be provided free of charge.
- Certain injuries, diseases and occurrences should be reported to the Health and Safety Executive.
- First aid facilities should be provided.
- A safety representative should be consulted about issues affecting health and safety in the workplace.

Finally, it states the legal duties of employees.

- Employees should take care of their own health and safety and that of others affected by their actions.
- Employees should cooperate with their employer on health and safety.

Product marking

Many items that are used every day have been tested for safety by the British Standards Institution (BSI). An item with a BSI Kitemark means that the BSI has independently tested and confirmed that the product complies with the relevant standard and is safe and reliable. Manufacturers pay for this service and their products are tested and assessed at regular intervals. Products are not legally required to carry a Kitemark, but many everyday appliances such as glass, electrical plugs and crash helmets have them.

Many products such as toys must meet legal requirements before they can be sold within the European Union and must carry a CE mark. This mark shows that the product meets European rules but it is not a safety or quality mark. Some products carry both a Kitemark and a CE mark.

The Kitemark

Product safety markings

Functional Skills

ICT: Developing, presenting and communicating information

English: Speaking, listening and communication

You could present your findings for this task in the form of a table. You could include pictures of the toys, using the Internet, alternatively you could take photographs of the toys that show the Kitemark and include them in your document.

When you discuss whether the items you have found conform to British Standards make sure you present your information clearly and always respond in an appropriate way.

COSHH

The COSHH (Control of Substances Hazardous to Health) Regulations 2002 cover substances which can cause ill health. COSHH lays down a step-by-step approach to the precautions to prevent injury or illness from dangerous substances. Such substances must have particular labels on them, which show the substances are dangerous and need to be kept in special containers and carefully stored.

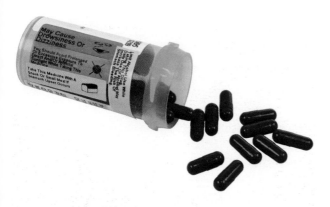

The labelling of hazardous substances

Regulations covering manual handling and risks associated with lifting and carrying children

Caring for children and young people naturally involves lifting and carrying of babies and children, as well as equipment. Incorrect lifting techniques can result in serious back injuries as well as the risk of fractures and sprains to limbs. Such injuries account for approximately 25 per cent of all injuries reported each year.

The Manual Handling Operations Regulations 1992 supplement the general duties placed on employers and others by general Health and Safety regulations.

You should always take care to protect yourself when lifting children or equipment by following good practice.

Best practice checklist: Lifting technique

Do you think about your lifting technique every time? Observe your colleagues to see if they are following the correct procedure:

✓ stand in front of the child or object with your feet at shoulder width apart

✓ always bend your knees, not your back and keep your back straight

✓ assess the weight of the child or object

✓ make sure you are firmly holding the child

✓ always test that you can lift safely before attempting to lift

✓ avoid twisting or bending as you lift.

Be able to recognise and manage risks to health, safety and security in a work setting or on off-site visits

Potential risks to health, safety and security

Any setting or **activity** carries a level of **risk**. By identifying and reducing risks in advance, full use can be made of the setting or activity to maximise the value to and enjoyment by the children in your charge.

The spider diagram below shows the different types of risks you need to consider.

Different types of risks you need to consider

Hazards in the work setting or in off-site visits

Effective management of risk should become automatic as you become more experienced. For every activity you plan, you should think about the **hazards**, the **likelihood** of the hazard occurring and the **control measures**.

If you see a hazard as you go about your everyday activities there is one simple rule: deal with it! This can be as simple as moving a toy left on the floor or cleaning up spilt water.

Over to you

Write down all the everyday hazards you can think of that you see in one day in your setting, then identify what should be done with each of them.

Case study: Risk assessment for an outing

Jason is planning an outing with a colleague to the local woods with two groups of children from his childcare setting. He hopes that he can include some nature work, physical skill development and art work with the children. The two groups he is planning to take are: six 4-year-olds from the pre-school group and eight 7–8-year-olds from the after-school group.

1. How might Jason carry out a risk assessment?

2. List the different safety risks for each of the groups.

3. What will Jason need to think about for each group?

4. How much freedom should each group be given when they are in the woods?

Health and safety risk assessments

Risk assessment forms are used to assess hazards and identify control measures for all activities and outings. They often include a **rating** for the risk. They should be simple and easy to complete like the example below.

Table 1: Examples of risk assessment for two common activities for younger children

Activity	Hazard	Control measures
Junk modelling		
Use of scissors	Sharp points and blades	Very young children use round ended scissors. Make sure children know how to use scissors safely
Containers and other materials being used	They may have rough or sharp edges that could cause injury	
	The materials used may have held food or unsafe substances (e.g. cleaning fluids)	
Cleaning up after the activity	Wet surfaces and floors present a risk of slipping	
Outing to the park		
Walk to the park	Traffic dangers	
	Child wandering off and getting lost	
Use of play equipment	Broken or damaged equipment	
	Equipment not suitable for age of child (e.g. very high slide)	
Recent rain	Lack of waterproof clothing (wet, cold children)	
	Effect on play equipment	

Visits or outings have different risk hazards from indoor activities in a controlled environment. Staff have a responsibility to ensure that outings are properly planned and carried out. If a proper risk assessment is carried out, and all reasonably practicable measures are taken to deal with the identified hazards, the scope for incidents should be minimised. The government provides comprehensive guidance for the organisation of visits, to help systems and procedures to be set up that support people leading visits. Ask in your setting to see this guidance, or look at the relevant website for your country (e.g. www.dcsf.gov.uk in England). The best way to assess risk for an outing is to make a provisional visit yourself.

Monitoring and reviewing risk assessments

A good risk assessment is only valid at the time it is carried out. Although the setting, outing or activity may be one you have used many times, one very important factor will change – the children taking part. Effective risk assessments must take account of each child taking part and the number of children.

Once you have started the activity that you have risk assessed it is important that you monitor the risks you identified and, if anything changes, you should review and change the plan. This is particularly important if you change your plans in any way.

After any activity that has been risk assessed, make sure that you review the assessment: were you correct in identifying the hazards? Were there any extra risks? This will be useful for the next time you carry out that activity.

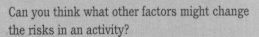

Reflect

Can you think what other factors might change the risks in an activity?

Did you think about the weather for an outdoor activity, time of day, or what the children had been doing before?

Why would these factors matter?

Case study: A trip to the art gallery

Georgia had carefully planned an outing to the local art gallery for the reception class with the class teacher. The children really enjoyed the short walk to the gallery and the time drawing the sculptures. The class was supposed to be having their picnic lunch at 12 o'clock, but at that time the gallery was having a special one-hour session for the children to have a go at making mini sculptures themselves. The teacher and Georgia decided to stay and let the children join in and delay their picnic. The session went on longer than planned and the children did not have their lunch until 1.30pm.

What changes would Georgia have needed to make to the risk assessment?

Be able to support children and young people to assess and manage risk for themselves

Balanced approach to risk management

Any activity a child does involves some risk – even something as simple as painting. If the activity is well planned and organised, with thought given to possible risks, the likelihood of an accident or injury should be minimal. The secret is to balance the risk of an activity against the benefit to and safety of the child.

Risk and challenge are important to a child or young person's development. Avoiding all risks and challenges would result in a very timid adult lacking in many everyday skills and abilities. It would be very easy to respond to all the risks to which children are exposed by not allowing them to explore or experiment. But think about how that would affect their development. Children need to explore their environment – it is one of the ways in which they learn — but it needs to be a 'safe' environment where risk is controlled by adults. It is important that children are given the freedom to develop their skills, with adult support but not too much intervention.

Understanding the stage of development a child is at and their individual needs can help you to provide the right amount of risk in activities. For example, children under the age of 8 years cannot safely judge the speed or distance of a car on the road; so a child under eight should never be allowed to cross the road alone.

Case study: Helping Josh to enjoy physical activity

Josh is 4 years old and has epilepsy. His parents are very reluctant to let him go on the climbing frame in case he has a fit and falls. Josh gets very upset that he can't join in with his friends.

1. How could you deal with this situation?
2. What steps could you take to let Josh develop his skills through climbing and at the same time reassure his parents concerns?

The dilemma between the rights and choices of children and young people and health and safety requirements

The UN Convention on the Rights of the Child clearly identifies the rights of children and young people to learn and develop into adults and be protected from harm.

Children learn by trying out new experiences and making choices. But they do not have the skills and judgement always to make safe choices. Carers have the responsibility to identify potential hazards in any situation and to judge when it is safe to allow a child to undertake an activity or make a choice. Some children need this freedom to explore risk even more than others. For example, a disabled child may be restricted in play at home because of parental concern that the child could hurt themselves. In a well-controlled setting the child can be encouraged to explore and try out new skills.

Over to you

Many children and young people have access to the Internet and it can be a source of learning and enjoyment. However it is also full of danger in terms of possible e-bullying or making contact with potentially dangerous adults. Children and young people have the right to learn and use technology: how can you support this yet protect them at the same time?

Supporting children and young people to assess and manage risk

Children are usually very good at deciding what is safe or not. Using large play equipment is a good example of how children assess and manage risk. Without adult or another child's interference most children will not stretch themselves beyond their capabilities. For example a child will not climb up a climbing frame if they are not happy at getting down it. However, parents or carers who are overly cautious about children may stop a child trying things out. We have all heard parents calling out 'Don't do that — you might fall!'

Using large play equipment is a good example of how children assess and manage risk

Best practice checklist: Supporting children to manage risks

✓ Let young children take appropriate responsibility for safety decisions in a controlled environment.

✓ Increase levels of risk as children grow and mature.

✓ Support and help parents to encourage their children to manage risk for themselves.

✓ Be aware of timid children who are reluctant to take risks and help them to develop the skills.

✓ Most children have an inbuilt level of self-protection.

Reflect

Can you think of a time when you have encouraged a child or young person to assess and manage risks themselves?

What was the situation?

What happened?

Did the child take the right decision and actions? Did you have to intervene?

Would you have done anything in a different way?

a blocked airway that needed little skill to open. A valid paediatric first aid certificate is a requirement for many child care jobs. If you do not have one, find out how you can take a recognised course, such as those run by St John Ambulance or the Red Cross, as this will give you the confidence to deal with incidents when they happen. For information on allergies see Unit EYMP3 page 269.

Understand appropriate responses to accidents, incidents, emergencies and illness in work settings and off-site visits

Policies and procedures for accidents, incidents, emergencies and illness

Young children frequently do have accidents. A child who has been injured will be very frightened and upset, as indeed will any other children who are in the area. Your main responsibility is to know what to do in an emergency, and to carry out the required actions calmly and confidently so that you meet one of the prime aims of first aid, which is to preserve life and to prevent the effects of the injury becoming worse than necessary.

The correct actions after an accident can save life. For example, people have died unnecessarily as a result of

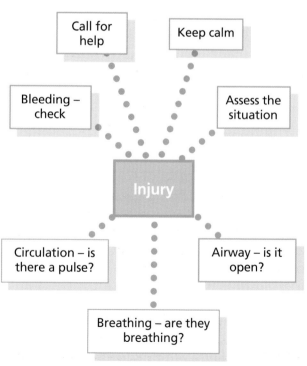

Basic First Aid

Case study: An accident during outdoor play

You are in charge of a group of six children. During outdoor play Ashok trips and falls onto a rough stony surface. You see that he has a nasty cut on his leg and blood is pouring out of the cut.

1. What do you do immediately?

2. What, if anything, do you do with Ashok's leg?

3. What do you do with the other children?

4. Who do you contact first and how?

A named person should be responsible for checking the kit and replacing missing items, although anyone using an item from the kit has a responsibility to report this.

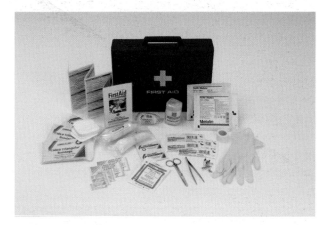

A well-equipped first aid kit

Dealing with Ashok's leg is only part what you should do. After initial first aid, he may need to go to hospital to have the cut attended to. The next important action is to inform his parents or carers. All children will have a record of emergency contact numbers.

The emergency contact number may not be the child's parents, because work commitments may make it difficult for them to be contacted. It may be that of the child's grandparents or aunt for example – it should be someone who is usually easy to contact, and who in turn can contact the parents.

The person in charge must get in touch with the emergency contact as soon as possible and inform the relevant person of the incident, and where the child is being taken. Obviously, someone the child knows well should go to the hospital with him or her until the parents or other carers arrive. This will help to reassure the child, and be a point of contact for the parents when they arrive.

Ambulances

When dialling 999, always have ready the details of the accident and injury, the age of the child and of course where the injured child is. In serious incidents involving breathing difficulties or severe bleeding, an ambulance should be summoned as soon as possible – preferably while first aid is being given.

First aid kits

All children's settings should have a well-equipped first aid kit that is easily to hand in the case of an accident. All staff should know where it is. Always make sure you know where the first aid box is kept, and what is in it.

Over to you

Find out where the first aid kit is at work. Is it easy to find?

Who is responsible for ensuring the kit is full and in a good state?

Find out where asthma inhalers are kept for each child who has asthma – read the policy for dealing with an asthma attack.

Do the contents match those in the photo? Is anything missing? Are there any extra items, and if so what are they for?

Recognising signs of illness

Occasionally a child may arrive at your setting apparently well and happy and later in the day give cause for serious concern, perhaps even as a result of a life-threatening illness. Obviously, if a child is unwell parents are contacted so that they can take the child home and to the family doctor if needed. But it is nonetheless important to recognise when a child is seriously ill so that rapid action can be taken if needed.

Call for medical help or an ambulance for any child with these symptoms:

- difficulty in breathing
- floppy or unresponsive

- unconscious

- five minutes after the start of an asthma attack, if symptoms are not relieved by the child's inhaler

- suspicion that the child may have meningitis — see below.

Meningitis

There are many illnesses that give rise to a need for immediate action but the most common is meningitis. There are several strains of meningitis and the immunisation programme offers protection from some of them. However, if you suspect a child may have meningitis do not wait and wonder about immunisation: get medical help immediately.

Make sure you are aware of the common signs and symptoms of meningitis and septicaemia, which are shown in the diagrams below.

Both adults and children may have a rash. One sign of meningococcal septicaemia is a rash that does not fade under pressure (the 'glass test'). The rash is caused by blood leaking into the tissues under the skin. It starts as tiny pinpricks anywhere on the body. It can spread quickly to look like fresh bruises. The rash is more difficult to see on darker skin. Look on the paler areas of the skin and under the eyelids. If someone is ill or obviously getting worse, do not wait for a rash. It may appear late or not at all. A fever with a rash that does not fade under pressure is a medical emergency.

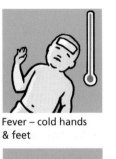
Fever – cold hands & feet

Refusing food or vomiting

Fretful, dislike of being handled

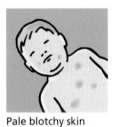
Pale blotchy skin

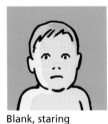
Blank, staring

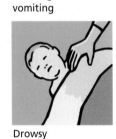
Drowsy

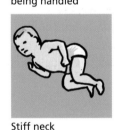
Stiff neck

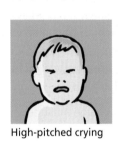
High-pitched crying

The signs of meningitis and meningococcal septicaemia in babies and very young children. (Source: Meningitis Trust)

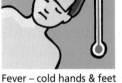
Fever – cold hands & feet

Vomiting

Headache

Stiff neck

Dislike of bright lights

Joint/muscle pain

Drowsy, difficult to wake

Confusion

The signs of meningitis and meningococcal septicaemia in older children (and adults). (Source: Meningitis Trust)

The glass test: a rash that does not fade under pressure will still be visible when the side of a clear glass is pressed firmly against the skin

Over to you

Find out what the emergency procedure is at your setting.

How is the alarm raised?

Who contacts the emergency services?

Who takes out the registers and checks them?

What are the safest exit points?

Where is the assembly point?

How often is there an emergency practice?

How are visitors to the setting made aware of evacuation procedures?

How are children reassured during evacuation practices?

Are there regulations and notices on view?

Emergency procedures in your setting

As part of the Health and Safety at Work Act 1974 and the associated regulations, your setting — if it employs five or more staff — will have a safety policy. The policy will cover emergency procedures in the event of a fire, accident or other emergency. There are many different types of emergency and it is important to know what the different procedures are — especially for fires, security incidents or if a child goes missing.

Evacuation procedures

There are many reasons why a building may need to be evacuated (for example in the event of a fire, a gas leak, a bomb scare). All adults need to know what to do. In most settings, one member of staff is responsible for these procedures and will need to make sure that all staff are aware of the evacuation procedures. Practices need to be held regularly and signs and notices must be kept in place. Drills and practices should always be taken seriously so that any difficulties can be reviewed.

In case of fire

- Close doors and windows and try to get the children out of the premises by normal routes.

- Do not leave the children unattended.

- Do not stop to put out the fire (unless it is very small).

- Call the fire brigade by telephone as soon as possible as follows: lift the receiver and dial '999'; give the operator your telephone number and ask for 'Fire';

when the brigade replies give the information clearly (for example, 'Fire at the First Start Nursery, 126 Beach Drive, Blackpool AB2 6PY, situated between the clock tower and the promenade'). Do not replace the receiver until the address has been repeated by the fire operator.

Fire practice

- Have a fire drill every three months.

- If there are problems with the procedures repeat the drill or seek advice from a fire officer.

- Reassure children during a practice by staying calm and explaining what is happening.

- Praise children and thank them for their help in carrying out the evacuation.

- Provide an absorbing activity such as reading a story or playing a game to help the children settle down quickly.

Missing children

A child should never go missing from a care or education setting if all procedures are followed. A small child should not be able to open gates or doors, and any adult going through them should follow all precautions to ensure they are properly closed and locked. Strict

Fire safety is of paramount importance

procedures that only allow the collection of children by parents or authorised carers should be followed. On outings, always ensure there is an adequate ratio of adults to children. However, if a child does go missing the alarm should be raised immediately and the setting's procedures followed. This should include:

- making sure all the other children are safe (i.e. with responsible adults)
- making sure any external exits are secure
- informing the person in charge
- starting a systematic search, based on where the child was last seen, and with whom, and make sure all areas are covered
- informing the child's parents
- informing the local police.

Procedures for recording and reporting accidents, injuries, signs of illness and other emergencies

Under certain circumstances accidents may need to be reported to the Health and Safety Executive, particularly if the child is seriously injured. Examples of this would include:

- a major injury (such as fractured limbs, electric shock, unconsciousness)
- if the child is absent through the injury for more than three days.

More information is available on the HSE website for education settings (www.hse.gov.uk/services/education/index.htm).

Even a minor accident requires an entry to be made in the accident book. For more serious incidents a full report is needed. After any such event, the person in charge should examine the circumstances to see what could be done to prevent something similar occurring again. Preventive measures may be as simple as having more adults supervise the children at outdoor play, or there may be the need to change equipment or to put further safety protection in place, such as more matting under swings.

Reflect

Fatalities on educational visits are very rare. It was estimated that across England there were 7–10 million pupil visits involving educational/recreational activity in 2003. Each year, on average, there are three or four fatalities.

(Source: Health and Safety Executive, http://www.hse. gov.uk/services/education/schoolvisits.htm)

Functional Skills

English: Writing

Produce a letter for the parents which includes all the relevant information about the outing that you have been asked to arrange. Think carefully about the layout of your letter and what it has to include. You could either handwrite or word process your letter but take care with your spelling, punctuation, grammar and sentence structure.

Getting ready for assessment

Your manager asks you to arrange a half-day outing for a group of children from your setting. This is as a summer treat at the end of a summer play scheme for children aged 4 to 11. Some parents will be coming along as well and will bring their younger children. You can use the setting's two mini buses as transport if you need to:

In total there will be 20 children aged 4 to 11 years and 6 young children aged 12 months to 4 years. There will be plenty of adults available for the outing, including the qualified staff from the setting.

1. Outline your plans for the outing, including where you will go, how you will get there and the activities you intend to offer.

2. Explain how you will find out about any potential hazards or risks relating to the outing.

3. What aspects of health and safety legislation do you need to consider?

4. Produce a risk assessment for the outing.

5. Using examples, how will you encourage the children to assess and manage risk themselves?

6. What actions will you take if a child falls and injures themselves while you are out?

Check your knowledge

1. What does COSHH stand for?

2. Name two other regulations that cover health and safety in children's settings.

3. List six routine daily checks you should make of the indoor and outdoor environments in your setting.

4. Identify two ways in which you can make sure children are secure in your setting.

5. List three aspects of welfare covered by the statutory requirements of the EYFS.

6. Give three examples of how you might assess the risk of particular activities, taking the children's age into account.

7. Why is it important to record accidents and incidents?

8. List six items from a first aid kit.

9. What should you do in the case of an accident before you start to give first aid?

10. List three key signs of meningitis in a baby or young child.

My Story

My name is Jane. I work in a large setting that has a nursery school, primary school and has a range of out-of-school provision. We have children from age 3 to 11 years coming to our school and we pride ourselves on meeting the needs of all our children, including several with disabilities including mobility and special educational support needs. I love the school grounds: as well as large garden areas where the children help to grow vegetables, the school is surrounded by woodlands and has a stream running through it. The head teacher has been keen to use the grounds and woods as much as possible to give the children an outdoor experience. All the groups and classes spend time in the outdoor environment.

We make the best use of the grounds and what they can offer by doing careful risk assessments for the area and different groups of children. By making sure that we have the right control methods and discreet boundaries we work with the children to help the understand the risks. Assessing each age group and group of children allows us to make sure we have appropriate levels of supervision so that children can feel in charge of their surroundings.

Video Corner

▶ **Clip 2: Kitchen safety**

Play this video clip on your CD-ROM and then answer the questions below.

Cooking is a potentially hazardous activity.

1. What are the hazards?

2. How can you make this enjoyable activity into a safe one that promotes learning?

3. What safety aspects would you have to consider for children aged 3 years and children aged 6 years engaging in cooking activities?

Viewpoint

A two-year-old girl attending a pre-school in Southampton left and walked half a mile back to her home in February 2006 without being missed. She had crossed a busy road before reaching her garden and finding her parents. http://www. healthandsafetybusiness.com/Spring06.html

How do you think this potentially tragic situation coud have happened? How could it have been prevented?

CYP3.5

Develop positive relationships with children, young people & others involved in their care

Working with children and their families is both fascinating and rewarding because, to a large extent, it is all about human relationships. Children flourish when they feel relaxed with the people who are caring for and educating them. They also need to feel that their parents and other adults around them are comfortable with each other. In some ways, creating the emotional backdrop is as important as any curriculum, play opportunity or theory of development. It requires an understanding of how best to promote positive relationships. This unit explores the importance of relationships and has strong links with SC1 Communication as relationships and communication are closely tied.

Learning outcomes:

By the end of this unit you will:

1. Be able to develop positive relationships with children and young people

2. Be able to build positive relationships with people involved in the care of children and young people.

Be able to develop positive relationships with children and young people

Working with children requires us to build relationships with them quickly, but also in ways that are professional. This learning outcome requires you to understand the importance of these relationships and asks you to reflect on your practice in relationship to your work with children.

Building and maintaining positive relationships

The quality of relationships that we have with children and young people has a huge effect on the way in which we can work with them.

Positive relationships with children and young people are important because:

- when children feel comfortable with us they can separate more easily from their parents
- children are more likely to participate in the play and learning activities if they are secure emotionally

- when children have strong relationships, they are less likely to show unwanted behaviour as we can recognise and meet their needs
- children's language develops more quickly because they feel confident talking to us
- practitioners can plan more accurately as they understand children's developmental needs and know their interests
- practitioners are able to respond to children more effectively because they can recognise their expressions and emotions.

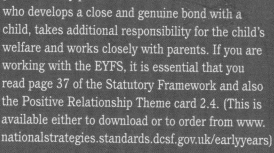

EYFS in action

The EYFS has as a statutory component the requirement for all children to be allocated a key person. A key person is someone who develops a close and genuine bond with a child, takes additional responsibility for the child's welfare and works closely with parents. If you are working with the EYFS, it is essential that you read page 37 of the Statutory Framework and also the Positive Relationship Theme card 2.4. (This is available either to download or to order from www. nationalstrategies.standards.dcsf.gov.uk/earlyyears)

Make a list of ways in which you could tell whether a child and a key person have developed a strong relationship.

Observe one of your key children. Consider whether a strong relationship has developed.

*The EYFS requires all children to be allocated a **key person***

Key term

Key person: a person who has a special relationship with the child and their family and who acts as a surrogate attachment figure when the child is separated from parents and carers

How relationships are built and maintained

There are some factors that seem to underpin a strong relationship. The spider diagram below and the text which follows look at these factors.

Communicating effectively

One of the most important aspects of building a relationship is to find ways of communicating effectively. As we will see below, the style and way that we might do this will change according to a child's age and stage of development. Communication is not just about words — see Unit SC1 on communication; it is also about our facial expressions, body language and gestures.

Identifying and sorting out conflicts and disagreements

Groups of children, like adults, will have their disagreements. As children become older these can become more serious and are not simply squabbles. In order for children and young people to trust us, it is important that we can identify difficulties and help them wherever possible to find ways through them. It is essential that children and young people perceive our way of doing this as fair.

Being consistent and fair

Children and young people rely upon us. This means that it is essential that day after day, we are consistent. Consistency means not just keeping behavioural boundaries in place, but also making sure that we do not have significant mood swings, for example one day being excitable and funny and the next being quiet and withdrawn.

Children also need to know that we will be fair with them. We will listen to what they have to say before jumping to conclusions and we will try to make sure that their needs are taken into consideration.

Fairness is also something that adults need as well. Parents will want to see that the way that their family is being treated is comparable with others, while staff members need to feel that their workplace is a fair one where everyone is expected to pull their weight.

Showing respect and courtesy

Children and young people will need to receive respect and courtesy from us in order that they can extend these skills to others. From the earliest age, we should be using markers of respect in English such as saying please and thank you. We should also speak to children and young people using voice tones that are warm and courteous.

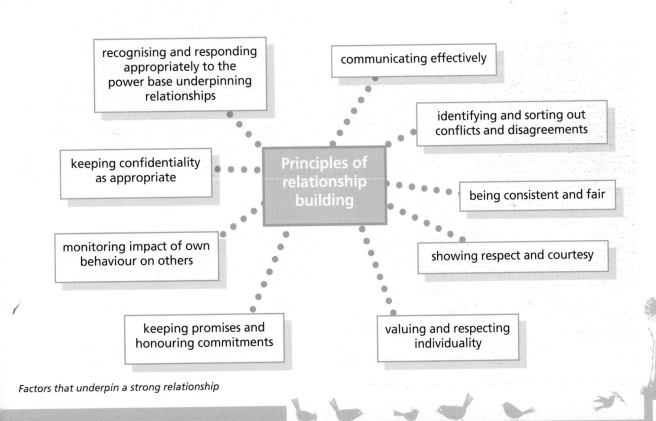

Factors that underpin a strong relationship

Valuing and respecting individuality

Recognising others' **individuality** is the basis of anti-bias practice (see Unit SC2). Children, young people and other adults will all have different strengths, talents and attitudes. They will also respond in different ways. Valuing and respecting their individuality means showing that we are comfortable with their differences. With young children it also means acknowledging that they may have particular interests and then building upon these by, for example, saying, 'I know that yesterday you enjoyed playing with the bucket outside and so today I have brought a scoop for you to try out.'

Key term

Individuality: the uniqueness of a child or young person

Keeping promises and honouring commitments

Small things matter enormously to children and young people. The promise of a turn on the tricycle tomorrow will be remembered as will talk of buying some card for a craft activity. Children and young people need to know that they can rely on us and part of this is keeping our word. Not keeping promises or honouring commitments mean that a child or young person will tend not to trust us again or may keep some distance from us.

Reflect

Have you ever been promised something that has not materialised? How did this make you feel? Did it affect how you felt towards the person or organisation?

Monitoring the impact of your own behaviour on others

Part of working professionally with children, young people and their families is to monitor and then, if necessary, adapt our own behaviour. You may notice, for example, that a child moves slightly back when you talk to them. Noticing this is important. It might be a sign that the child finds you too overpowering and so you will need to alter your style slightly to be gentler.

Keeping confidentiality as appropriate

While we can never promise to maintain confidentiality if children reveal that they have been abused, or that there is a danger that they may be harmed, keeping confidentiality is an important part of working with children, young people and others. Confidentiality is essentially about trust and respect. Parents and other professionals will often give you **confidential information** on the basis that it will be helpful to you when you work. They do so trusting that this information will not be passed on to others, to become the source of gossip or interest. If you breach confidentiality, you will break that trust. When trust between you and others breaks down, so too does the relationship.

Key term

Confidential information: that which should be shared only with people who have a right to have it, for example your lead practitioner, supervisor or manager

Best practice checklist: Confidentiality

✓ Do not gossip about children, their families or people you work with either inside or outside your workplace.

✓ Never give families' or work colleagues' contact details to others without consent, unless requested by the police or social services.

✓ Keep written information that you have been given or written in a secure place yourself.

✓ If you are unsure about whether you have the authority to pass on information, ask your supervisor, parent or other professional who has provided it.

✓ Do not take photographs of children and young people without the necessary consents.

Functional Skills

ICT: Developing, presenting and communicating information

Confidentiality is extremely important for you – both as an employee and also a student practitioner. You could design a poster to display in your classroom to remind your peers of the key facts about confidentiality.

Holding and cuddling a baby can help the child to feel wanted and reassured

Recognising and responding appropriately to the power base underpinning relationships

Few relationships are genuinely equal in terms of power. Someone may have more resources, experience or skills. They may equally have power as a result of their position and role. It is important to understand this in terms of our relationships with children, young people and others. With children and young people, it is particularly important that our power is not abused as it is given to us to protect and nurture them. This means not 'ordering' children about, but ensuring that we are always fair, respectful and courteous.

Build relationships with children of different ages

The way that we build relationships with children and young people changes according to the age and stage of a child. Responding to a 14-year-old boy in the same way as you would a 3-year-old is obviously not going to work. It is also important when building relationships with children and young people to think about their needs and interests.

Building relationships with babies

While all children will need to establish a sound relationship with early years workers, for babies it is an absolute necessity. Babies need to form an 'attachment' or special bond with an early years worker in order to compensate for the absence of their parents (see attachment theory in Unit SC3). The EYFS uses the term 'key person' to describe the role of a person who will take particular care of a baby or child and develop a special relationship with them. Constancy is particularly important: while babies are capable of making more than one attachment, they do need to have one particularly strong relationship. Children should, however, be encouraged to develop positive relationships with other members of staff so that in the event that their key person is absent, they feel comfortable and secure.

Physical contact

One way you can make a strong relationship with a baby is through physical contact; simply holding and cuddling a baby can help the child to feel wanted and reassured. While babies do need some time on the floor and to play, it is important that they do not have prolonged periods when they are not handled.

Body language and responsiveness

Babies quickly tune in to the human face. They recognise the adults they enjoy being with and with whom they have a special relationship. Babies need eye contact and to be responded to quickly. A baby who is crying may need to be picked up and rocked, while a baby who tries to attract your attention with babbling and smiling needs the adult to respond positively.

Skills builder

Observe babies or toddlers in your setting.

Can you see how often they make eye contact with their key person?

What happens when their key person picks them up or smiles at them?

Functional Skills

Maths: Analysing and Interpreting

English: Writing

If you were to complete this task over a set period of time (see Unit CYP3.2 for further guidance on a suitable method of observation) you could track your results in a table. From these results you would then be able to analyse the data you have collected in order to see how often this happens and if it happens at certain points, for example just before a snack or at lunch time, and then you could write a conclusion of what happens once the child has been acknowledged or picked up.

Using everyday routines

Relationships do not just happen. Babies learn about the people they enjoy being with through everyday events, such as nappy changing, feeding and playing. It is therefore good practice for the same person to change the baby's nappy each day and to take on other physical care tasks. During care routines, the baby needs eye contact, cuddles and plenty of response. These are important times for babies and actually have more effect on them than more structured activities such as hand printing.

Case study: Babies need to form an attachment

Leman is a childminder and looks after three children during the week. The youngest, Damien, is 4 months old. He comes for three mornings a week. Leman has arranged with Damien's mother for him to come on the mornings when she does not have any other children arriving early. This means that she can focus her attention on him.

1. Why do you think the childminder wants to spend time with Damien on his own?

2. What might be the advantages to Damien?

3. How might Leman be able to build a strong bond with Damien?

Songs, rhymes and repeated actions such as peek-a-boo for older babies are ways in which babies learn about play.

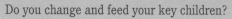

Reflect

Do you change and feed your key children?

How much physical contact do you have with the babies in your care?

How do you know that they have a strong relationship with you?

Building relationships with children aged 1 to 3 years

Like babies, children under the age of 3 years need to have a strong attachment to one person in the setting. Distress at leaving parents continues until most children are nearly 3 years old and can be avoided only when the child has a settled relationship with an alternative adult. This means that children need a very effective key person. To avoid the child becoming distressed, it is good practice that a good relationship is established before the child is left by the parents. This can be achieved by encouraging parents to come into the setting several times before children are left, so that children can get to know the person who will be looking after them.

Best practice checklist: Building relationships with children

✓ Allocate each child a key person.

✓ Work with parents closely to find out about their children's needs, interests and language.

✓ Allow children to familiarise themselves in the setting before expecting them to take part.

✓ Make sure children have a sufficiently strong relationship with their key person in the setting before they separate from their parents or carers.

Physical contact

This remains important for the young child. Toddlers, for example, clearly signal when they wish to be picked up by raising their arms; 2-year-olds may want to sit on your lap. Physical contact is important to young children and you need to ensure that when children want to have some physical reassurance, they get it. It could even be argued that depriving young children of physical contact when they seek it is tantamount to emotional neglect. Interestingly, these years are also a time when children can alternate between clinginess and independence. It is not uncommon for a 20-month-old child to want one moment to be carried and the next to be put down on the floor. Respecting such wishes is very important. This is one way in which children instinctively learn that they have rights over their bodies.

Responsiveness

Children of this age also need you to be responsive to them. They may tap you on the back or point out things. It is important that you are able to respond to them with a smile, a cuddle or a gesture as otherwise they soon learn not to bother trying to make contact.

Building relationships with children aged 3 to 6 years

From around the age of 3 years, children often become more confident about being with people they do not know so well. This can vary according to individual children's experiences, but, on the whole, children find it easier to separate for brief periods from their parents. Children in this age range are also becoming more aware of other children and gain pleasure from playing with them.

Between 3 and 6 years, children are becoming more aware of other children

Reassurance and approval

While younger children will often seek physical contact with you, in this age range they will gradually instead look for verbal reassurance and approval. This is linked to their language development. Children who come into the setting and do not speak the language, or who have some language delay, may still need opportunities for physical reassurance. Reassurance and approval are important as children are beginning to develop an awareness of themselves, and it is important that their self-concept is a positive one. You may give reassurance and approval by smiling, praising a child or simply being alongside children as they try out something new. Interestingly, if you observe children of around 3 years of age, you may notice that even when they are engaged in play with other children, they look around at odd times just to see where the adults are. They may also be keen to show you what they have been doing or enjoy some friendly interest.

Listening to children

Babies and very young children need you to acknowledge them and physically reassure them, but by 3 years of age they will need you to listen to them. With their growing language skills, children begin to enjoy chatting and expressing their ideas. They may also ask questions and will want a proper response. Children are quick to sense those adults will spend the time listening properly to them.

Building relationships with children aged 7–11 years

In this next phase of childhood, children need adults to talk, but particularly to listen to them and explore their ideas, feelings and thoughts. Unlike younger children, who will often spontaneously talk to an early years worker, older children may not always make comments and talk at the time, but after reflection may need to talk things through. When you work with older children, it is important therefore to find time to listen to them when they need you. Reassurance and approval remain important for children aged 7–11 years, and it is important that, at times, this is given unconditionally, as children who learn that they are valued only if they are achieving or pleasing an adult can lose confidence. During these years, it is important that children learn that they can develop their own views and opinions and that you are interested in hearing them.

Building relationships with young people

Young people still need good relationships with adults. In many ways these relationships are as important as ever. Young people are likely to be undergoing significant

You can build good relationships with young people by respecting their views, giving them time and responsibility

changes in their lives as well as physically growing up. They need to be able to turn to adults for advice, reassurance and to be understood. Young people are quick to identify adults who will listen to them and empathise. It is important for adults not to dismiss young people's problems out of hand, however trivial they may seem. When young people feel that they are not being listened to, they often stop communicating altogether. This is worrying, as many young people 'warm up' by talking generally before deciding whether or not to talk to an adult about some deeper issues that are affecting them. You can build good relationships with young people by respecting their views, which may be different from yours, and also by giving them plenty of time and also responsibility.

Case study: Rachael

Rachael is 15 years old. Her parents have recently split up and she is missing her dad. She finds it hard to talk about the situation at home to her friends. She attends a youth club on Wednesday and Saturday evenings. Rob, the youth leader, has noticed that she has changed quite a lot in the last few weeks. She seems moody and does not want to be involved with the activities. Tonight, he asks her if she would lend him a hand sorting out the snacks and drinks. She agrees. He is hoping that by talking generally about other things, he might find out what has been upsetting her.

1. Why is it important that Rachael finds someone to talk to?

2. Why did Rob not ask Rachael directly what was wrong?

3. Why might it take several sessions before Rachael is ready to talk?

Evaluate your own effectiveness

The wonderful thing about children and young people is that they are all different. This means that we need to adapt the way in which we approach and communicate with them according to their age/stage of development, needs and personality. Not so long ago, some adults working with two children of exactly the same age would have expected them to respond in similar ways, and a child who did not respond as the adult expected might have been seen as 'shy', 'sullen' or 'difficult'. Today, it is appreciated that it is more appropriate for the adults to change the way in which they work, rather than to condemn the child. An important starting point is therefore to consider how effective our relationships with children and young people are. Interestingly, some tell-tale indicators of the strength of our relationships with children and young people can be seen through some everyday activities.

Use the Reflect activity below as a tool to consider the relationships that you have with individual children.

Adapting our style

If we conclude that our relationship with a child is not as strong as we would have hoped, it is important to be ready to adapt our style of working. A good starting point is to observe someone in the setting or another adult involved in the care of the child and reflect on the skills being used. It might be that the other adult is calmer, shows more facial expression or praises more. Smiling is particularly important when it comes to relationships. When we are less confident and comfortable with children and young people, it is likely that our behaviour shows this. Smiling, being positive and acknowledging the child are all clear signs to the child that we are enjoying being with them. When adults are not sure about how to approach a child, these types of signals become less frequent.

Reflect

For each child or young person that you work with, consider the strength of the relationship they have with you. Use Table 1 below to identify how well the relationship is being built.

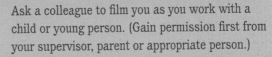

Skills builder

Ask a colleague to film you as you work with a child or young person. (Gain permission first from your supervisor, parent or appropriate person.)

Use this observation to consider how relaxed you and the child seem.

Think about what you are doing together and whether this activity is working well for both you and the child.

Table 1: The strength of your relationship with the children you work with.

	Always	Sometimes	Never
Greeting Does the child or young person seek you out soon after coming into the setting? Does the child or young person like to tell you when they are leaving the setting?			
Seeking help Does the child or young person seek you out quickly if they need help or have had an accident?			
Smiling and eye contact Does the child or young person often make eye contact with you or smile while you are with them?			
Looking for company Does the child or young person seek you out to involve you in play, chat or an activity?			
Absence Does the child or young person miss you when you are not in the room (babies and toddlers) or are absent for a few days?			

Functional Skills

ICT: Developing, presenting and communicating information

English: Speaking, listening and communication

Tip: it is important to remember that ICT is not just about using a computer.

After doing this activity you could discuss the relationship seen between yourself and the child and you could also discuss the effectiveness of using the video recorder as an ICT tool.

Getting ready for assessment

Write a leaflet for a new practitioner about how to build positive relationships with children. Your leaflet should contain information about the following:

- The importance of building positive relationships with children

- How relationships can be built and maintained with children of different ages

- The importance of listening to children.

might, for example, be brought into a nursery by a childminder or au pair; or a childminder might find that a reception-aged child will attend school in the morning but come to her in the afternoon. Some children with additional needs may also have a range of others involved in their care such as a speech and language therapist or a social worker. This means that we must be able to establish effective relationships with a range of people — from children's immediate families through to colleagues and other professionals. The skills that

We need to be able to establish effective relationships with a range of people

Be able to build positive relationships with people involved in the care of children and young people

Children do not come through the door alone or by themselves and it is rare that we are the only ones involved in a child's education and well-being. A child

are required to do this are covered in Unit SC1 on communication and also considered in Unit CYP3.7.

The key to building relationships with other adults is mutual respect and the understanding that although our approaches may vary, everyone involved is working towards the same end — the welfare and education of the child. It is also important to remember that relationships are built on trust and information that is given in confidence must remain confidential unless there is an issue about child safety. (See also Unit CYP3.3.)

The spider diagram opposite above shows some of the people who may be involved in the care of a child or young person.

Diagram showing: **People who may be involved in the care of a child or young person** — Organisational managers and supervisors; Colleagues; Parents/Carers; Official visitors; Other visitors; External partners; Colleagues from other agencies and services

We are rarely the only ones involved in a child's education and well-being

Where we do not have strong relationships, there is a danger that information may be passed inaccurately or that it is withheld because we may not be not trusted. This has to be taken seriously as, over the past few years, some child deaths have occurred because people caring for children have not worked properly together. Where parents are concerned, it is essential that we build positive relationships so that we can work closely together with them to benefit the child in a variety of ways. This should include settling the child in, sharing developmental information and also learning about children's interests.

The spider diagram below shows the benefits of establishing a good relationship and lines of communication with others who may also have a role in supporting the child.

The importance of positive relationships with other people involved in the care of children

The professional and positive relationships we develop will ensure that good communication is possible in order to support the needs of children and their families.

Diagram showing: **Benefits of positive relationships** — Information can be shared quickly between adults; Skills and ideas can be shared; Children are given consistent care; Children's welfare can be properly monitored; Children's needs and interests are identified; Plans for children's care and education are more effective

Positive relationships are essential for good communication

Case study: Connor

Connor is 3 years old and lives with his mother who works part time. He attends a children's centre for five mornings a week. On Thursdays, his grandmother, who he adores, picks him up and he spends the afternoon with her. On two other afternoons, he is with a childminder who has looked after him since he was a few months old. She also has him overnight if his mother is doing a late shift. Connor has learning difficulties, which are affecting his speech. A speech and language therapist works with him in the children's centre. As Connor has been identified as a child with additional needs, he also has a social worker. Recently, Connor has been quite aggressive with some of the other children in the children's centre. You are his key person.

1. Why is it essential that Connor has a strong relationship with you?

2. What are the barriers that might prevent communication between those who care for them?

3. What are the consequences for Connor if those involved in his care do not communicate with each other?

Reflect

Make a list of the children that you work directly with. Next to each child's name, see if you can list other people who are important in their lives or in their care.

1. Do you know how to contact them if required?

2. How often do you communicate with them?

3. On a scale of one to five (five being the highest), how well do you know them?

Reflect on what you could do in order to improve your communication and contacts with them.

Functional Skills

ICT: Developing, presenting and communicating information

Sometimes email can be a good form of communication between people who you do not see often or who belong to other agencies. Is there anyone on your list with whom email would be a beneficial way of communicating?

It is important that you understand the importance of email and how to send one.

vested interest in their child's welfare and education. This means that parents should command our respect and this should be shown in the way that we view our work with them.

In settings that have strong relationships with parents, parental participation and involvement is fundamental. Parents are seen as equal partners with valuable knowledge and information about their children to share. They are viewed as the experts when it comes to knowledge about their child. Such settings constantly look for ways of spending time with parents, as time is a key consideration when it comes to building relationships. Parents are invited in to observe their child, to help and to work in the setting and also to support the planning. In addition, settings will find ways of encouraging parents to be involved with fundraising and some of the management tasks within the setting.

Reflect

How does your setting involve parents in the care and education of their child?

Are parents given opportunities to feed back about the service that your setting is providing?

How are comments by parents received?

How is information shared between parents and staff?

Building relationships with parents and primary carers

It is essential that we build positive relationships with parents and primary carers so that we can work closely together with them to benefit the child in a variety of ways. This should include settling the child in, sharing developmental information and also learning about children's interests. Relationships with parents and primary carers are particularly special and so it is worth considering some of the factors involved in a little more detail.

Firstly, it is worth understanding that parents and primary carers usually have strong emotional attachments to their children. They are children's 'safe bases' and have a

Pressures on parents

Understanding the pressures on some parents is important in order to empathise with them. Modern parenting can be competitive. Some parents report feelings of anxiety that their child may be 'lagging behind' or that they are not providing sufficient opportunities. Some parents also work long hours and struggle to fit in time with their children and this again can make them feel guilty. The media also heightens parents' worries about being inadequate by often showing photos of 'happy families' or running articles about the perils of 'ready meals' or 'latchkey kids'. As well as external pressures, the intense nature of the attachment between parents and child can be overpowering for some parents as anger, pride, frustration and love provide a powerful cocktail of emotions. This may mean that some parents find it hard to cope with their children's demands and behaviour on occasions and may question their own ability to parent. In addition, parents may also have other pressures such as coping with illness, financial difficulties and their own personal relationships.

Over to you

Look at some of the Internet sites that support parents, particularly mothers, for example www.mumsnet.com

Can you see some recurring issues for parents?

Why is it important to be aware of the issues facing the parents that you work with?

Check your knowledge

1. Explain why positive relationships with children and young people are essential.

2. Give examples of ways that practitioners can build relationships with a toddler.

3. Give examples of ways that practitioners might build a relationship with a young person.

4. Explain the factors that might be involved in building positive relationships with children and young people.

5. Explain why it is essential for practitioners to keep their promises to children.

6. Explain why confidentiality is important when working with children and young people.

7. Outline ways in which a practitioner might identify that a positive relationship has been established with a child or young person.

8. Identify people who may be involved with the care of children.

9. Explain why positive relationships are important with parents.

10. Give examples of how positive relationships with parents may be established.

CYP3.6

Working together for the benefit of children & young people

This unit will encourage you to explore and understand how important it is in your role with young children to work effectively in teams of adults who have a variety of skills and experiences. You will find out what a multi-agency team is and how working together in this way can meet the needs of the children and their families who you work with. You will also find out how services working together in an early years setting, such as a children's centre, can enable practitioners to fully meet the needs of children and their families.

Effective communication is an essential part of your professional role. This unit will support you in developing the range of skills you need to develop as an early years practitioner working in a team.

You will also read about different ways in which you can record and share information with your colleagues concerning children in your setting.

Learning outcomes:

By the end of this unit you will:

1. Understand integrated and multi-agency working

2. Be able to communicate with others for professional purposes

3. Be able to support organisational processes and procedures for recording, storing and sharing information.

Understand integrated and multi-agency working

Multi-agency working refers to different services, agencies, teams of professionals and other practitioners working together to provide the services that meet the needs of children, their parents or carers.

The spider diagram below shows the adult professionals who may be involved in trying to work together to provide the best outcomes for young children.

Early years settings such as children's centres are integrated because they offer a variety of services in one building, such as integrated early education and childcare, a range of community and health services, outreach services that may entail visiting the child's home and even links to training and employment opportunities for families of children under five.

Some early years settings, such as nursery schools, may have a simpler form of **integrated working** by offering an extended day to support working parents, thus combining early education and childcare. In these ways different agencies can work closely together for the benefit of each child.

Key terms

Multi-agency working: different services working together to meet the needs of young children and their parents or carers

Integrated working: different services joining together to offer more effective care for young children

The importance of multi-agency working and integrated working

Children in their early years may have a range of needs and the way that we work together as practitioners can have a positive impact on their health, development and learning. Many early years settings, such as children's centres and extended schools, are responding to the wider needs of young children and their families. This holistic approach is a very important part of the government framework in England, known as Every Child Matters (ECM). The five outcomes of ECM state that we

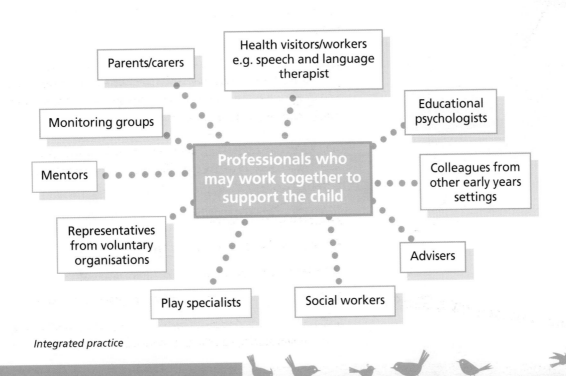

Integrated practice

should be working together to achieve the best possible outcomes for the children in our care starting in the early years. These outcomes are:

- be healthy
- stay safe
- enjoy and achieve
- make a positive contribution
- achieve economic well-being.

The Early Years Foundation Stage (EYFS) is clear that different professionals working together will help to improve outcomes for children in both their learning and development. It may be that records are shared or that observations of a child by a professional, such as a speech and language therapist or by a practitioner in the setting, may contribute to further assessment.

In the principle behind the theme 'A Unique Child' the EYFS guidance states that 'Every child is a competent learner from birth who can be resilient, capable, confident and self-assured'. Throughout the EYFS you will be encouraged to put this and the other three themes into practice, and make sure that your practice is inclusive.

Inclusive practice means that children's needs should be supported and valued so that they can access the curriculum of the setting they are in. This is an important part of the EYFS framework.

Inclusion is an important part of effective multi-agency working and you should ensure that the children you work with are welcomed and accepted as part of your setting. Working with other agencies to ensure this could range from ensuring a visually impaired child has ICT equipment adapted, so they can participate fully in activities, to ensuring that a child whose family is encountering financial problems can fully participate in activities such as outside visits.

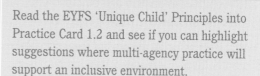

Over to you

Read the EYFS 'Unique Child' Principles into Practice Card 1.2 and see if you can highlight suggestions where multi-agency practice will support an inclusive environment.

Different professionals working together will help to improve outcomes for children in both their learning and development

How integrated working practices and multi-agency working in partnership deliver better outcomes

There are many outcomes for children that will be positive if the professionals working with the children and their families can share and agree upon the way they might assess, plan and implement for the child. Both the children and their parents can be involved in any plans to ensure that a child can achieve their potential.

Table 1 offers some different examples of how adults working together can improve the outcomes for the child.

If the outcomes for any child are to be positive it is important that all the adults involved understand what information can be shared and the importance of confidentiality.

Table 1: Positive outcomes as a result of multi-agency working

Example 1

A child who is looked after by a childminder may attend more than one setting. For example the child may have breakfast and tea with the childminder and go to a nursery during the day. Transitions can be difficult for a child in such cases; if the adults involved can share relevant information about key things that may have happened to the child, this can help to make the child's experience more positive. All information should be shared with the parent.

Example 2

If a child who attends a nursery in a children's centre is referred to a speech and language therapist they may be able to see them in the same building. The observation and assessment of the child's needs would become an easier and less daunting process if the services are in close proximity and can communicate with each other on a regular basis. It may also be easier for parents to be involved in the process if they do not have to take long journeys that may be difficult for a variety of reasons, such as lack of transport or living in a rural area.

Example 3

The adults working with a child attending a reception class with an extended day will be able to communicate more easily if the child is attending school and after-school provision in one setting. The local education authority behavioural support team will be able to hold meetings with all the adults involved with the child together and suggest a shared approach to managing the child's behaviour. A positive outcome will be possible if the adults working with the child on a daily basis, such as the parent, teacher and play worker, are able to communicate on a daily basis and have a shared approach.

Example 4

A young child whose family are refugees will need the teachers and adults working with them at school to understand their culture, the community they may be living in and their family's situation. It will be essential for social workers or workers from voluntary organisations to work together to support the needs of the child and their family. Although the school might not be able to support all the issues, which could range from housing to employment, they could be an important point of contact for the family.

Reflect

Think carefully about your experiences so far in early years settings. Can you think of an example where communication between different adults, including parents and professionals, could have been more effective for the child? Your example could involve a child who attends two settings, such as a playgroup and a nursery, or a child who has support from another professional such as a social worker or speech and language therapist.

Can you list three ways that you think the adults could have worked together more effectively?

You might like to reflect upon this with your line manager, a peer or mentor.

Functions of external agencies in the early years

There are a number of agencies which, although not part of the early years setting, may be brought in to support individual children and their families. They may work from either their own setting or might be integrated into a children's centre or school. They help to ensure that young children and their families can get the support they need so that children can have the best possible start in life.

Table 2 lists some examples of these external agencies and their roles:

Table 2: External agencies and their functions

External agency	Function
Behavioural Support Service (BEST) Specialist teachers Teaching assistants May work closely with a range of other practitioners including educational psychologists, education welfare officers and counsellors	A behaviour support service is part of the Local Authority (LA) and works in partnership with schools, within a framework of inclusion, to help them promote positive behaviour, and to provide effective support to pupils, parents and schools where behaviour is a concern and may have an effect on achievement. Parents and settings have the main responsibility for promoting positive behaviour. But LAs play an important supporting role, providing schools with some form of behaviour support service, advice to schools on developing and reviewing school behaviour policies.
Health care professionals Speech and language therapists Health visitors	They will probably be employed by the local primary health care trust and will support individual children and their families. The referral may have been made by a GP or awareness raised in a setting. They may also provide health screening for children. They will work closely with the setting and family.
Educational psychologists	They will be employed by the LA and support children who may have specific learning or psychological needs. They may be referred by the setting. They may work in independent offices or be situated in a school or children's' setting.
Advisers	There may be advisers for all aspects of early years ranging from parenting to local childcare options. Some advisers may be a part of the local children's information service or the early years department. They may work for agencies such as Jobcentre plus, supporting parents finding employment.
Social workers	Employed by social services they may be attached to a children's centre or work independently. They may support children and their families to improve their housing or support a family issue involving a health need, poverty, bereavement etc.
Play specialists	May support children in hospital or work with social services supporting children in difficult family situations.
Representatives from voluntary organisations	These could be organisations such as: National Association of Toy and Leisure Libraries – offering to make toys and books accessible to all National Children's Bureau (NCB) – working closely with professionals using research to affect policy and thus ensure children reach potential NSPCC – supporting children and families in threatening situations such as domestic abuse. Have school teams who work closely with practitioners supporting children with emotional and psychological issues. CHILDLINE – free helpline for children.

The government's vision, set out most recently in the Children's Plan, is that every child and young person should have the opportunity to fulfil his or her potential. Sure Start is responsible for changing the way services are delivered for young children and their families.

The aim of all Sure Start Children's Centres is to improve outcomes for all children by enabling families to access an affordable, flexible, and quality childcare setting for their child.

Local authorities (LAs) are responsible for setting up children's centres. They plan the location and development of centres in local communities, working with the following to deliver a range of services for children:

- parents
- private sector
- voluntary sector
- independent sectors
- primary care trusts (PCTs)
- Jobcentre Plus and other agencies, to deliver a range of services.

All these services may function together in three different ways.

Multi-agency panel

Practitioners work for their own agency but get together regularly to discuss children who may benefit from support from more than one agency. Sometimes the work is done by the panel members or sometimes they employ key people to lead a case; for example, the child of a family receiving support from social services with regard to housing and where the child also receives support for a medical condition such as asthma.

Multi-agency team

This may be a team such as the Behavioural and Education Support teams (BESTs) where practitioners

Over to you

The government has contracted with a partnership of private sector and public sector organisations, called Together for Children, to provide delivery support on the ground for local authorities. Visit the Together for Children website for LA resources, good practice, case studies and discussion forums.

If you look at the website Together for Children you can find out more about the functions of external agencies. For example they are leading Change4 life which encourages young people and their families to have a healthier lifestyle.

with different skills and expertise work together with individuals, small groups and families.

Integrated service

This may include a range of separate services that are working in the same location and which may have an overall manager to ensure that services are truly integrated. Sure Start Children's Centres and extended schools are an example of an integrated service for children in their early years,

Over to you

The NSPCC has 34 Treatment and Therapeutic centres in England, Wales and Northern Ireland. Most children and young people are referred to their services by social services, family protection police, and education and health services. Young people and children may refer themselves or be referred to these services and receive appropriate support depending on their needs.

Find out more about how NSPCC works with children, young people and their parents and supports early years professionals by visiting their website: www.nspcc.org.uk. It is important for your assessment that you are also aware of the needs of young people.

A children's centre supporting the whole family

Over to you

To show that you understand the functions of external agencies for young people, prepare a leaflet which clearly informs parents about three external agencies for young people, such as ConneXions, that are available in your area.

Visit your local authority website to find out more or go to your local library to find out about agencies for young people.

- Make the information clear, accurate and in user-friendly language
- Avoid using too much information
- Add addresses and contact details of agencies if appropriate
- Ensure that your leaflet is factual and positive
- Highlight the benefits of working together for young people

Functional Skills

ICT: Developing, presenting and communicating information

English: Writing

This assessment task will develop your ICT skills; you might use programs such as Word or Publisher to complete your leaflet. Think carefully about the layout and the style of writing. Remember you are writing to inform but with user-friendly language. Take care with your spellings, punctuation and grammar.

Common barriers to integrated working and multi-agency working

In your role as early years practitioner you will know that teamwork can sometimes be challenging. Multi-agency practice takes place where children spend most of their time and feel familiar – this could be a children's centre, school, village hall, health centre etc.

But it is important to understand what some of the barriers to effective working might be:

- where people have been clearly trained for a role they may find it odd to be managed by a person with different skills and expertise (which could happen in settings such as children's centres)
- they may behave in a different way in dealing with risks and have different priorities in their work with children
- they may not be used to sharing their expertise and knowledge
- each profession may have their own language – terms they use that are only recognised by their profession
- they have chosen a specific profession and may feel upset that they have to widen their working practice and find new ways of working.

In order for this to be successful it is important that each profession is respected and the knowledge they have is seen as a valuable asset to any multi-agency work. Professionals will need to have forums so they can share their practice with fellow professionals while opening their minds to consider a different way of working in multi-agency teams. There are a number of practical issues that will help to make multi-agency work run smoothly.

Best practice checklist: Effective multi-agency working

- ✓ If different professionals are sharing an office ensure that every member of the team has their own desk and computer, telephone etc.
- ✓ There must be a space that can be booked to hold meetings.
- ✓ There should be a suitable space, ideally two rooms, for group and individual work with children and parents.
- ✓ For multi-agency services based in settings such as a children's centre each service should have a dedicated telephone line for parents who want to contact them directly.

The key to removing barriers that may exist when different professionals begin to work together is to have a person to coordinate communication and activities. The person who takes responsibility for integrated services and support to children is called a lead professional. This individual takes the lead to coordinate professionals working together from different agencies. The lead professional acts as a point of contact for a child and their family when a range of services are involved and an integrated response is required.

Referrals between settings

If a child is already in a setting such as a day nursery or nursery school, it might happen that the parents and staff recognise that he or she needs support from another setting. For example, a child with hearing impairment may need to be referred to a support service for children who are deaf or hearing impaired. Panels are usually organised by local boroughs and are made up of different agencies. These panels determine the access that is available between settings for young children and enable referrals to be made.

Such panels aim to:

- support the early identification of children's needs

- ensure that a child's needs are identified and assessed quickly and referred to the appropriate setting

- monitor children's progress to ensure that provision can support the child's identified needs

- coordinate provision through the development of close partnerships between parents, settings and different agencies in the state, private and voluntary sector

- with parental agreement, support inclusion in mainstream early years settings and referrals between settings.

Early Intervention Teams have been set up in England to work with children with additional needs from birth to the end of the Early Years Foundation Stage.

You will have an early intervention team in your area that will be part of the multi-agency panel, enabling referrals to be made between settings. An Early Intervention Team:

- promotes inclusive practice

- provides advice, support and training to settings

- supports transition into school

- liaises with parents, carers and multi-agency professionals involved in supporting children and families

- ensures that parents are fully aware of and involved in any referral process.

Common Assessment Framework

The Green Paper Every Child Matters (DfES 2003) and the Children's Act 2004 outlined a Common Assessment Framework (CAF) as a way of providing early intervention for children before they reach a crisis point.

The CAF is a shared assessment and planning framework to be used by all practitioners working for children's services in all local areas in England and Northern Ireland. The aim of the CAF is to ensure an early identification of children and young people's additional needs and to ensure that agencies work together to meet them.

This common assessment is general and is meant to be accessed by all early years practitioners and improve communication between them. It may be the first type of assessment for a child who has more specific needs such as a child with Special Educational Needs who may

Early intervention is vital

be assessed according to the Special Code of Practice. The CAF is a key part of delivering services that are integrated, and are focused around the needs of children and young people. The CAF is a holistic approach to conducting assessments of children's additional needs and deciding how these should be met. It can be used by practitioners working on a daily basis with children.

As a practitioner working with young children you should know about the CAF and what a common assessment is. The diagram on the right outlines the three main steps in the CAF process,

First Step: Identify if a child may have additional needs using the CAF checklist

Second Step: Discuss the strengths and needs of the child using the CAF

Third Step: Decide what is needed to meet the needs of the child. A lead professional may be appointed

The three main steps in the CAF process

Case study: Supporting Emmy

Emmy has been attending Fernwood School reception class for two terms. She has displayed some behavioural issues and her parents and teachers are finding that the strategies they have in place are not working at home or in school. Her mum, Sue, has built up a good relationship with Ash who is Emmy's teacher. Ash has talked with the head of the school and they have agreed to fill in a CAF pre-assessment checklist form to see if they can receive some support from another agency. While Emmy was in extended care Ash and Sue filled in the form together. Sue wanted it to be recorded that she felt her other children were being affected by Emmy's behaviour, although she felt she had a very strong family unit. She was also finding the situation difficult to cope with as her husband was unemployed. Ash also told Sue that they would benefit from support from another professional such as a teacher from the local BEST team (Behavioural Education Support Team). They agreed to make a recommendation that Emmy would benefit from support.

1. Which of the five outcomes from Every Child Matters are Ash and Sue trying to achieve for Emmy?

2. Consider why Sue's involvement in completing the CAF pre-assessment checklist form could ensure positive outcomes for Emmy's development.

Best practice checklist: CAF pre-assessment checklist

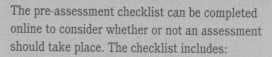

The pre-assessment checklist can be completed online to consider whether or not an assessment should take place. The checklist includes:

✓ Identifying details of child

✓ Record of evidence of:

    ✓ Child's health and safety

    ✓ Learning and development

    ✓ Impact on others

    ✓ Impact of poverty on child

✓ A recommendation as to whether or not a CAF assessment would help the child.

You can view a sample of this official pre-assessment checklist form on the Every Child Matters website. See www.everychildmatters.co.uk

Be able to communicate with others for professional purposes

There will be many times that you will be required to communicate with children, parents and a range of colleagues during your time as an early years professional in your setting. It is essential that you do this effectively to create positive outcomes for the children you are working with. In this section you will learn that communication takes on a variety of forms that you will be expected to use at different times. A lack of **communication** skills is so often referred to as a weakness in early years settings but is something that can easily be addressed. If there are any forms of communication that you find challenging then you must work on these and develop confidence in order to communicate more effectively.

The spider diagram below shows a range of the people who you might communicate with during a working week. In the centre of the web are the ways that you might use to communicate.

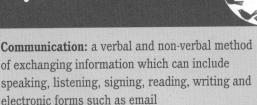

Key term

Communication: a verbal and non-verbal method of exchanging information which can include speaking, listening, signing, reading, writing and electronic forms such as email

Functional Skills

English: Speaking, listening and communication

Using the information in the spider diagram, can you match the different forms of communication to the relevant person with whom you would use it?

EYFS in action

The EYFS emphasises the importance of effective communication. If you read the Principles into Practice card 2.1 Respecting Each Other you will read that:

'There should be open communication to ensure that everyone's views are listened to and considered fairly, always keeping the needs of the children firmly in mind.'

Consider an example of how open communication in your setting had a positive outcome.

Professional colleagues from other agencies/settings

Parents of prospective children

**Verbal
Telephone
Email
Written
Video
Signing**

Children

Parents

Colleagues in setting

Visitors such as sales reps, trainers, students

Ways in which you might communicate

Before we think about different methods of communicating it is important to think more about who we communicate with during the working day. A good place to start is with the children. As with all effective early years practice your knowledge of child development will be useful. The subject of communication with children is dealt with in more detail elsewhere: see Unit SC1 Communication and Unit EYMP5.

Talking together

Communicating with adults

In this unit we have already discussed the range of adults who you may come into contact with. Communication is all about building a good working relationship. A positive atmosphere that has clear communication between adults can only be positive for the children involved. Clear communication between adults will be a positive model for communication by children.

Best practice checklist: When communicating with adults

✓ Listen

✓ Retain eye contact

✓ Avoid assumptions or jumping to conclusions

✓ Seek clarification if you do not understand something that someone has said

✓ Invite adults to express themselves by saying things such as 'I wondered what you thought about this...'

✓ Try not to see differing viewpoints as a threat but welcome differing views

✓ Try to use 'I' statements where appropriate

It is important to show respect for an adult by:

● respecting the fact that the other adult's views might be different from your own

● finding out how someone wants to be addressed such as Ms or Mrs

● never jumping to conclusions or assumptions about why someone says something

● always giving people time to talk and showing you are listening.

A great way to communicate positively with any adults is to start a statement with 'I'! This shows that you believe in what you are saying by owning the statement. For example: 'I am happy to come and meet you tomorrow' or 'I am happy to go outside today with the children'. Try this next time you are communicating with a parent or colleague and see if you feel clear and positive about what is said!

Active listening

This is an important element of communication skills with an adult or child. It involves thinking about what the adult or child is saying and showing that you understand. This actually means giving the child or adult you are communicating with your whole attention. The key is to make an adult or child feel relaxed and show that you do not want to rush anywhere. Where you talk is important. You may need to ensure you are in a quiet and relaxed place. Positive body language is a part of active listening – using your body to show that you are attentive. You can show you are listening by:

● leaning slightly forward to show that you are interested

● smiling if appropriate as this can make the listener feel comfortable

● nodding your head in agreement when appropriate

● avoiding crossing your arms as this can be seen as a barrier and a reluctance to listen

● engaging appropriate eye contact but do not overdo this as it can make some people feel uncomfortable.

Appropriate communication methods for different circumstances

You will use different methods of communication according to the situation. Some different methods of communication and when they should be used are shown in Table 3. However your communicate you should always be clear and confident.

It is important to be sensitive to adults who may not find it easy to communicate. You may sometimes need to use pictures and photographs or, for a variety of reasons, find another adult to translate for you. Beware of cultural differences or adults who have a different home language.

It is also important to understand that not every adult understands the written word, just as some may find the telephone difficult and prefer communication in person. These are all issues to be aware of in your communication with adults.

Table 3: Methods of communication and circumstances for use

Method of communication	Circumstances
Verbal	Interacting with children Interacting with parents and colleagues – discussion, giving information, meetings, feedback, receiving information
Written • Ensure letters are error free • Ensure they are correctly addressed • Ensure that you address the recipient appropriately • Ensure the content is clear and concise • Use official letter heading as appropriate	Letters, notices, permission slips, newsletters, labels, home school communication books, reports, forms, accident reports, notice boards, agendas, minutes, records of meetings, information such as policies and procedures, observations and assessments of children
Email • Ensure that you are respectful and not too informal, e.g. writing 'hi' to a parent instead of 'dear' • Avoid writing an email when angry as you may regret this later • Avoid sending too many emails • Only answer emails when not with children • Ensure that it is professional and free of errors • Messages are clear and concise • Ensure confidentiality by checking recipients and who is to be copied in	General message/ reminder to parents about an event etc; response to a communication from a parent or colleague
Computer/Internet • General and correct information on website • Be careful about placing images of children on the Internet	PowerPoint, other presentation of data to a group Interactive whiteboards Websites with interactive sections or giving general information on a daily or periodic basis Digital portfolios of children's observations to share with parents
Telephone • Be clear • Explain who you are and the reason for your call. • Ensure messages are recorded and get to the recipient in time • Ensure the recipient understands your message • Ensure that sensitive calls are made in a quiet area	Relaying or receiving information from parents, requesting information from parents and other sources, arranging meetings, ordering resources, arranging visits
Video	Conferences, training, record of children's learning
Sign Language	Children or adults who may have severe hearing impairment may use sign language. If sign language is taught early then a child will use it more naturally. There are different sign languages such as British Sign Language (BSL) or Makaton. Different countries have their own.

Skills builder

Use a digital recorder if your setting has one and record yourself talking to a child. Think of the right place to talk so that you can actively listen and encourage conversation. Try to let the child lead the conversation. Play back the activity to a colleague and discuss how effective the communication in the activity was? How could it have been improved?

Functional Skills

English: Speaking, listening and communication

When speaking on the telephone it is important to carefully consider the language you are using. You must be very clear when you speak as the recipient cannot see facial or hand gestures that may support what you are saying. Always listen carefully to what the other person is communicating so that you can respond appropriately and make sure you do not speak over them.

Appropriate communication methods

Before considering the types of communication methods that you may use in different situations it is important to remember that confidentiality must always be considered in any form of communication. As a practitioner you will have access to a range of information about children and their families and you must always know what it is you can share. Here are some key issues of confidentiality to remember when communicating with adults in whatever form:

- ensure that if you talk about sensitive issues you are in a quiet place
- be careful not to talk about work outside the workplace
- ensure that names are not identified on documents that might be shared in public

- always check if you are not sure that a piece of information is confidential
- be very careful about using photographs of children, ensuring that you have permission to do so
- be sensitive about talking about a child in your setting in front of other children and adults.

Case study: Indiscretion in the nursery

Cora is concerned about Brian, a 4-year-old in the nursery whose parents are going through a divorce. Brian's mother, Siobhan, has come in to tell her that Brian's father is no longer living at home. Siobhan is very upset. After she has gone, Cora talks in the corner of the room to another colleague about the situation, telling them the details of the divorce and how she feels that Brian's mother is not giving enough attention to Brian so he is very clingy and gets upset easily. She also says that she would have dealt with the situation in a different way and that she would have kicked the father out of the home a long time ago. Parents are collecting their children and Brian is playing nearby with a friend.

1. How did Cora breach confidentiality?
2. How might this conversation affect Brian and Cora's relationship with Brian's mother?

Reflect

Digital portfolios are increasingly being considered as a way of ongoing assessment for parents about their children's learning. Photos are also often posted on websites. Can you think of any advantages or disadvantages of this type of communication? You may want to discuss this with your colleagues.

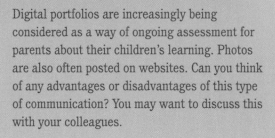

Getting ready for assessment

In your setting you will have the key person system to ensure that parents and practitioners can communicate clearly to ensure positive outcomes for each child. Key workers are responsible for a small group of children, communicating daily issues to the parents and acting as a point of contact. Talk to your colleagues about the key person system that you operate and how they feel that it enhances communication between parents and children. Perhaps, with your manager's approval, you could gain some views of parents about the system. Then write a brief report of how the key worker system helps your setting to communicate with parents. You could add some recommendations as to how the system could improve. In the next section you will learn about report writing skills.

Preparing reports

A report is a presentation of facts and findings, usually as a basis for recommendations; it is written for a specific readership, and probably intended to be kept as a record.

Consider the spider diagram below to find out what sort of reports you might write as part of your role.

To write a report successfully you need to: clarify why you are writing the report; plan the report and think about its contents — the structure.

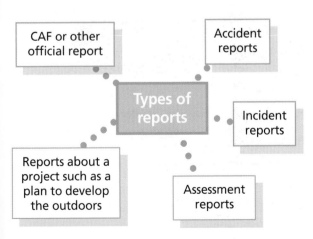

Reports you might write as part of your role

There are three types of report:

1. **Factual report** — to inform — such as an accident or incident report. This is a straightforward statement of the facts, giving an accurate record.

2. **Instructional report** — to explain: for example, when a change is introduced, such as a change to the curriculum, or a revised system of reporting about food quality, this will be written as an instructional report (step-by-step), telling people about the new procedures.

3. **Leading report** — to persuade people to listen your ideas such as developing your outdoor area. The leader wants to encourage people to support his/her idea. The writer of the report will lead people towards making a decision that he or she wants. This report needs a lot of evidence to be successful, such as examples of other outdoor areas and proof of positive outcomes from tried and tested outdoor developments.

A report will generally have the following features:

- Title page: a simple title page with writer's name, title, date; an indication of whether it is confidential

- Contents list: the contents of short reports may be shown on the title page. Longer reports should always have a separate page, listing the major sections, sub-sections if any, and appendices

- Introduction: this gives the aim and background to the report

- Main part of report: detailed facts and findings

- Conclusions: summarising main points of report

- Recommendations: make any recommendations, relating them clearly to what has gone before

- Appendices.

Some reports need detailed supporting information or perhaps information that only some readers need. All this goes in the appendices.

In some cases you may also need to include:

- References: this lists the books and articles consulted as a basis for the report, or those you want to suggest as further reading — or both

- Glossary of terms: this can be a help if your readers include non-experts as well as experts as it explains terms such as EYFS (Early Years Foundation Stage).

Many reports that you may write will be part of a requirement by the EYFS Statutory Framework and will be expected to be available for any Ofsted inspection. These will include:

- reporting accidents
- reporting injuries
- reporting concerns.

Functional Skills

English: Writing

When writing a report you must always keep your language formal and remember to think about and check carefully your spellings, punctuation and grammar.

Incident/Accident Report

Name of child:

Date, time and location of incident:

Description of incident:

If there were any witnesses, please list their names and contact details:

Name (printed): . . . .

Signature: . . . .

Date: . . . .

An example of a blank Incident/Accident report

It is important to remember that the Data Protection Act 1998 is concerned with personal information. Data protection stored about an individual must not be given to anyone without the person's permission or kept for longer than necessary. Everyone has the right to see any information that is stored about them.

Be able to support organisational processes and procedures for recording, storing and sharing information

Your setting will have clear guidelines as to how to record information and where to store it. You should also be clearly guided as to whom to share information with. You should most certainly share any information with your line manager or, in some cases, there may be a designated person to communicate with.

Over to you

In the case of any concerns about the safeguarding of children you should have a designated person in your setting who will gather information in confidence about a situation and consider if external support is needed. Find out who the designated person is in your setting and ask them about their role. Would this role change when safeguarding young people?

Listed below are points to consider when storing information:

- Is it in a confidential area if paper based?
- Who can access the information?
- Do computer systems storing information have limited access?
- Has the identity of the child been protected by not using real names, photographs and so on as appropriate?

- Have you considered the requirements of the Data Protection Act 1998?
- Have you used the agreed recording system?
- Have you made notes of all meetings?

Do computer systems storing information have limited access?

Contribute to the development or implementation of processes and procedures for recording, storing and sharing information

You can contribute to making the recording, sharing and storing of information a success by following the guidelines of your setting. Increasingly now, information is electronically stored so you have to ensure that it has limited access and is protected. You should follow these guidelines:

- Follow any written procedures such as a CAF referral.
- Record any information accurately in required format.
- Ensure reports are made to the designated person such as your line manager.
- Ensure all agreed people are informed.
- Ensure any information is shared as agreed by your setting.
- Always consider the safety of children when recording, sharing or storing information.

- Keep any notes away from public areas such as notice boards desks etc.
- Make sure that any information is recorded and agreed within an agreed time frame.
- Ensure storage is secure and confidential.

Maintaining secure storage systems for information

The spider diagram below demonstrates how you can ensure paper-based and electronic systems are secure.

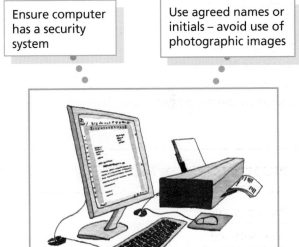

Ensure computer has a security system

Use agreed names or initials – avoid use of photographic images

Record as agreed

Ensure passwords are not shared

Ensuring the security of paper-based and electronic systems

Confidentiality versus the need to disclose information

As a practitioner you will most certainly have times when you are concerned about the importance of maintaining confidentiality but ensuring safeguarding the children in your care. You can always discuss such a dilemma with your line manager but, as a rule, always disclose something if you think that a child may be in danger. You will be doing the best for the child if you disclose such information of a sensitive nature even if you feel you are breaking a confidence.

Follow your setting's procedures regarding **disclosure of abuse**. Parents should have seen your setting's child protection policy which will state that information will be disclosed if it is deemed that a child is in any danger.

Key term

Disclosure of abuse: when a child tells or implies to you that he or she has been abused

When abuse of a child or young person is suspected:

- Do not promise to keep a secret.

- Ensure that you accurately record any conversations on an incident recording form.

- Share the information with the designated person in a confidential area.

- Ensure that you receive support as situations of this nature can be very upsetting and cause great personal strain.

- Remember that the CAF is there to help you if you are concerned about a child and need to assess their needs at an early stage.

Check your knowledge

1. Which government framework for children encourages people to work together from different professions?

    a) Every Child in Early Years

    b) Every Child Matters

    c) Children in Need

2. Which three of the following professionals might be working together in early years?

    a) Behaviour Support Specialist

    b) An educational psychologist

    c) A children's hairdresser

    d) A speech and language therapist

3. Which phrase below best describes multi-agency working?

    a) different services working together to meet the needs of young children and their parents or carers

    b) different services joining together to offer more effective care for young children

4. Briefly describe what the term 'inclusion' means.

5. List three external agencies which might support children and their families in the early years.

6. Name two examples of integrated services for children in their early years.

7. What do the letters CAF stand for?

8. Which of the following methods of communication would be most efficient to remind all parents about a forthcoming event in your setting?

    a) telephone

    b) email

    c) PowerPoint presentation

My Story

My name is Karen and I work in a room with 3–4-year-old children in the daycare setting in a children's centre. I have a great child in my class called Ho Jun who has a childhood illness that makes his bones brittle. He can easily break one of his bones at any time so we have to be very careful with him. His mother is naturally very anxious as he has already had two spells in hospital. Working in the children's centre here is a health visitor, Ellen, who has been really supportive of Ho Jun's mum and us. She has spent time observing him while in the nursery and has suggested some practical ways of us ensuring Ho Jun is safe but developing his independence and not being isolated from other children. Ellen has also given us lots of information about Ho Jun's condition and has talked to groups of our children so that they can understand more about Ho Jun. What I really like is that Ellen is always popping in to see us. She has listened to our concerns and supported Ho Jun and his mum so that we all feel more confident about Ho Jun's day with us. I also think that it has made me feel more confident about including children who have additional needs in to my setting as I now know that I can work together with other professionals such as Ellen to make it work.

Ask The Expert ...

Q I have been told that I could fill in a CAF pre-checklist for a child if I wanted to. Can I really do this?

A Yes, if you are concerned that a child may need some sort of additional support then this is a great way to do it. It is available online. You may find that, at the end of the process you, your manager and the parents don't think that you need to request any more help. Visit www.everychildmatters.org.uk

Q How can I find out more about other people in my area who work with children and who I might one day come into contact with such as behavioural support teachers or educational psychologists?

A The best thing is to go onto your local Children's Trust website and there you will find information about all of these people. Your Children's Trust has responsibility for all the services that support children and young people and they have a Children's Plan that shows how they intend to support children and their families.

Video Corner

▶ **Clip 3: Supporting Communication**

Play this video clip on your CD-ROM and then answer the questions below.

In this footage you can watch how childminders use sign supported speech with a child. When you have watched this consider:

1. How is eye contact encouraged?

2. How do the gestures and facial expressions reinforce the meanings of the words spoken?

CYP3.7

Understand how to support positive outcomes for children & young people

As an early years practitioner you will be involved in providing an environment appropriate for the children you work with. You may immediately think of the room you work in or the outdoor environment that the children play in, but the environment also involves the people who care for the child, the circumstances they live in and how these factors influence the child. It is important that you understand how all aspects of a child's environment can affect their lives, helping you to develop ways of working with each child to meet a range of needs.

Learning outcomes:

By the end of this unit you will:

1. Understand how the social, economic and cultural environment can impact on the outcomes and life chances of children and young people

2. Understand how practitioners can make a positive difference in outcomes for children and young people

3. Understand the possible impact of disability, special requirements (additional needs) and attitudes on positive outcomes for children and young people

4. Understand the importance of equality, diversity and inclusion in promoting positive outcomes for children and young people.

Understand how the social, economic and cultural environment can impact on the outcomes and life chances of children and young people

Social, economic and cultural factors

Many issues in our wider society will affect the lives of the young children you are working with. You may work with children whose parents are unemployed and find it difficult to find the money to buy clothes for their children or pay bills. Some children may suffer from a condition that affects their health or have a cultural background that excludes them from certain activities in your setting. As a practitioner, part of your role will be to be aware of the issues that can have a positive or negative influence on children's lives. You should ensure that this understanding is at the centre of your work and then you will be following the child.

Why does this matter?

It is important that you should continually consider the importance of the government framework known as Every Child Matters, which applies in England. You will read more about this in Unit EYMP3.

To understand how your work and that of others working with children can improve their life chances revisit the five ECM outcomes:

- be healthy
- stay safe
- enjoy and achieve
- make a positive contribution
- achieve economic well-being.

Table 1 lists a range of social, economic and cultural factors which might impact on the lives of children at

any time. Consider that key factors in children's lives can vary and that families and children may need support at certain times in their lives.

Case study: Craven Road Children's Centre

Grace is the manager of Craven Children's Centre, in an inner city area. As part of the centre she manages, Grace leads a team working with a group of children in a 30-place day nursery. Many of the children live in poor quality housing, many without gardens. There is a high rate of unemployment in the area. Grace and her team have worked to ensure that the children have nutritious meals, quality outdoor provision, and that the centre offers support to the parents about employment and developing their skills. Other agencies are on site to give support to the families if needed.

1. List the factors which may impact upon the lives of some of the children at Craven Road Children's Centre.

2. How have the team at Craven Road recognised the factors that may be having a negative effect on the children and their families?

3. How do you think that Grace and her team are supporting the families in a positive way?

4. What might the other agencies be on the Craven Road site? (See also Unit CYP3.6, where there is more information about multi-agency working.)

Poor quality or cramped housing conditions can negatively affect a child's development

Table 1: Social, economic and cultural factors that affect children's lives

Social economic and cultural factors	Possible impact on lives of children
Personal choice	Families may make the choice to live in a way that varies from the norm e.g. communal living, nomadic families or same gender parents. This may affect the way other families and society relate to such children; a child's schooling might be affected if they are part of a travelling community.
Poverty	A family living on a low income might not be able to provide for their children as hoped. Accommodation may be poor which can have an effect on the mental and physical health of children and their parents.
Housing and community	Poor quality or cramped housing conditions can negatively affect a child's development. Living in a community where children have challenging or anti-social behaviour can isolate families, making them reluctant to let their children play in the community. Rural communities can isolate families and make it difficult to access education or health facilities because of limited transport.
Educational environment	There are many different educational environments. All educational settings are regulated. A setting that does not meet statutory requirements may affect a child's development and potential.
Offending or anti-social behaviour	Such behaviour by parents of a child may result in a child being taken into care.
Health status	If a child has an existing condition, such as kidney disease or asthma, their education or home life may have to be supported accordingly. This could also have an impact on a child of parents with a health condition if the child is the carer.
Disability	The disability of a parent or child could affect educational provision, cause poverty or mean that the child is a carer. Support or respite care may be needed for the child or young person.
Health support	If a child or family member is receiving support for a health issue this could have an effect on income, continuity of care, education or development.
Addictions	Children living with addicted adults may be the main carer, isolated, under stress or experiencing poverty. If at school, their attendance may be affected. In some situations they may be taken into care.
Bereavement and loss	Losing a family member or friend can affect the emotional and physical health of children and their parents. Adults losing a child or partner may find caring for any remaining children difficult.
Family expectations and encouragement	There are many different types of parenting styles which result in a range of expectations. Such variations can be cultural. Inconsistency and a lack of support can lead to low self-esteem and challenging behaviour in children.
Religious beliefs and customs	Religious beliefs and customs may exclude children from settings or mean that they attend specific settings. Religious customs may mean that adults and children need time to celebrate or divert from the routine of the setting.
Ethnic beliefs and customs	This could affect the dietary needs of children, clothing, customs or other aspects of their lives.
Marginalisation and exclusion	Children can be marginalised or excluded for many reasons — financial, religious, ethnic, health or reasons of family status.

Over to you

Consider how a young child of 3 years and a young person aged 14, whose families are travellers, may be affected at school. You could visit the website www.gypsy-traveller.org.

The impact of poverty on outcomes and life chances

Poverty is on the agenda of the Every Child Matters framework, with one of the five outcomes stating that every child should 'achieve wealth and economic well-being'. This means it is important to ensure that children experiencing poverty have the same opportunities as their peers.

Reflect

Think about how poverty affects young people. Every Child Matters states that:

'Reducing the proportion of 16–18-year-olds not in education, employment or training (NEET) is a priority for the Government. Being NEET between the ages of 16–18 is a major predictor of later unemployment, low income, teenage motherhood, depression and poor physical health. No single agency holds all the keys to reducing NEET; LAs, schools, the Learning and Skills Council, youth support services and employers all have key roles to play.' (www.everychildmatters.org.uk)

Make a list of other ways in which poverty might have a negative effect on the life experiences of children and young people as they are growing up.

Lone parents often live in poverty as they are the only adult in the household earning an income

Parents, carers, families and the local community have an important role in reducing the effects of poverty on children and improving their outcomes. The government's Children's Plan, required by ECM and developed by each local authority, aims to develop and integrate services that can support children and their families. There are many reasons why a child lives in poverty although there is a clear link between poverty and employment. Even if one parent is working, a family can still be in a low income bracket. Lone parents often live in poverty as they are the only adult in the household earning an income and they may also have to pay for childcare in order to work.

Children are more likely to live in poverty if:

- they are looked-after children (sometimes called children in care)
- one or both parents are not in employment
- the parent is a teenage or lone parent
- parents are disabled, have mental health or addiction problems

- parents are from an ethnic or minority group (two-fifths of people in minority ethnic groups live in poverty, twice as many as in the indigenous population)
- they have a disability (a parent may not be able to seek employment as they may be a full-time carer for the child).

The income of parents can determine children's prospects of good health and life chances. Family income influences the type of area in which a child is brought up (inner-city/suburban/rural), the level of housing the family can afford to live in and the quality of food provided, as well as access to leisure facilities, outings and holidays.

The gap that exists between high and low income families in England and Northern Ireland is evident and such inequalities can affect children's life chances. The following factors can affect children's chances to 'achieve economic well-being' as stated in Every Child Matters.

- Infant mortality rates are more than twice as high in the lowest income group as in the highest.
- Child accident rates are many times higher, and the chances of poor health later in life are greater.
- Statistically, children from lower income families are more likely to have poorer health resulting from poor housing conditions, poor diet, stress or depression.

- Statistically, children from lower income families are less likely to achieve well at school due to lack of space to do homework, low self-esteem, low expectations by teachers and lack of funding for extra lessons such as music.

- Young adults may have less chance of employment in the future because of low achievement in education or may leave school at the minimum age.

- Statistically, children from lower income families are more likely to be involved in crime.

Best practice checklist: Working with children who may experience poverty

When working with children who may experience poverty it is easy to have preconceived ideas. Consider the following common assumptions about children from low income families (it is important that you try to avoid making such assumptions yourself):

✓ they are unhealthy

✓ will do badly at school

✓ will get into trouble at school

✓ are not loved or cared for by their family

✓ their parents have low intelligence

✓ their family is unhappy.

You should be aware of the possible negative effects of poverty in children in your care so that you can offer support if needed or work with other agencies. These may be:

✓ *economic deprivation*: as a low income can cause anxiety and not meet children's needs

✓ *material deprivation*: where children may not have basic childhood possessions, like toys, bicycles and games or limited essentials and everyday items

✓ *social deprivation*: may hinder children's chances to make friends or join in social activities

✓ *educational deprivation*: children may have limited opportunities at school, through a lack of money to pay for books or school trips, other social activities or uniform.

Personal choices and experiences

To ensure that children have the best outcomes there is evidence to show that they need to share in determining their future and should be given a voice to make choices and contribute their experiences. In order that children's services reflect the needs of the children in your care, they need to participate in these services.

The voice of children and young people was first championed in the United Nations Convention on the Rights of the Child (UNCRC), which was introduced in 1989.

Article 13 relates to the importance of children making choices. Much of our work with young children stems from this charter that is signed by many countries throughout the world.

The Every Child Matters framework ensures that policies and services are designed around children's needs and that by engaging young children they can make a positive contribution to their communities and futures. An ongoing

Charter of the United Nations

We the Peoples of the United Nations . . . United for a Better World

'Article 13

- The child shall have the right to freedom of expression; this right shall include freedom to seek, receive and impart information and ideas of all kinds, regardless of frontiers, either orally, in writing or in print, in the form of art, or through any other media of the child's choice.'

The voice of children and young people was first championed in the United Nations Convention on the Rights of the Child

dialogue with children and young people is essential for sustained services.

A framework called Hear by Right gives ideas to adults, young people and children as to how they can be involved in the services provided for them. Hear by Right has standards used by both statutory and voluntary sector groups, aiming to improve practice, actively involving children and young people as a way of developing each organisation's activities.

> The Hear by Right standards framework is designed to help secure sustained and beneficial participation of children and young people and to encourage continual improvement in an organisation's activities. It is intended to be applied to all services that affect children and young people, directly or indirectly. The framework encourages inclusion of a wide range of children and young people, while urging care in choosing approaches appropriate to different ages, abilities and understanding.

Hear by Right November 2009

In early years children can be given personal choices in their environment. The EYFS clearly states that a curriculum for children aged under 5 years should be a balance of adult-led and child-initiated activities; an environment needs to be rich in resources and displayed in such a way that the children can determine their own play. Children can be involved in observations, setting their own expectations of behaviour and goal setting. It is common to see agreed targets for behaviour in a setting created by adults and children. The experiences provided will contribute towards each child's outcomes.

The spider diagram above shows how involving children can make a positive contribution to their environment.

When safeguarding children, children's experiences and choices will also be considered to ensure a safe future for them.

There are several groups which have a wealth of experience in this area. These include:

- National Children's Bureau (NCB) www.ncb.org.uk
- Children's Rights Alliance for England (CRAE) www.CRAE.org.uk
- British Youth Council (BYC) www.byc.org.uk

- Develop children's communication skills
- Ensure choices are truly democratic
- Support children's rights
- Promote children's protection by ensuring their concerns are listened to
- Ensure legal responsibilities are upheld
- Make children and young people feel valued and respected by involving them in decision making
- Improve services by taking children and young people's views into account

Involving children can make a positive contribution to their environment

- National Society for the Prevention of Cruelty to Children (NSPCC) www.nspcc.org.uk
- Coram Family www.coram.org.uk
- National Council of Voluntary Childcare Organisations (NCVCO) www.ncvo-vol.org.uk/
- National Council for Voluntary Youth Services (NCVYS) www.ncvys.org.uk

Functional Skills

English: Reading

You could read the information that you find on the websites above, the information in this book and information from one other place – maybe a recent newspaper article – to find out as much as possible on the issue of safeguarding. Using the information you have gathered from all three of these sources, you could try writing a summary in order to develop your reading skills.

Understand how practitioners can make a positive difference in outcomes for children and young people

As a practitioner working with children, you will be aware that the support we give children to achieve is based upon best practice outlined in the framework Every Child Matters (ECM). Earlier in this unit you were reminded of the five outcomes of this framework:

- be healthy
- stay safe
- enjoy and achieve
- make a positive contribution
- achieve economic well-being.

In your area you will have a Children's Trust, ensuring that all people working with children and young people improve the lives of children across all five ECM outcomes. All Children's Trusts will have a board of representatives who ensure that services for children are accessible and developed in a comprehensive Children's Plan. A Trust is a partnership which brings together the organisations responsible for services for children, young people and their families, committing to improving children and young people's lives. Each Children's Trust will produce a Children's Plan, showing how they will improve the services for children and young people in your area.

The four themes of the EYFS will help you to achieve positive outcomes in all areas of your practice with children

Achieving positive outcomes for children and young people

We have already discussed the five outcomes in ECM. As an early years practitioner in England you will be working within the Early Years Foundation Stage framework (EYFS), which has four themes that link to the five outcomes of Every Child Matters. You should understand these themes as they will help you to achieve positive outcomes in all areas of your practice with children.

In Wales the Foundation Phase is a framework of learning for children aged 3 to 7 years and is based upon the idea that children need to learn actively.

In Northern Ireland there is a foundation curriculum for 5–7-year-olds based on experiential learning.

Look at Table 2 to see how the four EYFS themes and supporting principles link directly with outcomes of ECM.

To ensure that each child will *be healthy* it is important to remember that our health is influenced by our social, emotional, mental and physical well-being.

To achieve this outcome ensure that you have a clear understanding of how children develop. (See also Unit 3.1 where you can read more about the stages of development.)

You may be aware that the government has a focus on healthy living for young children. In many areas schools can achieve National Healthy School Status; this involves showing that their community has achieved standards in a range of healthy issues from diet to the environment. (You can find out more by visiting http://home.healthyschools.gov.uk/)

In your setting you may focus on healthy snacks and meals for the children in your care or provide information about vaccination and safety.

You are required to help children in your care to *stay safe* and ensure that they are safeguarded, know they have a voice and can be heard if they do feel in any danger. You should know the named person in your setting responsible for safeguarding children and to whom you can take any concerns. You should also be aware of the safeguarding policy that your setting has, outlining procedures for you to follow.

Over to you

Find out about children's physical development by reading the Practice Guidance for the Early Years Foundation Stage so you understand how young children grow and develop quickly in their first three years of life. By providing an environment that is secure and safe you will help them to meet their physical and emotional needs.

Table 2: The four EYFS themes and supporting principles linked to ECM

EYFS Themes	Supporting Principles	ECM
Unique Child	1.1 Child Development 1.2 Inclusive Practice 1.3 Keeping Safe 1.4 Health and Well-being	Make a positive contribution Make a positive contribution Stay Safe Be Healthy
Positive Relationships	2.1 Respecting each other 2.2 Parents as Partners 2.3 Supporting Learning 2.4 Key Person	Make a positive contribution Make a positive contribution Make a positive contribution Stay Safe
Enabling Environments	3.1 Observation, assessment and planning 3.2 Supporting every child 3.3 The learning environment 3.4 The wider context	Enjoy and achieve Enjoy and achieve Enjoy and achieve Make a positive contribution
Learning and Development	4.1 Play and exploration 4.2 Active learning 4.3 Creativity and Critical Thinking 4.4 Areas of learning and development	Enjoy and achieve Enjoy and achieve Enjoy and achieve Enjoy and achieve

So that each child can *enjoy and achieve* through their learning, you will be required to follow each child and become familiar with their needs. Your planning should be based upon what you observe the children doing rather than assuming that you know what they are interested in. To observe effectively you will have to ensure that you understand how children develop.

You should study the child development overview in the EYFS Practice Guidance and keep up to date with current research and practice by reading journals and attending courses and workshops. By understanding how each child develops you will be able to provide appropriate activities.

ECM outcomes form the basis of Ofsted inspections. The inspectors will want to know that each child's needs are being met by you and your team. They will want to consider the question 'What is it like for a child in this setting?'

Designing services around children and young people

The focus of ECM is providing a range of services to children and young people that are accessible and integrated in every area. Children's Trusts have been created by each authority, ensuring that children's services work towards the outcomes of the ECM framework. A range of services are available for children and young people. The spider diagram below informs you of the key issues when designing services to meet children and young people's needs.

EYFS in action

Carry out a holistic observation of a child in your setting playing in the outdoor learning environment.

What did you find out about the child by observing his/her play?

How did your knowledge of that child's stage of development help you to use the observation to plan for the next step in his/her learning?

How did you know at what stage of development the child is expected to be?

You could use the Practice Guidance to the EYFS to read about children's stages of development and help you with this assessment task.

Why does this matter?

Consider how children and young people's services are designed. After reading the spider diagram below read more detailed information in Unit CYP3.6 about children and young people's services, including children's centres.

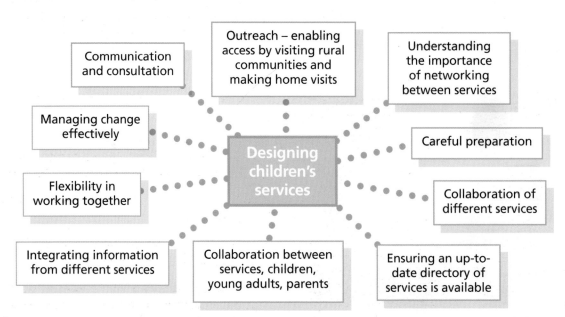

Key issues when designing services to meet children and young people's needs

The importance of active participation

In the past, services were provided for children and families without attempting to tune into what the children and families actually *needed* or wanted; **active participation** helps to overcome this and ensures that people are treated as individuals.

Key term

Active participation: gives children and families a say in how provision is made for them

The skills you need to promote active participation include:

- listening actively to what children and families say, and being ready to respond by changing day-to-day practice or the way that a setting is organised

- communicating openly with parents, and being ready to respect their opinions

- receiving communications from children, remembering that, in the case of young children, these communications be may non-verbal.

The value of active participation

When children and families are given the chance to participate actively, settings and practitioners adapt what they do and how they do it to meet needs and wants more effectively. The key benefits of active participation in early years settings include the following.

Listen to what parents tell you about their child

- The EYFS makes clear the special advantage of involving parents in early years settings: 'When parents and practitioners work together, the results have a positive impact on children's learning and development.'

- When children are supported to participate actively in their learning, they become more confident and able to tackle new ideas and situations. This means that a careful balance must be achieved between adults planning, initiating and leading activities and enabling children to have time and space to explore and discover through the play they initiate for themselves.

- As you develop skills of receiving communications from children, including babies, you will be more able to take their perspective into account and adapt your practice so you meet their individual needs more effectively.

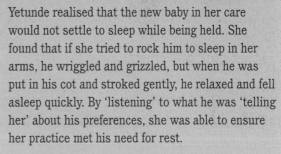

Case study: Yetunde listens carefully

Yetunde realised that the new baby in her care would not settle to sleep while being held. She found that if she tried to rock him to sleep in her arms, he wriggled and grizzled, but when he was put in his cot and stroked gently, he relaxed and fell asleep quickly. By 'listening' to what he was 'telling her' about his preferences, she was able to ensure her practice met his need for rest.

In what ways do babies and young children communicate their opinions?

Putting active participation into practice

Parents

There are many ways of giving parents the chance to play an active part in their child's setting. For example:

- in community pre-schools parents manage all aspects of organisation

- some settings encourage parents to join in play activities and experiences with their children

- most early years settings have regular dialogues with parents in some form, so they can explain what the setting is offering the child.

But participation depends on this being a two-way process, and as the EYFS says: 'Parents and practitioners have a lot to learn from each other.' Therefore good practice in planning learning opportunities for children includes valuing parents' contributions.

It is helpful when parents join in children's play

Children

Young children's learning is most effective when it is active, and when they are able to lead and direct their own experiences and play. The EYFS describes how active learning happens 'when children are keen to learn and are interested in finding things out for themselves'.

EYFS in action

Look at what card 4.2 has to say about active learning.

Look for ways that active learning is promoted in your setting. How are children helped to be 'at ease, secure and confident' so they can engage in learning? In what ways do adults 'challenge and extend their thinking'? How are children given 'independence in their learning'?

Monitoring and evaluating participation

As with all aspects of your practice, you need to **monitor** and **evaluate** how well you are promoting participation by analysing and thinking critically about your work.

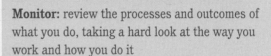

Key terms

Monitor: review the processes and outcomes of what you do, taking a hard look at the way you work and how you do it

Evaluate: identify the strength of your performance: how well you are doing, and how you could improve

Reflect

In what ways can early years settings work in what the EYFS calls 'true partnership' and engage with parents so they are able to participate and contribute their views and opinions on the way the setting works, such as the development of policies?

How can parents be enabled to learn about supporting their children's learning and development and contribute to planning what experiences their children will have in a setting?

Skills builder

Make a list of the ways you are encouraging parents' and children's participation in your setting. Discuss with colleagues how effective you think you are being and how you could develop your practice.

Support children and young people to make personal choices and experiences that have a positive impact on their lives

As an early years practitioner you will know that the environment you plan is one where children can feel safe, happy and challenged to achieve the best they can.

Why does this matter?

Providing the right environment will enable children to make choices that have a positive impact on their future lives. Read more about this in Unit EYMP2 about promoting learning and development in the early years.

Carefully consider the importance of making your setting warm and welcoming for children and parents and somewhere where they will want to be! All children will need an environment that encourages and provides:

- exploration
- experimentation

All children need an environment that encourages exploration

- problem solving
- taking risks safely
- a variety of activities
- accessible resources
- resources to meet individual interest
- language and interaction
- a welcome to families of all cultures and religions
- places to rest and eat
- an outdoor learning environment that is challenging and promotes learning.

EYFS in Action

In the Principle into Practice: Enabling Environments – effective practice is defined as ensuring you 'encourage children to help plan the layout of their environment'.

Consider an area in your setting that may not be used much or that children do engage in for long periods. Observe how the environment is used and then talk to the children about what they would like in the area. You will be surprised how good their ideas will be! If you decide to make changes, try to involve the children. Document this as evidence for assessment or for any future Ofsted inspection. Let parents see photos of how their children were involved in the change.

Child-centred curriculum

By encouraging them to be independent learners and problem solvers your curriculum will centre upon each child. This is hard work. The team has to be dedicated and focused to really consider the needs of all the children. You will need a lot of energy to work in this way! Consider how you will ensure that children have real choices and experiences.

Best practice checklist: A child-centred curriculum

✓ Follow each child's interest by observing regularly and using this to inform planning and the curriculum

✓ Meet regularly with your team to share observations

✓ Ensure each child has an individual learning plan

✓ Ensure that your environment is welcoming for families who may have English as an additional language by considering dual language notices and translators as appropriate

✓ Give children choices in their everyday lives – choosing when to eat – individual snack time

✓ Ensure you know how children develop and provide resources according to their age

✓ Ensure they have an indoor and outdoor environment rich with open-ended resources, encouraging problem solving and independence

✓ Celebrate achievements through child profiles, displays that reflect learning, photographic record etc

✓ Work closely with parents in all aspects of the child's development. Use the key person system so each child and parent has a special person to communicate with.

Functional Skills

English: Speaking, listening and communication

In the case study opposite Stefan attended the local youth forum to discuss the lack of facilities for young adults in their area. In your group you could organise a similar discussion. Remember to listen carefully to what people are saying so that you can respond in an appropriate way.

Consider how the outcomes from ECM can be used to support a play environment, and give choices and experiences to enable children to develop.

Table 3: Supporting a play-based environment

ECM Outcome	Supporting a play-based environment
Be healthy	Ensure the learning environment is healthy Ensure that physical exercise is part of any curriculum Encourage learning about a healthy lifestyle Ensure that the curriculum focuses on each child's emotional and social well-being
Stay safe	Ensure the setting meets regulatory standards Involve children and young people in creating a safe environment Implement policies and procedures to ensure safe play Ensure regular checking of environment and resources Ensure adults have regular and appropriate training
Enjoy and achieve	Provide children with a balance of child-initiated and adult-led activities Ensure children have freedom of choice and follow interests Allow children to challenge, be creative, explore and problem solve Support a range of learning styles and needs
Make a positive contribution	Ensure children and young people learn about their immediate and wider environment Create an environment that encourages choices and decision making Encourage children to explore own identity and culture through play Encourage exploration of new concepts Support children in gaining confidence about their own views and show respect for their contributions
Achieve economic well-being	Ensure that children's play encourages them to develop skills needed to experience an acceptable standard of living Ensure a curriculum full of rich learning opportunities Ensure each child reaches their full potential Ensure parents are engaged in their child's learning

Case study: Stefan joins parliament!

A group of 13–15-year-olds in a small rural community met regularly at a youth centre and decided to send 15-year-old Stefan to represent them at their local youth forum. At the forum they had discussions about the lack of facilities available for young adults in their area and felt that this contributed to the level of drug abuse locally. Stefan had recently been to Canada and had lots of ideas for activities and facilities that could be set up. He was elected as the representative from Devon, attending a meeting at the UK Youth Parliament where they had a discussion forum about the issues around drug taking amongst young people across the UK. Stefan was able to represent his peers in Devon and make a positive contribution to the debate.

1. How do you think that Stefan's involvement in the UK Youth Parliament might have a positive outcome on the lives of the group of young people in Devon?

2. Consider how young children could have a voice locally or nationally. Think of some examples.

Understand the possible impact of disability, special requirements (additional needs) and attitudes on positive outcomes for children and young people

The impact of disability

Children may have **impairments** which give rise to **disability**.

'Disabled children' include those with a wide range of impairments or conditions including 'hidden' ones.

Key terms

Impairment: describes a condition which is different from what is usually expected in a child at a particular age or stage of development

Disability: 'A physical or mental impairment which has a substantial and long-term adverse effect on a person's ability to perform normal day-to-day activities' (Disability Discrimination Act 1995)

Sensory impairment may consist of hearing loss (deafness) or restricted vision (blindness). A physical impairment and/or learning difficulties may be the result of a genetic inheritance, events before or during birth, an accident or a disease. Some children's disabilities relate to learning difficulties which may or may not have a specific title, such as Down's syndrome. For others, their difficulties are with emotional or social development, communication and interaction, and behaviour, including conditions such as autism. Each child is affected differently by their impairment or condition.

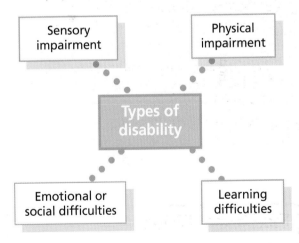

The term 'disability' covers a range of impairments or conditions, not all of which are visible

Disability has the potential to cause negative effects on children's life chances, including:

- Physical impairments and chronic medical conditions may compromise children's healthy development and disrupt their educational experiences.

- If adults focus on what is 'wrong' with a child and what they can't do, rather than on what they can do and are already achieving, and their potential to develop, learn and progress, disabled children's emotional well-being may be affected by poor self-esteem.

● Learning difficulties or difficulties with emotional or social development may hamper children's all-round progress.

● Families with a disabled child often experience financial difficulties which may restrict children's opportunities in life — not only of the disabled child but also of their siblings — and relationships within families may be destabilised by the stresses of caring for a disabled child.

Positive attitudes

A person is often disabled as a result of their impairment, unless:

● the environment where they spend their time is adjusted to their requirements

● appropriate resources and facilities are made available to them

● the attitudes of the people they encounter are positive and not based on limited assumptions about what they can and cannot do.

It is possible to avoid or reduce the impact of the impairment so the person can have opportunities to make choices, develop their potential, become independent and play a full part in society.

It is unhelpful to talk about disabled children as having 'special needs' since their needs are the same as those of other children. It may be necessary for us to go about meeting their needs in different ways, recognising that they have *specific* or *additional* requirements.

Media stories about disabled people often present them as 'tragic', victims to be pitied, and it is often assumed that disabled people will be helpless and dependent. Seeing disabled people in this way undermines the concept of disabled people as individuals who deserve respect for what they are capable of achieving. Low expectations about the potential of a disabled child, or being over-protective of them, can limit what they achieve. You should always keep a balance between being realistic about the limitations that a child's impairments may cause, while at the same time having high expectations for their progress and achievements.

Don't underestimate what disabled children are capable of

Case study: Attitudes towards disability

Sonali talks about one of the children she works with:

'Brandon is 6 and I try to persuade colleagues not to say things like 'developmentally he's like a 3 year old'. It's true that his cognitive development is at a stage we usually see in younger children, but his chronological age *is* 6, and in other aspects of development, he is like other 6 year olds. His interests are like those of other children of his own age, so it is important not to treat him as though he is only 3. If we talk to him in a babyish way or keep him only in the company of younger children, his self-esteem will be damaged and his development will be held back.'

Can you identify your own positive (and negative) attitudes towards the disability of children you work with?

If practitioners have positive attitudes about their capacity to provide for disabled children's requirements, and are ready to learn new skills such as sign language or using the Makaton system, the children have greater opportunities for making developmental progress.

Over to you

Find out about Makaton from www.makaton.org/

Not 'a Down's child' but a child with Down's syndrome – don't give children medical labels

Have a positive attitude to learning new skills

Models of disability

The **social model of disability** and the **medical model of disability** help us to understand the effect of disability on individuals.

Key terms

Social model of disability: recognises that discrimination against disabled people is created by society, not by disabled people's impairments

Medical model of disability: this treats the person as a sick patient and tends to focus on 'How can we make this person more normal?'

The medical model is a traditional view of disability, that it is something to be 'cured', even though many conditions have no cure. The problem is seen as the disabled person and their impairment, and the solution is seen as adapting the disabled person to fit the non-disabled world, often through medical intervention.

When medical labels are placed on the disabled person (for example, referring to people with epilepsy as 'epileptics'), the individual is seen merely as their impairment. Such labels can prevent us from developing a picture of the whole person, including their gender, ethnicity and culture, and social background.

The social model of disability is a more constructive approach to disability. It focuses our thoughts on addressing the issue, 'What do we need to do to enable this person to achieve their potential and have a fulfilling life?'

The social model puts the emphasis on the way in which society needs to change, in contrast to the medical model which expects disabled people to change to fit into society. The strength of the social model is that it identifies problems which can be resolved if the environment is adapted and the right resources are made available; whereas the medical model dwells on problems which are often insoluble. The social model asserts the rights of disabled people; it involves listening to individual disabled people to see what that person wants and, when there are barriers to their requirements, looking at ways of removing those barriers. The social model has been constructed and promoted by disabled people themselves, so it should be respected.

Reflect

How can the social model guide you in your work with children? How can you help to remove or reduce the disability resulting from impairments by:

- finding ways to adjust the physical environment in your setting?

- providing or adapting resources?

- organising routines and the way you work in a different way?

and, perhaps most important of all:

- not making assumptions about what a child can do, or may be able to achieve?

Over to you

Find out about Portage from www.portage.org.uk/

Research the availability of the services described above in your area. How accessible are they to disabled children and their families?

coordinated, 'family-focused' services. The programme provides parents with information about living with a disabled child and 'the system' — the many agencies they have dealings with relating to health, education, social care, benefits, housing, etc. It explains which professionals they may meet and how such agencies can provide support as well as giving information about sources of financial support and childcare.

Different types of support

The additional support which a disabled child may need will be specific to that child, depending on the nature of their impairment, and on the degree to which it has an impact on their lives.

For example:

- a child born with a cleft palate is likely to need speech and language therapy following surgery

- a child with epilepsy is likely to need regular monitoring from health professionals who can adjust medication appropriately

- a child with Down's syndrome may receive learning support in a setting from an additional adult

- a child with a hearing impairment may use the 'assistive technology' of hearing aids

- a child with learning difficulties may acquire new skills through a Portage programme developed in partnership with their family.

Perhaps the most positive development in recent years for young disabled children and their families in England has been the Early Support Programme which aims at early identification of children's impairments and better

The Early Support Programme aims at early identification of children's impairments and better coordinated, 'family-focused' services

Over to you

Find more information about Early Support on www.earlysupport.org.uk

Case study: The family file

Shania's parents find that the Early Support 'family file' is a great boon. They hold the file in which they and the professionals involved with Shania record information. This means that they do not have the frustration of having to 'tell their story' from the beginning every time they encounter a different professional or service. It also means that the professionals are aware of the advice and support being provided elsewhere and are able to identify priorities for their contribution as part of a whole strategy for Shania, planned jointly with her family.

1. Can you think of any other advantages to this system?

2. What problems might there be?

Understand the importance of equality, diversity and inclusion in promoting positive outcomes for children and young people

Equality, inclusion and diversity

We saw in Unit SC2 'Promote equality, diversity and inclusion' what is meant by these terms (see page 20).

If children are to achieve positive outcomes in life, it is essential that their rights are promoted and protected. They are entitled to:

- *equality*: opportunities to develop and learn, while their physical and emotional safety and well-being are protected
- *inclusion*: access to appropriate settings and the experiences they offer
- *diversity*: acknowledgement of and respect for their individuality.

These rights can be jeopardised through prejudice and discrimination (see Unit SC2, on page 21). When this happens, the chances of children achieving the outcomes envisaged by Every Child Matters are compromised. Protecting these rights can be hampered if practitioners fall into the trap of **stereotypes**.

Key term

Stereotypes: generalisations about a person and assumptions (usually inaccurate) that because they are part of a particular group, that individual will have certain characteristics and the same needs as all other members of that group, and will (or should) behave in a particular way

Stereotyping can lead us, without our realising it, into making assumptions about what an individual child can achieve, based on one aspect of who they are, and that prevents us from nurturing the all-round development of the child. This is likely to affect outcomes for them because, if we think about children in stereotyped ways instead of seeing them as unique individuals, we may be limiting the expectations and aspirations which we – and they – have for:

- their abilities
- how it is appropriate for them to behave
- their future achievements.

These limited expectations are likely to lead us into failing to offer challenging and stretching opportunities for learning so we do not encourage children to have ambitious aims for their future.

The key to steering away from stereotypes is to see each child as a unique individual, different from every other child. See Unit EYMP4.

Support children to steer away from stereotypes in their play

Promoting equality, diversity and inclusion

Promoting positive outcomes for children depends on promoting equality, diversity and inclusion in ways which are appropriate to their individual characteristics and requirements.

Positive images

You can help to overcome stereotypical expectations about children's potential and possible future roles by providing **positive images**.

You can provide positive images of a diverse range of people which show that, for example, black, female and disabled people can take on responsible, active and prominent roles in society, and male people can take on creative, caring and domestic roles. This helps children to develop strong expectations about their own future. It gives them positive ideas about what they will be able to achieve in life and the positions of influence and responsibility in society they will be able to take, whatever their ethnicity, gender, cultural or social background or disability.

Functional Skills

Maths: Interpreting

You could create a table to bring your findings together. From this table you could then calculate the percentage of resources and activities which are in your setting that do include positive images.

Combating stereotypes

Stereotypes about children's behaviour are just as common as expectations about what sort of activities and learning they will want to engage in and succeed at. Not all boys are aggressive, but society does seem to expect males to be more aggressive than females and, to some extent, will tolerate more aggression from boys and men than from girls and women. Stereotypes about what behaviour is appropriate or relevant for a child may have a limiting effect on their social and emotional development and on outcomes for their future lives. Practitioners should never accept that boys will be aggressive and girls won't; you have a key role to play in helping children to find non-aggressive ways of settling disputes and dealing with strong feelings.

A key element in promoting positive outcomes for children's well-being and ability to learn and achieve is to nurture their **self-esteem** and **self-confidence**. Children with high self-esteem are confident enough to tackle the new activities and experiences which will help them to develop and learn.

To help children feel good about themselves, it is essential to demonstrate that you respect each child as an individual, and also value their family. There are many different sorts of families with varying values, traditions and attitudes towards children. By welcoming

Reflect

Think about how gender stereotypes about children's behaviour might influence your own practice, leading you to have different expectations about the behaviour of boys and girls. (Be honest!)

1. Do you accept more aggressiveness and noisiness in boys' behaviour than in girls'? Do you emphasise controlled and quiet behaviour more to girls than to boys? Do you expect girls to be able to sustain quiet concentration more effectively than boys? Do you let things go further with boys before you intervene in a dispute than you do if girls are falling out? Do you think that boys won't talk with you about their feelings?

2. Have you observed such varying expectations based on gender in other practitioners?

3. What do you think might be the outcome of different expectations such as these about behaviour on gender lines? Will this influence you to change your practice?

Key terms

Self-esteem: valuing ourselves, and seeing ourselves as being of value in other people's eyes

Self-confidence: feeling able to do things and capable of achieving

and valuing all families equally in your setting, you show each child that you don't have negative opinions or feelings about their family. Children need to feel that their parents and the family unit they live in are respected and valued by the other people who are significant in their lives, especially their key person in their early years setting. When your manner towards parents and the way you refer to them in front of their children demonstrate that you respect parents' ways of life, you enhance

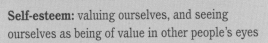

children's self-esteem; any indication that you don't quite approve of their parents, or regard their family as odd or 'not normal', will undermine children's emotional well-being.

There are many different sorts of families with varying values, traditions and attitudes towards children

One aspect of this is to show respect for their family's **culture.**

Key term

Culture: the attitudes and values underpinning patterns of tradition and custom which determine everyday aspects of life

Our culture is expressed in:

- how we see the role of men and women in society
- the way we bring up our children
- the language we speak
- what, when and how we eat
- how we dress
- how we wash and care for ourselves
- the way we decorate and furnish our homes
- the religious practices we pursue regularly

Our culture is expressed in how we dress

as well as:

- drama, music, dance, literature and art
- how we celebrate special occasions such as weddings and festivals
- our attitudes to death and dying.

It is equally important to show that you respect the composition of children's families so they know that they are valued.

Reflect

How does your practice demonstrate respect for the cultural background of the families you work with? In what ways does this help children's self-esteem and their confidence in learning?

Skills builder

Discuss with colleagues how you support various types of family, making it clear to them that you respect the way they live. Think about:

- single parents
- 'reconstituted' families containing step-parents and half-siblings or step-siblings
- same-sex parents
- extended families which include grandparents, aunts, uncles and cousins as part of regular daily life
- parents of mixed ethnicity
- teenage parents.

Functional Skills

English: Speaking, listening and communication

The Skills builder feature above is a great way to develop these skills.

Getting ready for assessment

Children and young people who are 'looked after' are more likely to be affected by poverty. To prepare for assessment visit the website www.poverty.org.uk and make a brief report on how the life chances of young people who are 'looked after' (14+) are affected by poverty. Include statistics from the website.

Functional Skills

English: Writing

ICT: Finding and selecting information

By writing a report you will be practising writing for a different purpose. A report is often a formal document so think carefully about your sentence structure, punctuation and grammar. When researching and using the information from www.poverty.org.uk make sure you reference it appropriately and are aware of any copyright material on the website.

Families come in many forms

Check your knowledge

1. What does ECM stand for?

2. List three social, cultural and economic factors that could impact on the lives of children and young people.

3. Which article of the UN Convention of The Rights of the Child relates to the importance of children and young people's right to make choices? 1; 7; 16 or 13?

4. What are the EYFS themes that relate to the ECM outcomes?

5. List the three skills you need to promote active participation.

6. Briefly describe the role of the UK Youth Parliament.

7. Give three examples of the negative effects impairment can have on a child's life.

8. Explain what Makaton is.

9. What is the strength of the social model of disability, compared with the medical model?

10. What is portage?

11. Give two examples of how stereotypical assumptions about a child might limit outcomes for them.

My Story

My name is Rashid and I work as an outreach worker for a national organisation. The idea is that we encourage families who are experiencing isolation and often poverty to attend local services such as our local children's centre. Recently I made a home visit to a lovely family who are originally from Pakistan and have 1-year-old twin boys who are quite a handful! The dad had been made redundant from the local engineering factory and they are finding it hard to cope financially. They have friends in the same road but the mum does struggle with understanding English. I was able to organise a translator for her so that she could take the children to the health clinic in the children's centre and she now attends a parent and baby group each week. She has also become involved in a Story Sack project; the group were delighted when they knew she had great sewing skills! The dad goes to JobCentre Plus where they are helping him to look for employment. They are also receiving advice as to the benefits they can claim while the dad remains unemployed. So while they are still experiencing problems they feel less isolated and are becoming integrated into the community, which seems to be helping the whole family.

Video Corner

▶ **Clip 4: Supporting differences**

Play this video clip on your CD-ROM and then answer the questions below.

In this clip you will see how families with different languages and cultures are supported in this early years setting.

1. How have they been welcomed to the setting?

2. Do you think that this setting has adapted to the needs of these families?

3. How is the setting having a positive impact on the children of these families?

Ask The Expert …

Q I understand that it is important for young children to be involved in making choices. I work with 3-year-olds. Surely they cannot do this?

A They can decide when they want a snack if you have snacks available all the time; they can choose who to play with and which activities to do. Three ideas already!

Q I would like to encourage the 5-year-olds I work with to help me redesign our classroom. How can I do this?

A Use a group time to ask them what they like and don't like. Ask them to make their own designs. Observe them using the classroom. Decide on an area you are going to change together and make a plan to involve them all. Photograph them making the change to share with their parents and to contribute to their learning records.

Q I know a 14-year-old boy who is very keen to make our environment a better place. There doesn't seem any way for him to do this? What can you suggest?

A That he finds out about his local youth forum which gets together to discuss various issues and have an active voice in the UK Youth Parliament.

Early Years Mandatory Pathway Units

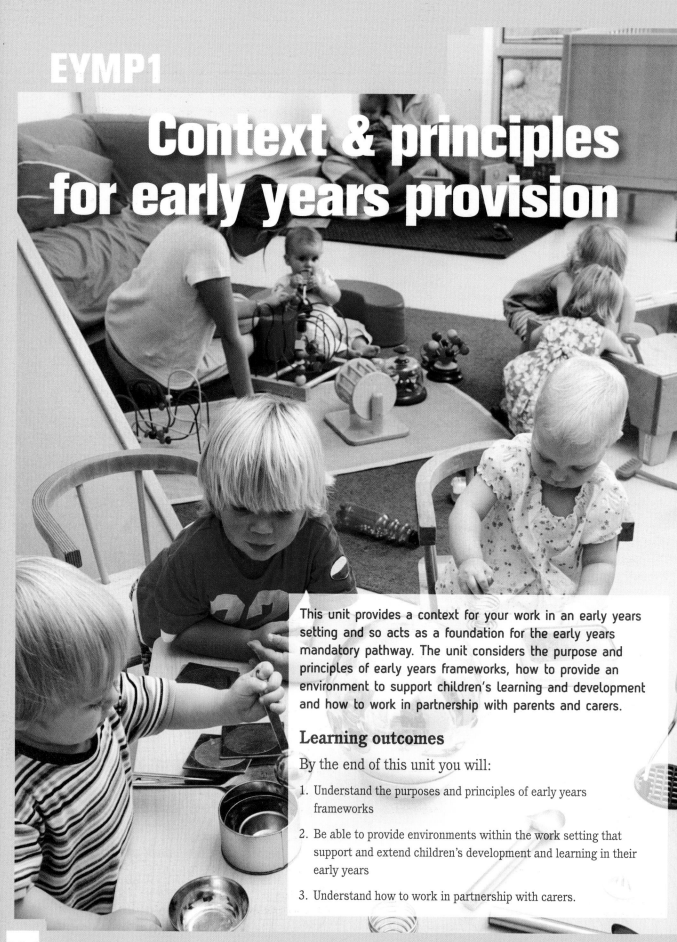

EYMP1

Context & principles for early years provision

This unit provides a context for your work in an early years setting and so acts as a foundation for the early years mandatory pathway. The unit considers the purpose and principles of early years frameworks, how to provide an environment to support children's learning and development and how to work in partnership with parents and carers.

Learning outcomes

By the end of this unit you will:

1. Understand the purposes and principles of early years frameworks

2. Be able to provide environments within the work setting that support and extend children's development and learning in their early years

3. Understand how to work in partnership with carers.

Understand the purposes and principles of early years frameworks

In recent times, the care and education of children has gained in importance as governments have realised its potential impact on children. This learning outcome requires you to have a knowledge of the purposes and principles of early years frameworks in the UK.

Principles of the early years frameworks in the UK

The four nations which form the United Kingdom have taken slightly different approaches to the planning and delivery of early years education. All four nations are in the relatively early stages of working with their frameworks.

England: EYFS

Since September 2008, England has introduced a statutory curriculum for children aged 0–5 years who are being cared for or educated outside their homes. The framework therefore applies to childminders as well as after-school clubs in addition to nurseries, pre-schools and schools, regardless of how they are funded. In addition to the 'education' programme that is outlined, the Early Years Foundation Stage (EYFS) also incorporates the welfare requirements.

Structure of the education programme

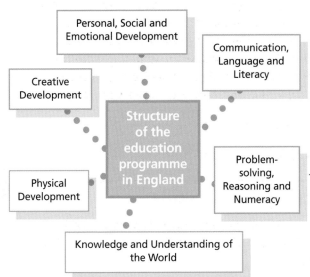

In England, there are six areas of learning which practitioners must plan for

Assessment

Children are assessed at the end of their reception year. The teacher completes an early years profile which consists of thirteen different scales that link to the early learning goals from the areas of learning. (See also EYMP2 page 233).

Wales: Foundation Phase

Since August 2008, the Welsh Assembly has been phasing in a statutory curriculum known as the Foundation Phase. This applies to children aged 3–7 years who are in receipt of local authority funding in schools, pre-schools, nurseries and childminders.

Structure of the education programme

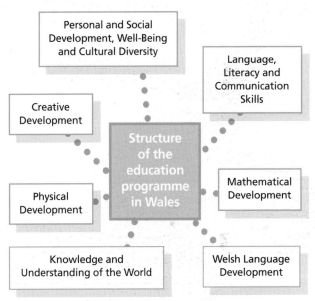

In Wales, there are seven areas of learning which practitioners must plan for

Assessment

Teachers at the end of the Foundation Phase assess children in three areas:

- Personal and social development, well-being and cultural diversity

- Language, literacy and communication skills in English or Welsh

- Mathematical development.

Scotland: Curriculum For Excellence

Scotland is in the processing of introducing a curriculum which encompasses children from 3–18 years. This is part of an overall strategic approach to education within Scotland and many elements such as assessment are still being developed at the time of writing. Underpinning the curriculum is the idea that children and young people should be given experiences in order to progress their development and, instead of working according to age, will be learning according to their own level.

Structure of the education programme

There are eight areas of experiences and outcomes. The experiences and outcomes are written at five levels and young children will be working at the first level known as 'early level'. In addition to the eight areas, practitioners at all levels have a responsibility to embed health and well-being, literacy and numeracy across the learning opportunities provided for children.

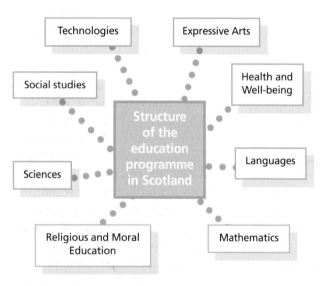

In Scotland, there are eight areas of experiences and outcomes

Assessment

At the time of writing, assessment arrangements are still being drawn up, although it is expected that settings will have responsibility for drawing up their own.

Northern Ireland

Before statutory school age, there is no specific curriculum, but once children are in statutory education, they will follow the Foundation Stage. The six areas of learning that form the basis of the curriculum are taken through into key stages 1 and 2.

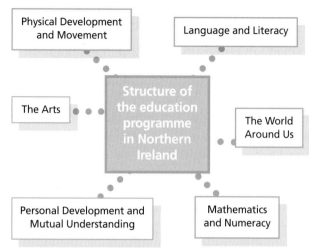

In Northern Ireland, there are six areas of learning that form the basis of the curriculum

National and local guidance and materials

To support the implementation of the national frameworks, each country has also developed guidance, information about the statutory elements, and training materials.

Over to you

Look at the following websites and choose the one most relevant to your work.

Explore the website looking at the range of materials and resources available.

England:
www.dcsf.gov.uk

Wales:
www.foundationphasewales.com

Scotland:
www.tls.gov.uk

Northern Ireland:
www.nicurriculum.org

Functional Skills

ICT: Finding and selecting information

Looking at each of the websites provides you with the opportunity to search the Internet and search within a site to find and select relevant information.

Common features of the early years frameworks

Each nation is developing its own approach to the care and education of young children, but it is worth noting that they all have some common features. These include the following:

- partnership and involvement with parents
- learning through active play
- need for children to have opportunities for child-initiated and adult-directed activities
- education programme is to be delivered holistically although divided into areas of learning
- importance of assessing children's individual needs.

There are also some differences particularly in the statutory nature of work with children under 3 years, as it is only England that brings work with children aged less than 3 years into a statutory education framework. The other home nations have good practice and recommendations for the under-threes.

Different approaches and influences on current provision

We have seen that all the four home nations are developing frameworks in slightly different ways. The development of the early years curricula has been significantly influenced by the following approaches:

- Reggio Emilia
- High/scope
- Montessori
- Steiner

A brief summary of each approach is given below although you may find it exciting and rewarding to do research further into them. As well as reading about the approaches, you may find that a pre-school, nursery or school in your area has adopted the approach within the EYFS.

Reggio Emilia

This is an educational approach inspired by a group of pre-schools in the city of and area surrounding Reggio Emilia in Italy. At the heart of the approach is a focus on partnership with parents and children aged 0–6 years being involved in their own learning.

The main features of this approach are that:

- children need some control over their own play and learning with teachers acting as a facilitator
- children learn through using all of their senses
- children need to learn from and enjoy being with other children
- children need a rich environment so that they can learn and express themselves in a multitude of ways.

Influences on the EYFS curriculum

- Practitioners are meant to provide opportunities for child-initiated play.
- There is a theme entitled 'Enabling environments' that prompts practitioners to think about how rich the environments are for children.
- There is an emphasis on sensory and outdoor play.
- There is an emphasis on children learning through play with other children.

High/scope

The High/scope approach began in the United States as a way of improving outcomes for disadvantaged children. It is an established model which stresses that children should be involved in decision making and take responsibility. Settings using this approach will typically expect that children learn to plan their own play and learning, review it and also report back to other children. Children are considered to be active learners and so play is used as the model for learning. Routines are also considered important so that children gain stability.

Influences on the EYFS curriculum

- Practitioners are meant to provide opportunities for child-initiated play.
- Practitioners are encouraged to talk to children about their learning.

Montessori

The Montessori approach or method originated with Maria Montessori, an Italian doctor who wanted to improve outcomes for children with disabilities. The approach stresses the importance of the practitioner as an observer of children who can support their learning sensitively by making appropriate interventions. The term 'play with a purpose' is at the heart of Montessori as equipment and resources have specific learning objectives and provide children with graduated challenge.

Influences on the EYFS curriculum

- Practitioners are meant to observe children individually in order to provide for their play and learning.

- Practitioners are meant to ensure that children are sufficiently challenged in order to progress their learning.

- The EYFS guidance gives suggestions as to what children need according to their stage of development.

Steiner

The Steiner approach has its origins in the work of philosopher Rudolph Steiner who founded a school after the First World War (1918) known as the Waldorf school. The Steiner approach emphasises the importance of fostering children's creativity and imagination, their understanding and exploration of the natural world and the importance of the practitioner as a role model. Routines form a key part of the kindergarten as does a blend of adult-directed and child-initiated play. Manufactured toys are not used as these are thought to inhibit children's natural curiosity and imagination. Formal reading and writing does not begin until children are 7 years old and there is an emphasis on working according to children's personalities.

The Steiner approach aims to foster children's creativity and imagination, their understanding and exploration of the natural world

Influences on the EYFS curriculum

- Practitioners are meant to plan adult-directed play and provide for child-initiated play.

- Play with natural objects is encouraged for babies and toddlers.

Common Core

The Common Core is the name given to six areas of skills, knowledge and expertise that the English government believes to be essential for all those working with children and young people. The Common Core was established as part of a range of measures taken following the death of Victoria Climbié, an 8-year-old whose death at the hands of her carers was considered to be preventable. The six areas are:

- Effective communication

- Child and young person development

- Safeguarding and promoting the welfare of the child

- Supporting transitions

- Multi-agency working

- Sharing information.

These areas underpin all initial training and form a major part of this qualification.

The introduction of the Common Core has affected the approach of settings working with children as it has encouraged greater multi-agency working and closer collaboration with other settings.

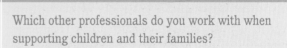

Over to you

Which other professionals do you work with when supporting children and their families?

A personal and individual approach to learning and development

All of the early years frameworks now focus on the needs of individual children. This is important as we know that children develop at different rates, they are all unique and will come from a range of backgrounds. This means that children will have different needs and interests and so will require a range of different opportunities in order to thrive. It is also worth noting that children are starting to spend longer periods away from their parents as a result of socio-economic changes and so extra care is required to support children's emotional well-being.

The EYFS stresses the importance of personalisation of learning and development experiences.

Case study: All change!

Castle Day Nursery had always changed babies' nappies on a rota system. Babies would have their nappies changed four times a day at set times by whoever's name was on the rota list. Since the introduction of the EYFS, the nursery has changed its procedures. Babies' nappies are changed only when they are needed and it is now the responsibility of the babies' key person to carry this out. Staff have found that it no longer feels like a chore and that they enjoy the time spent with 'their' babies. The staff have also noticed that babies seem much happier and that they communicate more.

1. Why did the nursery have to change its practice?

2. Why are staff enjoying nappy changing more?

3. What are the benefits for individual babies of this more personalised approach?

Be able to provide environments within the work setting that support and extend children's development and learning in their early years

We have seen that all of the early years frameworks in the home nations emphasise the importance of young children learning through play. This learning outcome requires you to prepare environments that will allow children to play and learn in ways that link to the early years framework that you are working with. In addition, you will also need to show that you can effectively evaluate the effectiveness of your provision.

Preparing environments for children

Preparing environments for children requires us to think carefully about their age/stage of development. You also have to ensure that the experiences and opportunities offered will deliver across the areas of development outlined in the framework of your home nation. Below are some suggestions of ways to prepare environments that particularly link to the EYFS.

Environments for babies 0–1 years

Babies need changing environments and it is essential that they spend time outdoors, but also in different rooms so that they can experience a variety of colours, smells, textures and noises. In many day nurseries, babies will have their own 'base' room but it is important that thought is also given as to how to provide variety for them by creating different areas within the room and looking for ways for babies to be taken out.

Babies need a variety of sound experiences but too much background noise may make it difficult for them to discriminate sounds effectively. Radio and background music should not dominate in rooms for under 3s or for any young children. Periods of quiet are really important and support a child-centred approach to the environment. Over stimulating babies and young children through any of their senses can lead to them becoming distressed.

Choice of resources

A good environment for a baby up to 12 months will include toys and resources that encourage sensory exploration. These need to be robust enough for a baby to mouth and handle. In addition, it is recommended that there are plenty of opportunities for treasure basket play as this single activity will cover many of the areas of development within the EYFS.

Sufficient floor space and opportunities to develop spatial awareness

Once babies are mobile they need sufficient floor space, but also a reason to want to move. This means that push-along toys, cushions and a variety of interesting toys and resources need to be laid out so as to create an

Once babies are mobile they need sufficient floor space

interesting environment. In addition, babies need to be at different heights and experience motion. It can be helpful to use baby swings and even just to pick up babies regularly as part of their routine.

Personalisation

The EYFS stresses the importance of personalisation of learning and development experiences. With babies aged up to 12 months, everyday care routines such as nappy changing, bathing and feeding need to be personalised and also seen as a learning experience.

Environments for toddlers 1–3 years

In this period of life, children's developmental needs are changing rapidly as they become more physically coordinated and develop language. Environments for toddlers need to be built around their observed interests, although often to start with we can create environments

Table 1: Play patterns in children aged 1–3 years

What you might observe		Ideas for indoors	Ideas for outdoors
Posting	Children are interested in putting things out of sight	Post box Cardboard tube and pompoms	Pushing objects through a fence
Dropping	Children are interested in watching things fall or drop down	Simple ball run Empty bucket with pine cones, shells	Bucket of water and assorted objects
Enclosing	Children enjoy wrapping things or putting things in and out of boxes	Small cardboard boxes with lids and items to put inside	Large cardboard boxes Fabric and dolls
Throwing	Children enjoy throwing items e.g. balls, bean bags	Soft balls and bean bags	Mixture of hard, soft, large and small balls
Climbing	Children look for ways of climbing onto things	Small steps, soft cushions	Steps Climbing frame
Connecting	Children try to build and join objects e.g. bricks, cardboard tubes	Wooden bricks Lego	Large bricks Cardboard tubes Metal tins, various
Crawling	Children enjoy crawling through and under things	Tablecloths draped over furniture	Tunnels
Snuggling in	Children like to settle themselves into tight spaces	Fabric draped over table Large cardboard boxes	Pop-up tents Large cardboard boxes
Transporting	Children like to carry items and materials from one place to another	Pushchairs Suitcases Brick trolley	Water, containers and a bucket for the children to take it to
Mixing	Children like to mix materials and resources e.g. stirring	Dough, gloop and materials so that it can be mixed	Sand, water and leaves in containers
Hitting and banging	Children like to bang two items together e.g. saucepan lids, knocking down a sandcastle	Hammer set Musical instruments Gong	Items that will make a sound if knocked together

The EYFS requires toddlers to have a rich outdoor environment

that we know are likely to appeal and which are based on common play patterns seen in this age group. It is expected within the EYFS that toddlers will spend time outdoors each day and that the outdoor environment will be a rich one rather than just an environment that focuses on physical development. In an environment for

toddlers, we must also be aware that they need quality sensory and exploratory experiences. This means that provision should be made for sand, water and dough and there should be opportunities for digging in materials such as gravel or bark chippings. In addition, to support toddlers' communication and literacy, the environment should also have attractive resources such as books, cuddly toys and puppets.

Table 1 shows some of the play patterns that you might see in this age group together with examples as to how you might cater for it in and out of doors. Note that this is not a definitive list, but can be used as a starting point when planning for this age group.

Environments for 3–5 years

Most settings organise their environments for 3–5-year-olds according to a mixture of play types, for example construction, sensory, imaginative play and the areas of learning within the EYFS. This is because unless thought is given there can be a danger that some aspects of children's learning are not provided for. The environment within the EYFS should be enabling so as to help provide for high-quality child-initiated play. This means that it should be set up in ways that allow children to operate within it with a minimum of adult assistance. (This does not mean that adults do not interact with children!) It

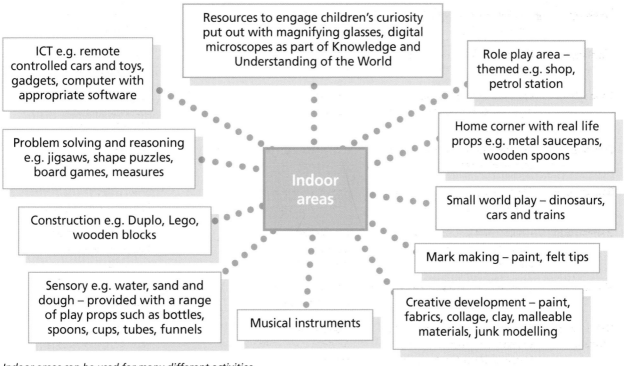

Indoor areas can be used for many different activities

is therefore important to think about whether there are sufficient resources available for children to access and whether the resources are providing play value. Many settings find that focusing on the 'accessories' of play can affect the quality of the play positively; for example providing real vegetables in the role play shop and real money in the cash register helps the children to engage better with the role play.

Indoors

Most settings will set out their provision in terms of distinct areas, although it is good practice for mark making, for example, to be available as part of several activities; for instance having notepads next to the phone in the role play area. In childminding settings, it will not always be possible for all areas to be accessible all of the time because of lack of space, but it would be expected that over a session several opportunities would be provided. The spider diagram on page 217 shows the areas that are commonly found in most settings for 3–5-year-olds.

Outdoors

The outdoors has received a lot of attention in the past few years as it is recognised that it is both an effective environment in which to learn, and a healthy one in which children can take exercise. Just as for the indoor environment, it is important that all of the learning areas are taken into consideration when planning. This means, for example, that you should think about how you would incorporate ICT outdoors, such as providing opportunities for walkie talkies. The spider diagram below shows some of the types of activities and areas found outdoors.

The role of the adult in preparing environments

To prepare effective environments for children requires not just a good knowledge of child development but also a knowledge of the individual children you work with. You might have observed that a child loves the sand tray and so use this as a starting point to think about how to enrich the activity, such as putting out different resources for the child to use, or preparing a separate tray of wet sand.

It is also important when preparing environments to imagine what children might do and check that it is possible. For example, if you set up a shop, children will need a purse with money, a bag, a check-out till, proper things to buy (small tins, vegetables or clothes in packets). You should also ask yourself if there are enough resources to make the play opportunity worthwhile for the child; for example ten wooden blocks on their own is not sufficient, and a little bit of water in the water tray will be of minimal use to a child who wants to scoop and pour.

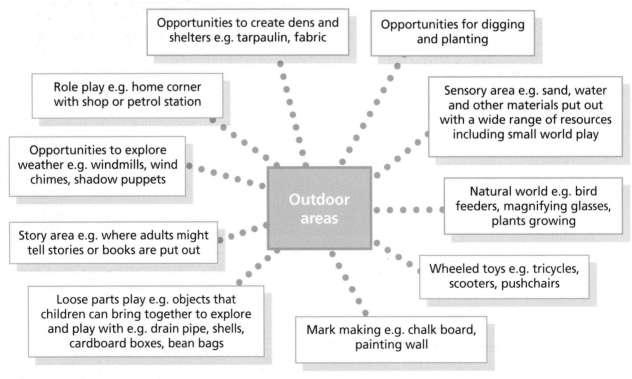

Outdoor areas also provide many play opportunities and different activities

Indoor play provision must be enjoyable for all children

It is also important to check that toys and resources are working properly, for example felt tips and markers must make a decent mark and powered toys should have batteries in them that work.

Finally, it is worth adding that, as part of the EYFS, children should have an active role in setting up and choosing what could be put out. In some settings, children are asked what they would like out for the next session, while in others, children 'pack' a shelf or suitcase ready for their play the next day.

Monitoring environments

It is not enough just to set up areas for children in order to enrich their play and extend their development, We also need to consider how well the areas are working in respect of the following:

● extending children's learning and development

● encouraging high expectations of their achievement.

This is important because one of the statutory requirements of the EYFS is that every provider must ensure that they have created an 'enjoyable and challenging' learning and development experience which meets every child's needs.

Extending children's learning and development

This means looking at how children are using play opportunities and considering whether they are sufficient to help them gain concepts, practise skills and whether the learning environment is delivering the six areas of learning.

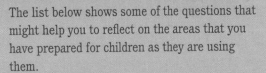

Reflect

Explain how you ensure that the environment you are providing for children is an enjoyable and challenging one.

Functional Skills

ICT: Using ICT

English: Writing

Why not ask if you can take some photographs using a digital camera of the environment you provide for the children? Leading on from this you could copy the images into a document and write some text about how you ensured the environment was challenging and describe the involvement the children had in choosing the activities.

Reflect

The list below shows some of the questions that might help you to reflect on the areas that you have prepared for children as they are using them.

How long are children concentrating?

How engaged are the children in the play/activity?

How does it meet each child's needs?

What else could be provided to make the play more meaningful?

Are there opportunities for children to interact with each other/adults?

What is the next step for each child?

Are children showing inappropriate behaviour? Why?

How will their play develop their knowledge, skills or attitudes within the EYFS areas of learning?

Encouraging high expectations of their achievement

Sometimes children can enjoy their play and learning, but if we analyse it we may see that it has become repetitive. We should therefore think about how to incorporate new resources, change the layout or add some more adult interaction in order for the children to make progress.

Although some children may struggle with the learning experiences for a variety of reasons, such as recognised learning difficulties, we should not label them as unable to achieve. Many children will respond well to the expectations of adults with whom they have a positive relationship. Undue pressure and unrealistic expectations will have the opposite effect and it is important that practitioners get to know their key children well and work sensitively with them.

Monitoring

There are many ways of doing this. We may informally watch children as they are playing or we may set about doing some recorded observations that focus on what children are actually doing during a session.

Group time sample

It is possible to observe children using a method that is a hybrid between target child and a time sample. Instead of sampling one child's activity over an extended period, several children's activities are considered. Although this method does not give in-depth information about a single child, it does provide an indication of how an environment is working overall.

Using this method:

1. Choose a time which you feel is working well in your setting, for example when the children are ensconced in play!

2. Draw up a grid.

3. Choose between 5 and 8 children at random.

4. At the start of the first 5-minute slot, write down where each child is.

5. Scan your setting during the 5-minute period and note down if a child moves from their activity/play.

6. At the beginning of the next 5-minute slot, look to see which children are still in the same place — you can draw

a line down to show this rather than writing out the name of the activity/play again.

During the observation:

1. Make a note of how engaged children are during their play/activity; for example 1 indicates not very interested, while 5 = highly engaged.

2. Make a note of what seems to have engaged the children.

3. Try to work out why children have moved — is it because the play/activity was no longer challenging? Was it because their friend moved? Or did an adult call them away?

You can also make notes of whether a child seems to be interacting with other children/adults. Indicate this by putting a C/A within a circle.

Reflect

Look back over the observation you have done. Could you see any patterns as to why children were engaged in play for a long period or on the other hand were leaving it? Consider whether there was sufficient challenge in the activities, what the children were gaining from it and how the activities could be extended or developed. If you repeat this several times, you could also learn about which areas of the environment are not popular with children or which areas attract children, or why children choose not to stay there.

Ensuring that the environment meets the needs of individual children

While we have seen the principles of providing environments for children, it is also important that time is spent reflecting on whether an environment is working for individual children. This means carrying out sensitive observations on individual children and considering how comfortable they seem and also how they engage with the environment. As children's rates of development differ, it is sometimes possible to find children who need more challenge and others who would benefit from slightly different types of play opportunities and resources. It is also essential that we consider whether children with additional needs or disabilities are able to benefit from what we are providing.

Over to you

Observe one child over a period of a session that you suspect is not fully engaged. Make a note of which activities, areas and play opportunities the child takes an interest in.

1. Can you work out how to improve the environment for this child?

2. Are there any changes that would also benefit other children?

Getting ready for assessment

Write a reflective account that shows how you can prepare and support children's play and learning. Your reflective account should include the following:

- a description of the area that you prepared
- an explanation of how the area was intended to support and extend children's learning
- an evaluation of how children used the area, the benefits to them and to what extent it met individual children's needs.

Understand how to work in partnership with carers

It is recognised across frameworks that parents have an essential role in the care and education of their children. This learning outcome requires you to understand how you might work in partnership with parents, overcome

barriers and also think about how multi-agency working links to our work with parents.

The partnership model of working with carers

Years ago, once parents or carers had handed their children over to the 'experts' in schools, pre-schools or nursery, they were often considered to be fairly surplus to requirements. Practitioners knew best! Today it is understood that the best outcomes for children are usually seen when parents and practitioners work together. This forms the basis of the model of partnership with parents or carers. The idea is that while parents and practitioners will have their own roles with children, they can come together to share ideas, information and thoughts about the best way forward for the children. Below are some of the ways which settings use to make partnership with parents or carers more than just an ideal.

Open door policy

As part of the partnership with carers model, the term 'open door' was coined. The idea is that carers do not have to make specific appointments to visit a setting, but know that they are welcome at any point.

Observations and assessments

Children's records and assessments made by practitioners used to be kept top secret. Now, it is understood that these not only need to be shared with carers, but also they should contribute to them. This is because children behave very differently with parents or carers and so practitioners can learn more about a child's development, interests and also needs. In some settings, carers are invited into the setting to observe their child.

Planning and decision making

Many settings not only share their planning with parents but also encourage carers to contribute with ideas and comments, for example suggestions related to the management of the setting or designing the learning environment.

Working alongside practitioners

Many settings invite parents to come and work alongside them, for example during open mornings, drop-in sessions and helping out generally. Parents may also continue activities that have been started in a setting at home.

Practitioners learning from parents or carers

It makes fairly good sense for practitioners to learn more about children by gaining information from carers. Parents or carers are, after all, the top experts when it comes to knowledge about their children. This approach is particularly crucial when children in a setting have a medical condition or disability as quite often carers will be able to help a practitioner learn how to work with their child.

The emphasis on personal and individual development

The four frameworks in the home nations have many similarities in structure as well as differences. All emphasise play as the medium for young children's learning. They also all stress the importance of observing children and working with them on the basis of their personal development. This personalisation of learning is interesting and links closely to inclusion and diversity as it is increasingly recognised that a 'one size fits all' approach does not work in the care and education of children.

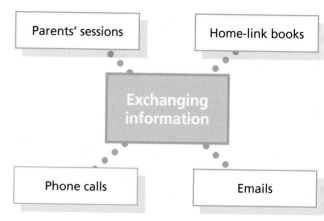

Key ways to exchange information and develop a relationship with parents

Over to you

Look at the early years framework that you are working with. Consider its key principles. In what ways can you see that there is an emphasis on structuring and delivering care and education in ways that meet individual children's needs?

Barriers to participation for carers

Partnership working can run very smoothly, but there are some potential barriers that practitioners need to be aware of and overcome.

Time

In the ideal world, carers will drop off and pick up their children and have plenty of time for discussions and joining in with our work. The reality is that some parents or carers are short of time and actually need to spend what time they have being with their children rather than

talking about them. It is important to recognise this and be sensitive as many parents can feel guilty that they are not able to do as much as they would like. Key ways in which we can exchange information and develop a relationship with parents include the following.

Home-link books

These are well established and can be a great way in which carers and practitioners can exchange information, comments and ideas on a daily basis.

Emails

Email exchanges can work well providing that consent and security issues are considered. In theory photographs can be exchanged as well as information, and parents may send in photos of their child at home or during an outing. Emails are increasingly being used to send out newsletters as well as plans and observations.

Phone calls

Although face-to-face conversations are ideal, a phone call can be an effective substitute.

Parents' sessions at a range of times

Parents' evenings or information about children's progress work well, but need to be held at times when parents or carers are available. Some settings also provide crèches or lists of babysitters to make it easier for carers to be involved.

Confidence

Some parents or carers can find it hard to be active partners in their child's care and education because they lack confidence. There are many reasons for this, although parents' previous experiences of education or interactions with other professionals are perhaps the most common. Some carers also feel that they do not have anything particularly to offer or that their views will not be of interest. To overcome this significant barrier, it is important that a parent's first contact with us is a positive one and that our communication skills are excellent. (See Unit SC1 on communication.) Some settings find home visits very useful in this respect as parents can see practitioners in a familiar environment and one they are in control of.

Language and literacy needs

Some carers may not feel they can be full partners if they cannot speak English fluently or find it hard to read and write English. Being sensitive to the language and literacy needs of parents or carers is therefore important. For some settings, this means encouraging carers to feel that they can bring along someone who can interpret for them. It also means that settings have to think about providing some alternatives to written information and must avoid putting carers on the spot in terms of asking them to read and write.

Disability

Some carers may have a disability, including a learning disability, which may create a barrier to partnership working. The way in which these barriers can be overcome will be very much dependent on the carer's individual needs; for example a carer with a sight problem may access information about their child using voice messages or large print. It is essential for settings to individualise their approach as a 'one size fits all' approach will not work. (See also Unit SC2 on diversity and inclusion.)

Culture

Some parents or carers do not have experience of the culture of working in partnership. They may not know what is expected and this in turn may create anxiety.

Supporting carers in partnership opportunities

Although we may do our best to create partnership working with carers, there will still be some people who do not wish to take up the opportunities or who may react negatively. It is important first to understand that they have the right not to participate should they choose not to and that they should not be put under pressure to do so. Taking this approach can reap some benefits as sometimes a more relaxed attitude can make carers feel more comfortable. In addition, it is important to see if we can find out if there are any particular reasons why our attempts are not working. In some cases, this may be about style, timing or accessibility. Where partnerships with carers are strong, it is useful to capitalise on this.

Parents or carers may have suggestions as to how they could be more fully involved or may have ideas as to how to engage with other parents. Many settings will therefore carry out evaluation questionnaires or have suggestion boxes in order to learn more about what they are doing well and which aspects of their performance they could improve.

Effective multi-agency working

In addition to settings working closely with families, we need to recognise that this should be taking place in the context of multi-agency working. This means that there is a role for all settings to signpost services and support that other agencies provide and also, if necessary, to help parents or carers to navigate their way through the different services. Finally, it is important to remember that information about children and their families should not be shared without the carer's permission, unless there are serious concerns about a child's welfare. Breaching children and families' confidentiality can undermine their confidence, not only in us, but will also jeopardise any situation in which they approach other professionals in the future. For more information about multi-agency working, see Units CYP3.6 and 3.7.

Check your knowledge

1. Outline the purpose of the curriculum that is used in your country.

2. Explain the main features of the curriculum that is used in your country.

3. Give one example of how the curriculum that you use has been influenced by another approach.

4. Give examples of areas within your provision that might extend children's learning.

5. Why is it important to prepare an area according to the age/stage of development of the children?

6. Outline the role of observation in preparing an area for children.

7. Why is it important to monitor and evaluate the effectiveness of an area?

8. Explain why partnership with parents is important.

9. Give two examples of possible barriers to parental participation.

10. Outline how common barriers to participation may be overcome.

Promote learning & development in the early years

For a number of years, it has been recognised that children's earliest experiences can shape their later attainment. In view of this, each of the four home countries of the UK have developed early years curricula. While each curriculum is different in style, they all aim to give children a range of stimulating experiences that will assist their development. For this unit, you are required to understand and be able to work with the early years curriculum for your home country, which in England is the Early Years Foundation Stage.

Learning outcomes

By the end of this unit you will:

1. Understand the purpose and requirements of the areas of learning and development in the relevant early years framework

2. Be able to plan work with children and support children's participation in planning

3. Be able to promote children's learning and development according to the requirements of the relevant early years framework

4. Be able to engage with children in activities and experiences that support their learning and development

5. Be able to review own practice in supporting the learning and development of children in their early years.

Understand the purpose and requirements of the areas of learning and development in the relevant early years framework

The Early Years Foundation Stage (EYFS) was introduced in England in September 2008. Its aim was to improve the quality of care and education for children from birth to the end of their first year in school. It is a statutory curriculum which means that all providers working with babies and children up to the age of 5 years have to follow it, including childminders, after-school clubs and crèches. The purpose of making it statutory was to ensure that all children were given the same opportunities for a high-quality education. It is unique, as although the other home nations provide resources and suggestions to help providers work with babies and toddlers, the EYFS includes the 0–3s in its education programme.

However, the EYFS is more than just an education programme as it covers the care or welfare requirements and sets out the staff ratios. This means that to work effectively with the EYFS, you must read both the information relating to the care and welfare requirements as well as the sections about the education programme. For this learning outcome you will need to show that you have understood the structure of the EYFS.

If you are working in Wales, Scotland or Northern Ireland, you will need to use the frameworks for your country.

- Scotland – Curriculum for Excellence – www.tls.gov.uk
- Wales – Foundation Stage – www.foundationphasewales.com
- Northern Ireland – Various – www.nicurriculum.org and www.early-years.org

Statutory Framework for the Early Years Foundation Stage

May 2008

Setting the Standards for Learning, Development and Care for children from birth to five

Every Child Matters
Change For Children

STATUTORY FRAMEWORK

department for
children, schools and families

Obtain a copy of the EYFS pack either by downloading it or ordering one

Areas of learning

There are six broad areas of learning within the EYFS education programme and they apply to all age ranges. Table 1 shows the six areas of development and the requirements for each one as stated in Part 2 of the Statutory Framework.

Table 1: Areas of learning in the EYFS

Area of Learning	Requirement
Personal, Social and Emotional Development	'Children must be provided with experiences and support which will help them to develop a positive sense of themselves and of others; respect for others; social skills; and a positive disposition to learn. Providers must ensure support for children's emotional well-being to help them to know themselves and what they can do.' Statutory Framework 2.7
Communication, Language and Literacy	'Children's learning and competence in communicating, speaking and listening, being read to and beginning to read and write must be supported. They must be provided with opportunity and encouragement to use their skills in a range of situations and for a range of purposes, and be supported in developing the confidence and disposition to do so.' Statutory Framework 2.9
Problem Solving, Reasoning and Numeracy	'Children must be supported in developing their understanding of problem solving, reasoning and numeracy in a broad range of contexts in which they can explore, enjoy, learn, practise and talk about their developing understanding. They must be provided with opportunities to practise and extend their skills in these areas and to gain confidence and competence in their use.' Statutory Framework 2.11
Knowledge and Understanding of the World	'Children must be supported in developing the knowledge, skills and understanding that help them to make sense of the world. Their learning must be supported through offering opportunities for them to use a range of tools safely; encounter creatures, people, plants and objects in their natural environments and in real-life situations; undertake practical 'experiments'; and work with a range of materials.' Statutory Framework 2.13
Physical Development	'The physical development of babies and young children must be encouraged through the provision of opportunities for them to be active and interactive and to improve their skills of coordination, control, manipulation and movement. They must be supported in using all of their senses to learn about the world around them and to make connections between new information and what they already know. They must be supported in developing an understanding of the importance of physical activity and making healthy choices in relation to food.' Statutory Framework 2.15
Creative Development	'Children's creativity must be extended by the provision of support for their curiosity, exploration and play. They must be provided with opportunities to explore and share their thoughts, ideas and feelings, for example, through a variety of art, music, movement, dance, imaginative and role-play activities, mathematics, and design and technology.' Statutory Framework 2.17

(Source: EYFS Statutory Framework)

Aspects of learning within the broad areas

To support practitioners in their delivery of the education programme, the EYFS pack contains Practice Guidance. This is an important document as it subdivides the areas of learning into their different components and also shows how to work with different ages.

Personal, Social and Emotional Development

Personal, social and emotional development is seen as essential because confident, secure children who know how to manage their own behaviour are more likely to cope with the demands of formal education.

This area of development is subdivided into six aspects as shown in Table 2.

Table 2: Aspects of personal, social and emotional development

Personal, social and emotional	
	Dispositions and attitudes
	Self-confidence and self-esteem
	Making relationships
	Behaviour and self-control
	Self-care
	Sense of community

Dispositions and attitudes is an important aspect as it is about interest, perseverance, levels of engagement and concentration. Embedding this into the way we work means making sure that we are providing sufficiently stimulating opportunities for children and also giving them the time in order to settle down and focus their attention. In particular, child-initiated play is essential in helping children work towards the early learning goals for this area.

Self-confidence and self-esteem is important because there is a link between self-esteem and children's achievement. Embedding this into the way we work involves more than just praising children; it also means helping them to learn that they 'can do' as well as helping them learn to express feelings and become thoughtful in relation to others. This might mean creating as part of the routine opportunities for children to help each other and of course child-initiated activities.

Making relationships is about helping children to socialise. This starts with ensuring that children have a settled and close relationship with a key person. Embedding this into the way we work means giving opportunities for children to play freely with each other and sometimes to stand back and see if children can resolve their own difficulties through negotiation; for example, agreeing whose turn it is, or what should the blocks be made into and so on.

Behaviour and self-control is about helping children to recognise and control their emotions and also show appropriate behaviour. In terms of our work, it means that children — even babies — need opportunities to help and take responsibility as this extends their locus of control; for example a baby may hold a rattle while we change the nappy whereas an older child might put out the beakers ready for a snack.

Self-care is about helping children to manage everyday tasks such as dressing and feeding. In terms of our work this means ensuring that we build sufficient time into the routine in order to allow children to practise and develop the self-care skills. Children can only learn to dress themselves if they are given the opportunity to practise.

Sense of community is about children learning that they belong to a group and that they develop respect for others. Embedding this into practice means we should check that our own way of working with other children, parents, staff and other people is inclusive. This is because children tend to learn their value system from key adults who interact with them.

Communication, Language and Literacy

This area of learning is essential for children's later academic achievement, but also for their ability to form relationships, manage their emotions and process information. It is divided into six aspects as shown in Table 3 below.

Table 3: Aspects of communication, language and literacy

Communication, language and literacy	
	Language for communication
	Language for thinking
	Linking sounds and letters
	Reading
	Writing
	Handwriting

Language for communication is about helping children to use language as a way of socialising and expressing their needs. To embed this into our practice means making sure there is sufficient interaction between ourselves and children. As children get older we also need to ensure that there are plenty of opportunities for

Development of communication skills is essential for children's later academic achievement

them to use language between themselves, for example in role play areas and at meal times.

Language for thinking is about looking at ways to help children use language to express their thinking, to predict and to reason. This is particularly important once children's speech has developed as it means they can learn to use language to 'figure things' out; reasoning, for example: 'If I put this here, the blocks might fall down.' One of the ways to embed language for thinking into our practice is to ensure that we draw children's attention to specific details and label things for children. For example, we might say 'That's a spotty looking dog. I think it's a Dalmatian.' We can also help children learn how to use their language for thinking by modelling our own thought processes: 'I know that Mark has had his lunch, but I'd better check that Bekir hasn't forgotten.'

Linking sounds with letters is at first about helping babies and toddlers tune into the sounds of English and then eventually helping older children, once they have begun to speak English, to link sounds with actual letters. Embedding this into your practice means introducing plenty of rhymes and songs to children of all ages; then, with children who are ready, you can start to draw their attention to letter shapes and sounds through games and activities.

Reading is about helping children learn to love books and to be motivated to look and eventually read them. Embedding this into your practice means you have to make sure that children have daily opportunities to share stories and books with adults. It is essential that this is a pleasurable experience and so matching children's stage of development to the correct language level of books is important, as is keeping an eye on the size of groups.

Writing is at first about mark making and gaining pleasure from seeing how marks can be made using a variety of materials. For older children, writing is something that they can be motivated to try because they have seen adults in the setting writing in front of them or scribing for them. Embedding writing into our practice means making sure that there are always pleasurable materials available for marking and also incorporating marking and writing into the play opportunities in and out of doors; for example providing clipboards and large white boards outdoors, shopping lists in the home corners and notebooks on the dough table.

Handwriting is not about tracing letters, but about helping children to develop their fine motor movements in preparation for later letter formation. Delivering this aspect involves providing tools for children as well as finding opportunities for mark making; for example, encouraging a baby to smear yoghurt on a tray.

Problem Solving, Reasoning and Numeracy

This area of learning is not just about maths but about helping children to problem solve and think about things logically. This area of development is divided into three aspects, as shown in Table 4 below.

Table 4: Aspects of problem solving, reasoning and numeracy

Problem solving, reasoning and numeracy	
	Numbers as labels and for counting
	Calculating
	Shape, space and measures

Numbers as labels and for counting: this aspect is about helping children to learn the names for numbers and eventually learning to count accurately. It means that children of all ages need to hear us sing counting rhymes and watch us count. It also means that as children get older we start to draw their attention to written numerals by writing them in front of them.

Calculating is not about sums. This is important to stress as some parents may feel that their babies are suddenly going to be learning their times tables! Calculating is at first about noticing reductions or increases — for example, 'Only one more spoonful left' or 'Would you like an extra piece of banana?'. The focus is to ensure that children also develop the mathematical vocabulary that they will need to talk about differences between numbers and groups, such as 'more', 'less' and 'same'.

Shape, space and measures is about exploring shapes and sizes through practical activities. For babies this might be treasure basket play, while for toddlers this might be watching how, when they drink, the amount in their beaker becomes less. Talking about clothes fitting, providing junk modelling and nappy changing (for example, asking whether this is the right size nappy to use) are all ways in which children learn to experience this aspect of learning.

Knowledge and Understanding of the World

This area of learning is diverse and helps children to gain an understanding of the world around them, that is, their immediate environment. This area of learning in the long term will link to the National Curriculum subjects of Science, History, Geography, Design and Technology and ICT. This area of learning is split into six discrete and very separate aspects of learning as Table 5 below shows.

Table 5: Aspects of knowledge and understanding of the world

Knowledge and understanding of the world	
	Exploration and investigation
	Designing and making
	ICT
	Time
	Place
	Communities

Exploration and investigation is about children learning by touching, feeling and observing

Exploration and investigation is about children learning by touching, feeling, observing and, in the case of babies, mouthing. It will eventually link to early science. Delivering this aspect means providing children with interesting materials and experiences for them to explore. For babies and toddlers, it may mean providing treasure baskets and **heuristic play.** It is worth noting that this aspect also links well to the 'Exploring media and materials' aspect of learning (Creative development).

Designing and making is about giving children the opportunities to make things that they have designed. Embedding this into practice might include doing some regular cooking activities with children as well as giving them plenty of child-initiated opportunities to use construction materials, sensory materials and loose parts such as cardboard boxes and fabric. For toddlers and

older children, this can link into 'Using equipment and materials' (Physical development).

ICT is about helping children of all ages find out about how to use ICT. In the early stages, it is about sharing with babies different toys and books which have microchips built in – such as books that make noises, toys that light up. Later it is about helping toddlers and older children learn how to control and use some gadgets safely such as turning on and using a programmable toy or noticing that a solar-powered calculator will only work when it is near light.

Time is the area of learning that will eventually lead to learning about history. In the EYFS, it is about helping children develop sufficient language so that they can explore the concept of time. For example, babies and toddlers need to hear the past tense before they can use it, while older children need language in order to sequence events. It is easy to embed into our everyday practice because it is about talking about what we are doing and also what we have done.

Place will eventually lead into learning about geography. As with Time, the earlier stages are about language – babies and toddlers, for example, will gradually understand and then use words such as 'in', 'out' and the names of places that are important for them: 'at home', 'in your bedroom', 'outdoors'. With older children,

Key term

Heuristic play: play with household and recyclable objects that encourage toddlers to explore

learning about Place is about thinking about what they can see, where they have been and what they like about their environment.

Communities is about helping children to explore cultures, beliefs and eventually may link into citizenship and religious education. As with other areas, there is an early focus on language — with children needing to be able to talk about themselves and their families before coming to understand the way in which people can lead different lives and can have different beliefs.

Physical Development

This area of learning is important as physical development allows children to do many other things such as write, explore and play. The concerns about child obesity and health mean that this area of development also has a focus on health. It is subdivided into three aspects as shown in Table 6 below.

Table 6: Aspects of physical development

Physical development	
	Movement and space
	Health and bodily awareness
	Using equipment and materials

Movement and space is about children gaining an awareness of how to use their bodies, as well as developing a sense of themselves in relationship to spaces — a concept known as spatial awareness. This is fairly easy to embed within our practice, providing we give children, of all ages, varied opportunities to experience and explore different types of spaces and sensations. Child-initiated play, particularly outdoors where children may have more space and access to a range of equipment, is essential in delivering this aspect.

Health and bodily awareness is about eventually helping children to make good choices about keeping themselves healthy. It covers food, hygiene and safety with the focus on children learning about making connections between what they do and eat and their overall health. In order to deliver this aspect, it is important that we provide nutritious food in the right portion sizes and also encourage children to enjoy foods that are balanced and therefore good for them.

Using equipment and materials particularly focuses on the hand—eye coordination and fine motor skills of children. This should be embedded into most of the activities and play opportunities that are available for children; for example, a baby playing with a rattle, a toddler who is trying to put a hat on a teddy or a group of children trying to make a hammock by tying fabric to a chainlink fence.

Creative Development

This area of learning is becoming of increasing interest as creativity, together with problem solving, is considered to be essential in supporting children's achievement, as well as their emotional well-being. There are three aspects within this broad area as Table 7 shows.

Table 7: Aspects of creative development

Creative development	
	Being creative — responding to experiences, expressing and communicating ideas
	Exploring media and materials
	Creating music and dance

Being creative — responding to experiences, expressing and communicating ideas is about the overall way that children might express themselves. This aspect of learning prompts us to make sure that children do get a wide range of experiences, materials and resources so they can find a way to express themselves. This means that, in your planning, you should have several types of provision available for children that will enable them to express themselves, including paint, drawing, junk modelling, musical instruments and heuristic play rather than a single adult-directed activity.

Exploring media and materials is about giving children a range of material for them to explore. To deliver this aspect of learning requires **sensory materials** as well as traditional 'art' materials and also opportunities for plenty

> ### Key term
>
> **Sensory materials:** materials that are usually tactile and will stimulate children's senses e.g. clay, cornflour, sand

Give children a range of materials for them to explore

of child-initiated activity. It has links with Exploration and Investigation within the Knowledge and Understanding of the World area of development.

Creating music and dance is a lovely aspect of learning. It is about children of all ages hearing and being able to respond to a range of music. Babies, for example, may wriggle on the floor to the sounds of a song that they like, while toddlers may bob up and down enthusiastically. This aspect of learning means providing ways of making sounds as well as responding to them, for example shakers, rattles and more sophisticated instruments that are tuned, such as glockenspiels. For this to be a creative experience for children, again it is essential for adults to be ready to take a step backwards and see what children want to do and how they respond.

Developing imagination and imaginative play is about making sure that children have plenty of opportunities to imagine and also to use role play. With babies, it might be about laughing when they see a puppet popping up and then down, while with toddlers we may see the beginnings of trying to make one thing stand for another. For example, the toddler takes an empty beaker but pretends that it is full and 'drinks' from it or makes a mark and imagines that it is a dog running around. With

older children we are likely to see a range of imaginative play including 'at home', superhero play and acting out stories that they have heard.

The interdependence of the areas of learning

Although six separate areas of learning are described in the EYFS, it is important to recognise that they are seen as interdependent. This means that good-quality activities are likely to cover more than one area of development and that neglecting one area of development is likely to create later difficulties. A good example of this is Personal, Social and Emotional development. If this area of development is not well supported, children will find it hard to concentrate, play with others and so make progress in other areas. Some settings therefore plan **holistically** and afterwards work out what specific areas have been covered rather than planning only for one area at a time. This approach is particularly useful if you work with babies and toddlers, as many everyday activities will support their overall development. For instance, taking babies on a walk outdoors will mean that they can communicate, learn about their immediate environment and develop spatial awareness as well as respond according to what they see.

Key term

Holistically: taken together as a whole

EYFS in action

Choose one of the following activities which are often available for 3-year-olds. Assuming that a 3-year-old is with other children at the time, consider what the child might be learning and link this to the EYFS areas or aspects of learning.

- Playing with dough
- Dressing up in the home corner
- Building a den outdoors

The documented outcomes for children

The EYFS was designed to ensure that all children — regardless of where they live, their family background or circumstances — would have access to a quality early years education. To be able to measure this and also to ensure that practitioners have a clear focus for their work, a series of outcomes is given for each area of learning. These are called the **Early Learning Goals.** The aim is that each child can meet them by the end of their reception year.

Key term

Early Learning Goals: targets in the Early Years Foundation Stage curriculum that it is expected that children at the end of the reception year will meet

These goals are important as they form the building blocks for children's later education. It is important that practitioners recognise that many of the Early Learning Goals are also associated with children's development and so while it is reasonable to expect children to meet them at the end of the reception year, they are not meant to be used as outcomes in nurseries or pre-schools. It is also worth noting that some children will for a variety of reasons not meet all of the Early Learning Goals as they may have specific health or learning difficulties or because they are simply younger than their peers.

Remember that children born in August will only just be 4 when they enter the reception class while other children may be nearly 5 years old.

Interpreting the Early Learning Goals

Many of the Early Learning Goals need to be interpreted carefully as they are not narrowly focused. For example, one of the Early Learning Goals for physical development is 'recognise the importance of keeping healthy and those things which contribute to this'. As this is a lifetime's research for some doctors, it is important to interpret this in terms of what might be reasonable knowledge for a young child.

Assessment and record keeping

Children's attainment of the Early Learning Goals has to be assessed at the end of the reception year. This is a statutory requirement and teachers will fill in a record showing how each child in their class is performing. This record is called the **Early Years Profile**. The child is assessed against 13 different scales each of which has nine points. The Early Learning Goals themselves are sometimes split or combined. Teachers are required to identify what children can do based on observations they have carried out during the reception year. There is a requirement that 80 per cent of these observations have been carried out while children are engaged in child-led activity. To ensure some degree of accuracy, the early years profiles are moderated.

Key term

Early Years Profile: a record to show how children are progressing towards the Early Learning Goals that is completed by reception teachers in England

Following is the assessment scale for social development which forms part of the Personal, Social and Emotional area of development. Points 4 to 8 are drawn from the Early Learning Goals. Points 1 to 3 describe children who are still working towards the goal, while children who score point 9 are working beyond the level of the Early Learning Goals for that area.

Social Development

1. Plays alongside others

2. Builds relationships through gesture and talk

3. Takes turns and shares with adult support

4. Works as part of a group or class taking turns and sharing fairly

5. Forms good relationships with adults and peers

6. Understands that there needs to be agreed values and codes of behaviour for groups of people, including adults and children, to work together harmoniously

7. Understands that people have different needs, views, cultures and beliefs that need to be treated with respect

8. Understands that he or she can expect others to treat her or his needs, views, cultures and beliefs with respect

9. Takes into account the ideas of others

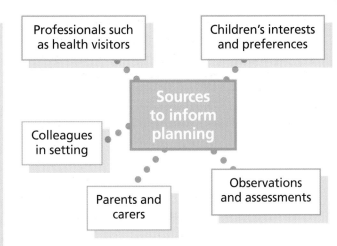

Different sources can be used to help with planning

Be able to plan work with children and support children's participation in planning

The EYFS requires practitioners to plan activities and play opportunities that will support children's learning while delivering the areas of learning within the EYFS. For this learning outcome, you will need to show that you know how to gain information to plan for an individual child and groups of children and that your planning is effective.

Sources to inform planning

The EYFS requires all practitioners to plan carefully so that individual children's needs are met and that the activities and play opportunities available might help children make progress towards the early learning goals. Planning based on observations in this way is a statutory requirement. (See the Organisation section of the EYFS

Statutory Framework.) Planning is also important given that the curriculum covers children from birth onwards and so activities must be selected according to children's stage of development. There are different sources that can be used to help us plan. The spider diagram above shows these.

Children's interests and preferences

All children have play preferences, toys and resources that are of special interest to them. Working out what children enjoy is important when planning for them as there is a statutory requirement for us to make their learning and development experience challenging *and* enjoyable. It is worth noting that 'enjoyable' is the exact word used. One way to work out what might be enjoyable for a child is to watch what they choose to play with and the way in which they play.

Observations and assessments

Observing individual children carefully to consider what they can do, and what their needs and interests are, is an important part of delivering the EYFS. It is expected that key persons in particular will have a major role in observing and assessing their children as they should be able to interpret what they are seeing. Observations have to be carried out in a range of situations and, once completed, time must be spent considering what has been learnt. Some observations will help us assess a child's stage of development and so will enable us to plan in a more stage-appropriate way, while other observations may help us to consider how the child is progressing towards the Early Learning Goals and whether any areas of learning are being missed. Most settings have a system to ensure that every child is observed regularly and that observations also focus on different developmental and learning areas. (See also Unit CYP3.2 on observing children, page 82.)

Parents and carers

In the EYFS, parents or other carers are seen as partners and their involvement is considered to be vital. Parents can tell us about what their child enjoys doing at home and also what skills and knowledge their child has mastered. Parents can also help us to work out what else a child needs to do. To involve parents, most settings try to exchange ideas and plans regularly. (See also Unit CYP3.5 pages 162–165.)

Colleagues in setting

In most settings the key person takes the lead on observing and planning for their children, but it is always advisable for colleagues to contribute to the planning process. This is because they may well have noticed things about particular children that others might have missed. Using information from colleagues is vital when children are engaged in free-flow settings, where children can go in and out of doors and their key person may not always be with them. Colleagues can also help us with ideas — especially if they are experienced.

Professionals such as health visitors

It is likely that some of the children we work with are also being seen by other professionals, such as health visitors, speech and language therapists or physiotherapists. Their ideas about how to plan activities and play opportunities for children will be important so that children have continuity of experience, especially where children need to master or gain specific skills.

Child's participation and involvement

It is important that our plans reflect children's interests and needs. This means not only observing children but also thinking about ways in which we can help children to tell us what they would like to do during a session or in future sessions. After all, it is the children who are most affected by what is on offer! With children whose speech is developing, we may need to find visual ways of helping them to express their opinions, for example showing children resources or having photographs of what is available so that they can point to them. With children who are talking well, we can ask them directly; although many children still find it helpful to 'see' what is on offer. As the EYFS requires that settings provide child-initiated play activities, it is important that we do find ways of helping children to play in their preferred ways.

Case study: Our toys have been stolen!

Sunshine day nursery has a lot of resources and toys but is tight on floor space. This meant that staff used to rotate the toys and resources: each day different things would be put out. A child, who had been enjoying playing with a dumper truck and the sand the day before, came into the room, looked around and began to sob. His key person asked him what the matter was. He said, 'Bad people have stolen our toys again.' The key person reassured him that there were no bad people but that the toys had been put away, and would come out on another day. He looked at her and asked why.

As a result of his comment, the staff team began to think harder about their system of rotation. They decided it would be better to ask the children during and at the end of the session what should be kept out for the next day. They photographed many of the toys and adult-directed activities to create a book so that children could also select what they would like to play with. Over the next few weeks, parents commented that their children talked about what they would be doing the next day on the way home and staff found that children were often far more engaged in their play than before. As result of these changes, staff have also decided that they will in future encourage children to be involved in choosing new equipment and toys and will also give the children a choice of possible outings.

1. Why is working with children in this way a more child-centred approach?

2. Why did the nursery find that children were more engaged in their play?

3. What skills are children learning by being more involved in the planning?

It is important that our plans reflect children's interests and needs

Support the planning cycle for children's learning and development

Although settings plan using different paperwork and styles, the EYFS is very clear that observations must form the basis of planning for individual children. There are two specific legal requirements in this respect which can be found in Welfare Requirements relating to the organisation of the setting.

'Providers must carry out sensitive observational assessment in order to plan to meet children's individual needs.'

'Providers must plan and provide experiences which are appropriate to each child's stage of development as they progress towards the early learning goals.' (page 37 Statutory Framework for the Early Years Foundation Stage May 2008)

Planning does not just relate to what happens indoors during adult-directed activities; the EYFS requires settings to have adult- and child-initiated activities both indoors and outdoors. In most effective settings, key persons undertake observations, talk to parents and use the other methods outlined above and then draw up individual plans for children. The level of detail within the plan is often variable. Using these plans, settings then work out what type of adult-directed activities should be offered and the type of activities and play opportunities on offer.

As children's tastes and play preferences can change quickly, most settings now use daily or short-term plans so that children's interests can be picked up on. This means that planning for children is part of a continual cycle whereby, each day, children's interests, reactions and learning are noted, planned observations are carried out and on this basis further plans are drawn up.

Planning for child-initiated activity

Planning for child-initiated play can be something of a contradiction as we may not know what children will choose to play with or how they might do so. Settings take different approaches in to how to deal with this, with many using **continuous provision** sheets which outline a range of play opportunities that can act as a basis for play both indoors and outdoors. The idea is that children can also add to the equipment and resources that are out and ask for anything that they need in addition. Other settings encourage children — the day before or on the day — to be part of the setting out of toys and equipment. This is seen as part of the learning for children.

Key term

Continuous provision: resources, toys and equipment that are put out for children to play with throughout the session

Indoor Continuous Planning Sheet – 3–4 years

	Monday	Tuesday	Wednesday	Thursday	Friday
Small World Play					
Role Play 1					
Role Play 2					
Board Games and jigsaws					
Sensory materials					
Mark making area					
Water					
Dough					
Sand					
Construction					
Exploration and investigation					
Creative area					
ICT					
Other					

This is an example of a continual provision sheet from a setting working with 2–3-year-olds. They have chosen to base the provision on patterns of play that their child regularly shows

Best practice checklist: Points to consider when planning adult-directed activities

✓ Is the adult-directed activity based on children's observed or expressed interests?

✓ How will the activity be engaging for the child?

✓ Is the activity developmentally appropriate for this child, regardless of their actual age?

✓ How does the activity link to the EYFS?

✓ What skills and knowledge will children gain from the adult-directed activity and why could these not be developed during child-initiated activity?

Planning for adult-directed activity

Adult-directed activities with children are a specific legal requirement as research shows that sustained quality interaction between adults and children can support children's cognitive and language development. Planning for adult-directed activities needs to be done sensitively and activities should not only be developmentally appropriate, but also interesting for the child or children. It is therefore good practice to base some adult-directed activities on the observed interests of children. For example, a child who has used the home corner to play shop may enjoy working with an adult to create a shop.

Be able to promote children's learning and development according to the requirements of the relevant early years framework

Although observation and planning are important, there are other ways in which practitioners must work to implement the EYFS. For this learning outcome, you will need to know how to promote children's learning within the EYFS and also be able to show that you can prepare, set out and support activities for children.

Promote children's learning within the EYFS

There are many ways in which the EYFS requires us to work in order to promote children's learning. The spider diagram below outlines some of these.

Organisation and management

in order to implement the EYFS, settings must have good systems in place in a range of areas. Staff in settings need to think about their overall routine and consider whether it provides opportunities for extended play for children. In addition, settings have to put into place an effective key person system, not only to comply with legal requirements, but also to ensure that someone is taking responsibility for the learning and development of each child. It is also important to consider how they will use spaces within the setting as there is a requirement to provide both indoor and outdoor play. Staff will have to work out how to create the observation and planning system so that children's interests and needs are individually met. For some settings, the organisation aspects of the EYFS have meant a series of changes and possible tweaks from their former practice, while other settings have needed to overhaul their approach completely.

Balance of child-initiated and adult-led play and activity

A specific legal requirement in the statutory framework is that providers must ensure there is a balance of adult-led and child-initiated activities. Adult-led activities mean those in which the adult steers the direction of the activity (for example, the adult asks a pair of children if they would like to play a game or organises an outing for the group). Child-initiated activities are those freely chosen by children and where they are able to play in their own way (for example, collecting some different types of tubing and dropping various objects down them).

No exact percentage of the time for child-initiated or adult-led activities is given, but settings do need to be aware of the balance they offer. Interestingly, many settings forget that time taken for registration, lining up, snack time or lunch time is actually adult-led activity unless systems are introduced to allow children to do these things when they wish, such as helping themselves to a snack, finding their name card and putting it in a box.

In addition, settings are required to make sure that adult-initiated and child-initiated play and activity is happening both in and out of doors. Traditionally, some settings have seen the outdoors as an area uniquely for child-initiated play.

Following children's interests and stage of development

We have seen that planning has to be based on children's interests and stage of development. This means that both adult-led and child-initiated opportunities have to be carefully thought through, especially when settings have mixed age groups or where children have been in the setting for a long period (if we are not careful the children may already have explored the opportunities on offer). It is therefore important to

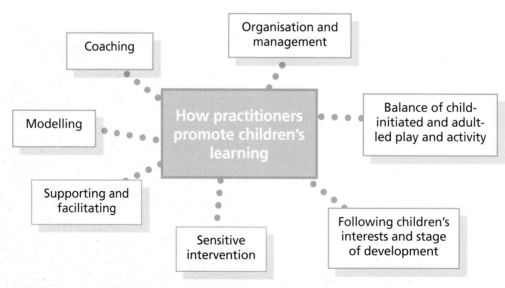

Some of the ways in which we can help to promote children's learning

think carefully about the opportunities that are provided for children and check that they are engaging.

Sensitive intervention

Child-initiated play does not mean that adults cannot become involved. Sensitive intervention can enhance a play opportunity for a child and thus become a deeper learning opportunity. There are no hard and fast rules as to when to intervene (aside from obvious issues relating to health, safety and anti-social behaviour) but there are some points to consider:

- How will you intervene without disrupting or changing the focus of the play?
- Does the child, or children, wish for you to become involved?
- How will you read the signals that children would prefer you not to be involved?
- How will your presence enhance the play opportunity?

Sensitive intervention should mean that children gain something which enhances their play and activity and that adults do not take 'ownership' of their play. This is something we will be considering further on page 242 of this unit in learning outcome 5.

Supporting and facilitating

Where children have good relationships with us, they should feel able to come to us for support. An example of this might be two children who are trying to build a den, but the fabric keeps slipping and they look to the adult for help. We should also be able to facilitate their play by working out what resources or help they need. With babies and toddlers, facilitating their play is quite a skill, as we have to work out what they would like us to do.

Facilitating children's play means finding ways to help them achieve their purpose

Modelling

It is easy to forget when working with children that modelling is an effective way to help children learn. Many children will watch what an adult does and then try to repeat the action, skill or words. This is a powerful method of helping toddlers to try out new experiences or to learn a new skill. Modelling is very useful to help children become interested in activities that they may not have noticed or explored before. This technique links to the social learning model that we looked at earlier (see Unit CYP3.1).

Coaching

Children can often do more than they think they can when given the support and encouragement of an adult. This means that one of the ways in which we might work with children is to act as a coach. Coaching is different to teaching. It is about helping children to feel confident enough to try something or to develop a little further. Adults have to be very sensitive when coaching as children must not feel that they are under pressure to achieve or that the adult is expecting them to do something that is out of their current ability range. Coaching as a way of working with children has links to Lev Vygotsky's theory of proximal development which we looked at earlier (see Unit CYP3.1).

Prepare, set out and support activities and experiences

As we saw earlier in the chapter, there are six areas of learning — each subdivided into several aspects of learning. For this assessment criterion, you will need to show that you can provide activities that encourage the learning and development with the children that you work with in each of these areas of learning. In order to do this you need to understand what type of activities

and resources are required for each child's stage of development. If you are working with the EYFS, you should refer to the Practice Guidance, which has ideas for ways of working with children, and will also help you to consider which stage the children have reached.

Below are some ideas of the types of areas and activities that many EYFS settings will provide for different ages of children.

Preparing and setting out the activities

Once you have selected an activity based on observations of a child or children, you will need to prepare and set it out. Ideally, children should be involved in this some of the time as this can enhance their learning. Most activities that engage children are often simple to set out and so, if your activity is time-consuming, do consider whether it is overly complex. Ironically, if it is too complicated it is likely to close down learning possibilities for children. Experienced practitioners have found time and time again that a couple of large cardboard boxes placed for children to discover result in more play, language and learning than a complex cooking activity.

Table 8: Types of areas and activities for children of different ages

Area of learning	Opportunities	Support/equipment and resources
Personal, Social and Emotional Development	Times for children of all ages to be involved with self-care Opportunities for children to play alongside and with each other Plenty of time for child-initiated play so that children can make choices and develop self-esteem Celebrations to help children learn about others e.g. birthdays, religious festivals	Environments in and out of doors where children can help themselves to toys and resources Adults who work sensitively to praise and acknowledge children's efforts and who help them to socialise with others
Communication, Language and Literacy	Plenty of one-to-one and small group interactions Time for children to share books with adults Opportunities to hear songs and rhymes — finger play for babies Opportunities to use tools including scissors. For babies and toddlers this might include toys that encourage fine motor movements e.g. rattles, pop-up toys	Attractive books A range of mark-making tools Adults who draw children's attention to the features of objects in the environment Adults who model listening skills and who acknowledge children's vocalisations and speech Adults who model reading Adults who model writing, painting and drawing

continued

Area of learning	Opportunities	Support/equipment and resources
Problem Solving, Reasoning and Numeracy	Opportunities to play with objects and group them Chances to measure and scoop materials e.g. sand, water Opportunities to be involved in problem solving e.g. how many spoonfuls do you need? Opportunities to sing counting songs	Jigsaw puzzles Construction toys Post-it toys Measuring jugs, tape measures, calculators, scales Adults who count objects with children Adults who draw children's attention to mathematical language e.g. saying 'all gone' to a baby when no more food is left
Knowledge and Understanding of the World	Opportunities to sort through and discover new toys and objects Opportunities to do be creative and make things of their own design Chances for children to play with or use appropriate gadgets e.g. digital camera Time to talk with adults about things that they have enjoyed or events in their family Opportunities for children to go on local outings and to talk about what they have seen Opportunities for children to come together and feel that they belong	Treasure basket play (babies) Heuristic play (toddlers) Collections of items Junk modelling, collage and art materials Resources that light up, make sounds Programmable toys Adults who provide rich resources for children to look at and explore Adults who facilitate children's interest in making things of their own design Adults who draw children's attention to the passing of time or what is happening outdoors
Physical Development	Opportunities for children to be mobile e.g. crawling, running, jumping Time for children to play in and outdoors with a range of equipment e.g. baby swing, wheeled toys, rocking horse Chances for children to use a variety of tools appropriate to their age e.g. spoon for a baby, scissors, grater, hole puncher	Climbing frame Balls, hoops, wheeled toys, see-saw, swing, balancing blocks Scissors, staplers, tweezers, paintbrushes, construction toys Adults who encourage children's physical movements (fine and large) Adults who draw attention to their bodily needs e.g. you might need the toilet, you look hot/cold etc.
Creative Development	Opportunities for children to touch, feel and explore a range of resource including traditional art materials Opportunities for children to hear stories Opportunities for children to hear, move and make music	Paint, clay, markers, glue, collage materials, dough, sand and water Musical instruments — and for babies, toys that make sounds e.g. rattles, shakers CDs and tapes, CD players Role play props e.g. kitchen equipment, items for dressing up Adults who encourage children to enjoy experiences rather than focus on end product Adults who model painting, drawing and other expressive arts

Case study: What went wrong?

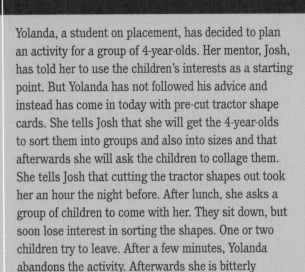

Yolanda, a student on placement, has decided to plan an activity for a group of 4-year-olds. Her mentor, Josh, has told her to use the children's interests as a starting point. But Yolanda has not followed his advice and instead has come in today with pre-cut tractor shape cards. She tells Josh that she will get the 4-year-olds to sort them into groups and also into sizes and that afterwards she will ask the children to collage them. She tells Josh that cutting the tractor shapes out took her an hour the night before. After lunch, she asks a group of children to come with her. They sit down, but soon lose interest in sorting the shapes. One or two children try to leave. After a few minutes, Yolanda abandons the activity. Afterwards she is bitterly disappointed as she feels she had put a lot of time into preparing the activity. Josh tells her that this is part of the learning curve of being a student. He points out a pair of children who are rolling toy cars down a slope

that they have made. He asks Yolanda to think about what they are learning and what extra resources would enhance their activity. The next day, Yolanda looks in the setting for a range of materials and resources including card, plastic sheets and guttering. She asks the children who were playing yesterday if they would like to make a slope for cars to race down. The children choose the cars and talk about how they could use the materials to make a slope. They ask Yolanda for some sticky tape. The children are totally engaged and Yolanda is impressed by the language that comes out of the activity and the concepts that the children have explored.

1. Why was the first activity not a success?

2. Explain how the second activity linked to areas of learning within the EYFS.

3. Identify three other types of activities that are simple to set up but can engage children.

Be able to engage with children in activities and experiences that support their learning and development

We can easily set out and plan activities but we know that children's learning can be greatly enhanced by sensitive adult involvement. This learning outcome looks at ways in which we can work alongside children and how, through our interactions, we can extend children's learning. See also Unit EYMP5 page 291 as this learning outcome has close links with it.

Engaging with children

Engaging with children is about finding ways to show that we are interested in their play and activity. It means going on a play or learning journey with them. This often means joining children rather than taking on a supervising

role and showing genuine interest in their 'discoveries' or what they are doing. As we saw earlier in this chapter, intervening sensitively is quite a skill and it will depend on what children are doing and their developmental needs. A toddler might, for example, want to 'feed' us play food and we might engage by taking the offering and showing enthusiasm using our facial expression and voice tone. For a group of children who are excited because we have put the sand on the tarpaulin on the floor, we may sit with them and listen as they pretend that they are on the beach. Engaging with children may also result in us

Reflect

Think about an activity when you engaged with children rather than supervised them.

How did this enhance children's concentration and learning?

What did you learn from the activity?

learning alongside them. The toddler may for example choose objects to 'feed' us that we would not necessarily consider, while the children 'on the beach' may show us how to make sand prints with their hands.

Functional Skills

English: Writing

Writing a reflection is good practice for writing for a different purpose.

Engaging with a child to support sustained shared thinking

Sustained shared thinking could be thought of as an extended conversation with children that helps them to develop their ideas. While chatting to children can promote their development and so is good in many respects, using this style alone will not necessarily help children to develop the skills of problem solving and reasoning. This is because a 'chat-style' conversation with a child might be short-lived or other unrelated topics of conversation may crop up. Sustained shared thinking helps children to reach conclusions and explore concepts at a deeper level. During this period, children are also processing information more effectively and often make connections with things that they have already learnt. This 'joining up' of ideas and concepts is extremely valuable.

Key term

Sustained shared thinking: ways in which children are encouraged by adults to use language to explore a topic, object or concept

In order for sustained shared thinking to take place, children have to be extremely interested in an activity or something that has occurred. Although we can plan some activities that might enable this type of conversation to take place, we also have to be ready to follow up on things that children are finding fascinating or interesting. Recognising the potential for sustained shared thinking is therefore essential. We also have to be ready to spend sufficient time with a child or group of children as the following case study shows.

Case study: Leaking boots

Jo is a childminder. On a Wednesday she looks after Curran aged 4 and his older brother who is at school. Today it is raining heavily and Jo makes a comment that when they pick up Curran's brother from school her feet might get wet. Curran stops playing and asks why. Jo says that her Wellington boots have started to leak. Curran tells her that she can wear his old ones as he now has a new pair. Jo says that she is not sure that they would fit her feet so Curran goes off and finds them. He comes back and puts one against her foot. He shakes his head and agrees that they would be too small. Curran then asks if he could look at her boots to see if he can find why they leak. He inspects them and declares that he cannot see any holes. Jo tells him that water can sometimes leak through very small gaps. She takes him into the kitchen and fills a washing-up bowl with water. She asks Curran if he would like to work out where the hole in the boot is where the water is coming in. The problem of how to fix the leaking Wellington becomes the major focus of their afternoon together. They try out a range of different ideas before going to the school to collect Curran's brother.

1. Why is this an example of sustained shared thinking?
2. What skills may Curran have learnt?
3. Why is it important for Jo to follow up Curran's interest?

Using language to support and extend children's learning during activities

We have seen that engaging with children and taking opportunities to promote shared sustained thinking is important, but a major way in which we do this is through the language that we use with children.

Mathematical language

If children are to understand many mathematical concepts and extend their thinking, the adults working with them must take opportunities to use mathematical language with them. This does not mean sitting children down and giving them a lecture, but instead using the words accurately in context. This draws children's attention to what they are seeing and can help them find words to express what they are thinking. Below are some examples of words and phrases that are helpful for adults to use with children or encourage children to use.

Size, shape and measure					
SHORTER THAN	SHORTEST	THE DIFFERENCE	THE SAME AS	LONGER THAN	LONGEST
BIGGEST	SMALLEST	THE FURTHEST	THE NEAREST	PATTERN	WIDE
NARROW	SPACE	GAP	DISTANCE	IN FRONT OF	BEHIND
NEXT TO	ABOVE	BELOW	INSIDE	OUTSIDE	NAMES RELATING TO SHAPES

Calculating						
MORE THAN	LESS THAN	TAKE AWAY	SUBTRACT	THE SAME AS	EQUALS NOTHING LEFT	ZERO
MOST	ADD	MORE	ADD ON	ALTOGETHER	FEWER	LEAST
THE DIFFERENCE BETWEEN	INCREASE	DECREASE				

Language of time									
BEFORE	AFTER	EARLIER	LATER	NOW	MORNING	AFTERNOON	YESTERDAY	TODAY	
TOMORROW	O'CLOCK	HOUR	MINUTE	SECOND	HALF AN HOUR	DAY	WEEK	MONTH	
CALENDAR	DIARY								

Open questions

Open questions have many uses when working with children. They are one of the ways that we can open up discussion and help children to communicate and think. Questions that have some speculation in them such as 'I wonder why...' are great starting points and also convey to children that we are not expecting a 'perfect' answer. They can be starting points for children to investigate or solve problems without support.

Open questions need to be used sensitively as they can make children feel inadequate if they do not have an immediate answer. When used well they can help children's curiosity, but if used with the wrong tone they can do the opposite. 'What are you doing?' could make some children anxious! This means that open questions usually work best when we are already involved with children's activities. Suggestions for ways to use questions are given in more detail in Unit EYMP 5.

Modelling language that is accurate and grammatically correct

Children can only repeat what they have heard and ideally when working with children we must do our best to speak accurately and also as grammatically correctly as we are able. Children, for example, who have never heard that 'water' has a 't' in it and instead hear it as 'war-a' will find it hard later on to spell. Most regions of the UK have their own 'dialect' and while it is important for their cultural identity that children learn the language for their region, it is important too that they can hear English in a more standardised form, which is used when writing.

Extending children's vocabulary

Most of us know far more vocabulary or words than we actually use in our daily lives as we all develop patterns

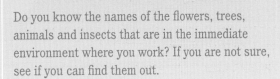

Reflect

Think about the dialect of your region. Do you recognise either of these?

Ain't it lovely? ⟶ Isn't it lovely?

I done it ⟶ I have done it *or* I did it

Over to you

Do you know the names of the flowers, trees, animals and insects that are in the immediate environment where you work? If you are not sure, see if you can find them out.

Functional Skills

ICT: Finding and selecting information

You could use the Internet to search for the names of the flowers, trees, animals and insects in your environment. Try using a variety of search engines to enhance your results.

or habits of using words. As with speech, children can only repeat and use what they have heard. This means that sometimes we must try to use the vocabulary that we know rather than constantly using simplifications. A good example of this is 'Put your coats on.' While we may know many specific words for coats, children may not. Asking children instead to put on their 'jackets' or commenting to a child about his new 'anorak' will mean that children will learn new words. This is essential as each word often has a slightly different meaning or provides a way of labelling an object with more detail. The more detailed vocabulary children develop, the easier it is for them to remember and talk about what they have been doing. Later, as children learn to read, having a wide vocabulary means that they not only read out words on the page, but also understand their meaning.

How many of these flowers could you name and help this child to learn?

Be able to review own practice in supporting the learning and development of children in their early years

In this unit, we have covered many of the aspects that you will need to support the learning and development of the children that you work with. In the final learning outcome, we consider what this means specifically in terms of the way that you work with children. You will need to show that you are able to reflect on your own practice and also demonstrate effective practice. This learning outcome also links to Unit SC3 Engage in personal development.

Reflect on own practice

A good starting point when reflecting on our own practice is to go back to the early years framework that we are using and consider whether we are delivering its aims and principles. Below is a series of questions that may help you to consider how well you know and understand the framework that you are using.

Reflect

Understanding the framework

What are the main purposes of this framework?

How do you measure children's progress in your setting against the framework?

How do your observations and plans link to the framework?

Are there any areas of learning that you not covering sufficiently?

Best practice checklist: Reflecting on your own practice

✓ Do you have individual plans for children based on observations?

✓ How do these plans translate into practice?

✓ How do you know that activities that you have planned for children will be of interest to them?

✓ How do you monitor the level of engagement that children show in adult-led activities?

✓ How do you ensure that children have rich opportunities for their child-initiated play?

✓ How do you engage with children?

✓ How long are your average interactions with children?

Once you have considered whether you really understand and are using the framework, then it is worth asking a colleague or someone that you feel comfortable with to give you some feedback about the way in which you work with children. You might ask them to observe or even film you during a particular activity. This may seem uncomfortable, but is likely to be the most effective way to find out whether you are putting into practice the principles that we have looked at in this chapter. It also gives you a 'baseline' so that in a few weeks time, you could then repeat a similar activity to see if your work with children has improved. You should look at your practice during child-initiated activity as well as adult-led activity as this often requires us to work in slightly different ways.

Once you have watched yourself or gained feedback from a colleague, you should then consider making an action plan using ways that were considered in Unit SC3.

Demonstrate how to use reflection to make changes in your own practice

For this assessment criterion, you will need to find ways of showing that you can reflect on your practice and then make appropriate changes. This should be a continuous process. A good starting point is to become aware of your current practice and consider how effective it is. You may wish to use the 'Best practice checklist' as a starting point for this.

Making changes

Once you have considered areas of your practice, you will then need to consider making changes. Some changes may require consultation with colleagues and so may require a little more time to implement, for example changing the system of planning. It is also useful to allow enough time for changes to 'bed down' before evaluating their effectiveness. A new role play area may at first be very popular with children because it is something new, but after a while may not be any more effective than the previous one. In the same way, staff may at first find a new planning or observation system difficult to use, but after a while may come to prefer it!

Getting ready for assessment

Ask a colleague to film you working alongside a child or group of children. Use this film clip to write an evaluation of your practice. Your evaluation should cover the following points:

- Your effectiveness in engaging with the child or children
- How effectively you supported their learning and developed their language
- Ways in which you could improve your practice with these children.

Functional Skills

English: Writing

By answering these questions in the form of a reflective report you could practise writing for a different purpose. You could organise your work into paragraphs based on the questions above. Take care with your spelling, punctuation and grammar.

Check your knowledge

1. Why is it important to read and understand the requirements of the EYFS?

2. Outline the six areas of learning in the EYFS.

3. Give examples of how you provide for Knowledge and Understanding of the World with the children who you work with.

4. Why is it important to use the outdoors as well as the indoors?

5. Explain what is meant by the term 'Early Learning Goal'.

6. Describe the importance of using the EYFS when planning activities.

7. Give three potential sources of information when planning for children.

8. Why is it important to provide opportunities for both adult-directed and child-initiated play?

9. Explain the importance of the adult using a 'modelling' style of working alongside children.

10. Describe how adults can support children's learning by using accurate language.

My Story

Working in the baby room

I have been working in the baby room for five years. Not everyone in my nursery likes working with babies, but I love it. I am key person to five babies. Two are full time at the nursery, the others come in on a part-time basis. We take babies from the age of 3 months, although most start with us at 6 months. It is important to be confident as babies seem to know if you are unsure. It also helps parents to leave their babies when they feel that the person who is going to look after them is relaxed and calm. I think that the most important thing in the baby room is to keep busy as otherwise it can be hard to keep talking to the babies. We take the babies for a walk a couple of times a day and we usually pop into the supermarket to buy the snacks for the rest of the nursery. You can see the babies looking around when we are in there and pointing at things. We give the older babies things to hold as well so that they can be involved with the shopping. The nice thing about working in the baby room is that you get to see 'your' babies develop and even when they leave your room, you still have a special bond with them when you see them around in the nursery.

Video Corner

> ### ▶ Clip 5: Outdoor play

Play this video clip on your CD-ROM and then answer the questions below.

Look at the way in which the baby can enjoy the treasure basket and ball out in the garden:

1. **Why is it important for young children to spend time outdoors?**

2. **What is of interest to these babies and young children?**

3. **Identify the role that the adult plays in this clip.**

Ask The Expert ...

Q How often should treasure baskets be put out?

A Treasure baskets can be put out every day, as they are a good source of stimulation for babies. It is important though that objects are changed so that babies have new items to explore, as like older children and adults they can become bored.

Q We have been told to take the babies and toddlers outdoors each day.

A It is important to take babies and toddlers out each day as it provides them with opportunities for fresh air, sunlight and also sensory stimulation. Just as adults do, babies and toddlers benefit from a change of scene and there should be new things for them to look at and talk about. You can also take babies and toddlers on simple outings such as a walk to a local park as well as play outdoors. Note that if you are working in England, it is a requirement of the EYFS for activities to be planned outdoors as part of the curriculum.

Q At what age should babies walk?

A There is no precise age when it comes to babies' mobility although it is likely that most babies are walking by 18 months. Some will crawl first, others will take a different route and may bottom shuffle first or simply begin by pulling themselves up to standing.

EYMP3

Promote children's welfare & well-being in the early years

Working with children requires us to have a mixture of skills and knowledge as not only do we need to promote their development, but we must also keep children safe and healthy. This unit looks at the principles of promoting children's physical welfare and well-being, including their nutritional requirements.

Learning outcomes

By the end of this unit you will:

1. Understand the welfare requirements of the relevant early years framework

2. Be able to keep early years children safe in the work setting

3. Understand the importance of promoting positive health and well-being for early years children

4. Be able to support hygiene and prevention of cross-infection in the early years setting

5. Understand how to ensure children in their early years receive high-quality, balanced nutrition to meet their growth and development needs

6. Be able to provide physical care for children.

Understand the welfare requirements of the relevant early years framework

Keeping children healthy and safe is so important that over time the four UK home nations have regulated the care of children in settings. To complete this learning outcome you will need to show that you understand and can follow the welfare requirements and guidance that apply to your setting and that you know about the lines of reporting within your setting.

The welfare requirements and guidance

To ensure children's health, safety and well-being, every home nation has sets of standards or welfare requirements which settings must meet. The standards vary from country to country but they all exist in order to protect children who are being cared for by people other than their families. It is essential that you obtain a copy of the standards or welfare requirements that apply in the home nation in which you work. If you work outside England, you should also make sure that you are referring to the standards that apply to the type of setting in which you work, such as daycare, pre-school.

Over to you

Below is a section on the welfare requirements in England. If you are working outside England, you will probably find that while there are many similarities, there are also some key differences. Look at a copy of the welfare requirements in your home country: http://nationalstrategies. standards.dcsf.gov.uk/earlyyears

Welfare requirements in England

In England, since September 2008, the welfare requirements are now part of the Early Years Foundation Stage. They have also been standardised so that all settings comply with the same welfare requirements. You will find the welfare requirements in the Statutory Framework section of the EYFS pack. The welfare requirements are compulsory, and it is essential that you have read them as your setting has a legal duty to comply with them.

You have a legal duty to comply with the welfare requirements

Safeguarding and promoting children's welfare

This is a significant section within the welfare requirements and covers many of the day-to-day activities that you are likely to be involved in, for example food and drink, behaviour management, medicines. This means that you should spend some time going through the **specific legal requirements** and **Statutory Guidance** to ensure that your personal practice is complying.

Key terms

Specific legal requirement: Requirements that have to be complied with in the way stated

Statutory Guidance: Guidance that providers must consider when complying with the legal requirements

The diagram below shows the general legal requirements and also the areas of specific legal requirements and guidance for all the areas outlined above.

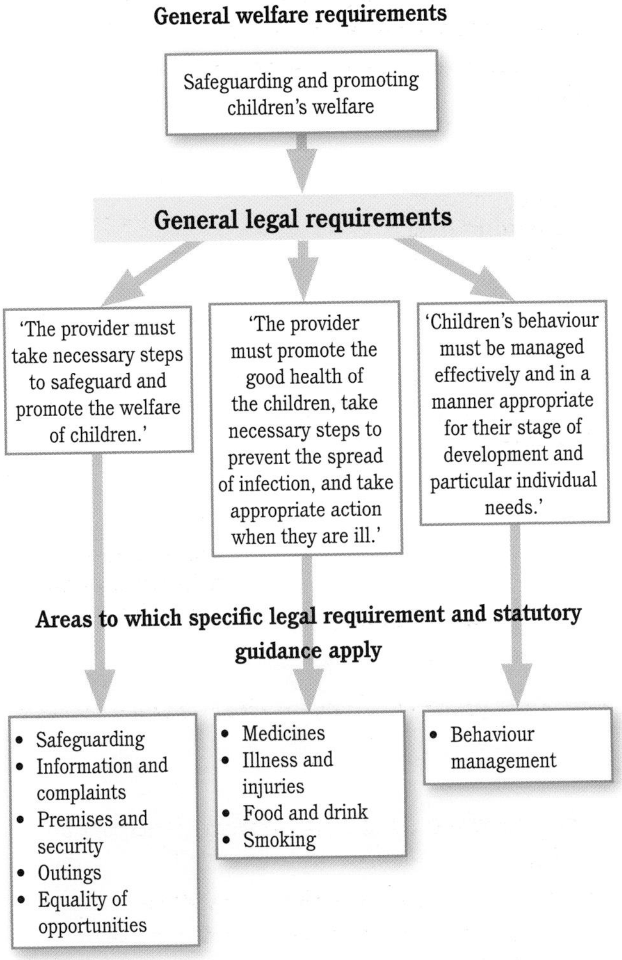

General welfare requirements

Safeguarding and promoting children's welfare

↓

General legal requirements

'The provider must take necessary steps to safeguard and promote the welfare of children.'

'The provider must promote the good health of the children, take necessary steps to prevent the spread of infection, and take appropriate action when they are ill.'

'Children's behaviour must be managed effectively and in a manner appropriate for their stage of development and particular individual needs.'

Areas to which specific legal requirement and statutory guidance apply

- Safeguarding
- Information and complaints
- Premises and security
- Outings
- Equality of opportunities

- Medicines
- Illness and injuries
- Food and drink
- Smoking

- Behaviour management

These legal requirements and guidance must be complied with

Suitable people

This section looks at the suitability of people to work with children and includes vetting procedures as well as issues such as training and fitness for work. It also covers child–staff ratios although the exact ratios are given in the document's appendix and are linked to children's ages and the qualification levels of the staff.

Suitable premises, environment and equipment

This section aims to ensure that children are looked after in premises and environments that are safe. As with the safeguarding and promoting children's welfare section, many of the legal requirements will apply to some of your day-to-day activities, for example checking that toys are safe and that the outdoor environment is clean.

Organisation

This is an important section within the EYFS as it relates not to the physical care aspects of working with children, but to the promotion of children's learning and development.

Documentation

This section looks at the documentation and records that all settings should have. You need to read this as you are likely to contribute to these records when, for example, parents tell you they are moving home.

Lines of reporting and responsibility within the work setting

If you work with children in a group setting, it is essential to understand the lines of reporting and responsibility. In some small settings, the lines of reporting might be quite obvious (for example, you may go straight to your supervisor or manager), but in large settings certain members of staff may be responsible for different areas, such as health and safety, and you should report any safety issues to that person.

If you are responsible for a particular area, for example, as the designated person who deals with any concerns regarding child protection, it is essential that you work with any new members of staff or volunteers so that they know when they should come to you. You may also have responsibility for training them.

Be able to keep early years children safe in the work setting

Keeping children safe is a major focus of our work and this learning outcome looks at some key aspects of this in our day-to-day work with children. For this learning outcome, you will need to show that you keep children safe in a range of situations and that you comply with the welfare requirements of your home nation.

Safe supervision of children while allowing them to explore risk and challenge

Supervision is a key way in which we can keep children safe. Everyone who is responsible for children must know where they are and what they are doing at all times. Sometimes, adults perceive that supervision is about preventing children from doing things, but it can also be viewed positively: often supervised children can be encouraged to do more interesting and challenging activities. For example, under supervision a 4-year-old might try to climb a tree or a toddler can be allowed to play with water. This is important as children need opportunities to explore and manage risk for themselves. We must avoid the temptation to constantly tell children that they must not do things, when in reality, providing we are there to keep an eye on them or to encourage them, they may be able to learn through having challenges. (See also Unit CYP3.4, where this is dealt with in more detail.)

Supervising children is also a real skill and we need to be flexible about how we manage this. There are times when we may try to be unobtrusive so that children can play 'in their own world', while at other times we may let children be aware that we are around so that they know we can support them. Ideally, much of our time should be spent in engaging with children, especially babies and toddlers, as this is not just a form of supervision, but is a key way in which we can support their learning.

Supporting children's safety when they move in and out of the setting

A potential area of weakness, when it comes to supervising children and keeping them safe, is when they are moving in and out of the setting or are on outings. It can be very easy in these moments for children to move out of sight or for an adult to make an assumption that another adult is with them. To avoid this happening, it is essential that we have clear systems in place for the following:

● receiving children into the setting

● ensuring their safety on departure

● during off-site visits.

Receiving children into the setting

At the start of a session, some settings can become very busy. Parents may be dropping their children off, sometimes with siblings in tow, and adults in the setting may be stretched because they are keeping an eye on

the children who are already there while at the same time greeting children and their parents/carers who are arriving. To avoid children wandering out, or staff not knowing which children have arrived, it is essential that clear systems are in place.

Register

All settings must register children on arrival. Some settings involve parents in this, but an up-to-date register is essential in case there is a fire and, most importantly, to ensure that staff—child ratios are correct.

Creating a system

There is no 'right' way to staff a group setting at the start of the session. Some settings stagger the arrival times of children; some have a dedicated dropping-off area in the building and others have a member of staff whose role is to oversee the entrance area and be aware of what is happening. The aim should be to create a system that helps children feel calm as they move from the care of their parents to their key person.

Remind parents not to keep doors open or let any children out other than their own

Entrances

It is important that we look for ways of reminding parents not to keep doors open or to let out any children other than their own. This in itself may not be adequate and so many settings also have doorbells or buzzers that indicate when a door has been left open or is being held open.

Reflect

Receiving children into the setting

Are there any times when the entrance door is in danger of being left open?

How would it feel if you were a child coming in?

How easy is it for parents to drop off their children?

How quickly are children registered and moved on to be with their key person?

How easy would it be to evacuate the premises if there was a fire?

Ensuring safety on departure

In the same way that we must create systems to help children on arrival, so we must think about children's safety as they leave the setting. In some ways this can be more difficult as often staff, children and parents are all tired and there are usually belongings to be collected. Many of the systems that are put in place for when children arrive should also be followed when children leave.

Register

It is important for settings to have a system in place to show which children have left the setting so that, if there is an emergency, time is not wasted looking for children who have gone.

Handing over children

It is essential that children are not released into the care of someone who is not their parent or carer unless prior notification, preferably written, has been given by the child's parent. (Note the welfare requirements with respect to this in the Safeguarding section in the EYFS) This is to prevent children from being taken by estranged parents who may not have access orders or others who may harm the child.

Case study: A helpful parent

It is 11 a.m., the boiler has broken and now it has begun to snow very heavily. It is agreed that the setting should close and already, without prompting, some parents have come to collect their children. One parent as she picks up her own child suggests that she should take her best friend's daughter as well. You know that they often do look after each other's children. The parent says her friend is attending an antenatal appointment and so will not have heard that the setting has closed. She points out that her friend will not mind and that it's silly for her to have to come out in the snow and risk falling when she is heavily pregnant.

1. Should you let this parent take the child?
2. How could you manage this situation to ensure the child's safety, but in a way that will support the child's mother?
3. How could this situation have been prevented?

Over to you

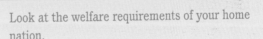

Look at the welfare requirements of your home nation.

Are there any specific requirements relating to the arrival and departure of children on the premises?

How does your setting comply with them?

Functional Skills

English: Speaking, listening and communicating, Reading and Writing

Working in small groups you could each get hold of a copy of your setting's arrival and departure policy. Together you could discuss the differences and similarities between the policies and maybe even create a new policy which combines elements from all of them.

During off-site visits

Off-site visits are when we take children off the premises, for example on outings. As outings can be hazardous, you may find that there are specific requirements relating to this in your home nation. In England, there are specific legal requirements and statutory guidance that should always be complied with.

Risk assessment

The starting point before any off-site visit or outing takes place is to carry out a full risk assessment. This has to be done carefully and thought needs to be given to the stage of development of the children that you are taking, the duration of the visit and potential hazards in the immediate environment (dogs, traffic, strangers, different road surfaces, for example). You should also think about how weather conditions might affect your visit. Doing a risk assessment will take a little time but is essential and, when done properly, it helps practitioners to focus on possible difficulties so that they are prepared. The risk assessment should, of course, detail the measures that will be put in place to minimise the risk to acceptable levels. (See also Unit CYP3.4 on health and safety.)

Parental permission

You must obtain written parental permission before taking any child off the premises. Some settings which make regular outings to the same place, such as twice a week to the local park, may ask parents to sign a consent form which applies to a period of time rather than to a specific day.

Staff ratios

The welfare requirements of your home nation often give minimum staff–child ratios with which you must comply when taking children off premises. These can change over time and so you must check the requirements carefully. It is worth noting that these are minimum figures and so you still need to consider whether more staff or adults are required. For adults who accompany children, such as volunteers or parents, you may also need to consider whether any vetting procedures are required. (In any case, volunteers should not be given sole responsibility of children.)

Emergency contact details

Contact details should be taken with you when children are off site. This is important so that parents can be contacted immediately in the event of an emergency.

Other essentials

Other essential items to take on an outing include a mobile phone, money, first aid kit and items relating to weather, such as sun hats or rainproof clothes.

Checking the inside and outside environments to ensure safety

As part of our duty to keep children safe, we are required to check that the environment the children are in is safe. This includes all indoor and outdoor areas and the equipment and materials used in them.

Most settings will carry out a full risk assessment on their environments at least annually, but will also carry out visual checks each day. In addition, new resources and equipment that comes into the setting should also be checked as this can create a hazard. Risk assessments must also be adapted to suit particular weather or other conditions, for example when it is icy or very hot.

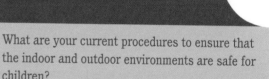

Reflect

What are your current procedures to ensure that the indoor and outdoor environments are safe for children?

How often are the environments checked?

Who needs to be notified if any hazards are identified?

How do you ensure that environments used by different ages of children are safe?

The importance of minimum requirements for space and staff ratios

As part of keeping children safe, we have to make sure that there is sufficient space for them and that there are sufficient adults to supervise and meet their needs. In general terms, the younger the children, the higher the requirement for both space and staffing. It is worth noting that while each home nation sets minimum standards for these, most settings will meet these easily.

Space

Accidents can easily occur when children do not have enough room to move safely. It is important therefore to ensure that rooms are arranged in ways to maximise space and that if there are any incidents where children have bumped into each other, thought is given as to how the layout could be modified to prevent further problems.

Staffing

Staff ratios need to be maintained at all times which means that staff who are included in the ratio are actively working with children. (Note that this is a requirement of the EYFS.) The ratios given by each of the home nations are based on the well-being needs of children, but also their safety. Babies and toddlers require significant levels of constant supervision.

Over to you

Each home nation sets its own standards regarding space and staff ratios. Find out about the minimum requirements that are set for the age group of children who you work with.

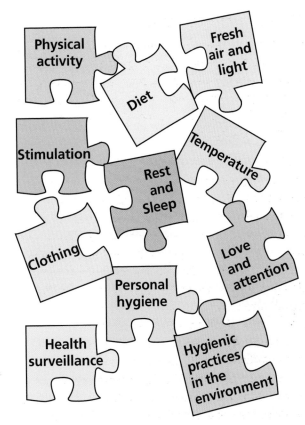

Many different components are required for good health

Understand the importance of promoting positive health and well-being for early years children

Promoting children's health

Health can be thought of a bit like a jigsaw puzzle as there are various components that need to come together in order to maintain good health and well-being both for children and adults. If one part is missing, health is affected. The diagram below shows some of the key components that need to be in place for children to be healthy.

Physical activity

Physical activity is essential for children of all ages as it helps to strengthen many parts of the body including the heart, lungs, bones and muscles. Physical activity is also linked to children's need for stimulation. In the past

Reflect

Physical activity

How much time do children in your setting spend engaged in physical activity?

Does it meet the British Heart Foundation's guide of 60 minutes a day of moderate intensity exercise?

How do you monitor that all children in your setting take exercise?

few years, there have been concerns that some children are not getting sufficient opportunities to exercise and experts predict that this may have both short-term and long-term consequences in terms of these children's health. (See also Unit CYPOP4.) This means that in the routines of our settings, we should think about how we can support children's activity both in and out of doors. This may include opportunities for walking and running about as well as through dance and physical play outdoors.

Fresh air and light

The need for fresh air is about children having opportunities to breathe more oxygenated air. Indoors this means ensuring that there is adequate ventilation – which also helps prevent the spread of airborne infections. Being outdoors in the fresh air seems to help children sleep and eat better. It also means that children have access to sunlight which can support their intake of vitamin D. It is important to take measures to protect children's skin from direct sunlight in the summer months, in order to prevent later skin cancer, but being out in the sunshine in the winter months is good for children. Light is also important to our health because it is linked to hormone regulation and this in turn can affect our sleeping patterns as well as our mood.

Diet

What children eat and drink has a pivotal effect on their health. We look at this as a particular aspect later in this unit, see learning outcome 5 on page 265.

Temperature

The body can control its temperature, but it can only do so to a certain point and the systems involved in this are still developing in children.

Room temperature: Ideally, indoor rooms should be 18–21°C to avoid children becoming too hot. In warm weather, this temperature may be difficult to maintain and so extra fluids must be offered and children may be encouraged to take off layers of clothing.

Room temperature and babies: Babies in particular are at risk if they become too hot, especially when sleeping. The foundation for Sudden Infant Death Syndrome recommends that rooms for babies when sleeping should be between 16 and 20°C.

Clothing

Children should wear clothing that is appropriate to the weather and the type of activities that they are engaged in. In hot sunny weather, clothing is needed to protect the skin from the sun, and in wet weather, clothing should keep children dry.

Stimulation

The healthy development of babies and children's brains requires that they must have opportunities for stimulation. This means providing play and activities as well as opportunities for sustained interaction and conversation with adults. We look at the importance of these in Units EYMP2 and EYMP5.

Rest and sleep

Sleep is an essential requirement for good health and development. Sleep appears to have many vital functions required to support a healthy immune system; it also aids the regulation of hormones and the processing of information by the brain. The effects of sleep deprivation on both children and adults are shown in Table 1. This is an area of continued research and so it is likely that further effects will be recognised in the future. Interestingly, for example, it was recently noted that there was a correlation between children who did not sleep sufficiently and obesity.

It is important that we help children who need a nap to do so

Table 1: The effects of insufficient sleep

Symptom	What it means
Behaviour and impulsivity	Children who are tired are likely to find it hard to control their behaviour. This is because lack of sleep impedes the function of an area of the brain that deals with our impulse control.
Emotional outbursts	Children who are sleep deprived are likely to have strong emotional outburst e.g. tantrums, tears and uncontrollable laughter. Lack of sleep seems to affect our ability to control our emotions.
Growth	Lack of sleep disrupts hormone regulation in the body. This includes growth and so growth patterns are likely to be disrupted.
Overweight	It has recently been found that children who do not sleep sufficiently are more likely to gain weight. This is thought to be linked to hormones connected with appetite and metabolism. Both adults and children generally crave calorie-rich foods when they are tired.
Concentration and hyperactivity	Children who do not sleep sufficiently are likely to show poor concentration and may show hyperactive behaviours. They may find it hard to settle to any activity.
Memory and learning	The brain uses the time when it is asleep to process information and children who are not sleeping sufficiently are likely to find it harder to store, i.e. remember, information. As memory, concentration and learning are interconnected, children's cognitive development can be affected by lack of sleep.
Illness	Sleep is important in helping the body's immune system to fight off infection and also repair cells. Children who do not sleep enough are more likely to have colds and other infections.

How much sleep?

The amount of sleep that any individual child needs will vary, but many researchers suggest that most children aged 1–3 years will need somewhere between 12 and 14 hours, with children aged 3–5 years needing around 11–13 hours. Sleep does not have to be taken in 'one go' and so many children meet their sleep requirements by having a nap.

Helping children to sleep

It is important that we help children who need a nap to do so. A dedicated space is required that is comfortable and where visual distractions, noise and light are minimised. Children should also have their own bedding to ensure hygiene. (Note that you should also check the regulations and welfare requirements relating to sleep in your home nation.)

Timing of naps

The timing of naps is crucial if children are to sleep later at night. Ideally, children should have naps in the morning or early afternoon and then have opportunities for physical activity, preferably outdoors, after they have slept. Not allowing children to sleep when they clearly need to is a hot topic and a recent intervention by Ofsted would suggest that the right of children to sleep outweighs the wishes of parents who may have instructed settings to keep their children awake. This is because sleep deprivation is thought to be akin to physical abuse.

Sleep safety

Areas in which children are to sleep have to be properly checked to ensure there are no objects that may suffocate or be a choking hazard for children. Rooms should also be well ventilated and regular monitoring of sleeping children is essential.

Preventing cot death

Cot death is still a serious issue although recent guidelines have reduced dramatically the number of infant deaths in the United Kingdom. It is essential that the latest guidelines are followed as they do change in response to research. You can find out about the latest guidelines by visiting the website for the Foundation for the Study of Infant Deaths (see below).

Over to you

Visit the Foundation for the Study of Infant Deaths and download their latest leaflet. www.fsid.org.uk

Love and attention

Children's emotional well-being is linked to their health. Babies and children can become depressed if they are not given sufficient love and attention. This means that children must have a key person who can establish a genuine bond with them so that they feel loved and nurtured. (This is discussed in more detail in the next section on Promoting children's well-being.)

Health surveillance

To maintain children's health, it is important that they are monitored regularly by health professionals. Health professionals also recommend that children are vaccinated against childhood illnesses and other diseases that could be fatal or leave children with long-term health problems.

Personal hygiene

To prevent possible infection, children need to be kept clean and this aspect is covered later in this unit (see pages 272–74).

Hygienic practices in the environment

To avoid children picking up an infection, a level of hygiene is required both in the immediate environment and in food preparation. This aspect is covered in learning outcome 4 on pages 260–64.

Promoting children's well-being

All of the frameworks in the home nations stress the importance of providing strong emotional support for children, as it is now recognised that children's emotional well-being plays an integral part not only in their ability to learn but in their overall health. In terms of practice, this means settings have to provide support so that children's attachment needs can be met.

Meeting the attachment needs of children in their early years

Children cannot thrive if they are not settled. It is understood that a poor separation experience – in which children become very distressed – may also do them long-term harm. The theory of attachment is straightforward and covered in Unit CYP3.1 pages 70–71. Essentially, young children need to form a strong relationship with their parents for their emotional well-being; but when parents are not available, a substitute relationship of a similar quality needs to be provided.

This role has become known as the **key person** role. Giving children stability in this way is so important that, in England, the EYFS states that the provision of a key person is a specific legal requirement for all children from 0–5 years in childcare and education settings.

Key term

Key person: a person who has a special relationship with the child and their family and who acts as a surrogate attachment figure when the child is separated from parents and carers

Making the key person system work

For the key person system to work, and to prevent children from suffering separation anxiety, it is important that a system of settling in children is put into place before separation actually takes place. The aim of the settling-in process is to make sure the children are totally relaxed and happy in our company so that there are no tears when the time comes for their parents to leave. This means that parents should visit the setting, and the key person should gradually get to know and play with the child, so that a relationship is built up before parents leave them with us.

Where settling in is rushed, or parents are encouraged to leave abruptly, children are more likely to show separation anxiety behaviours. These include distress, crying and anger. Although these can subside after a few days, children who are still not settled in may show a different set of behaviours which are akin to depression, including withdrawal, apathy, or total compliance. Sadly, some staff in the past have misread these behaviours and made the assumption that because children are quiet and submissive, they are settled in – when in reality children are under significant stress.

The key person role in day-to-day practice

We have focused so far on settling in. It is important, however, to be aware that children have enduring attachment needs. This means that key persons need to spend time with their key child on a day-to-day basis. In childminding settings, this is straightforward, but in group care and education, thought must be given to how often children will be with their key person (for example, meeting and greeting, nappy changing times, activities).

Shared key persons

To avoid children becoming distressed if their key person is not available, or to accommodate shift patterns or changing circumstances, settings can organise for children to have 'back up' key persons. It is important however that this is not watered down so that, in group care, children in reality do not have anyone who is of particular significance to them.

Roles of key health professionals and sources of professional advice

Health professionals have an important role in keeping children healthy and in supporting their families. In addition, they can provide us with information and general advice to ensure that we meet children's general and individual needs. Table 2 shows the role of some of the key professionals you may work with or contact for advice. Note that you must always obtain a parent's permission before referring children to another service.

Sources of professional advice

As childcare professionals we may be able to give families general advice, but it is important that we recognise the extent and limitations of our role. This means that we should always refer children onto other services, with parental consent, if there are health issues or other related problems. The first port of call for most families is to arrange an appointment with their family doctor as he or she is then able to refer them to specialists. In addition, we may be able to signpost parents to specific health services within the local community. To gain information about local health services for families in your area, you should contact your local NHS trust. Their contact details can be found in phone directories, online or from a GP's practice.

Table 2: Health professionals and their roles

Health professional	Role
Audiologist	Audiologists measure children's hearing levels
Dentist	Dentists specialise in the prevention and treatment of dental decay
Dietician	Dieticians work to promote nutritional well-being, prevent food-related problems and treat disease
General Practitioner (GP)	Doctors who provide a spectrum of care for families and are often the first person that families will take children to if they have health problems
Health Visitor	Health Visitors work with GPs to support families with young children. They advise on health and child development
Optometrist	They examine children's eyes, prescribe and fit glasses
Orthoptist	Orthoptists assess and manage a range of eye problems, mainly those affecting the way the eyes move, such as squint (strabismus) and lazy eye
Paediatrician	Doctors based in hospitals who specialise in working with children who have health problems
School nurse	School nurses work with school-age children; they monitor health and advise schools and parents about health topics
Speech therapists	Work with children who have speech, language and communication difficulties or delay
Physiotherapists	Aim to increase movement and coordination when children have problems as a result of injury, illness or a medical condition
Psychologists	Psychologists work with children who have behavioural or learning difficulties

Be able to support hygiene and prevention of cross-infection in the early years setting

As part of keeping children healthy, we must also make sure that the environment they are in is clean and that steps are taken to avoid cross-infection. To achieve this learning outcome, you will need to show that you can keep your setting clean and hygienic and that you can prepare and store food hygienically.

Keeping equipment and each area of the setting clean and hygienic

In order to keep a hygienic environment for children to play,in, it is important to have a regular system for cleaning surfaces, furniture and equipment. It is always easier to keep environments clean if time is taken at the end of the sessions to tidy away properly. Table 3 shows some of the regular cleaning and hygiene routines that should take place in a setting.

Table 3: Cleaning and hygiene routines

Item	Why it needs to be cleaned	Method
Toys, resources and play equipment that are frequently handled or mouthed	Bacteria can be transferred	Sterilise items that are used by babies. Wipe other items down with disinfectant
Cuddly toys and dressing-up clothes	Can harbour dust mites as well as bacteria and viruses	Wash at 60°C
Water trays	Damp areas allow bacteria, viruses and fungi to multiply	Water must be changed daily and tray must be cleaned with disinfectant
Feeding equipment	Spoons, bowls, beakers and other items are put in the mouth and handled	Sterilise feeding items for babies. Put other items in dishwasher or wash with hot water and rinse
Tables	Children may put items that have been on the tables in their mouths	Wipe with a clean cloth. A mild disinfectant can be used for tables used for feeding
Worktops	Food may be prepared on these surfaces	Wipe with a clean cloth. Disinfect surfaces that are used for food preparation
Fridges, freezers and cupboards	Food is stored in these. Fridges need to be cleaned each week	Wipe with a clean cloth. A mild disinfectant can be used if necessary
Toilets, hand basins, sinks	Toilets, hand basins and sinks are places where there is likely to be bacteria. They are also places with water	Wipe with a clean cloth. Disinfect surfaces that are used for food preparation
Nappy changing areas	Faeces and urine will contain bacteria	Disinfect every time a nappy change takes place
Bins	Items such as food, used tissues and nappies will have bacteria on them	Empty bins frequently. Place nappies in sealed bags in separate bins. Wash bins every day
Floors	Children will put their hands on floors when sitting or lying down. Food may be dropped on the floor. Dirt from outdoors may come in on shoes	Clean floors each day. A disinfectant should be used

Table 3: Cleaning and hygiene routines (continued)

Item	Why it needs to be cleaned	Method
Outdoors		
Grass and surfaces	Dogs, foxes and cats may foul these areas	Check for animal droppings. Pick up with disposable gloves and put in bag. Wash area with hot water containing disinfectant
Water trays, containers which have filled with water	Stagnant water can attract insects as well as bacteria	Tip out water and wash with warm soapy water, then rinse
Play equipment	Play equipment can become dirty or may have bird droppings on it	Check and if necessary wash with warm soapy water and rinse

It is important to have a regular system for cleaning surfaces, furniture and equipment

Preventing cross-infection

Bacteria, viruses and fungi spores can easily travel from one human to another and also from one place to another. Preventing cross-infection is therefore about preventing the spread of bacteria and reducing opportunities for the germs to enter the body. A good starting point is to understand the three ways in which germs enter the body.

Inhalation

Some germs are airborne and we breathe them. To reduce opportunities for infection, it is important that we ventilate settings by opening windows slightly. This is particularly important in the winter months when the air in rooms is likely to be warm and damp — conditions which allow germs to multiply rapidly. It is also important that children are taught to cover their coughs and sneezes and then to wash their hands.

Ingestion

Some germs enter our bodies because we literally swallow them. We may eat food that has bacteria on it, children may put their fingers in their mouths and babies may mouth objects. To prevent ingestion of germs from occurring it is important that children have good hand washing routines (see below) and also that objects which children frequently touch or babies might mouth are disinfected.

Inoculation

Some germs are able to infect us because they enter through broken skin, such as cuts or sores. To prevent this from occurring we need to prevent accidents wherever possible and treat any cuts promptly.

Hand washing

Hand washing is a key way of preventing cross-infection in settings. Both children and adults must get into the routine of thorough hand washing. The following spider diagram shows when children and adults must always wash their hands. We must also make sure that children use warm water and soap unless anti-bacterial gel is being provided instead.

After going to the toilet

Before preparing food

Before snacks, drinks and meal

Hand washing

After disposing of tissues

After playing outdoors

After coughing or sneezing

Hand washing is a key way of preventing cross-infection in settings

Waste disposal

Used tissues, food, nappies and other types of waste will all contain germs. This means that children should not have access to bins and that waste must be disposed of correctly according to its type.

The eight stages of handwashing

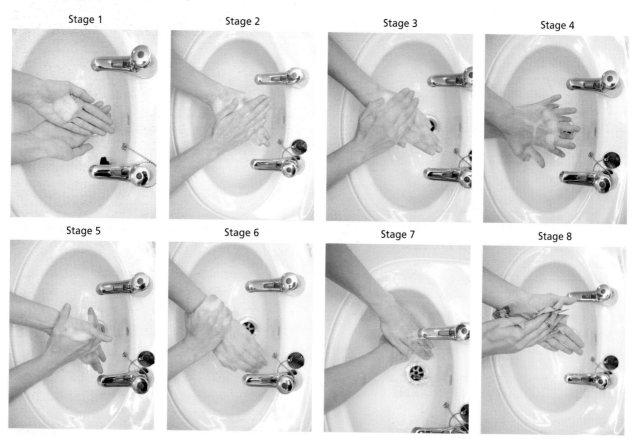

Stage 1 | Stage 2 | Stage 3 | Stage 4
Stage 5 | Stage 6 | Stage 7 | Stage 8

1) Wet your hands thoroughly under running water and apply liquid soap, 2) Rub your hands palm to palm, 3) Rub your right hand over the back of your left, change hands and repeat, 4) Rub fingers linked to your palms, 5) Rotate your right hand around your left thumb, change hands and repeat, 6) Rotate your right hand around your left wrist, change hands and repeat, 7) Rinse your hands thoroughly under running water, 8) Dry your hands thoroughly with paper towels

Managing children who are poorly

Most settings will have policies designed to prevent cross-infection when children are ill. These will outline the time period that children need to stay away in the event of them having some of the common childhood diseases. Policies need to reflect the latest medical advice, which can be found by contacting your local National Health Service trust. If a child becomes poorly while in the setting, it is important to keep them away from others to prevent cross-infection, while of course providing reassurance to the child and contacting the parents.

Reflect

Write a list of the measures that are taken in your setting to reduce cross-infection for the following:

- Changing of nappies/toileting
- Toys and resources
- Meal times
- Care of sick children

Safe preparation and storage of food, formula and breast milk

It is essential that food is prepared, stored and cooked hygienically as food poisoning can kill babies and young children. Each year there are many thousands of cases of food poisoning reported and far more go unreported. Food poisoning is considered such a problem that anyone who prepares food for public consumption is now required to have had training in food hygiene. If you are preparing snacks or meals for children, you should have had training in basic food hygiene.

Most food poisoning is caused by bacteria multiplying on food and then being eaten.

There are three principles involved in the prevention of food poisoning caused by bacteria:

1. Prevent the bacteria from coming into contact with food.

2. Prevent bacteria already present on food from multiplying and spreading to other items.

3. Elimination of bacteria on food.

Preventing the bacteria from coming into contact with food is an important first step. The kitchen area must be kept clean and anyone handling foods must have good personal hygiene. The first step that should be taken before touching any foods is to wash your hands with hot water and soap. You should also dry your hands carefully as bacteria thrive in warm and damp conditions.

Some raw products, such as meat, poultry and fish, are likely to contain bacteria. To prevent these bacteria from coming into contact with other foods, it is essential to use separate chopping boards and knives and also to wash your hands after touching them so that your hands are clean before you handle other products.

Best practice checklist: Preventing bacteria coming into contact with food

- ✓ Wash hands before touching foods and at the start of each part of the cooking process.
- ✓ Wrap and cover foods.
- ✓ Wash hands straightaway after touching raw meat, poultry and fish.
- ✓ Use separate (preferably colour-coded) chopping boards, knives and dishes for raw meat, poultry and fish.
- ✓ Keep raw foods away from cooked foods and store them separately.
- ✓ Regularly wipe and disinfect work surfaces, chopping boards and utensils.
- ✓ Avoid handling foods where possible – use utensils instead.
- ✓ Keep cuts covered – blue plasters should be used or disposable gloves.
- ✓ Tie back hair and keep nails short.
- ✓ Wear aprons and wash these in a hot wash.
- ✓ Change and wash tea towels and dishcloths frequently.

Functional Skills

ICT: Developing, presenting and communicating information

You could use this checklist of information to produce a health and safety poster for the kitchens all about good hygiene. Your poster could be produced in Word or Publisher. Maybe once you have completed it you could share it with your supervisor.

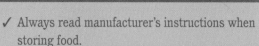

Best practice checklist: Correct storage of food

✓ Always read manufacturer's instructions when storing food.

✓ Read product labels to check how long opened jars can be used e.g. ketchup.

✓ Do not eat foods that are past their use by date.

✓ Once a tin is opened, store the contents in a covered container in the fridge.

✓ Do not refreeze foods once they have thawed.

✓ Keep fridges at 0–5°C.

✓ Keep freezers at minus18 to minus 23°C.

Preventing bacteria already present on food from multiplying is achieved by storing foods safely. This does not completely stop bacteria and mould from multiplying, but can slow it down. Bacteria and mould grow quickly at warm temperatures or in warm areas such as those warmed by the sun. The 'danger' zone is between 5 and 63°C as between these temperatures bacteria and mould can spread rapidly.

Storing baby milk

At the time of writing the focus of storing baby milk is on preventing food poisoning. This is because food poisoning in babies can be so serious.

Storing formula milk

The latest recommendation from the Department of Health is that formula milk should be made fresh rather than being made up in advance and stored. If this is not possible, for example because of an outing, ready to use liquid formula is recommended although this is quite expensive. If it is not possible to use this, it is better for boiled water (at least 70°C in temperature) to be put into

a hot thermos and then the formula to be made up when it is required.

Storing breast milk

Some mothers who are breast-feeding their babies will bring in expressed milk either frozen or fresh to be used in bottles. The Department of Health recommends the following guidelines for storage:

● up to 5 days in the main part of a fridge, at 4°C or lower

● up to 2 weeks in the freezer compartment of a fridge

● up to 6 months in a domestic freezer, at minus 18°C or lower.

Breast milk that has been frozen can be defrosted in the fridge. It can then be served straight from the fridge rather than warmed.

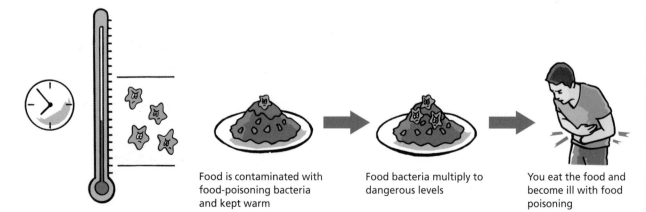

Food is contaminated with food-poisoning bacteria and kept warm

Food bacteria multiply to dangerous levels

You eat the food and become ill with food poisoning

How food is contaminated with food-poisoning bacteria

Understand how to ensure children in their early years receive high-quality, balanced nutrition to meet their growth and development needs

Food is an important topic at the moment as the UK is facing an increase in the numbers of children who are overweight or obese. As most early years settings serve snacks or meals, this means that we have to understand and provide healthy and nutritionally appropriate foods for the children that we work with. This learning outcome looks at factors to consider when providing food and drinks to young children, and links with learning outcome 6 in Unit CYPOP2 on physical and nutritional needs (see Unit CYPOP2 page 347).

Planning balanced meals, snacks and drinks

Planning balanced meals, snacks and drinks needs careful consideration and, of course, must be done in consultation with parents. Following is an outline of the principles of providing food for children and details of menu planning for children aged 3–5 years. More information about meeting the nutritional requirements for children under 3 years can be found in Unit CYPOP2 pages 347–49.

Understanding the principles of nutrition

The term 'balanced' diet is often used in connection with healthy eating. A balanced diet is one in which there are sufficient nutrients in the right quantities for children and adults. The 'eatwell plate' pictured on page 268 shows the five categories of nutrients.

For a diet to be considered balanced, all meals, snacks and drinks taken throughout the day, when considered as a total 'package', must provide children with sufficient nutrients.

Unbalanced diets

Where diets are unbalanced, children may have health problems. For example, too little iron in the diet may make children tired while too much energy-rich food or over-consumption of calories in the diet, even if the foods given are healthy, will cause the body to convert the excess energy into fat stores. This leads to children becoming overweight. Table 4 on page 266 gives some indication of the daily calorie intakes needed for children. The spider diagram below shows some of the effects of a poor diet on children's development.

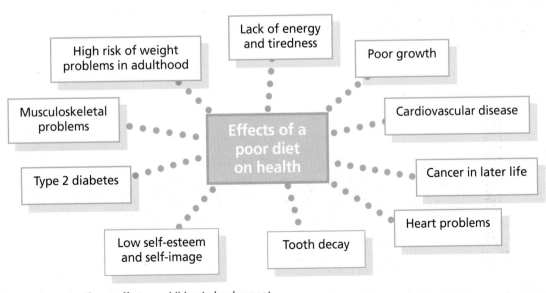

A poor diet can have significant effects on children's development

Factors to consider when planning a diet for children

There are many factors to consider when planning a balanced diet for children which contains sufficient nutrients and calories. It is important that adults who feed children have spent enough time reading food labels. This is not always easy as sometimes they are written in small print or percentages are given. You should ask yourself the following questions when buying food or preparing meals and snacks for children.

A traffic light food label

1. How much salt is in this product/meal?

What we call salt is a chemical called sodium chloride. Too much sodium is dangerous for both adults and children. Many commercially produced foods contain added salt, for example bread, baked beans. The maximum amount of salt/sodium that children should have each day depends on their age. On labels you should look out either for the salt or the sodium content.

- 1 to 3 years – 2g salt a day/0.8g sodium

- 4 to 6 years – 3g salt a day/1.2g sodium

2. How many calories will a portion contain?

Calories are a measure of the energy within food. The amount of calories that children need changes as they grow and will also depend on the amount of physical activity they take. The Table 4 shows the current calorie requirements of boys and girls at different ages. It assumes that children are physically active.

Foods vary in their calorific value. The physical portion size is not always a good guide as to how many calories there are in a meal: a plate of meat lasagne is much higher in calories than a plate of fish with rice. Foods that have high levels of fat in them will always be high in calories. It is important that children do not regularly exceed the recommended number of calories for their age as this will cause them to become overweight. Similarly, children who do not have sufficient calories in their diet will become underweight and may lack energy and also be prone to illness. Once you know how much a food contains in calories, you should then think about how this fits into the child's overall calorie intake. In general terms, the majority of children's calories should be taken at meal times; large quantities of high-calorie snacks and drinks should be avoided unless a child is underweight.

Table 4: Estimated average requirements for calorie intake

Age	Males		Females	
	(MJ)	(kcal)	(MJ)	(kcal)
0–3 mo	2.28	(545)	2.16	(515)
4–6 mo	2.89	(690)	2.69	(645)
7–9 mo	3.44	(825)	3.20	(765)
10–12 mo	3.85	(920)	3.61	(865)
1–3 yr	5.15	(1230)	4.86	(1165)
4–6 yr	7.16	(1715)	6.46	(1545)
7–10 yr	8.24	(1970)	7.28	(1740)
11–14 yr	9.27	(2220)	7.72	(1845)
15–18 yr	11.51	(2755)	8.83	(2110)
19–50 yr	10.60	(2550)	8.10	(1940)

Source: 1991 COMA Report on Dietary Reference Values (DRVs)

3. How much fat?

Fat is desirable as it is a source of energy for children, providing it is in nutritious foods such as full-fat yoghurts, milk and avocados. However, you should avoid foods with saturated fats wherever possible. Saturated fat is more likely to be found in commercially prepared foods such as pies or sausage rolls. This is one reason why home-cooked meals are considered to be better for children.

4. Is this food rich in nutrients?

Some foods are higher in nutrients than others. If a food is high in calories, it should ideally also be high in nutrients. Crisps, sweets and biscuits are not considered healthy foods for this reason because they are high in calories, but very low in nutrients other than fats.

5. How filling will this food be?

Children's stomachs have limited capacity. For very young children, it can be hard to make sure that they eat enough nutrients before they feel full. Some foods such as soup can quickly fill children up, but may not contain sufficient calories to be the main meal, while on the other hand, foods such as crisps may not fill children up but have taken up some of their calories.

Planning a balanced diet for children

Young children need to have a range of nutrients to satisfy the body's need for energy, growth and maintenance. When planning a balanced diet, it is important to look at children's intake across the day or ideally through the week. Children's intake of nutrients is likely to fall into three broad areas and it is important to consider all three when working out a menu for children.

Children's intake of nutrients is likely to fall into three broad areas

Drinks

The body needs fluids in order to prevent dehydration. This means that water must always be on offer for children throughout the day. In addition, we may provide other drinks for children, but it is important they are seen as part of the child's diet – drinks such as fruit juices, milk and smoothies all contain nutrients and calories.

Water

Children should learn to enjoy drinking water and should be served water at meals and at other times so that they become accustomed to it rather than to sugary drinks.

Milk

Milk is a healthy drink as it contains many nutrients that children need. It also contains calories and so must be monitored in terms of the overall calorie intake. A child who is underweight might be offered milk as part of a snack, but a child who is overweight should be offered water instead.

Fruit juices

Fruit juices are good for children, but must be given in moderation as the natural sugars in juice can cause dental decay. Juices are also calorific and, as with other drinks, must be included when considering children's overall calorie intake.

Smoothies

Smoothies are popular fruit drinks for children and can help children's overall fruit intake. However, they are high in calories and so should be included when calculating the children's intake. Like fruit juices, they also contain natural sugars which can cause dental decay.

Fruit drinks, squashes and fizzy drinks

These should not be part of children's daily diets as they are high in calories with minimum nutritional benefits. They also contain sugars which can cause dental decay. These type of drinks need to be seen as drinks for special occasions such as birthday parties.

Snacks

Young children's stomachs have limited capacity and so children may require snacks in order that they can take in sufficient nutrients. Like drinks, snacks should be seen as part of the overall food intake of the child and should be nutritious. The timing and quantity of snacks is crucial as children need to learn to eat well at meal times. Giving snacks too close to a meal can spoil children's appetites. Below are some examples of snacks that can be used with young children. Note however that where children are overweight, snacks should be chosen that are healthy, but not high in calories, for example slices of fruit and vegetables rather than a yoghurt.

Fresh fruit and vegetables

Slices of fruit and raw vegetables can make good snacks for children, for example carrot and celery sticks, slices of apples, pieces of orange.

Dried fruits

Dried fruits such as prunes, apricots and sultanas are nutrient rich and are liked by young children.

Savoury sandwiches

Savoury sandwiches can be used as snacks providing that quantities are small so as not to spoil children's appetite for their main meal (which is when the greatest proportion of calories should be taken).

Cheese and crackers

Cheese and crackers can be good for children in small quantities, although it is worth checking that the crackers are not high in fat and salt. Note that this is a high-calorie snack so should not be given to overweight children.

Popcorn

Plain popcorn is a good snack for children provided that no salt or sugar is added.

Yoghurt and fromage frais

Yoghurt and fromage frais are good snacks for children who are not overweight as they are nutritious. Choose yoghurts that are low fat and do not have added sugar.

Rice crackers and bread sticks

Children enjoy rice crackers and bread sticks and these are good snacks provided that the fat and salt level in them is minimal.

Meals

Children should have the majority of their calorie and nutrient intake at meal times. To help adults plan meals, the Food Standards Agency has produced the 'eatwell plate'. This can be useful when considering the composition of a healthy meal.

The eatwell plate can be useful when planning meals

It is important to plan meals carefully over a week to check that children will take in a range of different foods. It is, for example, currently recommended by the Food Standards Agency that children should have two portions of fish a week. Examples of menus and healthy meals for different ages of children can be found on the Internet, although it is always best to choose websites that are associated with the government or well-known voluntary organisations such as the British Heart Foundation.

Functional Skills

ICT: Finding and selecting in formation

Searching the Internet and researching healthy meals and menus will develop your ICT skills. Try to use a variety of search engines to broaden your results.

Food allergies or intolerances

For some children, it is essential to monitor their diet and the food that they eat has to be prepared and planned very carefully as they may have allergies, intolerances or medical conditions, such as coeliac disease or diabetes. You should take care to follow the parents' instructions relating to their child's allergies or intolerances; failure to do so could result in the child's health being endangered — possibly even in death.

Allergies

Contact with certain foods can be fatal for some children with allergies. This means that great care has to be taken and a system must be designed to prevent children from coming into contact with their allergen (for example nuts or dairy products). Where the allergy is severe, this may affect the food that can be prepared and eaten in the setting as some children can have a reaction just from being near other children who are eating a food containing an allergen.

Systems to prevent children from coming into contact with a known food allergen include photographs and names of the children in the kitchen, only key persons giving the child food and certain plates being used for particular children so as to provide a visual reminder. It is also essential that children are supervised when they are eating so that if an allergic reaction occurs emergency help can be called. Signs of an allergic reaction include swelling of lips or eyes, redness of the face, itching and difficulty in breathing. Children who have already had a severe reaction may be prescribed an EpiPen® and training is given to parents and the key person as to how and when to use it.

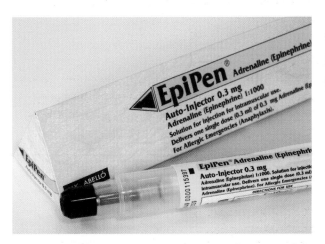

Children who have already had a severe reaction may be prescribed an EpiPen®

Intolerances

Food intolerances are not as severe as allergies, but can still be problematic for children. Food intolerances are generally identified by parents as they may notice that their child often has diarrhoea after having eaten certain foods. Because diarrhoea can have more than one cause, it is important that parents talk to their GP about suspected food intolerances.

Coeliac disease

This is a disease that is triggered by gluten which is found in wheat, barley and rye. Children with coeliac disease must therefore not be given anything that contains gluten. This means that some quite common foods, such as pasta, bread and toast, biscuits and cakes,

Children with coeliac disease must not be given anything that contains gluten

should not be given to children with coeliac disease — unless they are made with gluten-free products.

Diabetes

Diabetes is a condition where insufficient insulin or no insulin is being produced by the body, which means that it cannot properly regulate glucose. Diabetes in young children is a serious medical condition as they are likely to have Type 1 which requires daily testing of glucose levels in their blood and insulin injections. Children with Type 1 diabetes will have specific food requirements (meals and snacks to be taken at certain times) and you will need to follow a parent's instructions carefully.

Over to you

Find out more about supporting children with diabetes or coeliac disease by visiting Diabetes UK's website at www.diabetes.org.uk and/or the website of Coeliac UK at www.coeliac.org.uk (Helpline 0845 305 2060)

Dietary requirements of different cultural or religious groups

Food is linked to culture and religion and some families will have particular preferences or requirements that we must respect. As families can vary enormously in how strict they are about following any dietary restrictions or requirements, it is essential to find out directly from parents about what can be prepared and served for their children. Table 5 shows some of the common dietary requirements and restrictions.

Table 5: Some common dietary requirements

Food	Islam	Judaism	Sikhism	Hinduism (mainly vegetarian)	Rastafarianism (mainly vegetarian although take milk products)	Seventh-Day Adventist Church
Lamb	Halal	Kosher	Yes	Some	Some	Some
Pork	No	No	Rarely	Rarely	No	No
Beef	Halal	Kosher	No	No	Some	Some
Chicken	Halal	Kosher	Some	Some	Some	Some
Cheese	Some	Not with meat	Some	Some	Some	Most
Milk/yoghurt		Not with meat	Yes	Not with rennet	Some	Most
Eggs	Yes	No blood spots	Yes	Some	Yes	Most
Fish	Halal	With fins and scales	Some	With fins and scales	Yes	Some
Shellfish	Halal	No	Some	Some	No	No
Cocoa/tea/coffee	Yes	Yes	Yes	Yes	Some	No
Fast periods (for adults)	Ramadan	Yom Kippur	No	No	No	No

Vegetarians

Some families are vegetarian either because this fits with their religious beliefs or their own values. Vegetarians do not eat meat, fish, game or poultry although they will eat dairy products and eggs. A vegetarian diet can be healthy for children provided that it is carefully planned. As with all dietary requirements, it is essential to talk to parents about what foods they would like their child to be given.

Vegans

Vegans do not eat any foods derived from animals. This is quite a restrictive diet and one that health professionals do not recommend for young children because, unless supplements are taken or food is fortified, certain vitamins and minerals, such as iron, calcium and vitamin B_{12}, can be missing.

Over to you

Find out more about providing food for children who are vegetarian or vegan from The Vegetarian Society – www.vegsoc.org and The Vegan Society – www.vegansociety.com

Ethical and environmentally aware diets

Some parents have strong feelings about the conditions in which the food is grown for their children. They may require that foods are ethically produced, for example fair trade and/or organic.

Educating children and adults in effective food management

It is now recognised that just putting healthy food down on a plate in front of children is not always the best way to help them eat healthily. There are other issues involved in food management.

Portion control

It is important for us and for parents to understand how much food a child actually needs over the course of a day. Too much food, even if it is 'healthy', can cause weight gain in children; equally, insufficient food can cause children to be undernourished. A good strategy to help parents know how much food should be given to children is to prepare a sample day's food and work out its overall calorie content using food labels. Seeing how much food children of different ages need is more helpful than just being told how many calories they require. It is also important for us to be aware that 'healthy drinks' such as smoothies and fruit juices can be high in calories and so should be limited.

Case study: Overfeeding

Owen is 5 years old. At a recent appointment with the GP, Owen's mother was shocked to be told that her son was overweight. She had always been very careful about the foods she gave him and she thought that as a family they had healthy eating habits. The GP referred Owen to a dietician. During the appointment, Owen's mother realised she had been overfeeding him and was concerned also to find out that the smoothies she thought were healthy were so high in calories. After the appointment, she began to cut down on portion size and also on the number of smoothies and juices that Owen had each day. She began to read carefully the labels on food products to work out the correct calorie intake.

1. Explain why parents and practitioners need to be aware of portion control.

2. Why is it important to read the labels on food packaging?

Tackling under- and overweight children

It is now thought helpful for parents to be advised early on if professionals notice that their children are either under- or overweight. Interestingly, few parents recognise when young children are becoming overweight and often instead think of their children in terms of 'cuddly'. Parents of children over 3 years old need to realise that children should be beginning to look quite slim and by the age of 4 years the healthy profile of children is that they should look lean. There are now plenty of websites and leaflets from a variety of organisations that can help parents understand what a healthy weight is for their child. Once it is identified that children's weight is not at the expected level for their height, it is essential that professional help is sought. It is also important that young children are not made aware of any problems as this can lead to psychological issues with food later in life.

Over to you

Look at the following websites that may be used to help parents' awareness of healthy weight gain in children.

www.weightconcern.org.uk

www.bhf.org.uk

www.nhs.uk/change4life

Functional Skills

English: Reading

You could read the information on each of these three websites and then produce an information leaflet summarising your findings in order to enhance parents' awareness of healthy weight gain in children.

Food phobias

Ideally, food should be pleasurable for children and meal times should be relaxed social occasions where the focus is not solely on food intake. Unfortunately for some children and their families, food can become a battleground and as a result a child may develop a food phobia or other issues relating to eating food. Although many children have decided food preferences, and may decide not to try out new foods, we need to watch out for children who are becoming distressed by food.

We also need to look out for children who are becoming worried about what they eat, as some dieticians have expressed concerns that children are picking up adult anxieties about being overweight. If you notice that a child seems to have a difficulty with food, it will be important to stay relaxed and not create a tense atmosphere. You can try presenting foods differently or involve children in food preparation. If a low-key approach

does not work and parents report that they are also having difficulties, it will be worth parents getting some professional help via their family doctor.

Getting ready for assessment

Create a plan for a week that shows the meals, snacks and drinks for the children or child in your care.

Explain how your plan meets their individual nutritional needs based on current guidance.

Describe the steps you have taken to ensure that the plan meets parents and children's dietary needs and preferences.

Describe the steps that you would take if a child refused to eat food.

Be able to provide physical care for children

Providing physical care for children can support their health. This learning outcome links to Unit CYPOP2 and you will need to read pages 333–37 if you are working with children under the age of 3 years. This learning outcome requires that you can support children's personal care routines, understand how and when medicines can be given and protect yourself when lifting and handling children.

Supporting children's personal care routines

It is important to care for children's skin, teeth and hair as well as helping them to develop the skills of personal care. See also Unit CYPOP2 pages 333–37 and read this section alongside it.

Care of skin, hair and teeth

When helping to look after children's skin, hair and teeth it is important that you take into account the wishes and preferences of the parents or carers, particularly with regard to differences arising from ethnicity or culture.

Most parents of children from 3 years old will style and brush their children's hair at home. But it is important that we look out for head lice and find out from parents how they would like their child's hair to be cared for if we need to do so. For information about head lice see Unit CYPOP2 pages 334–35.

It is important that we look out for head lice (photo not to scale)

Sun awareness

It is now known that exposure to strong sunlight can cause skin cancers later in life. It is particularly important that children's skin does not burn. The current advice is that children should be kept out of strong sunlight in the summer months between 11 a.m. and 3 p.m. Shade should be provided and, if children have to go into the sunshine, they should wear sun hats, keep covered up and use sun cream if necessary. Some sunshine is important as it plays a major part in helping the body to create vitamin D, so it is advisable for children to have some exposure to sunlight out of these hours. See also Unit CYPOP2 page 333.

Care of nappy area

Children's nappies need to be changed promptly and the skin area needs to be thoroughly cleaned. See CYPOP2 pages 335–37.

Dressing and undressing

An important early skill is for children to be able to dress and undress themselves. This will not only help their physical development, but also their confidence. The process of helping children to learn to dress and undress can begin in a baby's first year of life as we may encourage them to push their arms into sleeves or at around 8 months to pull off their own hats and socks. For older children to learn to dress and undress, it is important that we give them plenty of time and also support. The ideal is for the child to do as much as possible, for example they may put on their coat, but we may do the zip up.

Children also respond to praise and acknowledgement of their efforts even when they have put the wrong shoes on their feet. Over time, it is important that we show respect for children's privacy, for example letting them pull down their own pants when going to the toilet.

Being able to dress and undress themselves increases children's confidence

Toileting

In Unit CYPOP2 page 338–40, we look at helping children to move out of nappies. In this section, we focus on helping children to gain independence when toileting. This is important as we need children to see this as a private activity for reasons connected to child protection. The starting point is to encourage children to do as much as they can and to teach them the skills

they will need. This might mean explaining to girls that they need to wipe themselves from front to back and showing this on a dolly. As soon as possible, children should be encouraged to wipe their own bottoms and parents should be encouraged to show their children how to do this. To help children learn that toileting is a private activity, it is important that the adult gradually withdraws by, for example, partially shutting the toilet door while standing outside and talking to the child.

Hand washing

Hand washing is an essential activity that children need to learn. It needs to become part of the physical care routine so that children automatically wash their hands after going to the toilet, before meals and after playing outdoors.

Supporting independence and self-care

We have seen that children's confidence can be boosted by encouraging them to take part in physical care routines. Many care activities also improve children's fine motor skills and are potentially good opportunities for children to learn concepts, for instance how water runs downwards. The key for adults is not to take over when children are trying to do things for themselves, but to just support sufficiently so that the task is possible for children; so a child might need an adult to brush the back of their hair but can do some at the front. It is also important not to undermine children's confidence or motivation by commenting that a task has not been done 'properly' although there will be many times when we will discreetly have to finish off a task.

The spider diagram below shows the many opportunities that occur regularly in most settings.

Encouraging and modelling good personal hygiene with children

Children find it easier to remember hygiene routines if they see adults involved in them too. This means that you should wear an apron if you are involved in a cooking or painting activity and also wash your hands thoroughly — preferably in sight of children.

Engaging with the child during care routines to support learning and development

Personal care routines do not have to be mundane and boring. They are often times when we can engage on a one-to-one basis with a child. The key is to be aware that these everyday activities are good learning opportunities. Some good examples include counting buttons on a coat, watching the way that water goes down a plug hole or noticing how our hands are dirty after playing with mud outdoors.

Regulations concerning management of medicines

Some children have ongoing medical conditions or infections that are controlled by medication and so parents may ask us to administer medicines; or in the case of children with asthma or allergies we may be required to keep medicines in the setting in case they are needed by a child. As medicines are a potential hazard, procedures should be put in place to ensure that correct dosages are given and they are kept out of reach of children when not being administered. The procedures to follow should comply with the regulations of your home country. The EYFS in England, for example, requires settings to do the following.

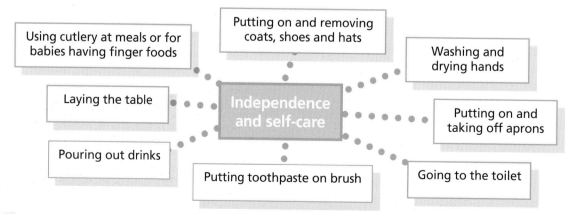

There are many opportunities for supporting children's independence and self-care in everyday activities

- Have a policy about the administration of medicines.

- Keep a written record to show what and when medicines have been given to children (which is shared with parents).

- Ensure that written permission from parents is obtained for each and every medicine prior to it being administered.

Most settings will also do the following.

- Find out from parents what the medicine is for, when it should be taken and in what circumstances. (This is particularly important for long-term medical conditions such as asthma, when it is essential that staff know what to do if a child has an asthma attack and which inhaler to use.)

- Check that medicines are in date before they are administered and follow the instructions given. (It is essential that parents bring in the medicines in their original packaging for this purpose.)

- Store medicines according to the instructions on the label and also out of reach of children. For children with asthma who need an inhaler nearby, thought has to be given as to how to keep other children safe, while keeping the inhaler accessible. (Some settings manage this by asking the child's key person to keep it with them, while others put it high on a shelf. Inhalers should always be marked with the child's name.)

Lifting and handling children and equipment in the work setting

In addition to caring for children, we also have to look after ourselves. Many back injuries occur each year through poor lifting and handling. It is therefore important to attend lifting and handling training if possible.

The following points should be considered when lifting and handling.

- Follow your setting's policy or procedures on lifting.

- Your employer should have carried out a risk assessment so that daily activities requiring you to lift and handle children and resources should have been assessed and, where necessary, written into a guidance policy.

- Think and assess the situation before lifting or moving children or equipment.

Some positions or situations are known to put stress on the back, so be careful when doing the following:

- movements where you lift and twist

- bending or getting into an awkward position

- handling loads that are heavy, cumbersome or difficult to grasp.

Actions you might take include the following.

- Consider asking someone for assistance.

- Reduce the size of the load, for example partially unpacking a box before lifting it.

- Lift safely by keeping the feet apart, bending the knees and keeping the back as straight as possible.

In addition, bending down to children can also cause back problems. Get into the habit of crouching down to be at the child's height rather than leaning over them.

Correct lifting procedures must always be followed

Over to you

Find out more about lifting and handling by visiting the Health and Safety Executive's website www.hse.gov.uk

Check your knowledge

1. Explain what the adult–child ratio is for the setting in which you work.

2. Describe three functions of sleep.

3. What are the three ways in which viruses and bacteria can enter the human body?

4. At what temperature range should fridges be kept?

5. How long can breast milk be stored in a fridge?

6. Give two examples of healthy snacks for children.

7. Why is it important to include snacks and drinks when planning to meet children's nutritional requirements?

8. Which foods must not be offered to a child who has coeliac disease?

9. Give three examples of how everyday care activities can be turned into learning opportunities for children.

10. Explain what should happen if a parent brings a prescribed medicine into the setting.

EYMP4

Professional practice in early years settings

You work in a very important profession. What you do at work and the way in which you do it will have profound and long-lasting effects on the lives of children. It will also have great significance in the character of local communities and our wider society in future generations, so it is important to understand how to work in professional ways.

Learning outcomes

By the end of this unit you will:

1. Understand the scope and purposes of the early years sector

2. Understand current policies and influences on the early years sector

3. Be able to support diversity, inclusion and participation in early years settings

4. Review own practice in promoting diversity, inclusion and participation in early years settings.

Understand the scope and purposes of the early years sector

Early years settings: scope and purposes

The early years sector in the UK at the current time is complex. Unlike in many other European countries, it was not developed by government policy in pursuit of specific aims, but emerged in an ad hoc fashion in response to families' requirements based on changing social and economic factors. For example, during the Second World War women were needed in greater numbers in the workforce to replace men serving in the armed forces, so nurseries were set up to care for the children whose mothers went out to work in factories and offices etc. However, when the war came to an end and the men came back for their jobs, the nurseries were closed.

In the second half of the twentieth century, public expenditure on early years provision focused on families who presented social need and difficulties – 'the deficit model'. Local authority day nurseries (later called family centres) and nursery schools catered primarily for children at risk of harm, mostly in urban and deprived areas. Otherwise, early years provision was in the private sector – childminders, nannies and a few private nurseries. They were regulated by the 1948 Nurseries and Childminders Act, which was followed by the stronger Children Act 1989 and the Care Standards Act 2000.

In the 1960s, the playgroup movement developed when parents took the initiative to set up and run provision for their own children to learn through play in village and church halls and other community facilities.

Families' requirements from provision for their young children vary:

- Some parents need their children to be in a setting where they will be safe and able to participate in play and learning experiences for all or part of the day, while the parents work or study.

- Some parents want to stay with their children while they socialise.

- Some parents want their children to spend time in a setting which offers services explicitly aimed at young children's learning.

- Some parents want their children to be in a small home-based group.

- Some families cannot afford to pay fees for provision.

Table 1: Early years provision

Type of provision	Timing	Age range	Venue	Charges to parents	Run by
Nurseries	Full or part time	Birth to school age	Own premises	Yes; some free hours for 3- and 4-year-olds	Private business
Childminders	Full or part time	Birth to school age	Childminder's home	Yes	Self-employed
Pre-schools (playgroups)	Part time	2½ years to school age	Community facilities	Free for 3- and 4-year-olds	Committee of parents
Nursery classes	Part time	2½ years to school age	State run or private schools	Free for 3- and 4-year-olds	Local authority or private business
Reception classes	School hours	4 and 5 year olds	State run or private schools	Free	Local authority or private business
Crèches	Part time	Birth to school age	Educational or employer's premises	Maybe	E.g. college, workplace
Parent and toddler groups	Part time	Birth to 2 or 3 years	Local community facilities	Yes (minimal)	Parents or local voluntary group
Children's centres	Full or part time	Birth to school age	Own premises	Free	Local authority

Consequently, the early years sector consists of various forms of provision which meet the needs of babies and young children, and of their families, in a variety of ways. Table 1 indicates some of these different types of provision.

Understand current policies and influences on the early years sector

Current policies, frameworks and influences

After a long period of political neglect, the early years sector has come on to the 'political radar' in the last 10 to 15 years, as the result of political responses to social and economic developments. Some of these are described below.

Growing demand

The demand for childcare in the UK has increased steadily since the early 1990s because the proportion of mothers of young children employed outside the home has risen to around 60 per cent of mothers of children aged under 5 years. This has been influenced by many trends, including the following.

- Women's rising career expectations and aspirations linked to the improvement of girls' educational opportunities and achievement of qualifications.

- Increases in the number of single-parent households dependent on the earnings of the lone parent, mostly headed by women.

- Government policies aimed at reducing child poverty which focus on reducing the number of parents dependent on benefits and encourage them to seek training and employment.

A significant proportion of this increased demand has been met by the private sector; there has been a rapid growth in the number of private nurseries since the mid-1990s.

Effects of quality early years provision on outcomes for children

It is now more widely known and understood that the early years are highly significant in determining outcomes for the rest of a child's life, laying the foundations for learning and behaviour. The Head Start programme in the USA provides education and health care for young children

in low-income families, with an emphasis on parental involvement. Research indicates long-term effects of this early intervention, with the children achieving better qualifications and employment prospects later in life, and being less likely to be involved in addiction and criminality or to become teenage parents. In the late 1990s, this prompted politicians in the UK to gain greater appreciation of the part played by good quality early years provision in affecting anti-social behaviour.

Social inclusion policies have sought to make sources of support available to all families ('universal') not just those on low incomes, in poor housing, with health problems, etc. ('targeted').

Key term

Social inclusion policies: aim to enable all people to participate fully in society

Some individuals experience social exclusion — they are not able to take advantage of opportunities open to others because of aspects of their social situation such as their educational progress and employment chances, where they live or the nature of their housing, or their disability or chronic illness, or their experiences of racism or other prejudice. Policies which take action to overcome these disadvantages promote social inclusion.

This was the impetus behind the Sure Start Children's Centres, aiming to offer services in every community as 'a one-stop shop' with health, early education and social care available to all local families from before birth.

Over to you

Use the Internet to find out more about the aims and successes of Sure Start.

Functional Skills

ICT: Finding and selecting information

Use appropriate search engines to locate and select relevant information about Sure Start.

Frameworks for early years provision

As the early years sector has expanded in recent years, there has been tension in the balance between *quantity* — making more early years provision available — and *quality* — ensuring that the experiences offered to young children support their well-being, development and learning in positive ways. To address this, frameworks for early years provision have been developed to set standards and guidance to providers.

Over to you

Find out about the early years framework relevant to where you work. You can find information on the Internet or in your local library.

In England, the *Early Years Foundation Stage (EYFS)* http://nationalstrategies.standards.dcsf.gov.uk/earlyyears

In Wales, the *Foundation Phase*. http://wales.gov.uk/topics/educationandskills/

In Scotland, *Birth to Three: supporting our youngest children* and *A Curriculum Framework for Children 3–5* www.ltscotland.org.uk/earlyyears/

See Unit EYMP1 page 211 for more information on the EYFS and other early years frameworks.

Evidence-based practice

Your everyday practice in your early years setting is likely to have been influenced by many factors, including:

- your training in working with young children
- your experience of working with different children and families
- your on-the-job learning from colleagues
- your reading and viewing of television programmes
- your personal experience — as a parent, perhaps, and as a child.

In addition, your professional practice should be '**evidence based practice**'.

Key term

Evidence based practice: practice which is influenced by objective evidence derived from research

Professional practice requires you to keep up to date with the reported findings of research studies and consider how it can be applied to your own work. However, care needs to be taken in interpreting what research tells us.

- Some studies are superficial — based on small numbers of children and situations.
- It is not uncommon for pieces of research to contradict one another.
- Research is often poorly reported by the general media.

An example of influential soundly based academic research on a significant scale in recent years is EPPE (Effective Provision of Pre-school Education) which has confirmed the value of early learning through 'guided play', especially for children from low-income families.

Over to you

Read about the EPPE project on http://eppe.ioe.ac.uk/

Look for information in journals about published research and use the Internet to follow up, thinking about what you find out, in the context of your previous learning and experience.

Functional Skills

English: Reading and Writing

Once you have read about various examples of research, you could write a short summary of what this might mean for your practice. This will help you to practise writing for a different purpose.

Case study: Kavitha's research

Read Kavitha's account of how learning about research influenced her knowledge and practice.

'Reading about how imaging and scanning techniques brought insight into human brain development, I now understand how important it is to make sure that babies and young children have experiences that help to connect **neurons** into the network of **synapses** that enable us to remember information and events and to make links between them. I can see why young children want to hear and do the same thing over and over again. When they repeat an experience, each experience builds on the previous ones and it strengthens the synaptic links. It also makes sense of why consistent people, environments and routines are so important for them. I'm really committed to the key person system now.'

1. What aspects of your practice are influenced by research evidence?
2. How could you find out more?

Key terms

Neurons: cells in the brain which transmit electrical impulses to other cells

Synapses: network of connections which enable neurons to transmit electrical impulses, so passing information from one part of the brain to another

Evidence supports the need for a key person for each young child

Be able to support diversity, inclusion and participation in early years settings

Diversity, inclusion and participation

We saw in Unit SC2 (equality, diversity and inclusion) that we can define the terms **diversity**, **inclusion** and **participation** as:

Key terms

Diversity: the differences between individuals and groups in society arising from gender, ethnic origins, social, cultural or religious background, family structure, disabilities, sexuality and appearance

Inclusion: a process of identifying, understanding and breaking down barriers to participation and belonging

Participation: concerned with giving children and families a say in how provision is made for them

Anti-discriminatory practice

We also saw in that unit that it is important that you base your work on **anti-discriminatory (or anti-bias) practice** in order to uphold children's rights to have

Key term

Anti-discriminatory (or anti-bias) practice: promoting equality of opportunity by –

- being positive about differences and similarities between people
- identifying and challenging prejudice
- taking positive action to counter discrimination.

equal access to opportunities for their development and learning and to be protected from the effects of prejudice and discrimination.

Being positive about differences

We looked in Unit SC2 at how to challenge prejudice and discrimination – see Unit SC2 page 27. It would be comforting to think that young children cannot be prejudiced, but the harsh reality is that they absorb attitudes from others, and this affects their behaviour. But children are less likely to develop prejudiced attitudes if they learn about differences in a positive way. Young children are very observant and notice differences between people from a surprisingly young age. We can help them to see these differences in a positive light, and enjoy the diversity of our society.

Talking about the differences between us

EYFS in action

The EYFS recommends that you 'Encourage children to recognise their own unique qualities and the characteristics they share with other children.'

Talk with a group of children about the ways they are different from one another. Who is tall, who has freckles, who has the darkest hair or the brownest skin? What colour eyes does everyone have? How does their hair grow? What sort of clothes do we and our families wear? What language(s) can each of us speak? Do we say words the same way, or do some of us have different accents? What are we each good at? Guide the conversation so the differences are brought out as interesting and enjoyable, not something to laugh at or be wary of.

Some practitioners feel uncomfortable in dealing with children's natural curiosity about people who are different from themselves and talking about variations in skin tone, hair texture, shape of features, physical abilities and impairments. If you respond readily to children's questions and comments about differences in gender, ethnicity, culture and family and physical appearance, you will help them to grow up with accurate information and help them to avoid stereotypes and prejudice.

Best practice checklist: Talking about differences

When you talk about differences with children:

✓ Don't ignore a child's question or comment, and don't change the subject. Talk to children openly and honestly. (If a child says 'That man is riding in a buggy like a baby', explain that maybe he finds it difficult to walk and the wheelchair helps him to get around.)

✓ Respond in a direct way, tailored to the child's stage of development; keep it simple. (If you're asked 'Why are Jamila's arms browner than Molly's?' it is usually better to say something like 'Because Jamila's mum and dad have darker skin than Molly's parents' rather than trying to go into a long explanation about skin pigment and sun levels in tropical countries.)

✓ Give some factually accurate information and introduce appropriate new vocabulary. (Respond to 'Parvati's mummy wears a funny long dress' by explaining that it's called a sari.)

✓ Offer reassurance if you think the child is anxious or concerned in some way. (If a child says 'I don't like that thing on Leo's leg', explain that it's called a calliper and is very helpful to Leo by making his leg stronger.)

Some practitioners find it helpful to use dolls (especially Persona dolls) or puppets to help these discussions.

Persona dolls can help to discuss differences

EYFS in action

The EYFS says: 'Children should be helped to learn to respect and value all people and learn to avoid misapprehensions and negative attitudes towards others.'

How do you help children to:

- understand the ways we are all different from one another?

- avoid developing attitudes that people who are different from themselves are strange or peculiar or odd?

- learn that none of us is inferior or superior to anyone else?

Avoiding discrimination

In Unit CYP3.7, we saw how stereotypical assumptions about children and families can limit expectations about children's achievements and outcomes. (See Unit CYP3.7 page 203.) To ensure that children do not experience discrimination based on such stereotypes, we should see each child as a unique individual. We each have a set of physical and psychological characteristics that makes

each of us different from all other people. Some of those characteristics may be similar to those of other people, but our own collection of characteristics is unlike anyone else's. Each of us also combines our own individual variation of ethnicity, cultural and social background, gender, age, sexuality, and perhaps impairment/disability; this is what gives us our unique identity.

We also saw in Unit CYP3.7 the part played by positive images in overcoming stereotypes. (See Unit CYP3.7 page 203.) To ensure that all children overcome stereotypes and have equal opportunities to participate in particular activities, anti-discriminatory practice involves giving some children positive encouragement by making it clear that it is entirely proper and acceptable for them to engage in certain activities, against the stereotype.

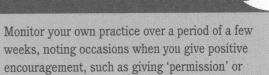

Skills builder

Monitor your own practice over a period of a few weeks, noting occasions when you give positive encouragement, such as giving 'permission' or reassurance that it is perfectly OK for:

- a disabled child to climb

- a girl to play with technological gadgets

- a boy to play in the home corner or wash up.

Also look for adults offering children a version of the world which challenges gender stereotypes with powerful positive images such as:

- a male practitioner cooking, reading a book or mending dressing-up clothes

- a female practitioner playing football or mending a broken chair.

The way learning opportunities are organised in a setting should take differences between children into account, and see beyond the stereotypes. For example, some studies have shown that there appear to be some differences in the way many boys develop from the way many girls develop, and that the differences in their play are not all derived from the pressures of stereotypes. Young boys may have their learning opportunities limited if they are required to spend too much of their day indoors, engaged in adult-initiated activities in which physical activity is restricted.

Functional Skills

Maths: Interpreting

You could create a tally chart over the space of the week to log how many times you either see or use positive images of gender stereotypes. At the end of the week you could interpret the data you have collated by considering whether one particular gender challenges the stereotypes more than the other. Does it happen specifically during one type of play, e.g. 5 per cent of the children that played with cars were female whereas 85 per cent of the children that played football were male?

Role models can challenge stereotypes

EYFS in action

The Early Years Foundation Stage (EYFS) says, 'Every child is a unique individual with their own characteristics and temperament'.

Discuss with your colleagues some of the ways in which your setting acknowledges this uniqueness and responds to each child as an individual. How do you take into account differences arising from gender, ethnicity, disability or cultural and social background?

Children's active participation

If practitioners give children the chance to contribute to small-scale decisions about everyday aspects of their life in their early years, they start to develop the skills they need for decision taking in later life.

When children are enabled to participate in the decisions that affect their lives, those decisions are more likely to have a beneficial effect because they take into account how the children feel. For example, when family courts make decisions about where and with whom a child should live, efforts are made to find out the wishes of the child, and then their perspective on the family situation can be taken into account. To be able to see things from a child's perspective and help them participate, we have to listen to the 'voice of the child'. 'Listening' to babies and young

Case study: Helping children to make decisions

Read the discussion below, in which Gemma and Kelly consider their efforts to offer the children more opportunities to lead and direct their own play in the nursery.

'I think we have become less intrusive in the children's play recently, and given them more chance to go where their interests are taking them. I notice they concentrate on an activity for much longer when it's what they've chosen for themselves.'

'We're getting better at giving them a choice of what they will do, and being less directive – we don't make all the decisions about what happens. I've noticed how much more confident B and F are about choosing for themselves, now it's become the norm; they're not waiting for us to make all the decisions for them. And C is much more ready to have a go at new things now she's had more practice at trying out equipment for herself independently.'

1. In what ways do you enable children to have choices about their play experiences and activities?

2. How do you help them to make decisions?

children involves tuning in to *all* the ways in which they communicate – including their non-verbal communication.

We also saw in Unit CYP3.7 the value of children's participation in determining what happens in their experiences of early years settings and the value of having the opportunity to be active learners. (See Unit CYP3.7 pages 193–94.)

Diversity, inclusion and participation in work with young children

Diversity, inclusion and participation have major implications for children's rights, so you should give them high priority in your work.

Diversity

As we saw in SC2, diversity is often the source of divisions and conflict in society (see Unit SC2 page 20), but early years settings can do much to enable young children to begin to view differences between people as interesting and enjoyable. A positive approach to celebrating diversity shows children that you value and respect them and their family, whoever and whatever they are, and also encourages them to have positive attitudes towards the wide range of ethnic, cultural and religious groups that make up contemporary British society.

One positive approach is helping children begin to learn about cultures other than their own and to show respect for the way other people lead their day-to-day lives. With younger children, your focus is likely to be on such aspects of culture as food, dress, stories and music.

Best practice checklist: Learning about other cultures

You should always avoid the following:

✓ References to 'funny' food or 'strange' music, or the suggestion that, for example, it is not very clean to eat with one's fingers. To help children grow up without developing prejudice, show them that you respect all cultures, not valuing one as better than or superior to another.

✓ Images and information about various cultures presented in an 'exotic' way, or talking about people who live in 'far-away-lands' – presenting them as very different from people who live in the UK, with peculiar ways of living their lives.

✓ The 'tourist curriculum' – giving children information only about the festivals of various cultures, or the sort of 'souvenir' aspects of life that get presented to tourists. Culture is not just about festivals and dress for special occasions – it is primarily about everyday aspects of life.

Inclusion

In Unit CYP3.7, we looked at some of the barriers to inclusion which it is necessary to overcome (see Unit CYP3.7 page 202); one barrier may be the appearance of your setting.

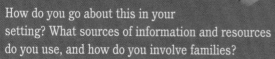

EYFS in action

The EYFS sets the goal: 'Begin to know about their own cultures and beliefs and those of other people.'

How do you go about this in your setting? What sources of information and resources do you use, and how do you involve families?

Learning about different cultures can widen children's horizons, making them aware of the wide range of ways people approach the events of everyday life; but there are potential pitfalls to be aware of.

Resources can provide a welcome

Reflect

Take a critical look at your setting. What visual messages of welcome are there for children and families of various ethnic, cultural and family backgrounds, and disabled children and parents?

- Will these children and adults find themselves represented in pictures on the walls and in resources like puzzles, small world figures and books?

- Are languages other than English visible?

- What cultures are reflected in:

  o resources like the cooking utensils in the home corner and dressing-up clothes?

  o the food provided for the children?

  o the festivals celebrated?

It may be necessary to make adjustments to the environment, resources and routines of the setting and your practice in order to include all children and families in a setting and to ensure that each child has an equal opportunity to benefit from their time there.

Keep thoroughfares clear for wheelchair users

Best practice checklist: Inclusive practice

Your inclusive practice can include:

✓ using variations in floor and wall texture to help children with sight impairments find their way around

✓ using carpets and soft furnishings to avoid hard surfaces and reduce the background noise picked up by the hearing aids of hearing-impaired children, helping them to focus on voices

✓ keeping thoroughfares clear of objects which may get in the way of wheelchair users

✓ using foam shapes to provide support for a child with cerebral palsy so they can reach play equipment

✓ providing access to frequent snacks for a child with diabetes

✓ seeing boys' fantasy games involving 'super-heroes' as creative and imaginative, not just noisy and disruptive and mostly about fighting

✓ providing paints in a range of skin tones so all children can depict themselves, their families and their friends accurately

✓ supporting children whose religious background requires them to keep their bodies modestly covered to engage in physical play.

Functional Skills

ICT: Using ICT

English: Speaking, listening and communication

You could ask to use a digital camera and take pictures of examples of inclusive practice within your setting (as long as you get permission from parents of children and from any other staff involved). You could put these images into a presentation and present your findings to the rest of your class.

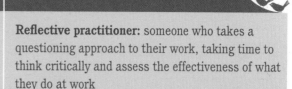

Participation

Your practice in promoting young children's participation focuses on:

- listening to children to discover their perspectives
- giving them the chance to practise making decisions and choices.

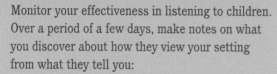

Review own practice in promoting diversity, inclusion and participation in early years settings

Reviewing practice

In Unit SC3, you learned about the importance for your professional practice of reflecting on your practice. Becoming a '**reflective practitioner**' can enhance the quality of your work as you:

- think critically about what you do in your work, analysing how you do it and why you do it that way

- assess the effectiveness of what you are doing at work and how you can become more effective.

Reflection or self-assessment is not something you do just once: it does not mean taking a snapshot of yourself on one day or one week in your working life. The questioning approach needs to become part of your whole working life — a habit you get into, something you do regularly and throughout your professional life. It is worthwhile to put in the time and effort this requires because you will:

- get a clearer picture of what you actually do in your work role and whether you are really being effective
- feel more confident about how you work with children and families — you will feel more sure about the things you are getting right, and more able to take on new developments, new roles and other changes
- be clearer about the things you are not so sure about or feel you need to learn more about
- reach higher standards in your work and provide a better service to children and families.

Reflective analysis

Reflective practice is not something someone else can do to you or for you — you have to take responsibility for your own professional development. The main route to becoming a reflective practitioner is to review and analyse your own practice, to **monitor** and then evaluate it. This means assessing the quality of your practice by asking yourself questions such as, 'Is what I do good enough – does it lead to the best possible outcomes for children and families?'

Key term

Evaluate: identify the strength of your performance – how well you are doing, and how you could improve

To monitor and evaluate your own work successfully, you need to be honest with yourself. Admit to yourself what you really do and say at work, not what you would like to be doing and saying, or what you think you *ought* to

be doing and saying. The feedback you receive from your manager or supervisor and other colleagues should help you to become a reflective practitioner.

Getting ready for assessment

Practice analysing your work practice concerning diversity, inclusion and equality. Monitor and evaluate your practice using the first format below.

Use your monitoring and evaluation to:

- identify your good practice – your strengths
- gaps in your knowledge and skills – your weaknesses or areas for development noting them in the second format below.

Some examples of what I have done:
- I learned from Q's parents that they use the traditional Chinese method of putting personal names after the family name
- I have arranged for Malathy's father to come in and play his sitar, Parminder's older brother to show us how to put on a turban, Zofia's mum to teach us all some Polish nursery rhymes, and Leah's mother to cook food at Hannukah for us
- I went through our books, puzzles and other materials with pictorial representations of families
- I intervened when I found two of our Muslim boys in floods of tears, looking really frightened, when a group of other children were threatening them and shouting at them 'Terrorists. Go home.'
- I spent time with the two Afghani refugee children who have just joined the nursery. They speak very little English and shied away from all the adults in the nursery.

My practice has been successful in these ways:
- Q's parents and I are much more at ease with one another; I think they feel I am showing them more respect.
- All children in the nursery are learning about aspects of life that are different from their own – and enjoying it.

But here are some examples of when things haven't gone so well:
- I thought the resources were OK until E pointed out that families are all shown as having a Mummy and a Daddy, and we haven't any examples of single parents, mixed-race families or extended families.
- I got so furious with the group of bullies that I didn't spend time comforting and supporting the two Muslim boys.
- I was totally unable to communicate with the new children or to involve them in any of the play activities.

My strengths	My areas for development
I'm good at communicating with parents and families, and listening to them.	I need to think in a much wider way about whether the nursery looks like a place that welcomes children from all sorts of backgrounds.
I have had success in encouraging members of the community to get involved in the nursery.	I need to keep calm when challenging discriminatory behaviour and make sure I support the children on the receiving end.
	I have little knowledge or understanding about refugee children or bi-lingual children.

Monitoring and evaluating your practice

Developing professional practice

Diversity and inclusion are areas of practice that many people find difficult and challenging to address, but throughout your career, it is your responsibility to plan how to develop and improve your practice (building on your strengths and tackling your weaknesses). You cannot take the view that you are ever 'fully trained' — there is always something new to learn which will make you better at your job.

You need to develop strategies for continuously changing and improving your practice, such as:

- finding and using learning opportunities such as formal courses leading to qualifications or workshops, seminars, and conferences

- 'on-the-job' learning such as:

  - shadowing — working alongside and observing the practice of other practitioners, in your setting or elsewhere

  - coaching — a manager or other colleague encouraging you to develop new skills, demonstrating or modelling aspects of practice for you, and giving you constructive feedback on your efforts

- researching up-to-date information through reading journals and magazines, using the Internet, or networking with other people in your profession.

Getting ready for assessment

After Izzy had undertaken a reflective analysis of her diversity, equality and inclusion practice, she booked herself in to a workshop on the challenges of working with refugee children who have been traumatised by their experiences and need sensitive support to build up their trust in unfamiliar people.

She set about finding articles and chapters in books among the nursery's resources about supporting bi-lingual children to extend their English, and arranged to spend time in a neighbouring children's centre, observing practitioners with experience of this.

Look back at your analysis (monitoring and evaluating) of your diversity, equality and inclusion practice, and identify aspects that present you with difficulty and challenge.

With the help of colleagues, identify strategies that could help you to develop and improve your practice.

Check your knowledge

1. State two purposes fulfilled by early years provision.

2. List the options open to parents seeking part-time care for a 1-year-old baby.

3. Describe two ways you can 'listen' to a baby under the age of 12 months.

4. What is meant by 'stereotypes'?

5. What is meant by 'positive images'?

My Story

'Our curriculum plan for this term in the pre-school has included talking with the children about differences in a positive way, having conversations about:

- the food the children eat at home
- their families
- special events their family celebrates.

Before we started I thought it might lead to the children focusing too much on the ways they were different – I prefer to think about what we have in common.

Parents brought in food for us to share. Some of the children were very reluctant to try new tastes but were interested in how the food looked and smelled. We had a lot of fun learning to eat with chopsticks, fingers and forks.

It wasn't always easy talking about families. I didn't want the children who live with single parents to feel that their families weren't as 'good' as two-parent families. But in fact their descriptions of their step- and half-siblings became intriguing, and several children were envious of those with several sets of grandparents. My qualms about Lauren talking about her two mums were quite misplaced: the children accept her family without much comment.

We all enjoyed Savita's and Abi's photos of their aunties' weddings – one in her red sari and one in her white dress. Some of the families are sharing with us all how they celebrate festivals. It's so interesting how many customs are the same in many festivals and cultures – giving presents, special food, visiting family, special songs.'

Viewpoint

Boys' Learning Styles

Are early years settings more suited to the way most girls learn than to the way most boys learn? Think about this in the context of your own setting.

There is a growing body of evidence and practitioners' observations that suggest that the 'natural' learning styles of boys seem to be exploratory and physical, involving movement. Boys need to play in these ways, yet such activities are often seen as noisy and disruptive. Do we try to control and suppress boys' boisterous play because we think learning is really only happening when children are sitting quietly? How can we acknowledge their need to learn in different ways?

Ask The Expert ...

Q What sort of decisions can I offer young children?

A Even very young children can make decisions about simple, ordinary aspects of their day, such as choosing what story they would like read to them, or selecting which piece of fruit to have for a snack. Young children usually find it easier to make decisions if they are not given too many options to choose between.

Support children's speech, language & communication

Speech, language and communication play a pivotal role in our everyday lives, although it is easy to take them for granted. Being able to let someone know how you feel, understand what someone is saying or simply ask for directions in a busy place all require the ability to communicate. For children learning to use speech, the acquisition of language and communication is an ongoing process. In this unit we explore its importance in relation to children's overall development and consider ways in which adults can support children to acquire it.

Learning outcomes

By the end of this unit, you will:

1. Understand the importance of speech, language and communication for children's overall development

2. Understand the importance and the benefits of adults supporting the speech, language and communication development of the children in your own setting

3. Be able to provide support for the speech, language and communication development of the children in your own setting

4. Be able to contribute to maintaining a positive environment that supports speech, language and communication.

Understand the importance of speech, language and communication for children's overall development

Speech, language and communication are closely tied to other areas of development. This learning outcome requires you to understand and be able to explain the links between speech and development and the likely impact of any difficulties that children may have in acquiring speech, communication and language.

Understanding the terms

In this unit the terms *speech*, *language* and *communication* are used. It is important to understand what is meant by each of these terms.

Communication

Communication is about the way that people send signals to one another. Communication can be seen as an umbrella term because it encompasses both language and speech and also includes facial expression, gesture and body language.

Language

Language is something very specific. It is a set of symbols – spoken, written or signed – that can be used and understood between people. Language can be quite abstract and we often forget this. A child has to learn that when the sounds of C-A-T are made, the speaker is referring to a cat even if there is not one in the room!

Linguists also suggest that the main feature of a language is a series of rules that users have to understand and use, but once mastered allow a user to convey anything they wish. At first children cannot use the rules. Toddlers begin by just pointing at objects and saying one word, but after a while they learn how to construct sentences.

Speech

Speech is essentially vocalised language. It is usually learnt before the written form of the language. In speech, the symbols are not written or signed, but spoken as sounds. The number of sounds that children need to master will depend on the language that they are being exposed to. English has over 40 different sounds or phonemes.

Key terms

Communication: a way of sending signals to other people; includes body language, facial expression, gesture and language

Language: structured communication with rules and a set of symbols that are spoken, written or signed

Speech: vocalised language

Listening

Listening is about being able to hear and more importantly understand the speech of others. It is sometimes referred to as 'receptive speech'. Babies begin the journey of learning to speak by gaining some 'receptive speech' and learning what specific words and phrases mean.

The diagram below shows the relationship between speech, language and communication.

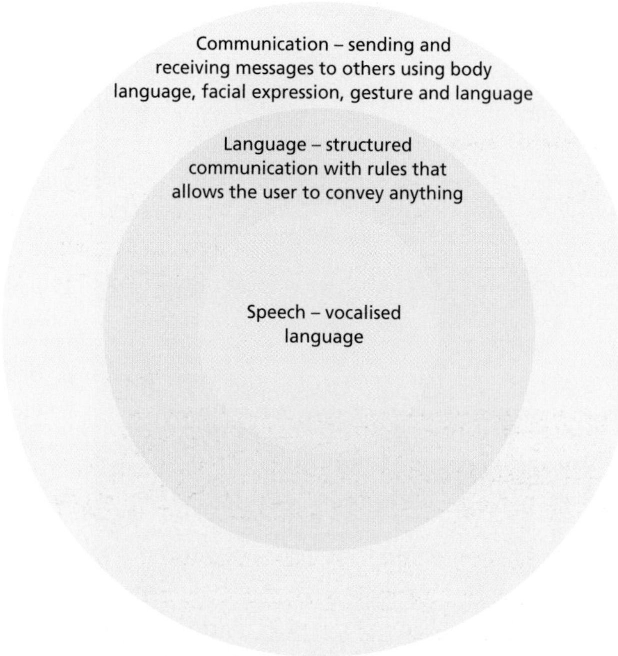

Communication – sending and receiving messages to others using body language, facial expression, gesture and language

Language – structured communication with rules that allows the user to convey anything

Speech – vocalised language

The relationship between speech, language and communication

Speech, language and communication needs

This term is used to refer to any difficulty that a child has in any of the three areas; for example a child might have difficulty in producing certain sounds and so have a difficulty with speech, while a child who does not make eye contact or enjoy being with others may have a more global communication need.

Understanding how children develop communication and language

As soon as babies are born, they begin to learn how to communicate. At first they cry and so learn that their cries can be understood or at least are responded to by adults. Very quickly babies' cries change depending on their needs. Most parents soon work this out and learn

Table 1: Stages in language development

Stage	Age	Features	Comments
Pre-linguistic			
Cooing	6 weeks	Cooing	Babies make cooing sounds to show pleasure. These early sounds are different from sounds made later on mainly because the mouth is still developing.
Babbling (Phonemic expansion)	6–9 months	Babies blend vowels and consonants together to make tuneful sounds e.g.ba, ma, da	Babbling has been described as learning the tune before the words. The baby seems to be practising its sounds. Babies increase the number of sounds or phonemes. This is sometimes called phonemic expansion. All babies, even deaf babies, produce a wide range of sounds during this period.
Babbling (phonemic contraction)	9–10 months 11–12 months **(echolalia)**	Babies babble but the range of sounds is limited	The range of sounds or phonemes that babies produce becomes more limited and reflects the phonemes used in the language that they are hearing. At this stage, it would in theory be possible to distinguish between babies who are in different language environments. At 10 months babies are also understanding 17 or more words. Babies' communication skills have also developed further. They now know how to attract adult's attention by pointing and raising their voices. They can also understand a lot of what is being said to them through word recognition, but also by reading faces.
Linguistic stage			
First words	Around 12 months	Babies repeatedly use one or more sounds which have meaning for them	The first words are often unclear and so gradually emerge. They are often one sound, but are used regularly in similar situations – for example 'baga' to mean drink and cuddle. Babbling still continues.

continued

Key term

Echolalia: a baby's babble – meaningless and automatic repetition of vocalisations made by another person

Table 1: Stages in language development (continued)

Stage	Age	Features	Comments
Holophrases	12–18 months	Toddlers start to use one word in a variety of ways	Toddlers use holophrases to make their limited vocabulary more useful for them. One word is used in several situations, but the tone of voice and the context helps the adult understand what the toddler means. Most toddlers have at least 10 words by 18 months. By this time toddlers have often learnt how to get adults' attention and how to make them laugh.
Two-word utterances – telegraphic speech	18–24 months	Two words are put together to make a mini sentence	Toddlers begin to combine words to make sentences. They seem to have grasped which are the key words in a sentence – 'dada gone' or 'dada come'.
Language explosion	24–36 months	A large increase in children's vocabulary combined with increasing use of sentences	This is a period in which children's language seems to evolve rapidly. Children learn words so rapidly that it becomes hard for parents to count them! At the same time the child uses more complicated structures in their speech. Plurals and negatives begin to be used, e.g. 'no dogs here!'
	3–4 years	Sentences become longer and vocabulary continues to increase	Children are using language in a more complete way. Mistakes in grammar show that they are still absorbing the rules and sometimes misapplying them! Mistakes such as 'I wented' show that they have learnt that 'ed' makes a past tense. These types of mistakes are known as 'virtuous errors'. By this time, children are able to use their communication skills in order to socialise with others in simple ways. They may, for example, repeat a question if they think they have not been understood.
Fluency	4–6 years	Mastered the basic skills of the language	Children have mastered the basic rules of English grammar and are fluent, although will still be making some 'virtuous errors'.
Speech maturity	6–8 years	Mastered the reproduction of most sounds	During this period, children's speech becomes clearer as their tongue, teeth and jaw develop. Children begin to use language to get their point of view across to others, although some do this by simply raising their voice! In this period, children's level of language is key to their acquiring the skills of reading and writing.

whether a baby is tired, bored or simply hungry. Babies also quickly learn to study faces, tone of voice and body language and soon begin themselves to respond to these communications – babies will cry if they hear angry tones or smile in response to an adult smiling at them. This means that by the end of their first year of life, most babies are skilled communicators. They are able to point at things that are of interest to them, turn their heads away to show they are no longer hungry and recognise when adults are happy.

Alongside learning these skills of communication, babies are also learning about language – usually in its spoken form. Table 1 outlines what you might expect to see in terms of children's language development.

Communication, language and speech supports other areas of development

Being able to communicate – and, better still, being able to use and understand speech – opens doors in terms of children's overall development.

Learning

There are many debates as to what is 'learning', but for our purpose we will limit this to children's overall cognition. The term *cognition* covers a multitude of different tasks, but is mainly about our ability to process and use information that we have gained. For example, a child might see that leaves are falling off trees and get told that this is because it is autumn. The child might then see more leaves falling off a tree. She may remember and make a connection between what she saw earlier on and what she is seeing now. The word *autumn* may also be remembered and so she might point and say proudly to the adult with her — 'Look those leaves are falling too! Is that because it's autumn?' Later on in the day while having tea, she may tell her mother that in the park leaves are falling off the trees because it is autumn.

This example illustrates the way in which for learning to take place, the child has to remember what they have seen earlier, make connections to what they are now seeing or hearing and then come to some conclusion. The ability of the child to 'label' it as autumn will help her enormously and she is likely from this point on to notice falling leaves and make the association over and over again. She can also talk and think about 'autumn' without needing to be in the park.

'Those leaves are falling too! Is that because it's autumn?'

At this point we can begin to understand the limitations of body language, facial expression and gesture when language is not available. Although they allow for instant communication, they cannot help a child to understand what is being seen or provide a way in which afterwards the child can communicate what she has seen. This means that children who only have the basic communication skills of body language, gesture and facial expression find it difficult to communicate concepts.

Emotional development

Being able to control your own emotions is a major part of emotional development. Babies and toddlers struggle with this, but as language develops they find it easier because they can express their needs. Tantrums and other outbursts linked to frustration, jealousy or anger tend to diminish as children find ways of talking through how they are feeling. This is one reason why it is thought good practice to 'name' emotions when working with young children, so that they begin to understand what they are feeling and have ways of expressing it other than through physical reactions alone.

Behaviour

Being able to manage your own behaviour is about self-control. Young children are very impulsive and find it hard to control their behaviour but, once language is mastered, children's behaviour changes. It would seem that the acquisition of language helps children to think things over. They focus more on the consequences of their actions and they also internally begin to remind themselves of what they need to do or what they should not do. Interestingly, the start of this process can be observed when a toddler goes up to something that they have been told not to touch, points to it and says 'no'.

Social development

Emotional development is linked to being able to control your own emotions and social development builds on this, as it is about being able to recognise emotions in others and learning to adjust your behaviour accordingly. It is also about understanding what the social codes are in any situation and behaving appropriately. This means that good communication and language skills are important. Children need to 'read' the faces and body language of others and respond appropriately. Because play is the main medium of socialisation with other children, language skills also become important from around the age of 3 years, as children tend to use speech to talk about what they are doing or, as they get older, explain the 'rules' of any games.

The impact of communication, language and speech difficulties on development

We have seen above the importance of communication and language for children's overall development. Where children have difficulties, there are likely to be many effects on their development, although the extent to which children are affected will very much depend on the

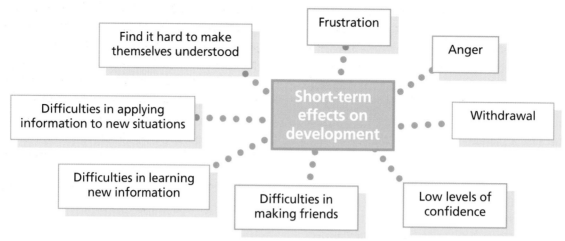

Short-term effects of language difficulties on development

nature of their difficulty, its severity and how the child is supported. The spider diagram above shows some of the immediate possible effects on children. Note that these are very general terms as there is clearly a big difference between a child who has a slight speech impairment and can otherwise use language and a child who is not using and understanding any language.

The longer term developmental consequences in children who have difficulties with their communication, speech and language are in some ways harder to predict but again, in general terms, we may find that children later on have:

- lower self-esteem

- not achieved their potential

- found it hard to make and maintain relationships

- become isolated

- not reached independence

- developed antisocial behaviour in some cases.

Getting ready for assessment

Create an information pack which will help a student understand the importance of speech, language and communication.

Your information pack should contain the following:

- An explanation of the terms:
  - ○ speech
  - ○ language
  - ○ communication
  - ○ speech language and communication needs
- An outline of how speech, language and communication skills support children's overall development
- A description of the potential impact on overall development where children have speech, language or communication difficulties.

Understand the importance and the benefits of adults supporting the speech, language and communication development of the children in your own setting

We have seen that children who have difficulties with their speech and communication skills may be disadvantaged when it comes to their overall development and even life outcomes. For this learning outcome, you will need to show that you understand ways in which adults can support children's communication and also how individual children's speech and language development may be taken into account when planning activities. This learning outcome has links with other units – Units CYP3.1 and CYP3.5.

Ways to support and extend speech, language and communication

Many babies and young children attempt to communicate either using body language or by vocalising sounds and words. It is important for adults not only to acknowledge these communications but also to look for ways of supporting children so they can make progress. There are many ways in which we can do this.

Words and levels of language

One of the skills to acquire when promoting children's language is to quickly work out the level of language we need to use with children and also the style we need to adopt. Babies, for example, need us to use exaggerated facial expressions and to point to objects that we are talking about in order for them to work out our meaning.

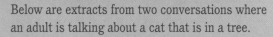

Reflect

Below are extracts from two conversations where an adult is talking about a cat that is in a tree.

Conversation A

Adult: 'Look! (Adult points to the tree) Look! Cat! There's a cat! He's up in the tree.'

Conversation B

Adult: 'Come and look at this. There's a cat in the oak tree next door. I wonder what he's doing up there?'

In which conversation is the adult talking to a baby?

What are the features of this conversation compared with when the adult is talking to a 4-year-old?

Interestingly, linguists have found that adults seem automatically to be able to change the structure of their language when working with babies in order to simplify it. This seems to be particularly important so that babies can focus on the key words in a sentence and so begin to associate these words with meaning. The term 'parentese' is often used to describe the style that adults adopt with babies and toddlers. With older children whose language is developing, our style needs to change once again and instead of simplifying our language we may set out to enrich it so that a 4-year-old's vocabulary can develop.

Questions

Questions play an important part in stimulating and extending children's speech. They can show children that we are interested in what they are doing or thinking. The way that a question is formed can change a child's likely response and so it is important to be aware of the different styles.

Rhetorical questions

Rhetorical questions are not really questions as the speaker tends to answer them! For example, 'You would like a go on the swing, wouldn't you?' This type of question is useful when working with babies and toddlers as it helps adults to sustain a commentary while they are busy with the child who may not otherwise be able to say very much. Rhetorical questions can help babies and toddlers feel involved, providing that the adult uses eye contact while talking. The commentary style is one that seems to be very helpful in allowing babies and toddlers to 'hear' language, although the commentary has to be directed at them. Rhetorical questions are not helpful with children who already have speech as they simply deny children the opportunity to answer.

Closed questions

Closed questions prompt short answers, for example. 'Did you enjoy that?' and so they are useful as a way of engaging a child. We will often need them when working with babies and very young children who can then use one word answers, body language or gesture. With children who have limited language, however, it is important for adults to extend the conversation from a closed question, as the example below shows:

Adult to a 16-month-old: 'It's time to sort out your nappy. Do you want to hold the cream for me? (*toddler nods*) Here you are then – *Careful* – it's heavy.'

Closed questions can also be 'safe' for children who are feeling anxious, or who do not know us, and should be seen as starting points in conversations. With older children, the amount of closed questions that adults use needs to be monitored as they do not extend language and can actually prevent children from getting a chance to express themselves.

Open questions

Open questions prompt longer answers and can help children to think, for example 'What shall we do today?' Open questions work well when children feel comfortable with the adult and also when they have sufficient language to be able to communicate.

Using questions

It is often suggested that closed questions are 'bad' and open questions are 'good'. The reality is often much more complex and the use of questions really depends on the language level of the child and how comfortable the child feels. Many skilled communicators switch between open and closed questions, but what distinguishes their use of questions is that they are genuinely interested in what the child is saying. Poor communicators ask questions blandly without really wanting to know the answer. This means that using questions only to ascertain a child's knowledge, for example 'What colour is this?' can actually prevent children from wanting to talk.

Best practice checklist: Using questions

Look at the effect that your question has on a child. Consider the following:

✓ Do they seem to understand your meaning?

✓ Do they need thinking time?

✓ Do they look worried?

✓ Do they look bored?

✓ Does your question stimulate and advance your conversation with the child or does it make it stilted?

Conversations/interactions

When language use is looked at in settings and in children's homes, it becomes clear that some adult language is used just to 'organise' children; for example,

'Have you put your coat on?' Tthis type of language is essential, but it is not useful in extending and developing children's language. For this to happen, children need some genuine time interacting or talking to an adult.

Interactions with babies and toddlers

For babies and toddlers, early interaction is often quite playful. With a baby we may play a game like 'peepo'. With a toddler, we may find that they give us a toy, we say thank you and then they take it away! These early interactions may not seem important, but they are essential as babies and toddlers are learning the early skills of having fun when communicating. They are also learning about turn-taking, eye contact and interpreting expressions. Other interactions of this type may also include songs and rhymes. Babies and toddlers also need to hear a 'running commentary' whereby the adult talks to them as if they could answer (for example, 'Let's go out now, shall we?').

Conversations with children

Children who have speech need times when they can chat to adults. Note that most children like to be doing something or have something to show the adult for this to take place. This often requires the adult to sit down or take the time to show children that they are available. Good conversations do not work when the adult is moving and cannot make eye contact or is distracted. For learning outcome 3, you will need to evaluate your practice with children; so in preparation for this you should begin to think about how often you sit with children and chat to them as they are playing or are involved in a day-to-day activity.

Information and activities

Language rarely develops in a vacuum. Children and adults need to have something to say to each other.

This means that many settings will work on children's language by planning activities or having books that will prompt children's speech. With babies and toddlers this might mean putting out an 'experience' for them such as a basket with a lid on that contains toys or a teddy. With older children, a variety of activities can be used to stimulate language, although it is always important for adults to build on children's existing interests as well as providing new things for them.

Work with parents/carers

Many parents and carers undervalue their role in promoting and extending children's speech and language. They are much more likely to have 15 minutes a day in which they can chat to their child without interruption, for example on the walk home, or at bath time. As parents often have a strong relationship with their children they are also able to 'tune' into them and adapt their language. This means that parents have the potential to be brilliant language partners for their children. In view of this, many settings provide sessions for parents to let them know about the importance of their role and also to build their confidence. Where a child has a specific speech and language need, both setting and parents will need to work together with a speech and language therapist.

Positive effects of adult support

When adult support is provided for children there are many positive effects. The diagram below shows some of the effects.

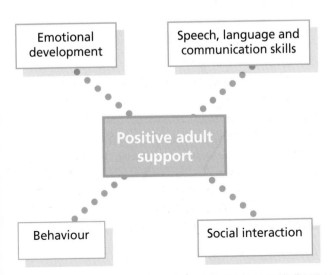

Adult support can have positive effects on a child's language and behaviour

Speech, language and communication skills

Very quickly, if high-quality support is given, children can show progress in their speech, language and communication skills. This means that working with children can be very rewarding and parents often delight in the improvement that their children are showing.

Social interaction

At the heart of social interaction is children's ability to communicate. This means that positive support can quickly make children more outgoing and also confident in their interactions. Many practitioners report that once children have more speech and language, they are able to play more easily with other children.

Behaviour

Many children who are finding it difficult to communicate and speak will show aggressive, uncooperative and frustrated behaviour. Being able to communicate effectively can make an enormous difference to children's behaviour. Parents also note that when they are spending more time communicating with their children, their children show less attention-seeking behaviour.

Emotional development

Positive adult support also helps children's emotional development. Not only do children become more confident, they also find through words ways of controlling their emotions and expressing their needs.

Providing for children with different levels of language

Children of the same age will often have different levels of language. This clearly means that we need to identify children whose language is atypical in order that they can gain additional support, but we also need to think about how our practices and procedures support children.

Settling in

We have already looked at the importance of the **key person** who can act as a safe base for children and help them to feel secure. See Units CYP3.1 page 80 and EYMP3 page 258. For children who do not have spoken language, either because of their age or because of an additional need, it is essential that time is taken for them to get to know their key person before any separation takes place. The key person also needs to find out from the child's parents how they communicate with the child and to learn these skills. Children who are speaking well and can understand us still need a similar level of care and attention, but they may find it easier to settle in as they can articulate their feelings.

Grouping children

Many group care settings will have moments when children are put into groups – at lunchtime or for a story. It is important that thought is given to ensuring that children who have language needs are grouped sensitively and carefully so they have the opportunity to interact and be involved.

It is important that thought is given to ensuring that children who have language needs are grouped sensitively and carefully

Activities

When activities and play opportunities are planned, children's level of language needs to be considered. Certain activities require a high level of language and so may not be appropriate for a child whose language is still developing, for example '20 questions' or 'I Spy'. Language is also needed for role play and so it

is important to think about whether children who want to join in role play need support. The ability to process language also means some activities which require children to listen need also to be carefully thought about, particularly if there are no visual stimuli which will help children to work out the meaning.

Be able to provide support for the speech, language and communication development of the children in your own setting

We have considered how to support children's language in general terms, but in this section we look at practical and more specific ways. This learning outcome also considers how we might evaluate our practice. In order to complete this learning outcome, you will need to demonstrate that you can work effectively to progress children's speech and language.

Methods of providing support

The starting point of supporting children's language is to consider their age, their current level of language as well as their interests, and also any specific need.

Age

Children's age has to be considered in relation to the way we work with children. Babies and toddlers have emerging language and so rely on our facial expressions, gesture, tone and body language to help them understand us. In the same way, they also need to use these communication tools and we have to learn to interpret them correctly. By the age of 3 years, most children will have developed sufficient language to form sentences and so again our style will need to change.

Specific needs

It is important for anyone working with children to know what the expected milestones are in relation to the children they are working with. This is because children must quickly be identified so that they can gain the necessary support. Table 1 might be useful in this respect. For some children, speech and language therapists may give us specific suggestions as to the type of work that a child needs, for example exercises or rhymes to help a child with pronunciation. Other children with cognitive needs alongside language needs may also be using Makaton, which is a series of signs that create visual cues to help them understand the meaning.

(See also Unit CYP3.1 page 76 for more information on the importance of early intervention.)

Abilities

Children come in all sorts of shapes and sizes and it is the same with language. Some children have language delay, while other children get off to a flying start and they are hungry for attention and language opportunities. For these children, we have to think about how challenging activities and language opportunities, such as stories, are. For other children, we have to think about how we can use their interests and existing skills to bring language in. For example, if a child loves playing with a train set, we may sit with them and create the sounds of the train in order to encourage some vocalisation.

Home language

Today, many children learn English alongside a home language. Being able to speak two or more languages from an early age is a wonderful opportunity and so it is important not to make parents or the child feel that there is a problem! We do however need to understand how much English a child has and also how strong their home language is. It is also worth finding out how parents use their languages: some parents will choose only to use their home language with their child, others will split languages up (one parent speaking only in the home language, while the other speaks in English) and finally some parents will 'slide' between two languages.

For children who come into a setting without English, but otherwise used to talking in their home language, we need to be aware of the emotional impact this may have. It is why the key person system is so important – as it is one way in which we can reassure the child. For these children, progress in acquiring English can be very rapid which is why it is not a problem for parents to speak only

their home language. Some linguists take the view that in many ways this is desirable so that the child can gain competence in both languages. Where young children are not making progress in either their home language or English, it is often worth suggesting to parents to make clearer distinctions in their language use so that the young child or baby can work out which sounds and words belong to which language (not starting a sentence in one language and finishing it in another!). It is also worth remembering that children who are learning more than one language are just as prone to hearing loss, sight problems and communication difficulties as other children and so, if a child is not making progress, it is also worth exploring these possibilities.

Gaps in vocabulary

When working with children who have more than one language, it is important to be aware that they may have specific gaps in their vocabulary. This is because most language is learnt in context. For children who have more than one language, this can mean that words relating to activities and objects in the house are learnt in the language of the home, while activities and objects in the setting will be learnt in English. Therefore some children will not know the words for otherwise common household objects in English, such as tea towel or pillow, nor will they be able to talk about what they have done in the setting to their parents as they may not have the words for 'sand' or 'dough' in their home language. It is important to be aware of these gaps and plan activities accordingly.

Specific skills to support children

Adapting own language

As we saw earlier, it is important to adapt our style and language to suit the needs of children. With children who have an additional language, but no English, we may for example need to provide more facial expression, point to objects and simplify our sentences in a similar way to how we work with babies. This style allows them to break into the meaning of words.

Scaffolding children's language

Children need to hear language and phrases before they can use them. Scaffolding children's language involves talking to children in ways that will help them afterwards repeat key words or use whole phrases. The key person is essential in this respect as they are likely to spend more time with the child and can also develop language routines, for example saying the same sentence or words during everyday routines such as greeting and at the end of the session.

Recasting and expanding statements

As part of scaffolding children's language, adults should always acknowledge children's vocalisations or attempts at communication and either recast the sentence, so that it is grammatically correct, or expand the sentence so that the child is hearing a fuller sentence. As vocabulary and concepts are often learnt in context, expanding a sentence from a child can mean that they can learn more.

Reflect

Look at the two conversations below. Which adult is helping to extend and scaffold a child's language while the child is playing with dough?

Conversation A

Child: 'Look!' (*Child has rolled the dough out into a sausage shape.*)

Adult: 'Very nice.'

Child: 'Yum yum.' (*The child pretends to eat it.*)

Adult: 'Don't put it near your mouth!'

Conversation B

Child: 'Look!' (*Child has rolled the dough out into a sausage shape.*)

Adult: 'You've made a wonderful thin sausage. Who's that for?'

Child: 'Yum yum. I like saus..ssies.' (*The child pretends to eat it.*)

Adult: 'I like sausages too. It's a shame that we can't eat these though. They're too salty and salt is not good for us. It would make you poorly.'

Which conversation is likely to extend a child's language?

Why is it important to follow a child's interests?

Functional Skills

English: Speaking, listening and communication

You could use these conversation examples as starters for discussion. You could share your similar experiences in small groups and discuss how you felt your conversation extended the child's language.

Giving children time to communicate

Many adults forget that children need time to 'process' the words and visual cues before being able to reply to a question or respond to a communication. A common mistake therefore is for adults to 'fill' the gap immediately, assuming that a child has not understood or cannot think of anything to say. This means that in reviewing our language practice, it is worth thinking about how much 'time' we give children in order that they can communicate with us.

It is particularly important to remember to give children time when the children are learning English and they already have another language. They may know what they want to say, but need a moment to put together their words. Interestingly, many toddlers and young children also process things after a few hours. This can mean that a toddler who did not seem responsive when he fed the ducks may later on point to a photograph and become very excited and try to talk about the ducks. This is one reason why it can be useful to repeat activities that children have obviously enjoyed, but not necessarily said much about at the time. It is also another reason why using photographs and film clips can support children's interactions.

Facilitating communication between children

Children's social skills and language are connected. Sometimes the role of the adult is to help children connect with each other so they can communicate. One of the best ways of doing this is through simple activities that are pleasurable for children. Pairs of children cooking, for example, or playing a lively game can work well as children may be encouraged to listen to each other and to enjoy being with each other. Working with large groups has to be carefully organised as children who have strong language skills will find it hard not to shout out or dominate. As young children are 'external thinkers' (meaning that they often vocalise their inner thoughts), it can be hard for them to wait and some would argue that it is unfair to expect them to do so. In addition, children who have a stutter can feel under pressure if a group of children have been told to be quiet to listen to them. This in turn can make their stammer or stutter worse.

Best practice checklist: Facilitating communication

✓ Think about group size when facilitating communication.

✓ Avoid competitive language situations when children are encouraged to be the first to say something.

✓ Look out for pleasurable activities that pairs of children can enjoy doing alongside an adult.

✓ Match children carefully so that a good language user does not dominate.

✓ Praise children for playing/working together.

Learning through play

Play is not just a medium through which children learn physical and social skills, but it can be used to develop language. A key skill for adults to master is the ability to play with children in ways which allow children to still have ownership of it. Role play is often used with older children to help them develop vocabulary and sentences; but with babies and young children, language can be learnt through games such as 'peepo'. In order that play is a good vehicle for language, it is important that the materials and resources which are available for children are interesting and satisfying; for example, sufficient sand to scoop or build something, sufficient water and interesting containers for children to use for pouring. To promote language, many practitioners also look for ways of introducing new materials or props into children's play – as this gives children something to talk about.

Working with parents, carers and families

As we saw earlier in the unit (page 299), parents need to be involved in supporting their children's language as they are often more aware of their child's language level and have potentially more one-to-one time available. Parents may sometimes need some support to know how to maximise language opportunities and so some

settings put on workshops where parents and children can come and play and learn together. These can give parents more confidence as well as an understanding of their important role in promoting their child's language.

Interests of children

Children tend to talk more about things that excite and interest them. This means that adults need to be flexible when working with children and be ready to talk and explore things that children have noticed or are interested in. For example, an autumn walk during which the practitioner was hoping to talk about the different types of leaves might have to be put on hold if the children have found a large cobweb and are interested in hunting for spiders!

Day-to-day activities

It is sometimes easy to forget that everyday routine activities can be fascinating for children when adults allow them to be properly involved. This can mean that adults need to allow more time and value these moments in the day instead of just trying to 'get through them'. Tidying up can either be a quick routine task, in which children hardly say anything, or can be a time when adults and children really talk about where things go, why some things seem to 'travel' and which items no one has played with. Some settings organise tidying up so that children work with their key person. The spider diagram below shows some everyday activities that have the potential to extend children's language.

Language can be developed and extended in many ways

Supporting speech, language and communication in your own practice with children

Working with children one-to-one

Children's language can improve dramatically when they spend time in the company of sensitive adults who respond to them carefully. The term 'language partner' is often used in this respect. A language partner is good at picking up on individual children's interests and is ready to allow conversation to follow the child's interests. Chatting with children as they are playing or when we are carrying out an activity is important: just sitting children down to talk can feel very unnatural and forced. But one-to-one time is very valuable because children can talk at their own pace and do not have to compete with other children who may also interrupt them. Ideally, one-to-one work in EYFS settings should be carried out by the child's key person as this is a way of strengthening the relationship and also because the child should have an existing bond with them.

Working with groups

Working with groups of children is a juggling act. Children's language levels are often different and this means that they process information at different speeds and in slightly different ways. An organised walk to the shops may mean that one child notices a post box, while another child might be more interested in holding the shopping bag or noticing a yellow car. If groups are too large, or the activities that the adult is doing are not developmentally appropriate, the adult may find that they tend to 'close down' opportunities for speech rather than open them up. They may resort to closed questions so that all the children can say a single word. This can mean that some children lose out as they do not get opportunities to hear or speak in full sentences.

Ideally, we should make sure that the group size is developmentally appropriate. For example, 3-year-olds are often best, in a maximum group size of three or four, while only older children can cope with a group size of eight. Children who are younger than 3 years tend not to find group work easy at all and may show this by walking off or wriggling!

Best practice checklist: One-to-one and group time

✓ How much one-to-one time do children in your setting have with an adult?

✓ How often can children spend time in pairs or by themselves with an adult?

✓ What size groups do you have in your setting?

✓ How do you ensure that they meet the language needs of all the children?

Evaluating practice

There are many ways in which we might evaluate our practice with children. Firstly, it might be possible to record ourselves as we work with children. This will help us to hear the tone of voice we are using with children, and how much time we give them to respond. In addition, we might also follow children's progress where we have given them additional support. Recording children using an MP3 player can give us a baseline assessment of what they can do and then recording them again in the same situation can help us to see how much progress has been made. In addition, we have to learn to reflect on how to work with individual children. Some children enjoy a puppet or love to talk as they are cooking, while others seem to talk more when we join them as they are playing. This means that, to work effectively with different children, we need to reflect on their reactions and adapt accordingly.

Over to you

Choose three children to work with over three weeks. With permission from parents, assess their current level of language by, for example, carrying out a recording. Work out how their language level relates to the expected development for their age. Make a plan of how you might work with these children.

Be able to contribute to maintaining a positive environment that supports speech, language and communication

As well as the skills that adults show when working with children, it is also important to think about the wider environment as this can impact on children's development. In this learning outcome, you will need to show how your setting's environment works to support children.

The importance of the environment

It is important not only that we can work effectively in terms of our skills with children but that the physical environment, including the play and activities, creates opportunities for language. Children and adults need something worthwhile to talk about and so environments that are boring or stagnant or activities that are repetitive or unchallenging may result in minimal language use. Having said this, environments that are loud and chaotic are also not helpful in providing support for interaction between children and adults, as children may not be able to focus or make themselves heard. Adults may also become distracted if they can see that mayhem is happening on the other side of the room and this can prevent sustained interaction. We need to work towards providing environments, both in and out of doors, that work well in terms of communication and which meet the range of children's developmental needs. We also need to think about the activities and resources that are available for children. Ideally, these should enable interaction because they are challenging and interesting for children.

Case study: Focusing on the environment

Sarah, the manager of the Busy Bee pre-school, and her staff team decided to focus on the communication and language skills of the children in their setting. As well as attending training which helped them to think about the skills of interaction, they also decided to consider the environment they were creating for the children. This made them aware that the noise level in the hall where they worked was very high. They decided to make more use of the outdoors and also to put down rugs in some areas indoors and to create some small spaces. After a week they found that the noise level had dropped considerably and that the quality of interactions had improved.

1. Why is it important to think about the environment when focusing on children's communication and language?

2. Why should the outdoors be thought about as well as the indoor environment?

Activities and resources should enable interaction because they are challenging and interesting for children

Key factors that support an effective speech, language and communication environment

There are a range of factors that can support a setting in providing an effective communication environment. The spider diagram below shows these.

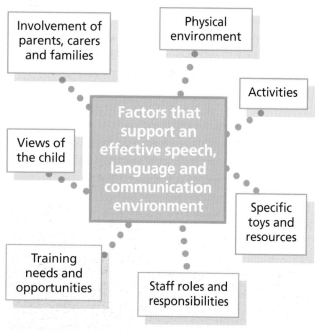

An effective communication environment is supported by a number of different factors

Physical environment

The physical environment needs to be thought about carefully. The following aspects are particularly important.

Light

Babies and children need to see our facial expressions and body language as well as mouth movements. This means that good light is important. This becomes absolutely essential where children have a hearing loss or visual impairment.

Sound and layout

Some settings have high ceilings that reflect sound and this can lead to environments becoming very noisy. Sound is also linked to layout and so thinking carefully about ways of laying out a room to prevent sound from travelling is important. Many settings therefore aim to create some small cosy spaces, as this helps to cut down the background noise. As with light, it is important

again to think about this particularly in respect of the following groups of children: babies and older children who need to carefully tune into the sounds of English, and children with hearing loss who otherwise may not be able to pick up what is being said.

Creating small spaces

Small spaces seem to have an impact on the ability of some children and adults to engage in sustained conversation. The cosiness means that children can feel more secure. Some settings create a range of different spaces – some for children only, so that children can learn to talk and communicate with each other.

Activities

Activities can be directed by adults or led by children; both are valuable.

Adult-led activities

Thought should always be given to the quality of adult-led activities. Some 'language activities' prepared by adults can actually create situations when children just have to listen passively and are hardly using language. The ideal language situation is one where children and adults can take part in sustained conversation with each other and also with other children. With many young children the ideal time for this is while they are quite active, for example involved in a cooking activity, pretending to be a customer at a shop or simply tidying away.

Child-led activities

Children are often more likely to communicate with us when they are doing something that is of interest to them. Child-initiated or child-led activities have the advantage that they are likely to be engaging for the child and we can join them either to act as facilitator or as a play partner. For child-initiated activities to be stimulating, it is important that they are satisfying for the child. Real props, sensory materials, and also the opportunity for children to explore, all seem to be helpful in this respect. As children's speech and language develops, many will enjoy imaginative play and for this to work well children will need good-quality props.

Specific toys and resources

There are few toys which in themselves can 'do' language, but there are some toys and resources that can be great motivators for children. These include phones, walkie talkies, gadgets that allow children to record themselves and puppets. In addition, some children like listening and playing with books and puzzles that make sounds.

Staff roles and responsibilities

When there are large numbers of children within a setting, it is important that children do not 'slip under the radar' just because they are self-sufficient and no particular trouble to anyone. Many settings work effectively to prevent this from happening by using the key person system to double up as a language partner system. The key person takes responsibility for the language development of their key children and routines and systems are put in place to ensure that children do have time to talk and to be with adults. In addition to the key person working, the staff team also have to think about the routines of the setting. Are there times when staff could carry out tasks with children 'in tow', for example putting out the snacks or sweeping the floor?

Training needs and opportunities

Training plays an important part in maintaining and also improving the quality of our language practice. Training may help us reflect on specific aspects of our work or provide us with ideas for activities, layouts or resources. In addition, some training needs to be specific to the needs of certain children that may be in our setting, such as Makaton, communicating using language systems such as the Picture Exchange Communication (PECS) System.

Views of the child

Learning to follow children's interests and allowing children to lead communication seems to be a key way

in which we can encourage children to vocalise and develop language. For some adults this requires learning to ask children more about what they would like to do or what they need. Children often have very clear ideas about what stories they would like to share, what they wish to talk about and who they want to share their spaces with.

Involvement of parents, carers and families

We have seen already in this unit how important it is to involve parents, carers and other family members in the support of children's communication and language skills. This may be through giving information sessions, providing resources and also through understanding that parents may be able to share their expertise with us.

Over to you

The importance of the key factors that we have looked at above are well researched. You can review the evidence for them by visiting the following websites.

www.ican.org.uk

www.literacytrust.org.uk

http://eppe.ioe.ac.uk/

Functional Skills

ICT: Finding and selecting information

English: Reading

The Internet is a vast resource of information but being able to select relevant information is a good skill to have. Once you have found the relevant information and read it you could summarise the main points, either in the form of a short written account or as a verbal discussion.

How settings use the environment to support speech, language and communication

For this assessment criterion you need to demonstrate that your setting's environment is supporting children's speech, language and communication. This means reflecting on the key factors outlined above. Try the 'Reflect' task on page 308 to help you with this.

Functional Skills

English: Writing

Reflecting on your own setting in this way provides the opportunity to write an informative document. Plan your reflective account carefully before you start to write it to ensure that your writing is kept clear and concise.

Reflect

Look carefully at your setting and the environment it is in.

- Does the layout allow for interaction? Think about noise, distraction and quality of light.

- Are there small spaces where children can talk to each other or come alongside children?

- Do toys and resources provide sufficient challenge and interest so that children have things to talk about?

- Where role play is provided, are there sufficient real life props?

- Do adults support and join in with children's play sensitively?

- Do the adult-led activities encourage children's interactions?

- How is the staff team organised to ensure that children's progress is monitored and that all children have opportunities for sustained interaction?

- How often do staff receive training about children's communication and language development?

- How do adults work with children in ways that are empowering e.g. following their interests, asking them for ideas?

- How do you involve parents in supporting their children's language?

Check your knowledge

1. Analyse the difference between communication and speech.

2. Identify three ways in which a child's speech and communication can support their development.

3. Explain the consequences on children's behaviour if speech and language are delayed.

4. Why is it important that adults working with children 'tune' into the level of the child's language?

5. Explain the importance of asking questions when working with children.

6. Analyse some of the specific skills that adults need to use when working with children.

7. Why is it important to give children sufficient response time when communicating with them?

8. Outline the role of play in supporting children's speech and language.

9. Discuss the elements of a supportive environment to promote children's speech and language.

10. Explain why it is important to work alongside parents in developing children's speech, communication and language.

My Story

Using MP3 Players

I work as a manager at a day care nursery. We take children from 3 months through until they leave for school. Some children can be with us for 60 hours a week and so we make language and communication a strong focus of our work. Last year we began recording babies and toddlers' progress using MP3 players. Every two weeks, the key person records their key children and puts the recording into the child's file on our laptop. This has been very popular with parents, but we have also found it a good way of noticing how much progress children are making. Staff have noticed in the baby room how the sounds of babbling change over just a few months. I think that it has also motivated staff to talk more and also to be aware of children's speech.

Video Corner

▶ **Clip 6: Babbling**

Play this video clip on your CD-ROM and then answer the questions below.

@ work

This baby is babbling.

1. Why is this baby mainly making sounds from the language which his/her carer uses?

2. Why is it important that babies' babble is acknowledged?

What other communication skills has this baby learnt?

Ask The Expert ...

Q We have one child who talks to other children, but avoids adults.

A This is not so much a speech or communication difficulty, but rather a relationship difficulty. Children who are comfortable with adults tend to talk to them a lot, so if a child is not talking to adults, consider how well settled the child is and also how well your key person system is working.

Q There is one child in our setting who talks very loudly all the time.

A Many children talk loudly when they are excited or if they are afraid that an adult is not giving them attention. If you have observed that this child usually talks loudly, you might need to consider whether the child is fully hearing. Loud speech can sometimes indicate that a child has hearing problems.

Q We have a 4-year-old who is hard to understand. At what age should a child speak clearly?

A Most children should be speaking fairly clearly at 3 years old, even if they may not be forming complex sentences. Children whose speech is unclear at 4 years may need additional support. They may not be hearing clearly or may need some work on producing speech sounds. Talk to the parents about referring the child on to a speech therapist.

Optional Units

CYPOP1

Work with babies & young children to promote their development & learning

Babies and children under the age of 3 years are at an exciting phase in their lives. During this period, their brains will develop rapidly and they will learn to move, talk and gain control of their bodies. This unit looks at ways in which we can promote their development and learning.

Learning outcomes

By the end of this unit you will:

1. Understand the development and learning of babies and young children

2. Be able to promote the development and learning of babies and young children

3. Understand the attachment needs of babies and young children

4. Be able to engage with babies and young children and be sensitive to their needs

5. Be able to work in partnership with carers in order to promote the learning and development of babies and young children.

Understand the development and learning of babies and young children

In order to work effectively with babies and children under 3 years, it is essential to understand their development. This learning outcome looks at the expected pattern of children's development and the factors that might affect it.

The pattern of development in the first three years of life

Babies and toddlers show amazing progress in all aspects of their development from birth to three years, considering they are born with simple reflexes and are quite helpless and dependent. It is essential to have a good understanding of the developmental stages in this age group in order to support their development. In Unit CYP3.1 we looked at general patterns of babies and children's development and the skills that they are likely to show, and in Unit EYMP5, we looked at the development of language. To complete this unit, you will need to revisit both of these units (see Unit CYP3.1 pages 49–60 and Unit EYMP5 pages 292–96.)

Over to you

Revisit Unit CYP 3.1 and check again the expected development for the age of children that you are working with.

Connections between development and learning

Development and learning are closely tied. Children need to develop certain skills in order for them to learn, but also the desire to learn something or achieve a goal can motivate a child to develop the necessary skills. A good example of this is walking. For a baby to begin to walk, a level of coordination and growth is required, but the baby must also have the desire to walk. During the process of learning to walk, the child will develop balance, strength in the legs and improved coordination. Once the child can walk, a whole new world can be discovered as the child can now reach things and see things from a different level. Therefore, learning to walk has improved both the child's physical development, and his or her cognition.

Variations in the rate and sequence of development and learning

It is not fully understood why some children appear to learn more quickly than others, but it is thought that there are both genetic and environmental factors at play.

Learning difficulties

Some children have learning difficulties that prevent them from learning in the same way – or at the same rate – as other children. The causes of learning difficulties vary and include chromosomal conditions, medical conditions and others that are not yet understood. However, although the term 'learning difficulties' is used, it does *not* mean that such children will have difficulties in learning in every area of their lives. So some children will learn some skills, for example the ability to draw or socialise, at the same rate as others.

Case study: Sophie's learning difficulties

Sophie is 4 years old. She has a chromosomal condition which makes it hard for her to communicate. She has not yet learnt to talk and her comprehension is limited. In many aspects of her cognition she is delayed, but her mother knows that in some ways Sophie is quite clever. She always seems to be able to find chocolate in the house – even when it has been hidden, she knows how to put on a DVD and can get adult attention easily.

1. Explain why it is important not to make assumptions about children with 'learning difficulties'.

2. Why is it essential to gain information about children's different strengths and abilities?

Giftedness

Some children are seen as 'bright' very early on. Adults may notice how quickly they remember things and how fast they are to learn new skills. For these children, it would seem that they are able to process information more quickly and effectively than other children of the same age. This is thought to be linked to the presence of a stimulating environment combined with a strong genetic component.

Stimulating environments and the acquisition of language

Children need stimulation so that their brains can develop (as outlined below on page 317). This means that children who have had many different opportunities and experiences are likely to learn and develop at a slighter faster pace. Language is a major factor in learning as being able to process and use language allows more information to be processed and stored in the brain. Because language acquisition is closely linked to the amount of time spent with an adult and the quality of interaction, some children may be advantaged if they are with adults who take time to interact with them.

Attachment

Emotional well-being (as we saw in Unit EYMP3 and will consider again later on in this unit) plays an important part in children's development. Strong attachments to parents and carers make it easier for children to learn as they are not stressed and this in turn can make it easier for the brain to thrive.

Strong attachments to parents and carers make it easier for children to learn

Learning in different ways

In Unit CYP3.2, we saw that children can learn in a variety of ways. They can copy adults and other children; they can also learn from their own experiences as they will repeat activities that fascinate them or are enjoyable. Interestingly, most of what babies and toddlers will learn comes from 'doing' rather than being 'taught' by adults. As children can learn in a variety of ways, it is important for us to provide them with a range of different opportunities and experiences.

The importance of play

Play is essential for children's development. Through play, children can develop a variety of skills that support every area of development. Good play opportunities allow children not only to have fun and to explore, but also to learn about materials, concepts and how to socialise. Play begins very early on in babies' lives as long as they have an adult who can engage with them. As children develop, they are able to choose and create their own play

Table 1: The role of play in supporting development

Area of development	Supporting role of play
Physical	A range of physical skills, including fine and gross motor skills, are developed as children make movements, balance or sit in order to play with toys or engage in games with adults
Cognitive	Children learn concepts and about the world around them by playing with materials, resources and learning by trial and error what things can do
Language	Play gives children a reason for talking and communicating. At first this is with adults, but as children can play together, they talk to each other
Emotional	Play is fun. It makes children feel happy and also helps them to feel powerful and in control. Play also helps children to learn about feelings; when they engage in role play they also learn about different perspectives
Social	From playing with adults, babies learn social skills such as taking turns and co-operating. They also learn to 'read' faces. With age and language skills, children also learn to play with other children

opportunities (see also Unit EYMP2 page 225). Table 1 shows how play supports many areas of development

Potential effects of pre-conceptual, pre-birth and birth experiences

All babies and young children show different rates of development, but some do so because of difficulties linked to experiences during conception, pregnancy and birth.

Pre-conceptual care

We know that even before a baby is conceived, the lifestyle of parents can have an effect on their potential development. This is because men's sperm and women's ova can be easily damaged. Would-be parents are advised to think about stopping smoking, about taking folic acid supplements, cutting down on alcohol and avoiding recreational drugs. They are also advised not to leave starting a family too late because not only does it become harder for women to conceive as they get older, but also the quality of a woman's eggs can deteriorate over time.

Conception

At the moment of conception, when a sperm and egg fuse, a transfer of genetic information takes place. The fertilised egg will have 23 chromosomes from the father and 23 chromosomes from the mother, which are used to determine its development. This mixing of genetic information is often described as nature's lottery, as some medical conditions and disabilities are the result of this genetic combination.

Pregnancy

Between conception and birth, babies can be affected by the health of their mother as well as her lifestyle choices. Stress, diet and alcohol are examples of factors that can affect development. It is now recognised that the first twelve weeks of a pregnancy is when the foetus is at its most vulnerable. During this time the foetus becomes recognisably human and all the organs are formed.

Smoking

Smoking restricts the amount of oxygen the unborn baby receives and affects growth and development. Babies born to mothers who smoke are therefore more likely to be lighter at birth and also premature. There seems to be other long-lasting effects on health as well. These include a higher incidence of cot death and a greater predisposition to asthma.

Substance abuse

The use of recreational and prescribed drugs can affect the developing foetus. Drugs enter the mother's bloodstream and then cross via the placenta into the baby. The effect of drugs can be devastating — especially in the first twelve weeks when the foetus is developing. Pregnant women are therefore advised not to take any drugs during pregnancy unless advised to do so by a doctor.

Alcohol

Alcohol can enter the foetus's bloodstream in the same way that drugs do. Again this can have a serious impact, especially in the first few weeks of a pregnancy when sometimes a mother may not even know that she is pregnant but the baby is at a critical point of development. During the rest of the pregnancy alcohol can affect the development of the baby and so doctors now advise that women should preferably refrain from drinking during a pregnancy. A specific condition known as Foetal Alcohol Syndrome, which is caused by alcohol during pregnancy, has now been identified. This condition negatively affects aspects of children's cognitive development including their concentration.

Infections

Some infections that a mother may pick up during pregnancy can affect the development of the foetus. The common cold is harmless, but food poisoning, rubella (German measles) or a sexually transmitted disease such as genital herpes can put the unborn baby at risk. Babies who have been exposed to rubella often have sight and hearing problems.

Maternal health

Most women should have healthy pregnancies, but some women can develop complications, including diabetes and **pre-eclampsia** (which can even be fatal). If left untreated, these conditions can affect the health of both mother and baby. This is why pregnant women are offered regular antenatal check ups.

> ### Key term
>
> **Pre-eclampsia:** a life threatening condition in late pregnancy that often requires babies to be born earlier

Maternal diet

The developing baby requires nutrients so the diet of the mother plays an important role throughout pregnancy – a malnourished mother is likely to give birth to a low weight or premature baby.

Diet is particularly important in the first twelve weeks of pregnancy when lack of a mineral called folic acid, found in green leafy vegetables, can cause spina bifida. Women who are considering a pregnancy are therefore urged to take a supplement of 400mcg of folic acid daily until the twelfth week of their pregnancy. Pregnant women can also become deficient in iron and so are encouraged to eat foods high in iron such as red meat, green vegetables, dried apricots and fortified breakfast cereals.

Overall, women do not need a 'special' diet when they are pregnant although they do need to eat a balanced diet. They should also be careful to avoid certain foods which could cause illness, for example:

- Unpasteurised cheese, soft cheese such as Camembert and Brie, and blue cheeses can contain the bacteria listeria, which can cause miscarriage, premature delivery or severe illness in a newborn baby. Listeria is also found in old cuts of meat, pâtés and smoked fish, or ready meals which have been pre-cooked and then chilled for some time before consumption.

A healthy diet is essential for both mother and baby

- Raw or partially cooked eggs should be avoided during pregnancy since these can cause salmonella food poisoning.

- Raw and undercooked meat and raw shellfish can also be a source of food poisoning so should be avoided during pregnancy.

Birth

The process of birth can present various dangers to both mother and child, which is why mothers are monitored before and during birth.

Assisted birth

Most women give birth vaginally but sometimes a **Caesarean section** is given. This is when an incision of approximately 20cm is made across the lower abdomen and the baby is delivered through this opening; the mother is given an anaesthetic beforehand. A Caesarean may be planned in advance (elective Caesarean), for example when a woman is carrying triplets, or may have to be carried out at short notice (emergency Caesarean) if there are difficulties when giving birth.

Key term

Caesarean section: a surgical procedure in which the baby is removed from the womb via the abdomen

Birth trauma

The main danger for babies during the birthing process is a lack of oxygen (**anoxia**). During labour, the oxygen supply to the baby might be interrupted for several reasons, including the umbilical cord becoming entangled or the baby being slow to breathe at birth. In extreme cases anoxia can be fatal or leave the baby with permanent brain damage. It is important to emphasise, however, that this is relatively rare and most babies are born safely.

Key term

Anoxia: a decrease in the level of oxygen

Prematurity and multiple births

A baby's development can be affected if they are born before the full term of the pregnancy. Full term is considered to be between 38 and 42 weeks, and so babies born before 38 weeks are considered to be premature. Premature babies account for around 10 per cent of all births. Some premature births are the result of medical intervention; for example in cases where the health of the mother is at stake or it is recognised that the baby or babies (in the case of multiple births) are not thriving. In other cases, women may go spontaneously into labour well before their due date.

Survival rates for premature babies have increased over the past few years as a result of technology and advances in medical understanding. This has meant that 90 per cent of babies who are born weighing 800g will now survive, although for some there will be some effects on their later development.

The extent to which development is affected varies considerably and is linked to how early a baby is born. The last few weeks in the womb are vital as they allow the baby's organs and nervous system to mature and the baby to gain weight. This gain in weight can help to control body temperature and makes the baby less vulnerable to infection. Babies born between 35 and 38 weeks are usually mature enough to feed and breathe independently and so development in the longer term is not usually affected. Babies who are born much earlier, such as at 25 weeks, will need significant medical support in order to survive and are usually placed in an incubator that is designed to keep the baby warm and free from infection. There have been significant medical advances in recent years in providing womb-like conditions, but very premature babies are at a higher risk of developing hearing or sight problems and also learning difficulties than those who are born full term.

Current research

The latest research into the development and learning of babies and young children centres on the brain's structure and function. It now seems clear that early stimulation – including experiences and language – are vital to the healthy development of the brain. This is because, while babies are born with 100 billion neuron cells, they need to connect together in order to function. Some of these connections are made as result of what a baby senses and experiences. It would seem that the more connections that are made, the better the outcome. As well as stimulation, it would also seem that sufficient sleep and a healthy diet makes a difference in allowing connections to be made. This is why physical care is also important in the overall health and well-being of babies and young children.

Keeping up to date with research

The scientific discipline that looks at brain development is known as neuroscience. Neuroscience is a relatively new area of research and has been helped by the technology of brain scans. It is therefore likely that as time goes by new information relating to the early brain development will emerge and so it is useful to keep up to date with this work. For more information about neuroscience and education visit the Teaching and Learning Research into Practice website (www.tlrp.org.uk)

Brain development

Brain development begins well before birth. Special brain cells known as **neurons** are formed between the

Key term

Neurons: cells in the brain which transmit electrical impulses to other cells

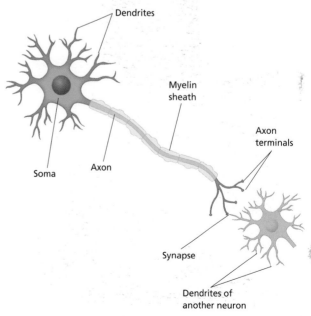

A cell of a neuron

tenth and twentieth week of the pregnancy. These cells are critical as they will eventually join together to allow the brain to function properly. The diagram on page 317 shows an example of a neuron cell. Connections are made between cells when electrical pulses pass between them via their **dendrites** and **axons**.

In the final two months of pregnancy, the dendrites and axons of the neurons develop and begin the process of joining up. Those that have not made sufficiently strong connections are killed off. This is thought to be one reason why some children are born with learning disabilities.

At birth, while neurons are present, many areas of the brain are not yet activated. This is because, as well as neurons needing to join together to create **synapses**, the axons of neurons need to be coated with a substance called *myelin* in order to work effectively. Myelin acts as an insulator and prevents electrical pulses from straying. The process of coating the axons is known as myelinisation and begins in the first few months of life, but is not completed until early adulthood.

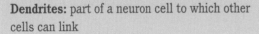

Key terms

Dendrites: part of a neuron cell to which other cells can link

Axons: part of a neuron cell which carries electrical impulses

Synapses: network of connections which enable neurons to transmit electrical impulses, so passing information from one part of the brain to another

Alongside myelinisation, the first two years also see the tripling of the brain's weight. This is a result of the axons and dendrites increasing in size and an increasing number of synapses being made. It is worth noting that the process of growth within the brain does not occur uniformly. For example, synapses made to enable visual processes are formed earlier than those for language. It is not clear if synapses follow a pre-determined pattern, but the role of external stimulation is definitely known to be important. At about the age of 18 months and thereafter, the brain 'prunes' unused synapses. Babies

who are stimulated and enjoy a rich environment of sensations and movement, particularly language, should develop strong and dense synapses that will cope with pruning. On the other hand, babies who are deprived of stimulation and language may lose out as pruning seems to take away synapses that are not used and it is now clear that these cannot be replaced later. A result of this research is that there is now a huge emphasis in the early years sector on creating stimulating environments and providing good sensory opportunities for babies and toddlers.

Be able to promote the development and learning of babies and young children

As we have just seen, it is now recognised that adults working with babies and children need to create learning environments which are stimulating and which will also promote their development. All of the current frameworks of the UK home nations encourage practitioners to observe and plan for the development needs of children and to create stimulating environments. For this learning outcome you will need to demonstrate that you can recognise developmental needs in the children that you work with, plan for them and also create environments that are stimulating.

Assessments of babies or young children

As part of our work with babies we need to assess their development and interests. This is important so that we can be sure that the activities we offer and our ways of working are meeting their needs. For example, when a baby can roll over, we will need to be extremely vigilant when changing their nappies on a high surface. Assessment is also an essential way of checking that the baby or child is making expected developmental progress. Early identification of developmental delay and subsequent support is known to be beneficial. In Unit CYP3.2, we looked at methods of observing children, and it is worth re-reading this before undertaking an observation of a baby. (See Unit CYP3.2 page 72.)

Checklists

Checklists are usually based on the milestones of expected development and can be helpful in reminding us which milestones the babies we are working with should be reaching. It is important that checklists are filled in accurately so that a picture of the rate of development can be built up. It is also usual to find that the developmental picture is not uniform — with babies sometimes reaching milestones in advance of their chronological age in some areas of development but not in others.

Snapshot observations

Many settings use a system of noting down odd incidents or glimpses of development throughout a session. These notes are used to build up a picture of development, and also to record a baby's play interests. Snapshot observations are popular with parents, as they seem less clinical than checklists.

Photographs and film

Photography and filming has become a cheap and easy way of visually recording babies and toddlers at different points in the day. It is a lovely way of sharing information with parents as they can see what their children have been doing and enjoying. As with all observation and recording methods, it is important that care is taken about obtaining permission from parents and also that photographs and films are properly stored. Permission is also needed from other parents of the setting as it is hard to film only one child without others coming into view.

Recording speech

We have seen in Unit EYMP5 that language development is a critical area for babies. Language development needs to be recorded in order for it to be easily assessed. To do this, you can use an MP3 player, dictaphone or tape recorder. Catching babies' and toddlers' vocalisations on a recording enables us to listen to and identify changes in vocalisations and check that they are developing. This can be a useful tool in identifying hearing loss.

Indoor and outdoor environments

It is important that a great deal of thought is given to the environment we provide for babies and toddlers, as

Skills builder

With permission from your supervisor and the child's parent, observe over a few sessions one child, aged under 3 years, who you are working with.

Work out the developmental skills that this child is showing in different areas.

How does this child's development compare to the expected development for his/her age group?

their needs are different from those of older children. They should not merely be given a watered-down version of what we might provide for older children. The key to providing a good environment is to think about how it can be varied and stimulating. This is particularly important for babies and toddlers who spend a long time in the same environment each week. It is also important that we provide environments which are safe, but not sterile or boring in feel.

Table 2 indicates some factors that need to be taken into consideration when planning an environment for children and babies under the age of 3 years.

Equipment suitability, safety and hygiene

As we saw in unit EYMP3, it is essential that environments are kept clean for children. It is also important that age-appropriate toys and resources are available. Table 2 shows resources and materials that might be used with this age group.

Providing appropriate level of challenge

It is important that while we keep babies and young children safe, we also think about making sure that the play and activities we provide are challenging enough. In some ways this is about varying what is available as well as assessing children's stage of development and considering what their next steps are. When planning activities, it is also worth noting that babies and young children can look at and explore objects or engage in physical play that might seem risky or too difficult, but with an adult supporting them such activities will instead just be challenging. For example, a toddler might help to wash up or a baby may be put in a baby swing.

Sensory stimulation

Babies and toddlers are still exploring their environment using their senses of touch and sight and often their mouth. They are also likely to enjoy some time on the floor. Having a range of different floor coverings in the setting — some lino, carpet and even tiles — can in itself be stimulating. If this is not possible, consider bringing in some different textured

Table 2: Suitable resources and materials for 0–3 year olds

Toys and equipment	Suitable for	Role of adult	Skills developed
Mobiles	All babies and toddlers	Make sure that they are out of reach	Build an awareness of colour, shape and stimulate vision
Pop-up toys	From around 6 months	Show how the toy works. Encourage the child to do it for themselves. Look out for more complex wind-up and pop-up toys for toddlers	Encourage learning about shape, size and also cause and effect. Develop fine motor movement and hand–eye coordination. Promote language and communication development
Posting toys	From 3 months	Show babies by putting objects inside. Encourage toddlers to do it for themselves	Encourage learning about shape, size and also cause and effect. Develop fine motor movement and hand–eye coordination. Promote language and communication development
Bathtime and water toys	From 6 months	Use at bath time or in washing-up bowls. Make sure play is supervised	Encourage learning about shape, size and also cause and effect. Develop fine motor movement and hand–eye coordination. Promote language and communication development. Help emotional expression
Balls	From 6 months	Choose a ball that is appropriate to the age of the child. Roll balls to babies. Encourage toddlers to throw	Encourage visual skills, hand–eye coordination. Promote gross motor movements in mobile children. Encourage turn-taking as well as learning about cause and effect
Push and pull toys	Babies who are sitting or children who are mobile	Show the child how to make the toy move. Note that older babies walking might swing toys and this can be dangerous for other children	Encourage physical movements and coordination. Help children to feel in control. Encourage learning about speed, space and distance
Large wheeled toys e.g. brick trolley, sit and ride, tricycles	For mobile children	Observe children carefully to ensure the most appropriate equipment is provided	Develop gross motor movements. Help children learn about speed, space and distance. Encourage self-reliance
Toy telephones	From 9 months		Encourage imagination and language skills
Small world toys e.g. wooden animals	From 18 months	Make sure that the toys are suitable for the age of the child e.g. very small world toys can be a choking hazard. Sit on floor and play with toddler e.g. take the Noah's ark animals up the ramp, put play people in and out of cars or house	Develop fine motor skills, hand–eye coordination. Promote language development. Encourage imagination and creative skills

mats and rugs which can be put down; for example a door mat or a bath mat. To keep babies and children stimulated if they spend much of the time in the same room, it is important to change the pictures, the layout and the toys and resources regularly.

Some settings change the layout of the room during the day so that children feel as if they have 'moved' room. This links to the way that in the home setting, many children would move from their bedrooms to the lounge and maybe even into the kitchen. In addition both babies and toddlers need sensory activities. Examples of these are given on page 322 in this unit.

Quiet calming spaces

Babies and toddlers need quiet times and spaces where they can feel relaxed and cosy. Many settings now think about the layout and ensure that small enclosed spaces are provided so that babies can crawl into a tent or under a table that has a cloth on it. We also need to make sure that there is furniture that feels 'homely' and many settings have sofas where adults and children can share books or just cuddle up.

Environments planned and organised around individual needs

In group care, it is now realised that some routines are not primarily about the children, but about making the routines of the staff easier. While it is important to strike a balance, it is essential that everyday routines are based on what is best for individual children. This may mean that children have different meal times or that a baby's older brother is invited to eat alongside the baby.

Experiencing the outdoors

Being outdoors is a way in which children can be stimulated. A breeze on a child's face or the feeling of damp air is actually stimulation for the brain. The need for babies and toddlers to spend time outdoors is now considered to be so important that it is part of the legal requirements in the EYFS framework in England. With non-mobile babies, being outdoors might mean being taken for a walk in a pushchair or, in warmer weather, sitting on a rug outdoors. For mobile children, it should be a chance for them to be actively playing outdoors as well as visiting local parks or playgrounds. The environment we create outdoors needs to reflect children's play needs and interests. For example, a toddler might be interested in throwing things or moving

This setting understands the importance of trying to recreate a family mealtime

things from one place to another, and the outdoor environment is ideal for this.

Planning play-based activities and experiences based on assessment

It is important that we watch the type of play that babies and toddlers are engaged in so that we can provide play experiences that will be of interest to them and will also enhance their development. In Unit EYMP1, we looked at play patterns that we may observe in toddlers which can be a good starting point for planning activities for them (see Unit EYMP1 page 216). In addition, we need to think of other activities that babies and toddlers might enjoy. Below are some examples of popular activities for babies and toddlers.

Treasure basket play

A particular type of play known as treasure basket play is usually recommended for babies. It has its origins in traditional ways that babies were cared for when toys were not available. Treasure basket play is easy to prepare and plan for. A range of natural materials, objects and artefacts are put together in a basket that the baby can easily reach into. The aim is that the baby can take things out and explore them using all senses, including the mouth. This means that objects need to be kept clean and, importantly, checked as a choking hazard.

Babies enjoy this activity because it satisfies their curiosity and gives them plenty of stimulation. During the activity they learn about texture, shape, size and also how to make connections. Babies will often spend quite long periods of time engaged in this play. The role of the adult is also interesting. Instead of interacting or showing the baby objects, the adult should stay close by and be there for reassurance rather than to be actively involved in the play. This is a good time to observe babies' development, but also to notice what items are intriguing them.

To maintain the baby's interest in the activity, it is important that new objects appear in the basket, especially ones that will support any play themes that they have shown interest in, such as trying to stack objects or post them.

Examples of items that might be included in a treasure basket are:

- Ball of string
- Natural sponge
- Wooden spoon
- Metal biscuit tin
- Rubber plunger
- Corks
- Cardboard tubing
- Orange
- Coconut
- Metal teaspoon
- Leather purse
- Rubber plug

Babies can take things out of the treasure basket and explore them using all senses including the mouth

Heuristic play

Heuristic play is used for toddlers and is a progression from treasure basket play. The objectives are similar, but the materials used no longer have to be natural and man-made materials can be added. Toys are not included as the idea is that by playing with a selection of objects and materials, babies and toddlers can discover for themselves what they can do. During heuristic play, toddlers are able to explore in their own way the materials presented. They often make connections while they do this — for example, that corks fit into a plastic bottle, that metal tins can be used to make towers.

Key term

Heuristic play: Play with household and recyclable objects that encourage toddlers to explore

Sensory activities

Babies and toddlers enjoy learning by using their senses particularly taste, touch and vision. Below are three examples of sensory activities that children enjoy.

'Gloop'

This is cornflour mixed with water. It is suitable for babies and toddlers as both groups enjoy its gloopy texture. Toddlers are also likely to enjoy mark making with this mixture if it is spread thinly on a plastic tray.

Cooked pasta

Babies and toddlers enjoy touching, playing and eating cold cooked pasta. This is suitable for older babies and toddlers, although it is important to check that children do not have a wheat allergy.

Water

Water play may happen during bath time for babies, but toddlers will also enjoy playing with washing-up bowls or in paddling pools. It is of course essential that, where water is used, adults are in constant supervision and then remove the water when it is not in use.

Benefits of sensory activities

Sensory activities build on young children's desire to learn through their senses. Through sensory materials, babies and toddlers learn about textures, cause and effect and also learn to be independent. Sensory activities also promote babies' and toddlers' co-ordination and fine motor development. They also help babies and toddlers to concentrate as well as express themselves.

Getting ready for assessment

Carry out some observations on a child who you work with.

Create a plan based on the child's interest and also their developmental stage.

This plan should give examples of resources, play opportunities and activities tailored to meet the particular child's needs.

Ask a colleague to film or observe you with the child while you are carrying out an activity/play opportunity.

Then write a reflective account based on their observation that includes:

- An evaluation of how engaged the child was during the activity
- How well the activity/play opportunity promoted different aspects of their development
- Your role in supporting the child.

Tailoring activities to babies' needs

For this assessment criterion, you will need to show that the activities and experiences you provide are tailored to meet babies' or young children's needs. This means observing children once again to check that the activities and experiences are engaging for them. In some cases, it might be worth asking a colleague to observe you working with the child, as we know that, for babies and toddlers, it is not just the play experience or resources that matter most; it is the interaction and engagement of the adult who is with them.

Understand the attachment needs of babies and young children

Babies and young children's development is closely tied to the quality of the relationships that they have with others. This learning outcome looks at the importance of the key person system and the effects of poor quality attachments. This learning outcome links to Unit EYMP3 (see Unit EYMP3 page 258).

The key worker/person system in early years settings

As part of their survival mechanism, babies and toddlers do not like to be separated from their parents or primary carer. Children and parents tend to show signs of separation anxiety when they are not together and this can create stress for both. In order to prevent children and their parents from being stressed, it is essential that babies and young children are supported by a key person in a setting who will act as a temporary substitute for the care, love and attention that is usually provided by the parent. When the key person system works well in a setting, both parents and children are able to feel comfortable and relaxed during their time apart.

The importance of loving, secure relationships

Good relationships are essential for the well-being of most people. The same is true for babies and young children. When babies and young children feel valued, secure and can trust the people around them, they are likely to thrive. Certain areas of development are linked to the strength of attachment that children have with those around them, especially emotional and language development. We also know that children learn from those they have a strong bond with and so cognitive development can also be linked to strong relationships. This is equally true of relationships with their primary carer (for example, their mother or father) as well as with their key person in the setting. When babies and children have poor attachments or relationships with these adults, they are likely to find it hard to settle, to concentrate

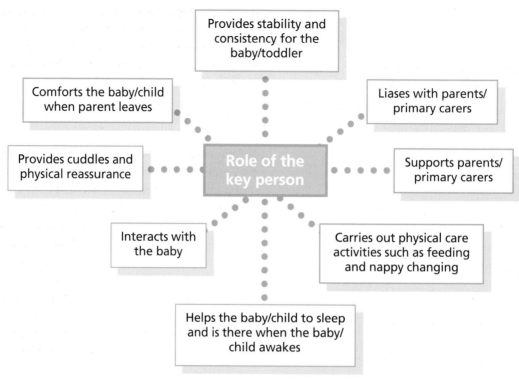

Provides stability and consistency for the baby/toddler

Comforts the baby/child when parent leaves

Liases with parents/ primary carers

Provides cuddles and physical reassurance

Role of the key person

Supports parents/ primary carers

Interacts with the baby

Carries out physical care activities such as feeding and nappy changing

Helps the baby/child to sleep and is there when the baby/ child awakes

The key person system helps both parent and child

and enjoy being in the setting. If poor attachments exist between parents and children, children are more likely to show poor behaviour and concentration and this in turn affects their learning.

Over to you

Observe one of your key children. Look to see if you can identify any of the classic signs below that may indicate they have a strong attachment with you:

- Actively seek to be near you

- Cry or show visible distress when you leave the room or (for babies) if you are just out of sight

- Show joy or relief when you appear, for example when they first see you or you come back from a break

- Acute awareness of your presence – for example, looking up at you from time to time, responding to your voice, following your movements.

When babies and young children feel valued, secure and can trust the people around them, they are likely to thrive

Possible effects of poor-quality attachments

It is important for everyone working with babies and children to understand the effects that poor-quality attachments can have on the development of babies and children. In relation to the parent–child attachment, these have been well researched since the 1960s, but there is also now research to show that poor-quality settings can harm children.

Effects on social and emotional development and emotional security

Strong secure attachments help babies and children's emotional development as they learn to trust others. Where young children have a series of broken attachments or unsatisfactory ones, they begin to show antisocial behaviour and aggressiveness. There is evidence that suggests poor attachments may be linked to youth crime in later life.

Effects on ability to settle, take risks and make the most of learning opportunities

Children who have strong attachments find it easier to become independent and confident. It is interesting to note that children who have had 'successful' separations from their parents are more likely to cope with transitions, for example going into reception class, moving room or moving house. Children who have had 'unsuccessful' separations and who have been distressed seem to have deep-seated although often subconscious memories of their distress and this seems to hold them back. They are less likely to settle, to take risks and therefore unable to make the most of learning opportunities offered to them. Interestingly, the recent work on the brain seems to show that traumatic events early in childhood are stored deep within the brain.

Possible effects on short- and long-term mental health

Babies and young children can become depressed. This was not always recognised in the past but now has been confirmed by research. Withdrawn behaviour and listlessness often follows the period of visible distress when parents leave their child with adults to whom the child has no relationship. There is also good evidence to show that babies and children who have poor attachments can go on to have depression and other mental health issues later in life. This is particularly the case where there are problems in the parent–child attachment.

Effects on relationships with parents and professional carers

Children who have experienced poor attachments, or ones that have come to a sudden end leaving the child feeling bereaved, can find it hard to make new attachments. This is not a conscious decision as such, but the child might have learnt that people go in and out of his/her life and that to avoid pain it is better not to trust other people and make a strong relationship. Where children have been separated from their parents and have been distressed, it can also make them subconsciously angry with the parents as they may feel abandoned. Parents who 'just disappear' to save the pain of saying goodbye, also run the risk that their children do not learn to trust them.

Be able to engage with babies and young children and be sensitive to their needs

Engaging with babies and toddlers is about promoting their language, following their interests and play and drawing their attention to things. It is essential that we find ways of doing this which are sensitive to their needs in order to make them feel emotionally secure and also to help them communicate. Below are some key ways in which we might engage with babies and young children.

Time to process and respond

Babies and toddlers need time to process information before they can respond. A good example of this is when we smile at a 6-month-old baby and it takes a moment before they beam back. During this time, the baby's brain is processing the information that is gained from looking at your face and only once the information has been processed can the child respond. The same occurs with toddlers, especially when we ask them questions. Sometimes adults can unwittingly rush babies and toddlers or fill the gap assuming that they cannot respond.

Cuddling and talking

Most adults are able to adapt their style of speech to suit babies almost instinctively. This is sometimes dubbed 'parentese'. The pitch of the voice becomes higher, key words are emphasised and the facial expression is exaggerated. It is also clear that physical interactions such as cuddling and holding are important. For the adult, it makes it easier to switch into 'parentese', while it helps the baby to feel reassured. It also becomes easier to talk to a baby when you both 'know' each other. This is why it is essential for language development that babies have their own key person with whom they have a special relationship (see page 323).

Toddlers also need physical contact with us, but it is important that we 'offer' this and allow toddlers to decide if they feel like taking up our offer. As with babies, times when we are physically close to toddlers are likely to help us engage sensitively with them.

Running commentary

One of the ways in which adults can support early language is by talking to babies, even when their responses may seem limited. This type of talk is sometimes referred to as a running commentary: the adult talks to the baby about what they are doing and tries to include the baby. You may find yourself doing this while involved in some of the routine physical care aspects of working with babies, such as nappy changing and feeding.

Drawing attention to objects and games

Another way of helping babies and toddlers break into the code of language is by drawing their attention to things. You may, for example, hold a rattle in front of the baby and shake it while talking about it. In the same way, you might carry a baby over to a window, notice and point out a passing cat and then talk about the cat. From around the age of ten months, most babies who have had their attention drawn to things begin to reciprocate this movement. They start to point out things to us, such as a favourite toy on a shelf or their bib. With toddlers we will need to keep doing this, but also be ready to acknowledge what they want to show us.

Rhymes and songs

Singing and saying rhymes to babies and toddlers is a traditional way of providing emotional reassurance, and also helps to develop language. It is important that babies and toddlers have individual times when their key person holds them and uses songs and rhymes. It is also necessary for rhymes and songs to be repeated often so that the child can predict what is going to happen and become familiar with the sounds, rhythms and tunes.

Playful activity with babies and young children

Babies and toddlers are playful, but need a partner to play with. The adult is usually this partner and, from early play experiences, babies and toddlers learn a significant amount including social skills which will later help them to play with other children. Following are examples of some play activities that adults can use with babies. With toddlers, it is useful to play alongside them and follow their interests, for example pretending to drink from a cup or rolling a ball to and fro with them.

Posting and dropping

Once babies reach the age of about 8 months, they enjoy watching things drop and posting things. They may throw a spoon down from the highchair, watch you pick it up and once it is returned to them throw it down again. This is a simple game and many babies will enjoy playing it ten or more times! You can also provide tubes, tins and containers for babies and toddlers to drop objects into. Again, they will drop an item into the container and then a few moments later retrieve it. Look out for containers that make a noise such as a metal tin or for objects that make a sound as they land, such as a bunch of keys.

Peepo

From around the age of about 7 months, babies enjoy finding things that they know to be there. You might, for example, pull a hat down over your face and then pull it back up and smile. If you do this repeatedly, the baby will start to learn that you are there. At first they may just look, but eventually they will start to join in by pulling off the hat and 'finding you'. From this, you can start to 'hide' the baby. Gently pull the hat over their eyes (not their whole face), wait a moment and then pull it back up to 'find them'. As with other simple games, repeat this several times. You will probably find that

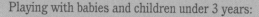

Repetition of an activity is valuable for toddlers

Best practice checklist

Playing with babies and children under 3 years:

✓ Observe the child's current interests and use these as a basis for play.

✓ Allow the child to repeat games and movements.

✓ Play at the child's pace. Be ready to stop if interest wanes.

✓ Draw the child's attention to things.

✓ Smile and acknowledge the child.

Skills builder

Observe an adult playing with a baby.

1. What do you notice about the baby's facial expression?

2. What skills do think this baby is learning?

3. How is playing helping the baby to feel secure?

babies then begin to show you that they like hiding by pulling the hat over themselves.

Knocking down

Knocking down is a simple game where a pile of objects is built up so that the baby can watch it and then eventually join in knocking it down. Stacking beakers, small boxes and wooden bricks can all be used. You begin by piling up the objects and then show the baby how they can be knocked down. As with many simple games, you will probably need to repeat it a couple of times so that the baby can understand the game. You can then look out for signs that the baby is ready to do the knocking down.

Responding to how babies express their emotions, preferences and needs

One of the most important things that anyone working with a baby has to do is to learn how the baby communicates. Very early on, babies, for example, differentiate their cries. Some cries mean they are tired,

while other cries indicate that they are bored or want some company. Responsive care means being good at recognising what a baby needs and attending to them quickly. The following points are important in being able to demonstrate that you are skilled in responsive care.

Responding sensitively, consistently and promptly

Babies are very responsive to the atmosphere generated by adults. They notice tone of voice, body language and even the way they are being handled. This means that when we respond to a baby's cry or smile, or carry out a nappy change, we need to be sensitive to them. As we see below, it is also important that we are consistent and are prompt at meeting their needs. For some people, responding to babies becomes easier with practice. They are able to complete nappy changes, bathing and preparing feeds more efficiently and so gain confidence. This confidence is often picked up by babies who often settle with people who seem comfortable with them.

Responding to individual needs and preferences

Babies, like adults, are unique individuals. Some babies like to have their cheek stroked if they are finding it hard to fall asleep; others are soothed by being rocked. It is therefore important that our responses to babies are based on their individual needs and preferences. This is one reason why the key person approach is so important as, over time, the key person will know exactly how to respond to their key children. It is also why we need to work closely with parents, as they will be able to share information about their babies' needs and preferences.

Consistency of response

In their first year of life, babies are learning whether the world they have been born in is a place to be trusted or one where things keep changing and people's responses are unpredictable. This means that the way in which we respond to babies has to be consistent so that they can feel secure.

Managing situations to avoid delay

Babies cannot be put on 'hold'. Their needs are urgent and we have to respond promptly to them. It is also important for us to predict what their needs will be and, in the case of feeding and nappy changing, to have everything ready or on standby.

We have to respond promptly when babies need us

Managing transitions for babies and young children

Once babies and toddlers have settled into the setting, there is a likelihood that they will still need at sometime or another to make a transition. A member of staff may leave; in group care they may move into another age group; and children in home-based care may need to adapt as other children come into the setting. Transitions can be difficult for babies and children. The old adage that they are flexible is not quite true!

In order to support babies and toddlers we need to take things at their pace and try to gradually introduce the new person or new child who will be with them over a few days. This is important because it allows children to build up a relationship before being expected to make a change. This is particularly important if children are to change key person or carer.

Rest and sleep

In Unit EYMP3, we looked at the importance of sleep for children's overall health. It will be useful to re-visit this unit, see Unit EYMP3 pages 256–57, before looking at the assessment criterion in this unit.

Babies and toddlers' brains are developing quickly in the first few years of life. Their brains are also taking in vast quantities of new information as they experience

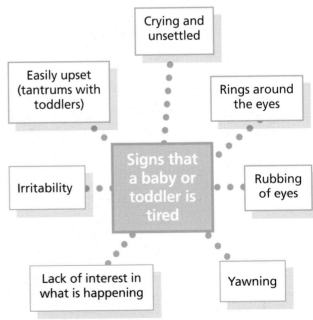

These signs of tiredness should not be ignored

new things every day. Scientists believe that sleep has an important function in allowing the brain to develop and 'bed down' or consolidate learning and memories. This means that babies and children under the age of 3 years have a requirement for large amounts of sleep. They are likely to need at least 12 hours sleep, and very young babies are likely to need even more. Sleep is often taken by babies and young children in a combination of short naps and one long sleep, which is hopefully at night. Sleep is a routine and it is important that we support parents in building this routine by keeping as far as possible to the same sleep patterns that the child has at home.

Babies and children under the age of 3 years will find it easier to sleep if there is a quiet and darkened room for them. It is important that adults putting babies and toddlers to sleep are calm and relaxed as this can help babies and toddlers to fall asleep. It is usual for key

persons to help babies and very young toddlers fall asleep, as this can be a time when children show some separation anxiety. (For more information about putting babies to sleep safely see Unit CYPOP2 page 343.)

Children do not need constant stimulation during the day. Some quiet periods need to be built in where activities allow children to rest so that they are not physically active. This does not mean these activities should be boring! Favourite stories and rhymes are examples of restful activities; and babies can be put in a buggy for an outdoor walk. When toddlers need a quiet time, we might sit and help them with a simple jigsaw puzzle. Note, while rest is important for babies and toddlers, it is important not to assume that it can replace sleep.

Be able to work in partnership with carers in order to promote the learning and development of babies and young children

It is hard for parents and carers to leave their baby in the care of someone they do not know – it often feels strange and can make parents very anxious. This is because attachments between babies and their carers are reciprocal. This learning outcome looks at the importance of the parents or carers in the lives of babies and young children and ways in which we might work in partnership with them. This learning outcome has strong links to Unit SC1 and it will be important to re-visit that unit. See Unit SC1 Promote communication, page 2.

The primary importance of mothers, fathers and carers in the lives of babies and young children

In Unit CYP3.1 pages 70–71, we looked at the importance of attachment and it will be important to re-visit this to help with this assessment criterion. Parents and other carers, such as grandparents or foster parents, are key people in children's lives. They have the closest and strongest attachments to the children and these will

Stories and rhymes are examples of restful activities

usually be lifelong attachments. Parents and key carers act as safe bases for children. They are people to whom the child can turn at any point for reassurance, love and boundary setting. Parents and key carers are also people who protect their children and will defend them. The strength of emotion between parents or carers and children is one that has to be understood and respected if we are to work effectively with them. It means that parents will notice and be annoyed if their child has come back with a jumper on the wrong way or has not had their nappy changed. This level of attachment brings many benefits for a child, particularly emotional benefits. Feeling loved and special helps children to gain confidence and self-esteem and this in turn is vital in terms of socialising with others and also being ready to learn.

Exchanging information with mothers, fathers and carers

To work effectively with parents and carers it is important that we develop a strong partnership with them. They need to know that their child is going to be nurtured — not just looked after. To do this well you will need to gain information from parents and carers about their baby's needs, interests and 'little ways'. You will also need to know about any medical condition or allergy the baby has. This type of information must be written down so there is no confusion and the key person can use it when planning activities and carrying out care routines such as feeding.

Once you have begun to take care of their baby, parents will want (and need!) information about what has happened during the session. Details of naps, food and nappy changing are very important and it is usual for this information to be written down each day. Parents and carers also need to know what their child has been enjoying during their day. In the same way, it is useful if parents can tell us about what their child has been doing or showing an interest in while away from the setting.

There are many ways of sharing information with parents, especially now digital technology has become cheap and easy to use. This means that some settings now email photos that they have taken of the children in their care and send home CDs that have film clips and sound recordings on.

Reflect

How do you currently exchange information with parents?

How do you evaluate whether the information you provide to parents is useful to them?

Evaluating ways of working in partnership with parents

Exchanging information is important, but there are other ways in which we can work in partnership with parents and carers. At the heart of these lies an understanding that parents are the experts when it comes to knowing about their child. Below are some ways in which settings and key people can work in partnership with parents.

Involving parents in observing their children

Parents have a vested interest in seeing how well their baby or toddler is developing. This means that parents should be shown observations that you have carried out and may also be encouraged to observe their child and feed back information about what they are doing at home. This is important as parents will be doing slightly different things with their babies and toddlers and this is reflected in the skills that the children show and also their interests.

Involving parents in planning with you

Observations, as we have already seen, have little value unless they are used to inform planning. This is an area that we can share with parents as they may have different perceptions about a child's needs and may also have a range of ideas as to the type of activities the child will enjoy.

Involving parents in the running of the setting

Settings that work well with parents actively look for ways of involving them in the running of the setting. This may include volunteering and fundraising, but also taking on some specific roles, for example being responsible for producing newsletters.

Involving parents in the recruitment of staff

Some settings use parents in the recruitment process of new staff. These settings recognise that parents are the key users of the service and so, by having a parent representative on the interview panel, they can gain a parental perspective.

Asking parents for feedback

It is easy for staff to take parents' views for granted or to make assumptions about what parents want. Settings that work genuinely with parents encourage honest feedback in order to try to improve their work.

Check your knowledge

1. Give two reasons why some children may not show the expected pattern of development.

2. Explain why play is important in the development of babies and children aged under 3 years.

3. Why are would-be mothers encouraged to take folic acid supplements?

4. Describe how smoking in pregnancy might affect the baby's health and development.

5. Give two examples of play or activities that might support the learning and development of a baby and a toddler.

6. Why is a key person important for babies and toddlers?

7. How does attachment between parents and children affect their development?

8. Describe two effects of poor attachment on the development of a toddler.

9. Why is it important that babies and toddlers have sufficient sleep?

10. Describe one way in which we might work in partnership with parents.

CYPOP2

Care for the physical & nutritional needs of babies & young children

Babies and young children are vulnerable and very dependent on their parents and carers. Therefore, as well as providing for babies and children's learning and development, it is also essential that we support their physical care, keep them safe and meet their nutritional needs. This unit looks at ways in which we can meet these fundamental needs.

Learning outcomes

By the end of this unit you will:

1. Be able to provide respectful physical care for babies and young children

2. Be able to provide routines for babies and young children that support their health and development

3. Be able to provide opportunities for exercise and physical activity

4. Be able to provide safe and protective environments for babies and young children

5. Be able to provide for the nutritional needs of babies under 18 months

6. Understand how to provide for the nutritional needs of young children from 18–36 months.

Be able to provide respectful physical care for babies or young children

This learning outcome looks at ways in which you might provide physical care for babies and children and the importance of doing so with respect and in line with parental wishes.

Culturally and ethnically appropriate care

Every parent will have their own way of caring for their child. This will depend on their culture and personal preferences, and also on their child's skin and hair type. It may also depend on the religious practices or traditions of the child's family and any particular medical needs. Parents may therefore ask us to use certain products — or not — as the case may be. They may also need to show us how they manage aspects of personal care. It is essential that we work closely with parents and respect their knowledge and decisions about their child.

Skin

Skin is the largest organ in the body and has a very important role. One of its functions is to be a barrier against bacterial, viral and fungal infections. If skin is not properly cared for, infections can enter the body. This means that, as part of our care of babies and toddlers, we must help to keep their skin clean.

Face and hand washing

Babies and toddlers will need to have their hands washed frequently as they are constantly putting them in their mouths and so may introduce infections. Learning that hands have to be washed before eating is important and we can introduce this concept early on to babies. To avoid skin chapping, hands and faces must also be dried carefully. It is likely that babies and young children will also need their hands washing after eating, as they are likely to use their hands to eat with. Babies and toddlers often dislike having their faces washed. This is partly because, if it is done roughly, it feels as if they are being smothered. It is very important not to rush face washing

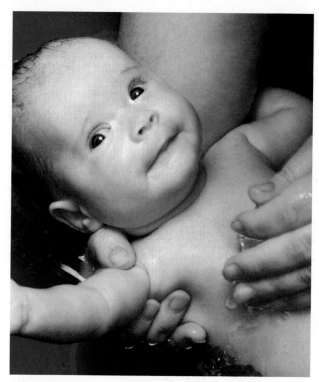

Keeping skin clean is a key way of reducing the risk of cross-infection

and take care only to wipe half of a child's face at a time.

Bathing

Keeping skin clean is a key way of reducing the risk of cross-infection. Not all settings take responsibility for bathing babies, but if you work in home-based care you may need to do this. It is important to check with parents about any products they would like you to use or preferred ways of bathing the baby. It is worth noting that not all families will bath their baby as they may prefer to use a shower so that there is running water.

Sun protection

Babies and young children's skin is very sensitive and can be easily burnt in strong sun during the spring and summer months. As exposure to the sun can cause skin cancers, it is vital to protect young children. Ideally, we should keep them out of the sun and in the shade, and when in the sun they should wear a sun hat, sunglasses and their body should be kept covered up. For the latest advice about skin care in the sun, visit the SunSmart website which is run by Cancer Research and gives more information about protecting babies and children.

Procedure for bathing a baby

Checklist	Step-by-step procedure
Essential items: • Clean nappy • Clean clothes, including vest • Cotton wool or baby wipes • Bag or bucket for waste materials such as dirty nappy and wipes • Towels • Shampoo *Non-essential items:* • Thermometer to check temperature of water • Barrier cream • Soap or bubble bath • Talcum powder (Skin products should be used only after checking with parents as the baby may have a skin allergy.)	• Prepare all the equipment and fill the baby bath with warm water which should be no more than 38°C as a baby's skin is very sensitive. Always check that the water is not hot and ideally use a bath thermometer. (Always fill up with cold water first and then add some warm water afterwards.) • Put the baby on a flat surface, undress him/her and take off the nappy. Clean the nappy area. • Wrap the baby gently but securely in a towel, so that the arms are tucked in. Wash the face with moist cotton wool. • Hold the baby over the bath and wash the head and hair. • Take off the towel. Holding the baby securely under the head and round the arm, lift him/her into the water. • Use your spare hand to wash the baby. • Lift the baby out of the bath, supporting under the bottom, and quickly wrap him/her in a warm towel.

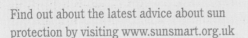

Over to you

Find out about the latest advice about sun protection by visiting www.sunsmart.org.uk

Does your setting have a sun protection policy?

Hair

The care of children's hair will depend on their hair type and also the preferences of parents. Most parents will style their children's hair at home, but occasionally we may need to do this for the children. It is important to follow parents' preferences and also use the same tools as them, for example a wide-toothed comb or a soft brush; or hair oil rather than shampoo.

Head lice

Over the past few years, head lice have made a come-back and few children will escape them during their childhood. Head lice are small grey-brown wingless parasites that live on and suck blood from the scalp. Checking for head lice should be done weekly and is usually the responsibility of parents, although it is important for us to recognise signs that a child may have head lice (see also Unit EYMP3). Look out for the following:

• children who scratch their scalp

• white egg cases that look like dandruff, but do not move. These are the 'nits'

• sight of lice moving in their hair.

Treating head lice

There are various methods of treating head lice and parents will need to decide which ones they wish to use. They include using a chemical solution that can be bought from pharmacists, combing them out or using an electric comb.

Preventing head lice

Head lice spread by moving from one head to another. If there is an outbreak of head lice in your setting, it is important to inform parents so that everyone can check their hair. This includes the adults! It is also advisable for hair to be tied up wherever possible to prevent the spread.

Teeth

As soon as babies have their first teeth, we should start to brush them. This is essential to prevent dental decay. Contrary to popular belief, care of children's first or milk teeth is as important as care of their adult teeth. Without good dental hygiene, children's teeth can decay in the gum.

Care for children's first or milk teeth is as important as for their adult teeth

It is recommended that babies and children have their teeth brushed once in the day and again last thing before bedtime. It is important that teeth are cleaned after meals and at times when the child will not be eating again for a while or drinking anything other than water or milk, so that the teeth have a period when they can stay clean. In some settings, children brush their teeth or have them brushed after breakfast or lunch. If children have their teeth brushed in group care, it is essential that each child has their own toothbrush. This should be rinsed thoroughly after use. Toothbrushes for babies and children should be small and soft. We should brush their teeth gently and in circular movements.

Best practice checklist: Caring for children's teeth

✓ Brush teeth with a small-headed toothbrush after meals.

✓ Brush teeth gently in a circular way.

✓ Avoid sugary drinks, sweets and snacks between meals.

✓ Only use the toothpaste provided by parents.

✓ Make sure that there is sufficient calcium in children's diets.

Nappy area

In many settings, parents provide nappies for their children. Like many areas of physical care, this will be linked to parents' preferences — some parents may choose cloth nappies that are washable. Nappies need to be changed promptly and regularly so that babies do not develop a rash. It is important that you carefully follow the procedures in your setting for changing nappies to prevent cross-infection. Disposable gloves and aprons should be worn and then taken off when finished. This is to avoid any traces of urine or stools being passed to babies via your hands or clothes. Dirty nappies must be immediately disposed of; in many settings there will be bags or a special bin for their disposal. The area where you have changed the baby needs to be cleaned thoroughly so that it is ready for the next change.

Taking account of parents and carers' preferences

Before we begin to care for babies and young children, it is essential to find out how the parents or other carers wish us to provide physical care for their child. Some parents may, for example, want their baby to have a dummy to get to sleep; others may wish for barrier cream to be used at nappy changes. Some parenting and child-rearing practices are cultural or religious in origin, while others might be social. A parent may, for example, feel that they want their child to have only environmentally friendly or ethically made products such as nappies or skin products because of their social conscience. It is important that preferences are respected, as we should be aiming to work alongside parents.

Nappy-changing procedure

Checklist	Step-by-step
This is a simple guide to changing nappies. Nothing beats practice or being shown by a supervisor.	
Changing mat	Wash your hands; put on disposable gloves and apron.
Disposable gloves	Undress the baby as needed and lie the baby on mat.
Apron	Undo nappy – if removing a terry-towelling nappy, close pin or fastener and put somewhere safe.
Clean nappies	Gently lift up baby's legs by ankles.
Nappy fastener and plastic pants if required	Wipe off faeces using cotton wool or baby wipes.
Cotton wool or wipes	Remove soiled nappy and waste materials.
Bucket or bag to dispose of soiled nappies and waste products	Thoroughly clean the genital area.
Spare clothing for baby	Make sure that the skin in the nappy area is dry.
Barrier cream (to prevent nappy rash)	Put on barrier cream if desired by parents and then put on clean nappy

The main exceptions to this would be when parents' wishes run counter to professional practice and are detrimental to their child's health or the health of other children. An example of this might be if parents were to insist that their 4-month-old baby should be put down to sleep on its front, when professional advice to avoid cot death is that the baby should be put on its back. In such cases, it is usually possible to talk through the reasons why we cannot respect requests.

Below are examples of the questions that we might need to ask parents:

- Do you use barrier cream, oil or any particular skin product on your child?
- Does your child have a particular comforter or toy that you use as a distraction during a nappy change?
- Do you have a particular method of caring for your child's hair or skin?
- Do you use a dummy with your baby? If so, in what situations?

Respectful and personalised care

It is essential that we find ways of making physical care routines as pleasant and enjoyable as we can for babies and toddlers. We can do this by having everything ready, making it into a game and encouraging wherever possible

babies and toddlers to be active in some way, for example holding the clean nappy or wiping their own face. It is important that we understand that some aspects of physical care are not particularly enjoyable for children and that we must be gentle and sensitive with them.

It is also useful to give toddlers advance warning so that they know ahead of time that they will have their nappy changed or that we are going to clean their faces. Rushing children or being rough with them during physical care routines makes babies and children anxious and can make them fearful in future.

Best practice checklist: Respectful care

✓ Do not approach from behind when wiping babies and young children's faces.

✓ Encourage children to be active and do as much as they can.

✓ Give toddlers advance warning that a physical care activity is to take place.

✓ Don't rush the process.

✓ Talk and reassure babies and toddlers about what is happening.

Procedures that protect babies, young children and practitioners

In the past couple of years, there have been cases of women abusing young children and taking advantage of being alone during physical care routines such as nappy changes. It is therefore essential that everyone in a setting is aware of the setting's procedures for safeguarding children and also what they should do if they suspect a member of the team is abusing children. The policies and procedures in the setting should link to the regulations and requirements of your home nation. These should not only protect babies and children, but also prevent false allegations of abuse from others, for example giving clear guidance about what to do if a third party (such as a parent) makes an allegation about a member of staff. Most settings now make sure that staff involved in intimate physical care are monitored by others and also carry out physical care near or in sight of other staff.

Be able to provide routines for babies and young children that support their health and development

Routines are about the way in which we organise the everyday care and stimulation for babies and young children. This learning outcome looks at the ways in which we might plan and implement routines that meet the needs of babies and young children. We also consider how we might help children to move out of nappies.

Daily and weekly routines

Looking after babies and toddlers requires good organisation and planning. The planning of care and activities should act as a framework for your day-to-day work and for a weekly routine. Routines should be based around the needs of individual babies and toddlers. The starting point for developing plans should be the information that you gain from parents and carers about their children and the ongoing observations that you carry out.

As babies and toddlers develop quickly, so the routines and plans will change. What is suitable for a young baby of 3 months will not be appropriate for a mobile and active 11-month-old child. The spider diagram below shows the factors that need to be taken into consideration when planning daily and weekly routines for babies and toddlers.

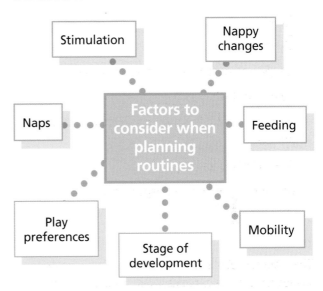

There are several things to think about when planning routines for babies and toddlers

Stimulation/naps

Stimulation during physical care should be part of the everyday routine, as well as planned activities, toys and resources. Because outings and visits need to be planned ahead, they will need to go into the weekly routine.

It is also important to allow time for naps and rest for babies and toddlers, as these are an essential part of a young child's routine. Toddlers are busy little people and even if they do not actually sleep, they must have some quiet times and restful activities during their day.

Nappy changes

Nappy changes must be regular to avoid nappy rash and nappies must be changed immediately after they have been soiled.

Feeding

Babies need to be fed regularly and it is important that you are organised so that they are not kept waiting and hungry. Once babies reach 6 months old, they will need to be weaned. It is important to find out from parents about any food preferences or dietary needs that a baby has. As advice about feeding babies can change, it is also important to keep up to date with the latest guidance. When planning daily routines for toddlers, time has to be built in to allow them to feed themselves and also to recognise that they may eat quite slowly.

Mobility

The physical development of babies affects the type of play that they can engage in as well as the safety precautions that we need to take (see the section on safety later in this unit, page 341). It is important when planning for babies and toddlers that they are given sufficient time and space in order to move freely.

Play preferences

When planning activities it is important to consider children's play preferences. These will change over time as the child develops. Babies and toddlers will quickly develop a preference for favourite games, songs and toys. It is important to introduce new activities in order to keep stimulating their development.

Stage of development

It is essential to observe babies and children's individual development, but also to understand what they will be mastering next. In this way we can ensure that the right toys, games and equipment are ready.

Showing respect and sensitivity during everyday care routines

Earlier in this unit, we looked at the importance of showing respect when working with babies and young children during physical care tasks. This is fundamental to the way we should work with babies and young children in every aspect of our practice and this includes planning routines. It is expected that the key person will play a major role in the different aspects of the routine, such as nap time and feeding. This is important as the key person will get to know the child well and be sensitive to their particular needs. Patience and good communication skills play an important part in the way we work with babies and toddlers. See also Unit SC1 pages 4–10 about communication and Unit CYP3.5 pages 158–60 in relation to building strong relationships with this age range.

This practitioner is making the child feel comfortable

Effective toilet training

Somewhere in the third year for most children, they will be ready to come out of nappies. This is a major developmental step both physically and emotionally for toddlers and so needs to be handled very carefully. As with other areas of physical development, there are some children who are ready quite early, even from 15 months, but others may be much later and will not be ready until they are nearly 3 years old. As with other aspects of care, it is important to work in partnership with parents; toilet training will be less stressful for everyone if similar approaches are being taken at home and in the setting.

Recognising that a child is ready to move out of nappies

Timing is a key component in helping children to move out of nappies. If pressure is put on children too early, it is more likely that they will have many 'accidents' and be stressed. Leaving toilet training too late is not advisable either, because success in leaving nappies seems to help build children's self-esteem. It is interesting that when children are really ready for toilet training, they are often able to complete the process within five days or so and thereafter have few accidents. When children are not ready, the process can take much longer and will also be much more stressful for both the child and the adults.

Look out for signs that a child is ready to come out of nappies. These include the following.

Extended periods when a child's nappy is dry. This shows that their bladders are starting to develop. Look out for a dry nappy after a nap.

Awareness of bowel movements and emptying of the bladder. In order for toilet training to be successful, the child has to be aware of bowel movements or that they are emptying their bladder. As modern nappies are very efficient, this can be a problem and so you could sometimes consider using cheaper nappies so that the child becomes more aware. Note that nappies need then to be changed promptly to prevent nappy rash.

Sufficient language to talk about what is happening. Children need to be able to communicate that they need to use the toilet or to understand when we ask them if they need to go.

Physical signs. It is not enough that a child is motivated or interested in leaving nappies, their body needs to have achieved a sufficient level of maturation. A good sign that a child is ready to be toilet trained is if they can climb stairs using alternate feet, i.e. one foot per step. This seems to be a reliable indicator and is widely used in parts of Europe to assess a child's readiness.

During toilet training

During the process of toilet training, the following points are important.

Encouraging and praising

It is important that children are praised for having a 'go' even if they do not perform. We should always encourage children, but it is important that they do not feel too pressurised as this can backfire. Star charts or the promise of presents can create a 'high stakes' atmosphere. This in turn can make the child feel stressed, which may mean they do not notice the signals that they need to go or may become too anxious to 'perform'.

Treating the child with respect and avoiding guilt

Children need to feel confident that we will not be cross with them if they cannot 'perform' or if they have the odd accident. If children are made to feel guilty, or are worried, there is a likelihood they will find it hard to relax enough to allow the urine to flow or to pass a bowel movement.

Working in partnership with parents

As with every area of personal care, we have to work closely with parents. In some cases, we may help parents to realise their child is ready for toilet training, while in others we may have to point out the disadvantages of beginning too soon. It is important, however, that everyone involved in the child's care tries to take a similar approach so that the child does not become anxious.

Flexible personalised approach

There is no 'single' right way in which children can be toilet trained. Some children prefer to use a toilet rather than a potty, others have to hold a toy and some children like to hear the sound of running water. Understanding and being sensitive to the needs of each child is therefore important and we must also gain information from parents to allow for a personalised approach.

Timing

As we have seen already, it is essential to get the timing right so that toilet training only starts when the child is ready. There will be times, however, when it is recognised that the child is not ready and so we must be prepared to abandon attempts and try later. As this can happen quite often, it is one reason why toilet training needs to be low key – so that if a child needs to go back to nappies, they do not feel like a failure.

Being positive and supportive to the child's efforts

When children first start toilet training, they often get their timing wrong. This means that they may reach the potty or toilet too late and it can make them feel very distressed. It is therefore important to stay positive and also praise children's attempts. Accidents need to be cleared away and the child changed without any fuss so that they do not feel guilty.

Structuring physical environment to facilitate training

It is important that we make it as easy as possible for a child to get to a potty or the toilet. At first this means having one close by at all times. It is also helpful if the child's clothing is either simple for them to remove themselves (no fiddly dungarees!) or in summer, when it is warmer, kept to an absolute minimum.

Avoiding confrontation

Children do not deliberately set out to have accidents or to sit on the potty and not perform. It can be annoying if a child has an accident, especially if it is only a few minutes after they have been asked if they need the potty. Getting annoyed with the child, or asking them why they did not go before, will not help and will just make the child feel stressed.

Fluids and fibre to prevent hard stools

Diet and drinks are important factors in toilet training. Children need sufficient water or other drinks in order for them to experience having a full bladder, and also to prevent them from becoming constipated. It is important that children should be given foods, such as fruit and vegetables that contain fibre, which will also help avoid constipation and prevent hard stools as well as contributing to a healthy diet and lifestyle for the future.

Be able to provide opportunities for exercise and physical activity

Opportunities for exercise and physical activity are important for babies and young children as they need to gain control over their bodies in the first few years of life. This learning outcome looks at the importance of exercise and physical activity as well as ways in which we can provide it.

The importance of exercise and physical activity

In Unit EYMP3 we saw the benefits of physical activity and exercise for children (see pages 255–56). We know that physical activity strengthens children's fine and gross motor movements as well as building up muscles and lung function.

For babies and toddlers, providing for physical activity means giving them sufficient floor space and time outdoors so that they can move. Pre-mobile babies need time on their stomach to build up the muscles and strength in their neck, hands and back which is necessary to help them learn to crawl. This is important, as crawling is thought to contribute to babies' brain development.

With toddlers, it is important to understand that they need 'stop, start' opportunities for physical activity and exercise. This is because they do not yet have the stamina to maintain constant movement. This is why toddlers often alternate between wanting to walk and then sit in their pushchairs. The spider diagram below shows some of the ways in which babies and toddlers might engage in physical activity.

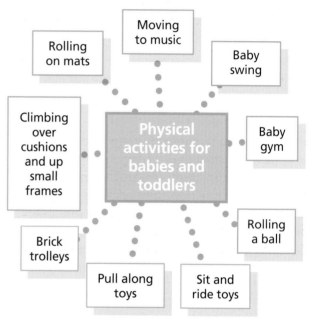

Babies and toddlers can enjoy these physical activities

Supporting babies or young children's exercise and physical activity

As well as providing opportunities for babies and young children to have physical activity, we must also find ways of encouraging them. As with other areas of development, this is closely linked to our relationships with children and our ability to encourage and support them. It is important that we praise, acknowledge and create playful opportunities so that they enjoy movement and are keen to try different things. It is also important not to rush children or to force children to do something they are not interested in.

Be able to provide safe and protective environments for babies and young children

Babies and young children are at high risk of having an accident. This is because they get engrossed in exploring their environment and do not have an understanding of what might be dangerous. This learning outcome looks at how we can provide safe and protective environments for babies and young children.

Policies and procedures

Every setting should have a health and safety policy and is also obliged to carry out risk assessments on the environment, including the furniture and equipment. (This is a statutory requirement in the EYFS framework in England.) It is vital to follow your setting's policies and procedures in order to prevent accidents from occurring. The spider diagram below shows the key dangers for babies and toddlers.

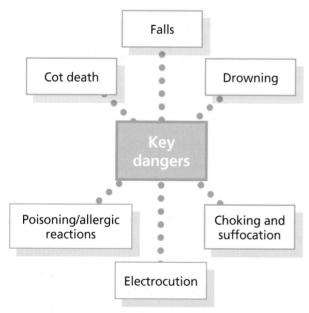

Babies and toddlers are at risk from these dangers

Preventing falls

It is essential that we are aware of areas in the environment that might cause a baby or toddler to fall. Falls can be fatal as they can result in a head injury.

Best practice checklist: Preventing falls

✓ Never leave a baby unattended on a raised surface, such as a changing area.

✓ Do not use baby walkers.

✓ Always use the available harnesses and straps on equipment such as highchairs or pushchairs.

✓ Install and use safety gates.

✓ Keep the floor area fairly tidy.

✓ Remember that non-mobile babies can often roll or wriggle.

✓ Supervise toddlers who may sometimes try to tip out a baby from a piece of equipment.

Preventing choking and swallowing objects

Babies and toddlers often put objects into their mouth in order to explore them. This increases the risk of a choking incident. Babies from around the age of 9 months also have a tendency to look out for and pick up tiny objects that they can spot, such as pins or buttons, which they may then put into their mouth. We therefore need to take preventative measures to avoid accidents. Many 'harmless' objects have the potential to cause suffocation or choking, including carrier bags, soft toys and cushions or pillows.

Feeding

When they are first weaned from the age of 6 months, babies can tend to choke a little on their food. It is important therefore only to put small amounts onto the spoon and to be ready to remove a baby quickly from the harness in a highchair. You should learn the first aid technique to stop them from choking. It is also important that the foods given to babies are suitable for their stage of weaning. Babies can, for example, easily choke on a grape or a piece of apple until such time as they are chewing well. Cutting up fruit into smaller pieces can be a preventative measure.

Preventing burns, scalds and electrocution

Once babies and toddlers are mobile, they become extremely adventurous and interested in their

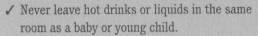

Best practice checklist: Preventing choking and swallowing

✓ Make sure that toys and equipment are 'age' appropriate by reading manufacturer's advice.

✓ Keep floor areas properly clean and vacuumed.

✓ Check that objects in the environment do not pose a choking hazard.

✓ Keep pins, needles and other sharp items in separate areas – out of sight and out of reach.

✓ Make sure that home-made garments are strong and properly made, for example check that buttons are properly sewn on.

✓ Keep plastic bags and wrapping away from babies and toddlers.

✓ Always supervise babies and toddlers at meal times.

Best practice checklist: Preventing burns, scalds and electrocution

✓ Never leave hot drinks or liquids in the same room as a baby or young child.

✓ Do not leave matches, lighters or pills/tablets near children, for example in a handbag that they might reach into.

✓ Check carefully the temperature of feeds and food.

✓ Use a temperature gauge to check the water when washing babies and children.

✓ Use safety gates to prevent children from straying into the kitchen area.

✓ Use safety covers to protect electrical sockets.

✓ Do not encourage babies or toddlers to touch or become interested in electrical appliances such as televisions or DVD recorders.

environment. They start to look into bags and notice what adults do with objects. They become interested in turning things on and off and, if not stopped, will try to poke things into electrical appliances or plugs. They also start to pull themselves up using furniture. This increases the risk of many types of accidents including burns, scalds and electrocution. It is therefore important to supervise them extremely carefully at all times and not to underestimate their abilities. Scalding incidents sometimes occur because adults miscalculate the temperature of food at meal times or water when preparing a bath.

Preventing drowning

It may seem incredible, but babies and children can drown in as little as 5cm of water. This means that babies and toddlers must *never* be left unsupervised when there is water around. This includes bath time and also when there is a water tray or a paddling pool provided.

Safety equipment and features

To keep babies and children safe, we can use a variety of safety equipment. Safety equipment must not be seen as a replacement for good supervision and care although if adults remember to use it consistently it can be very

helpful. Table 1 shows some common types of safety equipment that you might use in your setting.

Table 1: Safety equipment and purposes

Equipment	Purpose
Socket covers	To prevent children from putting their fingers into sockets
Safety gates	To stop children from climbing stairs and from going into areas that pose a danger e.g. kitchen
Corner protectors	To put on furniture with sharp edges
Cupboard and window locks	To prevent children from gaining access to chemicals, cleaning products or other dangerous items and from falling out of windows
Finger guards	To prevent children's fingers from getting trapped in doors
Reins and harnesses	To prevent children from falling out of highchairs, pushchairs or from running into the road
Smoke detector	To raise the alarm if there is a fire

Supervision and risk management

Children in this age group should never be left unsupervised unless they are asleep. This is because at this age children do not have safety sense and are keen to explore and try things out. When we are supervising children, we must keep a balanced attitude towards risk so that the children are in stimulating environments. This may mean holding a child's hand as they climb up stairs or being behind a baby so that it does not fall when taking its first few steps.

Sudden Infant Death Syndrome

Sudden infant death syndrome, sometimes called cot death, is the sudden and unexplained death of a baby. At the time of writing there are over 300 such deaths in the United Kingdom each year, although as a result of recent research and campaigns, the number has been decreasing. Most deaths occur in young babies, but there are some deaths in babies over a year old. The following factors seem to be important in preventing cot death.

Smoking

It is important that those working with babies do not smoke near them or closely handle them immediately after having a cigarette. This is because it takes twenty minutes for an adult's breath to get back to normal; before this time, a baby would be breathing in the adult's smokey breath which will have less oxygen in it and may also have some quite dangerous chemicals.

Temperature

Babies should not become overheated. Care should be taken to check that they are not too hot. The Foundation for Sudden Infant Death Syndrome recommends that rooms should be between 16 and 20°C. This may feel quite cool. In addition, they suggest that blankets rather than duvets should be used to prevent the baby from overheating.

Sleep position

Babies placed down to sleep on their front are at more risk than those placed on their back. The recommendation is that babies should be put on their back with their feet touching the base of the cot. This is often referred to as the 'feet to foot' position. Babies should be tucked in with their shoulders and heads above the sheet and blanket to prevent their head from getting covered up.

Dummies

It is recommended that babies are settled to sleep with a dummy for the first six months. This seems to help their breathing. For speech and communication development, it is suggested that they are weaned off it between six and twelve months.

Getting ready for assessment

During a session with babies or toddlers, make a note of what you do to ensure their safety. Write a reflective account about the session which includes the following:

- How you ensure that the environment is safe
- Safety measures you took to avoid possible accidents, including the use of equipment
- How you supervised and engaged with the child or children
- Measures that you take to prevent cot death if you work with a baby.

Be able to provide for the nutritional needs of babies under 18 months

For babies to grow and develop normally, they need good nutrition. This learning outcome focuses on providing nutrition for babies under the age of 18 months and looks at the latest government guidance on how to prepare feeds and wean young children.

Nutritional needs of babies

Over the past five years there have been significant changes to guidance issued by the Department of Health in relation to the nutrition of babies. It is important to understand the current guidance and also to keep up to date with it. Ideally, you should only refer to information that comes from the National Health Service, the Department of Health or government agencies such as the Food Standards Agency. Below is outlined some of the guidance that is currently being given.

Breast milk

Breast milk is considered to be the best source of nutrition for babies as it is easily digestible and contains all the nutrients in the right quantities for the first six

months of life. Breastfeeding is also a key way in which strong bonds can be formed between mother and child.

The spider diagram shows the benefits of breast milk.

Formula milk

There are many reasons why parents may use formula milk with their child, including difficulties with breastfeeding, or the mother being unwell after birth, but the ideal is always breast milk. A significant recent change to practice is the recommendation that formula milk should be made up only at the time of a feed rather than being made up ahead and stored. This is to prevent food poisoning. This latest recommendation means that unless ready-to-use liquid feeds are used, which are quite expensive, using formula milk for 'convenience' purposes is not as attractive.

Weaning

There have been significant changes to thoughts about **weaning**. It is now recommended that babies are only weaned after the age of 6 months (see section on weaning below on page 345).

(see section on weaning below on page 345).

> **Key term**
>
> **Weaning:** the process of encouraging babies to move from a milk-only diet to taking in other foods

Vitamin supplements

Vitamin drops containing vitamins A, C and D are recommended for breast-fed babies from the age of 6 months and formula-fed babies from around 12 months. These should be taken until children are 4 years old. For low-income families these are provided free.

Peanuts

Advice has changed and unless a child or their family have a history of allergies such as **eczema**, hay fever or food

> **Key term**
>
> **Eczema:** a common skin condition characterised by intense itching and a rash

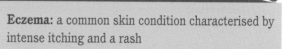

Spider diagram:

- Has the best balance of nutrients and prevents babies from becoming overweight
- Allows mother and baby to bond
- Is easy for the baby to digest
- **Breast milk**
- Prevents constipation
- Is hygienic
- Contains antibodies from the mother

Breast milk has many benefits

allergies, peanut products such as peanut butter can be introduced after the age of 6 months, although the child should be observed in case of an allergic reaction. Whole peanuts are a choking hazard and should not be given.

Over to you

Visit the following website:

www.food.gov.uk

Is your setting following the latest nutritional guidance for the age of children that you are working with?

How do you help parents to know about the latest guidance?

Preparing a plan for weaning

The starting point is to understand that weaning should take place at six months. It is important to wean babies at this point as their stores of iron from birth will have depleted and they need foods alongside milk to gain the iron, as well as other nutrients. It is also important to find out from parents about any dietary requirements or preferences they have that may be linked to cultural, religious or social beliefs, for example, the eating of meat and fish, preparation of foods (see Table 5 in Unit EYMP3 on page 270). Some parents may also want to bring in foods from home because ideally babies should be weaned on the foods they are likely to eat as part of their family's diet.

The Food Standards Agency suggests that weaning is a four-part process. Table 2 summarises these stages. More advice can be found by visiting the website at www.eatwell.gov.uk

Allergies

It is usual to introduce new foods alongside foods that the baby has already had in order to check the child does not have an allergy. If an allergic reaction is suspected, it is important not to give any more of that food. It is also essential that babies are always supervised while they are feeding so that if a child has a violent reaction, such as difficulty in breathing or goes into **anaphylactic shock**, emergency help can be summoned immediately.

Table 2: Stages of weaning

Stage		Foods to offer
Stage 1	This stage is about helping babies to get used to the sensation of solid foods. Offer foods during one normal feed, either in the middle or at the end. Quantity of milk feed (500–600ml) remains the same.	Pureed vegetables Pureed fruit Cereals (not wheat) e.g. baby rice, maize
Stage 2	This stage is about increasing gradually the number of solid feeds and introducing small quantities of new foods. The aim is for babies to have solid foods three times a day. Quantity of milk feed remains the same.	As above but also: Pureed meat, poultry Pulses e.g.beans Full-fat yoghurt, fromage frais Sauces made with full-fat milk e.g. cheese sauce
Stage 3	Introduction of lumpier foods and finger foods and also vitamin drops containing vitamins A, C and D for breast-fed babies. Quantity of milk feed remains the same.	2 servings a day of foods high in carbohydrates e.g. potatoes, yams 2 servings a day of foods high in protein e.g. eggs, meat, fish, tofu, beans Fruit and vegetables to be part of 2 or more meals a day
Stage 4	Introduction of minced or chopped foods. Increasing quantities of food so that the baby has three main meals a day. Milk remains important (500–600 ml a day).	3–4 servings a day of foods high in carbohydrate 3–4 servings of fruit and vegetables 2 servings of foods high in protein Fruit and healthy snacks if baby is hungry between meals

Note: Salt, honey or sugar must not be added to or already in any of the foods

Key term

Anaphylactic shock: a severe allergic reaction which can be fatal

Reporting to parents

It is essential that we work closely with parents so that they know how much food their child has had over the day and also what they have enjoyed or disliked.

Foods to avoid

Table 3 shows foods that must not be given to children under 12 months. Note that nutritional advice can change and it will be essential to regularly check the latest advice.

Preparation of formula feeds

Powdered formula feeds can cause food poisoning unless they are prepared properly and given to babies in sterilised bottles. They also have to be made up strictly in accordance with manufacturer's instructions.

Best practice checklist: Preparing formula feeds

✓ Wash hands thoroughly before washing bottles for sterilising and before making up feeds.

✓ Thoroughly clean all surfaces that bottles will touch.

✓ Always make up fresh feeds rather than storing bottles.

✓ Make sure that bottles are sterilised.

✓ Boil water (including bottled mineral water) to make the bottle with.

✓ Allow the boiled water to cool slightly but not less than 70°C.

✓ Follow manufacturer's instructions as to how to make up the feed and the quantity required.

✓ Cool bottle rapidly.

✓ Check that bottle is lukewarm before giving to baby.

✓ Throw away any feed that is unused after 2 hours.

Table 3: Foods to avoid for babies under 12 months

Food	Reason for avoiding
Salt	Salt can cause problems for the kidneys and later health problems. Do not buy foods that have salt in them or add salt when cooking.
Honey	Sometimes honey can contain bacteria that are dangerous to babies. It can also cause tooth decay.
Sugar	Sugar can cause tooth decay, and also gives babies a liking for sugary foods later on.
Whole or chopped nuts	These can be a choking hazard.
Raw eggs or partially cooked	Eggs are a good source of protein, but must be thoroughly cooked as they may contain bacteria which can cause food poisoning.
Shark, marlin, swordfish	Fish is good for babies, but these fish can contain mercury and should be avoided.
Low fat, low calorie foods	'Diet' low-calorie foods are not good for babies because they need foods that have plenty of nutrients. Low-fat dairy products also need to be avoided as the babies need full-fat versions e.g. full-fat yoghurt.
High fibre foods	Bran, wholemeal pasta and brown rice are good for adults but are very high in fibre and stop babies from digesting other nutrients. Wholemeal bread is fine.
Cow's milk	Cow's milk is not suitable for babies under 12 months. Full-fat milk can be introduced after this time.

Types of formula milk commonly available

Where breast milk is not being used, there is a range of formula milks available. Table 4 shows the types of formula milks that might be used and summarises the main features of each.

Table 4: Types of formula milk

Type	When to use
Whey dominant milks	These formula milks are closest to breast milk and are favoured by health professionals who suggest they should be used until a child moves onto full-fat milk at 12 months.
Casein dominant milks	These formula milks are marketed at 'hungrier' babies or older babies. They are closer to cow's milk. The milk is harder to digest and babies do not become as hungry because digestion takes longer.
Follow-on milks	These formula milks are marketed at babies aged over 6 months and contain higher levels of iron. Health professionals say that main benefit is for babies over 12 months. These are not necessary if babies are having a good diet.
Soya milks	These milks are used with babies who have dairy allergies or whose parents have religious or social beliefs (e.g. vegans). They should only be used after consultation with a family doctor or medical practitioner and are not usually suitable for babies under the age of 6 months.

Understand how to provide for the nutritional needs of young children from 18–36 months

Young children learn some of their attitudes towards foods in this period of their life. They also begin to develop tastes and preferences for certain foods. It is essential that we plan menus that are nutritionally balanced for this age group. This learning outcome looks at preparing menus for young children. It also considers the importance of following parents' wishes to meet children's dietary needs, taking into account any food allergies.

Nutritious meals for young children

From the age of 18 months to 3 years children are growing rapidly in height and should be very active. They therefore need a diet that contains enough energy as well as sufficient protein, which helps growth. When planning menus for children aged from 18 to 36 months, it is essential to ensure that they are having a 'nutrient dense' diet. Nutrient dense foods are those that are high in calories, but critically are also high in nutrients such as protein, vitamins and minerals. Foods that are high in calories, such as sweets and crisps, or are high in saturated fats, are of little food value because they contain few nutrients but they still take up space in children's limited stomach capacity. This means that fried foods, pies and sugary puddings and drinks should only be offered very occasionally. In addition, children in this age range need to be eating fruit and vegetables. This is a different diet from adults who often have to watch the amount of fat and calories they eat and may, for example, have skimmed milk or eat a lot of high-fibre foods.

Working with parents

Ideally, we should provide foods for children that will be similar to those they eat at home. It is therefore good practice to involve parents in meal planning. Parents may provide suggestions and even recipes for the foods that make up their meals at home. In group care settings, this might mean that children will have the opportunity to sample many different types of meals.

Foods to avoid

There are still some foods that should not be given to children under the age of 3 years. They are the same foods as those shown in Table 3 on page 346 with the exception of cows' milk which can now be offered, although it should be full fat until the age of 2 years and thereafter semi-skimmed (providing that children are otherwise eating well). Skimmed milk should not be given to children unless under advice by a medical practitioner.

Drinks

The best drinks for children are milk or water as they do not cause dental decay. It is also important that young children have sufficient water to prevent them from becoming constipated.

The best drinks for children are milk or water

Introducing new foods

It is important that children are introduced to new tastes in this period, particularly fruit and vegetables, so that later on they enjoy having them in their diet. It is also important to encourage but not to force children to eat new foods. Put a small quantity on a plate and sit with children and eat alongside them to act as a role model. It is also helpful to praise children for trying out new foods.

Empty plates

It is important that children do not learn that they have to finish everything on their plates as it is essential that children learn to stop eating when they are full. We need to take a relaxed attitude to meal times and make sure that

Case study: Providing nutritious meals for young children

Little Gems nursery decided to review its food policy. The cook and the manager agreed to look at the quantity and types of food that were being served at meal times and snacks. They also visited the Food Standards website and gained meal planning information from the Caroline Walker Trust. In addition, they consulted with parents to gain their views and feedback. Finally, they observed and talked to children about which meals and snacks they most enjoyed. As a result of their review, they began to give children two portions of fish each week and also made sure that new foods were introduced every week. In addition, the nursery began also to introduce more cooking activities with the children which proved very popular. As part of an inset training day, staff also looked at portion sizes for children which they shared with parents.

1. Why is it important to regularly review the types of food and snacks that are served?

2. Why is it essential to check that meals and snacks are in line with current government recommendations?

3. Why was it a good idea for the nursery to work closely with parents and also to take into account the views of children?

portion sizes are realistic for the age of the child. If a child is not hungry at a meal time, avoid giving large snacks or any treats so that they are ready for their next meal.

Vegetarian diets

Some families will want their children to follow a vegetarian diet. You can find out more about planning for a vegetarian diet by visiting www.eatwell.gov.uk and also the Vegetarian Society, see www.vegsoc.org

Food allergies and intolerances

It is important when planning meals, snacks and drinks for young children that we are aware of children who have allergies, intolerances or special dietary requirements. This means having a system in place so that food is always prepared and served correctly. See Unit EYMP3, pages 265–72, where we looked at common food allergies, intolerances and other dietary needs. It will be important for you to re-visit these pages in order to achieve this assessment criterion.

Over to you

Plan a nutritionally balanced menu for a week for children in the age group 18–36 months. See Unit EYMP3 pages 265–72 to consider the overall calorie intake for the age of children that you are planning for.

Reflect

What systems are in place to prevent children being served food that is not appropriate for them?

How is information gained and shared with parents about their child's food needs?

How do you manage meal times so that children with dietary needs do not feel excluded?

Check your knowledge

1. Why is it important to ask parents about their child's needs and preferences in relation to physical care?

2. Explain the ways in which we might keep a child safe from the effects of the sun.

3. Describe ways in which we may care for children's teeth.

4. Explain what has to be considered when planning a routine for a child.

5. Describe ways in which we might recognise that a child is ready for toilet training.

6. Give some examples of ways in which we might provide physical activity for a toddler.

7. Describe the latest advice to prevent Sudden Infant Death Syndrome.

8. List five foods that should be avoided for babies aged less than 12 months.

9. Identify the difference between whey dominant formula milk and casein dominant formula milk.

10. What is meant by the term 'nutrient dense' and why is it important in young children's nutrition?

CYPOP4

Promote young children's physical activity & movement skills

Physical development and activity plays an essential part in children's health and also in many areas of their development. In this unit we look at the importance of physical activity and movement in children's early years as well as ways in which we can plan and carry out activities to promote it.

Learning outcomes

By the end of this unit you will:

1. Understand the importance of physical activity and the development of movement skills for young children's development, health and well-being

2. Be able to prepare and support a safe and challenging environment for young children that encourages physical activity and the development of movement skills

3. Be able to plan and implement physical activities for young children

4. Be able to build opportunities for physical activity into everyday routines for young children

5. Be able to evaluate the effectiveness of provision in supporting young children's physical activity and movement skills.

Understand the importance of physical activity and the development of movement skills for young children's development, health and well-being

Physical activity is recognised as being an essential component in children's overall health and well-being. This learning outcome looks at the reasons behind the importance of physical activity as well as how it develops in children.

Effects on short- and long-term health and well-being

Unfortunately, at the time of writing, many children are not as physically active as they need to be in order to prevent many harmful short-term and long-term effects on their health. The current guidelines for physical activity suggest that children should be spending a minimum of an hour a day engaged in physical activity. This can be through play, walking or structured activities.

Short-term health

Physical activity helps children to build muscle, develops the skeletal frame, develops the heart and lung function and also plays a part in the prevention of obesity which, as we will see below, is linked to long-term health conditions. Children who are sufficiently active are likely to get to sleep more easily and also sleep for longer. Where physical activity is taken outdoors, children are also less likely to develop infections such as colds and flu.

Long-term health

Physical activity in young children can not only support health in the short term, it can also give children a

positive attitude towards sports, playing outdoors and walking. It is important to build these good foundations in young children, because the overall trend is for children to become less active as they get older. Getting children into the habit of physical activity early on is therefore very beneficial.

If children are not doing sufficient physical activity, they are more likely to become overweight or obese. This in turn is linked to serious diseases such as Type 2 diabetes, cancers and heart disease. Worryingly, it is estimated that as a result of poor diet and lack of physical activity around one-fifth of children in the UK are already showing early signs of heart disease by the age of 12 years.

For adolescent girls who do not take physical exercise, there is also an increased risk of developing osteoporosis later in life, which is a disease that makes bones brittle and more likely to break easily.

Well-being

As well as providing short-term and long-term health benefits, physical activity is also important to children's overall well-being. If physical activity is taken out of doors, children benefit from being out in the fresh air and in an environment that can make them feel free. Children also benefit emotionally and socially as they learn new skills and develop confidence in playing alongside others.

The development of movement skills

This unit primarily concentrates on **locomotive** and **gross motor skills**. These are the ones required to move and also to make arm and leg movements needed, for example to throw or kick a ball.

Key terms

Locomotive: large movements that allow babies and children to gain mobility

Gross motor skills: whole limb movements

The spider diagram looks at some of the main movement skills that children will develop.

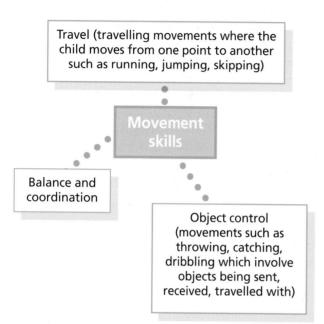

Travel (travelling movements where the child moves from one point to another such as running, jumping, skipping)

Movement skills

Balance and coordination

Object control (movements such as throwing, catching, dribbling which involve objects being sent, received, travelled with)

Children need to develop these movement skills

In order to achieve the physical skills required for the areas in the spider diagram, a mixture of movement skills need to be acquired in the right order. They include the following.

Hand–eye coordination. Many activities require hands and eyes to work together. To catch a ball, for example, the brain needs to take information from the eyes and use it to inform the movements that have to be made with the hands.

Foot–eye coordination. Children have to learn to guide their feet. Climbing stairs and kicking a ball require this type of coordination.

Balance. Balance is a complicated skill, although it is one that most people take for granted. The ability to balance develops with age, with most children relying on visual input to balance.

The development of these skills follows the development of the central nervous system (principally the brain and the spinal cord) in babies and young children. The central nervous system is responsible for collecting, interpreting and sending out information to all parts of the body.

Information is constantly collected via the body's senses of taste, touch, smell, sight and hearing. This information is then transformed into electrical pulses that are carried by the nerves, up through the spinal cord and into the brain. From the information that is received, the brain then responds and sends out instructions to muscles, glands and organs using the network of nerves again. The whole process is surprisingly quick, which means the body can take action against possible danger; for example, a person will almost instantly withdraw their hand from something that is very hot.

In babies and young children the central nervous system has to mature. At first babies are reliant on the many survival reflexes they are born with. These are automatic reactions, but in order to gain control, the central nervous system has to learn how to interpret and control these responses.

Gaining physical control

The rate at which babies and children gain control over their bodies varies enormously, but it is recognised that there are three key principles that underpin the gaining of this control.

1. Development follows a definite sequence
Movements and control develop in a certain pattern, which means that babies cannot walk before learning to sit unsupported.

2. Development begins with the control of head movements and proceeds downwards and outwards
Babies first gain control of their head and top of the spine before other parts of the body. This is thought to be a survival mechanism as it is important for babies to be able to turn their heads to feed.

3. Development begins with uncontrolled gross motor movements before becoming precise and refined
Babies gain control over their arms before managing to control their hands and fingers. This principle is an important one to remember when teaching children new skills, such as handwriting, as it means that they will need to start by making large letter shapes before using pencils to make much smaller ones.

Table 1 shows the expected physical development of babies and children, although it is worth noting that the rate of physical development does vary enormously between individual children.

Table 1: Expected physical development of babies and children

Age	Hand—eye coordination	Movement skills
3 months	Can find hands and bring to mouth Looks at and plays with fingers	Kicks legs strongly and moves arms Movements less jerky although not coordinated Can lift and turn head from side to side when lying on front
6 months	Grasps objects Follows adults' movements	Beginning to roll over Pulls up legs with hands when on back Pushes head, neck and chest off floor when on front
9 months	Bangs objects together	Sits up well unsupported Reaches out for toys May be crawling or shuffling on bottom
12 months	Picks up objects with thumb and forefinger Points to objects Holds cup with help	Mobile either crawling, shuffling or rolling Sits up unsupported for long periods Walks with assistance Tries to crawl upstairs
15 months	Holds and drinks from cup with two hands Builds tower of two bricks	Crawls downstairs feet first Walks independently Seats self in small chair
18 months	Threads four large beads Turns door knobs and handles Pulls off shoes and hats	Bends down from waist to pick up objects Squats down to look at objects Rolls and throws a ball Walks downstairs with adult help Pushes and pulls toys while walking
2 years	Uses a spoon to feed him/herself Puts on shoes Builds a tower of five or six bricks	Kicks a ball that is not moving Climbs on low climbing frame Walks up and downstairs confidently
3 years	Uses a spoon and fork Puts on and takes off coat Turns pages in a book one by one	Walks and runs forwards Walks on tiptoes Throws large ball Kicks ball forward Jumps from low steps Pedals and steers tricycle
4 years	Buttons and unbuttons own clothing Puts together 12-piece jigsaw	Walks on a line Aims and throws a ball Bounces and catches a large ball Runs, changing direction Hops on one foot Pedals and steers a tricycle confidently
5 years	Forms letters Dresses and undresses easily Cuts out shapes using scissors Draws around a template	Skips with a rope Runs quickly and is able to avoid obstacles Is able to use a variety of equipment e.g. swings and slides Hits ball with bat or stick

Links to other aspects of development

It is easy to forget the way we use our physical skills to support many everyday aspects of our lives. To read this page, for example, you have reached out and picked up the book and have turned pages. The development of movement skills gives children this same independence. Over time, they are no longer reliant on adults to physically feed them, clothe them and move them from one place to another. This gives children great confidence and also allows them to learn because they

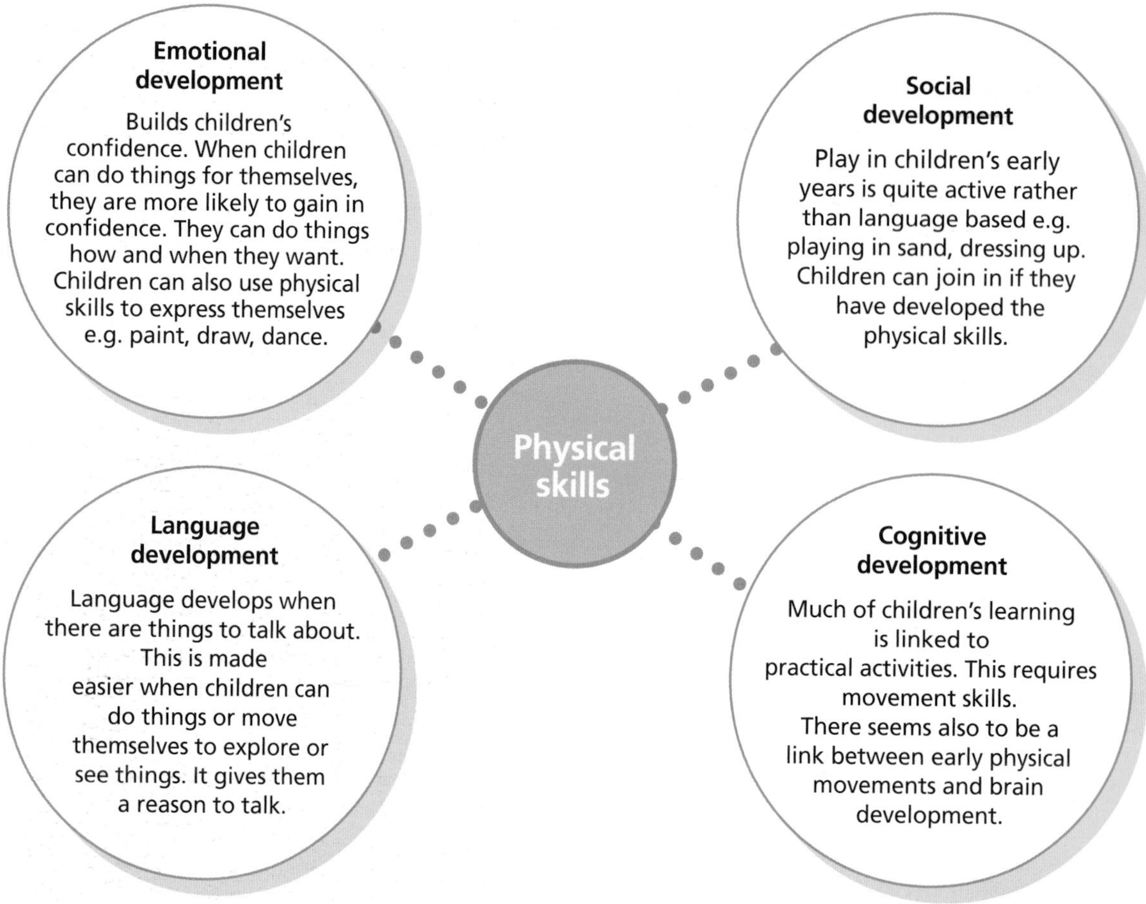

Emotional development

Builds children's confidence. When children can do things for themselves, they are more likely to gain in confidence. They can do things how and when they want. Children can also use physical skills to express themselves e.g. paint, draw, dance.

Social development

Play in children's early years is quite active rather than language based e.g. playing in sand, dressing up. Children can join in if they have developed the physical skills.

Physical skills

Language development

Language develops when there are things to talk about. This is made easier when children can do things or move themselves to explore or see things. It gives them a reason to talk.

Cognitive development

Much of children's learning is linked to practical activities. This requires movement skills. There seems also to be a link between early physical movements and brain development.

Physical skills link to many other areas of development

can now explore. Children are also able to use their new-found skills to play more challenging games and also to play together. The diagram above shows how physical skills link to other aspects of children's overall development.

Skills builder

Observe three different physical play activities that are available for children in your setting.

Identify what type of physical skills children are developing.

Consider how these play activities are promoting other areas of children's development.

Be able to prepare and support a safe and challenging environment for young children that encourages physical activity and the development of movement skills

Children need a good-quality environment in order that they can take part in physical activity and develop their movement skills. This learning outcome looks at ways in which we might prepare an environment, the benefits of natural outdoor environments and how we can keep children safe.

Preparing the environment

Every child needs opportunities for physical activity, including children with disabilities and children who may have additional needs. The term 'environment' needs to be thought of as both indoor and outdoor spaces. The following factors are important when preparing an environment.

Space

How do you ensure that some areas are large enough for children to move, for example space for babies to crawl, or older children to run? For children who have mobility needs, additional space may be needed as they may use special equipment.

Variety

You need to look at what is available in terms of equipment, resources and activities which will allow children to develop both fine and gross motor and movement skills. This is important as children need to develop a range of skills. For children with specific needs or a disability, they may need particular practice at some skills.

Interest

What is available that is exciting, challenging and of interest for children? Children's interests change and so does the way they play as they develop. It is important to prepare environments that are enjoyable for all children, for instance, both boys and girls.

Developmentally appropriate

How do you ensure that the environment is developmentally appropriate? It is important to consider carefully how to create environments that are challenging, but also developmentally appropriate. Equipment, activities and resources that are too easy will not provide sufficient challenge, but if they are beyond a child's developmental stage they will create frustration.

Indoor and outdoor environments

It is important not to think of physical activity as being just for outdoors. Physical activity, including movement skills, should also be part of the indoor environment. This might mean thinking about creating areas or times when children can move to music or setting up enjoyable physical challenges, for example creating tunnels that children can use to go from one area or place to another.

Meeting the needs of all children

Although it is accepted that all children develop at different rates, some children may also have additional needs or a disability that may require specific equipment or adaptations to the layout. A child with a visual impairment may need us to mark clearly the steps on a slide so that they are easily distinguished. In addition, where your setting has different ages of children, it is important to think about providing spaces and equipment suitable for babies and toddlers.

Meeting the needs of all children

Integrating physical activity into play

Ideally, the environments that we create for children should be rich ones so that opportunities for physical activity can be naturally occurring. For example, if there is a mound outdoors, children will probably use it as part of their play – playing hide and seek around it or rolling toys down it. If a tunnel is created which leads to a small den, children will automatically enjoy crawling or crouching in it or, if a role play area consists of both a shop and a home, children are likely to use a pushchair or tricycle to go from one place to another.

Keeping children safe

There is always a tension between allowing children opportunities to develop their physical skills and keeping them safe. In the past few years, there has been a huge emphasis on safety, but it is now recognised that keeping children safe at all costs can be detrimental to their health and well-being. Many children now prefer to be indoors rather than outdoors and sitting rather than engaged in physical activity. The latest thinking about safety is that our duty is to take reasonable care of children. This means identifying possible risks and taking reasonable steps to prevent accidents from occurring. This is usually done in the form of a written risk assessment although it is important to carry out mental risk assessments all the time.

Learning from children

There are times when we will have to intervene because children's actions are not safe, for example they are throwing stones at a door and watching them bounce. Although this is not a safe activity, it might be telling us that we have not created a sufficiently interesting or challenging opportunity for children to throw things. Our next step should be to consider how we can provide a throwing activity that is as interesting as – but safer than – the one they have created.

Over to you

Look at the following situations and analyse the physical skills that the children are enjoying. Consider how to re-create the activities in a safe way.

- Two children are trying to lift up a manhole cover.
- A child is walking up the slide.
- A child is jumping from the top step of the slide to the ground.

The importance of natural outdoor environments

Natural outdoor environments include fields, woodland, moors and beaches. For children they represent a wonderful playground that changes every time they visit according to the weather and the season. Today it is recognised that, whenever possible, children should have access to these types of environments so that they can enjoy and learn about nature. Such environments encourage children to move and practise skills. They may, for example, want to climb on a wall, over a fence or up a tree. They may enjoy running and making footprints in the sand or rushing to hide behind shrubs. Unlike man-made or artificial environments, natural environments can also be very challenging – the terrain underfoot might be uneven, there might be large pools of water to avoid or jump into, or natural barriers to climb on, and so children are likely to gain confidence as well as develop better coordination.

Case study: Balancing risk and challenge

Jo is a childminder who lives in a rural area. There is a paddock adjoining her property which the owner allows her to use with the children. The children love playing in the paddock. They run through it, take carrots to the horses and play hide and seek in and out of the trees. Jo remembers playing in a similar field as a child and believes that it is important for children to have the same sense of freedom. She has carried out a risk assessment which she reviews regularly. She is always with the children, but she has mapped out certain areas where they can play by themselves while still in sight. She always stays with the children when they feed the horses and makes sure that the children do not stand behind them. There are some trees that the older children can climb and she helps the younger children get to the lower branches.

1. Why is it important that children can play outdoors?

2. How is Jo balancing risk and challenge?

3. Why is it important that she regularly reviews her risk assessments?

Be able to plan and implement physical activities for young children

Although many children are naturally active, it is important to think about creating a range of different opportunities for them to develop physical skills. This means that planning for their development is important. This learning outcome requires you to plan opportunities for physical activities for young children and to implement the plan.

Opportunities for physical activity

As we have seen in other units, observation is the key to planning for young children. It needs to be the starting point so we can work out what children enjoy doing and also ensure we are planning opportunities that are developmentally appropriate. The latter is very important as we know that physical development in young children is sequential.

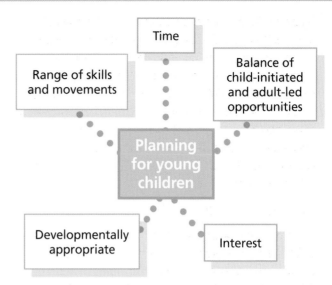

Planning for physical activities

Planning for children's needs

Once you have observed children, the next step is to plan to meet their needs. The spider diagram shows the factors that need to be considered when planning for young children.

Time

How much time is available for children to enjoy physical activity? Children need to play at their own pace. Some children are 'slow to warm up' and so take a while before they know what they wish to do or master a skill. This means that in your planning you should allow sufficient time for children to join in.

Balance of child-initiated and adult-led opportunities

When planning to meet children's needs, there must be a balance of child-initiated and adult-led opportunities. If you are working in England, this is a requirement of the EYFS. It is important in any case as children tend to need time to discover new skills for themselves and also to play in ways that are of interest to them.

Interest

What are children naturally interested in doing? How can this be incorporated or developed further in the planning? Children need to be motivated in order to practise and develop skills. Play is a key way in which children learn and so most planning should look at how children are playing and consider how physical activity can be incorporated.

Developmentally appropriate

In the same way as when creating an environment, activities must be developmentally appropriate for children. For children with disability or additional needs, this might mean seeking further information or advice from parents or other professionals such as the child's physiotherapist.

Range of skills and movements

It is important that opportunities and activities allow children to experience and practise a range of skills and movements. While this unit focuses on movement skills, it will also be important to consider children's fine motor movements.

Planning for non-mobile babies

Babies who are not yet mobile still need opportunities for physical activity. This might include activities to encourage babies to move their hands and legs, for example a baby gym, or grasping a rattle. Babies who are not mobile also need to have time each day lying on their front. This will help them to build up the muscles in the neck and back which will help them to crawl. Babies who are not used to being on their front will need short periods at first so that over time they can become used to it. It is important for adults to put objects for them to reach or hold so that they do not become frustrated. Adults should also get down and play with them. In addition, our plans should include movements that adults do with them which will help babies enjoy movement and gain other skills, such as balance and spatial awareness. Below are some ideas that should be planned daily to help babies enjoy movement.

Rocking: Being rocked by an adult helps babies' balance and spatial awareness.

Swinging: Having the opportunity to be in a baby swing promote babies' balance.

Being held high: Being held high helps babies to see the world from a different perspective.

Bouncing: Being gently bounced while being sung to can help babies to gain a sense of rhythm, for example 'Humpty Dumpty'.

Baby swings promote balance

Sitting on a lap: Sitting on a carer's lap strengthens babies' muscles which will help them to sit.

Being carried: Babies enjoy being carried on a hip. It gives them another view of the world.

Planning for toddlers

Toddlers enjoy exploring and are also keen to practise their new-found skills. They will need opportunities to walk and climb but also throw and transport objects. The table below shows some of the toys, activities and equipment that might be included when planning for this age range.

Table 2: Toys and activities for toddlers

Equipment and activities for fine motor skills	Equipment and activities for movement skills
Books Shape sorters Posting toys and activities Threading toys Playing in water Playing with sensory materials e.g. cornflour and water 'gloop'	Rocking horses Sit and ride toys See-saws Low climbing frames Slides Large balls Brick trolleys Pushchairs Wheeled toys Catching bubbles Rolling balls

Planning for 3- to 5-year-olds

Most children in this age range have become fairly coordinated, but will need support with their fine motor skills. They will also need varied opportunities for movement skills, which should be incorporated into their play wherever possible. Some adult-directed activities can be used to ensure that all children develop a range of movements and skills.

Table 3: Equipment and activities for 3–5-year-olds

Examples of equipment and activities for fine motor skills	Examples of equipment and activities for movement skills
Puzzles Bricks Construction toys Paint Sand and water play Dough and other sensory activities Dressing up clothes and props Small world play	Outdoor apparatus e.g. climbing frames, slides Wheeled toys including tricycles, scooters, wheelbarrows Balls, hoops and cones Pushchairs Cardboard boxes Fabric Parachute games

Table 4: Suggested activities to help 3–5-year-olds practise movement skills

Movement	Activity	Further opportunity
Jumping	Trampoline	
Bouncing	Moving to music	
Sliding	Slide	
Running	'Catch my tail'	
Dodging	'What's the time Mr. Wolf?'	
Crawling	Obstacle course	
Balancing	Wobble board	
Throwing	Throwing balls into paddling pool	
Catching	Catching bubbles	
Hitting	Golf clubs	
Kicking	Soft balls	
Transporting	Pushchairs with role play	
Swinging	Hammock	
Pedalling	Tricycles	

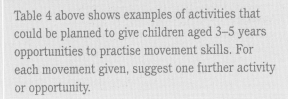

Over to you

Table 4 above shows examples of activities that could be planned to give children aged 3–5 years opportunities to practise movement skills. For each movement given, suggest one further activity or opportunity.

Planning for physical activities

Once you have identified opportunities that will promote physical activity in the children you are working with, you need to incorporate them into a plan. Your plan must:

• meet the individual movement skills needs of children

• include activities that promote competence in movement skills

• encourage physical play.

To ensure the above points are covered, you should base your plan on the observations you have carried out on the children you are working with. There is no single way of planning, but you might like to consider showing in your plan details of equipment, specific adult-led activities and child-initiated play opportunities. If you are working in England with the EYFS, you should also make sure that you show how individual children are being planned for. It is also good practice to involve children when planning activities. They may have ideas about what they would like to do or the equipment they would like to use.

Implementing planned activities

When implementing planned activities, you will need to watch children carefully. Their reactions will tell you whether your plan is developmentally appropriate, sufficiently challenging and also of interest to them. As you are watching children, you should also be ready to change, adapt or even if necessary abandon the activity. Being flexible and ready to change your plan according to the needs and interests of children is essential. It is also worth remembering that children are creative. They may adapt your planned activity to meet their own interests and develop the activity further, as the following case study shows.

Building children's confidence

Some children seem to be more confident than others. They may find movement skills easier or be more comfortable with risk taking. Other children may be hesitant and we will need to find ways of encouraging them. This may mean role modelling a skill or action or breaking it down into steps to make it easier.

Case study: The importance of working with children's interests

Phil brought in several cardboard tubes from a local printer. He put out some balls and showed the children how to roll the balls down them. The children did this for a little while, but one child picked up the tube and carried it across the outdoor area. Another child brought a wheelbarrow across and together they put the cardboard tube in it and began to wheel it around. They pretended to dig up the road and lay pipes. This was something the children had seen recently as the road outside the pre-school had been dug up and a new gas main had been laid. Two other children took the tricycles and pretended to be in their cars. Phil smiled and brought out a piece of paper and wrote 'Stop' and 'Go' on each side of it. He held it up so the children in the tricycles could pretend that they were at the temporary traffic lights. The next day, he brought in fluorescent jackets and hard hats so that the children could pretend to be 'workers'.

1. Why is it important to watch how children are playing?

2. What physical skills did the children practise when they 'diverted' the planned activity?

3. Why is it essential to be flexible when planning for children's physical activity?

Be able to build opportunities for physical activity into everyday routines for young children

In order for children to gain skills and also to build up their stamina, it is helpful if physical activity is incorporated into their daily routines. This learning outcome looks at the importance of building physical activity into everyday routines and considers how you might do this in practice.

The importance of physical activity in everyday routines

Getting children used to physical activity as part of their everyday lives will help them later on in life. It is also another way of helping children practise skills needed for independence. Ideally, it is worth working alongside parents so that children are active at home as well as in our settings. Children should also have time to play outdoors as well as go for a walk so that they are used to being outside each day (see also Unit EYMP2 page 225).

The spider diagram below shows some of the many ways in which everyday routines can be sources of physical activity.

Physical activities can be part of the everyday routine

How to provide opportunities in practice

For this assessment criterion, you will need to think about opportunities for physical activity with the children you work with. To do this, you might like to think about each part of a session and consider how much physical activity children take part in. If you are working with babies or toddlers, you could look at how much time these children are able to move around and how you could encourage them to join in with the everyday routines; for example you might ask toddlers to find their shoes or give babies spoons to hold as you are feeding them. It can also be useful to carry out an observation on individual children to see how much time in a session is spent engaged in physical activity.

Getting ready for assessment

Look at each part of your session.

- Consider how many opportunities there are for children to be involved in the routine activities that might provide opportunities for physical activity (pouring their own drinks, helping to tidy up).

- Consider whether the routine has sufficient opportunities for physical activity, for example time outdoors.

- Explain how the everyday opportunities that are available for the children you work with are important.

Be able to evaluate the effectiveness of provision in supporting young children's physical activity and movement skills

It is important for us to be aware of how effective our provision and practice is in supporting children's physical activity. This learning outcome requires you to consider your provision, identify ways of improving it and also reflect on your own practice.

Assessing effectiveness of planned provision

For this assessment criterion, you must reflect on your provision of physical activities for children and how you support confidence and progression in movement skills. This will include the environment that you have created and any planned activities, as well as opportunities for physical activity in everyday routine. To carry out this reflection, you should consider the following points.

Observe and assess children's participation and developmental progress

Look at a child or children and observe them over a number of weeks. Consider how interested they have been in opportunities for physical activity and also how they have made progress.

Gain direct feedback from children on their participation in and enjoyment of activities

Direct feedback from children can be verbal (listening to their comments, asking them questions) and also non-verbal: we can watch children's reactions, show them photographs or film clips and see if they show positive facial or other reactions to them. Babies and young children also have good memories and so can often point to equipment that they would like to use or to photos that show them engaged in activities, such as a photo of them in the paddling pool.

Gain feedback from parents, colleagues and others

It is useful to gain feedback from other people as they can see more objectively and give us their thoughts about our provision for children. Parents also have experience of seeing their child in other situations and so may be able to let us know if activities are sufficiently challenging.

Other ways of gaining feedback

It can be useful to film children using the environment as this can help us to see which children are accessing opportunities for physical development and whether there are any children for whom the environment and activities are not working.

In addition, it can also be useful to visit other settings that are working with similar aged children as this can provide us with ideas about how to use layout and equipment.

Area for improvement	Reason	Action to be taken	Resources, equipment required	Target date
Role play area	Not sufficient physical activity taking place	Create a petrol station so that children can fill up their 'tricycles'	Wooden crate, Hose pipe, Cash till	15th June
Snack table	Opportunities for pouring required	Put out jugs and beakers for children to pour themselves	Low table, plastic jug, beakers	2nd June

Action plan for future development

Identify and record areas for improvement

You should then use the feedback and information that you have gained to identify areas for future development. In some settings this might mean altering the physical environment, while in others it might mean changing the types of activities and play opportunities. You can present this information in the form of an action plan like the one above.

Reflect on own practice

The final assessment criterion requires you to consider your own practice in relation to supporting children's physical development. You will need to use the feedback you have gained and consider areas you have identified for improvement to help you reflect on your overall practice with children. Below are some questions that you might like to use to begin this process.

- Do you act as a good role model by, for example, joining in physical activity?

- Do you observe children's physical skills regularly?

- How aware are you of children's expected development?

- How do you adapt activities or opportunities to meet the needs of children with additional needs or disabilities?

- How do you ensure that both boys and girls enjoy physical activity?

- How do you plan activities to ensure that children are engaged in a range of movement skills?

- How do you ensure that there is sufficient challenge and variety in the environment for children?

- How often are children able to play in a natural environment?

Check your knowledge

1. What are the benefits of physical activity for children's short-term health?

2. Outline the sequence by which most babies gain control over their bodies.

3. Give three examples of physical skills that most 4-year-olds can demonstrate.

4. Describe the three principles of physical development.

5. Why is it important that activities are sufficiently challenging for children?

6. Explain the benefits of natural outdoor environments in relation to children's physical activity.

7. Why is it essential to observe children before creating a plan for physical activity?

8. Why is it important to provide children with sufficient time to enjoy a physical activity?

9. Give three examples of ways in which everyday routines can be used to promote children's physical activity.

10. Evaluate the importance of reflecting on opportunities for physical activity in a setting.

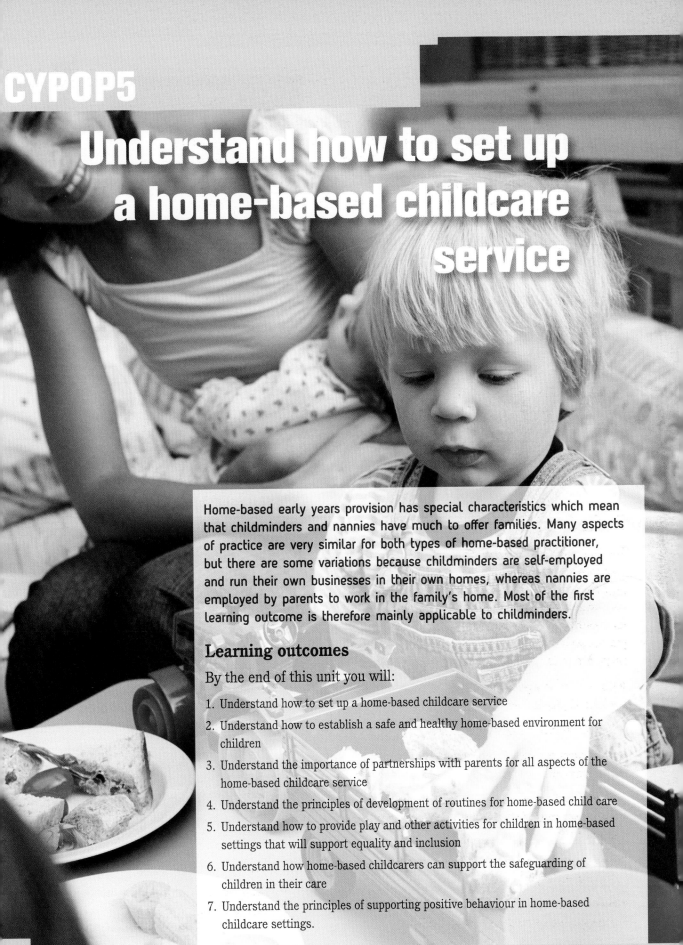

Understand how to set up a home-based childcare service

Home-based early years provision has special characteristics which mean that childminders and nannies have much to offer families. Many aspects of practice are very similar for both types of home-based practitioner, but there are some variations because childminders are self-employed and run their own businesses in their own homes, whereas nannies are employed by parents to work in the family's home. Most of the first learning outcome is therefore mainly applicable to childminders.

Learning outcomes

By the end of this unit you will:

1. Understand how to set up a home-based childcare service
2. Understand how to establish a safe and healthy home-based environment for children
3. Understand the importance of partnerships with parents for all aspects of the home-based childcare service
4. Understand the principles of development of routines for home-based child care
5. Understand how to provide play and other activities for children in home-based settings that will support equality and inclusion
6. Understand how home-based childcarers can support the safeguarding of children in their care
7. Understand the principles of supporting positive behaviour in home-based childcare settings.

Understand how to set up a home-based childcare service

Legislation and regulation

If you intend to become a childminder caring for children aged under 8 years, the law in the UK requires you to be registered; registration for nannies and for childminders caring for older children is voluntary. Responsibility for registration lies with different agencies across the UK:

- in England, the Office for Standards in Education (Ofsted) www.ofsted.gov.uk/
- in Wales, the Care and Social Services Inspectorate for Wales (CSSIW) http://wales.gov.uk/cssiwsubsite/newcssiw/
- in Scotland, the Scottish Commission for the Regulation of Care (the Care Commission) www.carecommission.com/
- in Northern Ireland, your local Health and Social Services Trust.

The regulatory bodies publish the standards you have to meet in order to be registered, and the registration procedures.

Policies and procedures

If you have written **policies** and **procedures** you can share them with parents, to make it clear to them how you intend to work. Registration may require you to draw up such documents.

It is best to keep policies and procedures simple. A policy written in straightforward language is more parent-friendly, and straightforward procedures are more likely to be useful.

Even when you take precautions, accidents may occur or a child may become ill when you are looking after them. Registered childminders are required to hold a current first aid certificate and be prepared to deal with an emergency, and other home-based practitioners should also complete such a course.

We will look at developing other procedures and policies for managing children's behaviour, for safeguarding children, and for equality and inclusion later in this unit.

Confidentiality and data protection

You learned about keeping records confidential earlier (see Unit SC1 page 15). Remember that any professional practitioner must be very vigilant about **confidentiality.**

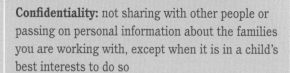

Key term

Confidentiality: not sharing with other people or passing on personal information about the families you are working with, except when it is in a child's best interests to do so

As you get to know families, you will acquire a lot of information about them – especially if you are a nanny, living with the family. You may be told some information directly (by parents or other professionals) and some of it you may pick up indirectly (sometimes from the children). Some of this information must be treated in a confidential way.

Best practice checklist: Confidential information

✓ You should always treat information about parents' relationship difficulties, financial and business matters, and health issues as confidential.

✓ When deciding what sort of information should remain confidential, think about how *you* would feel if such information about you and your family was general knowledge.

✓ Confidential information should only be passed to other professionals who 'need to know'.

You should only share or pass on confidential information if:

✓ parents have given permission for you to do so. If you feel that it would be helpful to share information about a child's progress with a health visitor, check with parents that they are happy with this.

✓ it is essential to do so in the interests of a child, for example if you suspect that a child is being abused. There may be circumstances when you should – in fact must – pass on information without any previous discussion with the parents, in the interests of protecting children from harm. A child's welfare must always take top priority.

You may find you experience pressures from other people which make it difficult to keep information confidential. For example, parents of other minded children, your friends, neighbours, even other childminders or nannies may be curious about the children you care for, and their families. They might try to get you to tell them things that should remain confidential, perhaps in a gossipy way. The checklist below shows an example of how you might deal with such a situation.

Best practice checklist: Maintaining confidentiality

If other people try to get you to share confidential information inappropriately:

✓ be firm in stating clearly that you cannot give the information they seek

✓ explain that it would be unprofessional to break a confidence

✓ bring the conversation to a swift conclusion

✓ if necessary, move away from the person.

Childminders' family members should also be careful about not passing on information about the children and families who come to their home.

If you record information about children and families, you must comply with the Data Protection Act 1998.

Over to you

Take a look at www.ico.gov.uk and read the section on data protection and your legal obligations to check that you handle families' personal information appropriately.

Ways of complying with the data protection provisions include:

- keeping written information about children and families securely in a lockable personal record box so no one in or visiting your home can have access
- using password-protected computer files to keep records.

Marketing

If you are starting out as a childminder, you need to develop a **marketing** plan.

Key term

Marketing: promoting your business to potential customers

Start by thinking about what parents want to know when they are making childcare choices.

Although you probably cannot afford glossy brochures and media advertisements, think about:

- cards or a simple but eye-catching computer-generated leaflet
- distribution to newsagents' windows, local facilities used by parents and parents-to-be, organisers of ante- and post-natal classes, personnel departments of local big employers, estate agents, job centres
- other childminders in the area – if they are full, they may pass on enquiries to you.

Over to you

Using the ideas above, draw up a plan about how you can promote your service.

Best practice checklist: Marketing your business

Include information about:

- ✓ the area you live in (not your exact address)
- ✓ times you offer your service
- ✓ the schools and pre-schools you can take and collect for
- ✓ your training and experience
- ✓ your registration and insurance
- ✓ the play activities you offer and any regular places you go such as the park or childminders' drop-in
- ✓ your 'unique selling point' (USP), what makes your service special, such as:
  - ✓ a home atmosphere
  - ✓ individual attention
  - ✓ part of the local community
  - ✓ brothers and sisters of different ages coming to the same place for childcare
  - ✓ your flexibility if you can work irregular or out-of-the-norm hours.

Financial planning

To be able to make an income from childminding, you have to plan how to handle your finances. It is up to you to set the amount you charge parents, but you need to think about:

- the expenses of running your childminding business, such as:
  - ○ meals and snacks, play materials, toiletries, safety equipment
  - ○ insurance and membership of NCMA, SCMA or NICMA
  - ○ stationery to run your business – account book, contracts, accident book
  - ○ phone calls and transport costs
  - ○ wear and tear on your home and extra heating

- how much money you want to be able to take out of the business as regular income for you and your family

- the 'going rate' in your area — what parents are able and willing to pay for the services of a childminder.

When you negotiate your charges with parents, make it clear what payment you expect for:

- absences of the child, illness (child's, parents', yours)

- unsocial hours

- retainers (to keep a place open, for example, during maternity leave).

To avoid any later misunderstandings, it is best to use a written contract (which both you and the parents sign) to detail what your charges are, and to make it clear whether the charges include:

- holidays (parents' and yours)

- outings and other extras

- food, nappies etc.

Over to you

Make notes on how you calculate how much to charge parents.

Agree a written contract with parents

Support and information

Your local authority early years service may be able to provide you with information and advice about many aspects of your work, but you may find that the most reliable and up-to-date sources of information about business issues are NCMA, SCMA and NICMA (see page 364), as well as other experienced childminders in your area. If you are a member of a childminding network, the co-ordinator will also be a good source of information.

Understand how to establish a safe and healthy home-based environment for children

You learned in Unit CYP3.4 about keeping children safe and healthy and we looked also at the policies and procedures (page 147) which cover how to deal with accidents, emergencies and illnesses. But there are some specific factors to take into account in a home-based setting.

Safe and healthy environment

Home-based practitioners provide meals and snacks for children, and this must be done in hygienic conditions.

Regular disinfecting of the seat and handle of the toilet, the door handle and taps in the toilet/bathroom is also necessary to help maintain a hygienic environment.

If there are pets in your home-based setting, take care to:

- clean the floor after a pet has been fed (to prevent bacteria multiplying or pests being attracted)

- keep pets' feeding dishes and litter trays out of reach of the children

- keep animals clear of fleas, wormed and inoculated

- exercise dogs away from the garden

- keep the sand pit covered when it is not in use to prevent animals getting into it

- never leave a child alone with a dog or other animal such as a reptile which might harm them.

Disposing of waste in a home environment must be done hygienically.

Best practice checklist: In the kitchen

✓ When storing, preparing and cooking food:

  ✓ cover or wrap food in the fridge and keep raw meat at the bottom (to prevent blood dripping onto other foods)

  ✓ never use food after the use-by dates

  ✓ take care to de-frost frozen food fully before cooking

  ✓ never re-freeze food that has been thawed.

✓ Keep implements and utensils used for preparing food, tea towels and working surfaces clean, and never allow pets on to working surfaces.

✓ Run the fridge at 4°C to 5°C, and the freezer at minus 18°C (to stop bacteria multiplying).

✓ Cover pet food stored in the fridge, and wash up and store pets' feeding bowls separately from utensils used by humans.

✓ Never change babies' nappies or put toddlers on the potty in the kitchen.

Best practice checklist: Waste disposal

✓ Empty rubbish bins frequently and clean them thoroughly.

✓ Wrap disposable nappies individually and put in the dustbin outside the house as soon as possible, not in the kitchen bin.

✓ Tip the potty down the toilet (not the hand basin).

Some common objects and materials found in the home can be harmful to children so must be stored out of their sight and reach:

● gardening, car maintenance and DIY equipment and materials

● medicines and tablets

● matches and sharp objects such as knives and razor blades

● household cleaners

● polythene bags

● alcohol and cigarettes.

Any house plants which could be poisonous may also need to be put on high shelves.

Supervision of children

An important aspect of your practice in maintaining children's safety and well-being is to supervise them. They may need:

● constant supervision: you watch them every moment, perhaps in direct contact with them

● close supervision: you watch them most of the time, ready to step in and take action if their safety is at risk

● general supervision: you check on them regularly, and keep a 'watchful eye' from a distance.

Reflect

Think about the different levels of supervision you give children, depending on:

● their stage of development and understanding (compare an inquisitive toddler's needs with a calm 7-year-old)

● what they are doing (think about a child learning to use a sharp knife)

● where they are (consider a visually impaired child outside the familiar home setting; or children who are taken on an outing)

● changes in their surroundings (when it has been raining or it is icy, outdoor play equipment may be slippery).

Equipment and safety requirements

When you buy equipment, always check for safety standards marking, such as the British Standards Institute, or the European Union CE mark.

Look out for safety markings, such as the Lion Mark, on toys.

Safety equipment like car seats should never be purchased from second-hand shops, car boot or 'nearly new' sales where you cannot be sure of the quality and safety of the equipment for sale.

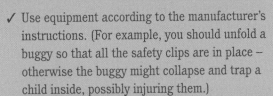

Best practice checklist: Using equipment safely

✓ Use equipment according to the manufacturer's instructions. (For example, you should unfold a buggy so that all the safety clips are in place – otherwise the buggy might collapse and trap a child inside, possibly injuring them.)

✓ Use equipment which is suitable and safe for the size and stage of development of a particular child: either too small or too big can be dangerous. (It would be unsafe to put an 18-month-old child into a car seat designed for a 4-year-old. Be alert to warning symbols on toys which say 'not suitable for children under 36 months'.)

✓ Make regular checks of toys for sharp edges, pieces working loose, etc. and repair them or throw them away; check that swings do not work loose; check that brakes are working properly on prams and buggies.

All equipment can be used in a safe or unsafe way. Make sure you familiarise yourself with the correct way of using and storing all the equipment you have.

Risk assessment

One of the statutory regulations you must comply with is to carry out a **risk assessment.**

A risk assessment involves taking a long hard look at the home environment, room by room, plus the garden, and

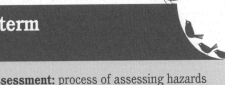

Key term

Risk assessment: process of assessing hazards and identifying control measures for all activities and outings

spotting potential hazards. When you have seen where all the potential dangers are, you need to decide what changes to make to reduce the risks you identify. It may help you to spot the danger points in a room if you get down to toddler height.

Case study: Manjit's risk assessment

Manjit is planning to start childminding in her home. She carried out a risk assessment, walking through her house and round the garden, noting all the potential hazards. She noticed:

- slippery rugs on her polished hall floor
- the kitchen doorway off the hallway
- the main staircase rising out of her sitting room
- the open fireplace in the sitting room where she sometimes lights a fire in cold weather
- several exposed power points
- a rickety garden fence
- a broken catch on the garden gate so it would not shut
- the pond in the back garden.

What actions should Manjit take now?

Over to you

The Health and Safety Executive (HSE) advises that risk assessment is 'common sense' and does not have to be overcomplicated; look at their straightforward Five Steps to Risk Assessment on www.hse.gov.uk.

Medication

You should never give a child any form of medication without the written instructions of a parent. You may not know about a child's allergies or possible reaction to medication.

Best practice checklist: Administering medicines

✓ Give the doses in the amounts and at the times set out in the instructions given by the parents.

✓ Make a note each time you give a dose of the amount and time, and get parents to sign your record to show they have seen it.

Understand the importance of partnerships with parents for all aspects of the home-based childcare service

The importance of partnerships

In Unit CYP3.5 you learned about the importance of forming partnerships with parents. Look back at Unit CYP3.5 pages 163–65, and then read the Reflect box below which will help you to consider why it is important in the context of home-based childcare.

Establishing and developing partnerships

The subject of building partnerships was discussed in Unit EYMP1. It is worth refreshing your memory – read Unit EYMP1 pages 221–23 again. The checklist below summarises the key points to bear in mind.

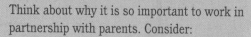

Reflect

Think about why it is so important to work in partnership with parents. Consider:

- the central role of parents in children's lives
- the attachment between parents and their children
- young children's needs for continuity and emotional security
- how children's learning is enhanced by their parents' involvement
- the need to exchange information with parents regularly.

One aspect of relationships with parents specific to the home-based setting is that parents come into childminders' homes and nannies work in parents' homes – so there is a lot of close contact. This can make it difficult for home-based childcarers to keep relationships with parents on a professional footing – business-like, but within a friendly atmosphere.

Best practice checklist: Partnerships with parents

To establish and sustain partnerships with parents, you need to:

✓ understand the central role of parents in their children's lives, and how demanding and challenging that role can be

✓ appreciate and respect families' different lifestyles, values and expectations for their children

✓ communicate effectively – openly and frequently – with parents

✓ base your relationship on trust and respect.

Build parents' trust in you

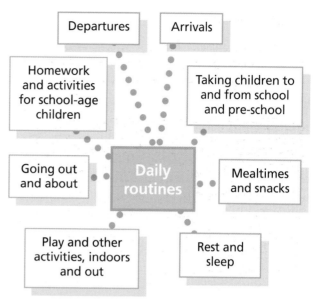

Daily routines can include many different activities

Understand the principles of development of routines for home-based child care

Establishing routines

The routines you establish will depend upon the number of children you look after and their ages, and how long you look after them each day.

Regular routines provide children with consistency but need to be flexible enough to accommodate spontaneous learning opportunities.

Best practice checklist: Routines

✓ Meet children's needs by:

  ✓ creating a relaxed atmosphere and unhurried pace

  ✓ timing meals to fit in with pre-school, naps and other parts of your routine

  ✓ giving them plenty of time for play.

✓ Comply with parents' wishes as far as possible, for example:

  ✓ either make sure the child has a long sleep during the day so they are awake in the early evening and the parents can enjoy their company, or avoid letting the child sleep for a long time during the day so they sleep in the evening and parents can have time for themselves

  ✓ give children food which complies with parents' requirements, such as a vegetarian diet, or one which relates to cultural or ethical considerations.

✓ Involve children in deciding what to do next – do they want to play in the garden or go down to the shops?

Adapting routines

As children develop and grow, you have to change routines to suit their changing needs.

Welcoming and valuing each child

Young children need support in making transitions from one stage of their life to another, from being at home with their parents to spending time in an early years setting. That is why emphasis is placed on settling children in to a new situation and giving them time to adjust to new surroundings and to develop trust in new people. As babies approach the age of 12 months, they may experience '**stranger anxiety**', and many toddlers feel '**separation anxiety**'.

Give the child individual attention to help them settle.

Key terms

Stranger anxiety: from the age of about 8 months, it is usual for children to become wary of people they don't know

Separation anxiety: under-threes often find it difficult to cope with being separated from the familiar adults in their lives

The strategies you use to welcome a child and make them feel confident in your setting will depend on their stage of development and previous experiences. The checklist on page 373 gives some suggestions of how you can help to smooth the transition process.

Case study: Nick's childminding routine

Nick began looking after Isla and Daljit when Isla was 8 months and Daljit 2 years old. He built a routine to incorporate their naps, taking them to the park for short periods when they were awake. Soon, Daljit just needed a short rest so Nick spent more time playing quietly with him at home while Isla slept, but they had no time deadlines. When Daljit started pre-school, and Isla was awake for more of the day, more time was spent playing with her, but they had to take and fetch Daljit at fixed times.

1. What further changes will Nick have to make to accommodate a busier routine when Daljit is at school and Isla at pre-school?

2. What factors will he have to take into account?

Best practice checklist: Helping with transitions

✓ Arrange for the child to spend time with you with a parent, and then, when they are ready, progress to short stays without the parent.

✓ Offer a calm and warm welcome.

✓ Give the child lots of individual attention, stay close by and offer reassurance.

✓ Make sure they have their comfort object or 'cuddly' if they need it.

✓ Give the child lots of information about what happens in your setting.

✓ Make sure they have familiar food and hear familiar language (for example, recordings of their parents' voices).

Reflect

Think about the play experiences and activities you provide. In what ways does this play offer children the chance to learn, by:

- having first-hand experiences of the real world?
- practising skills, and trying something out (an idea, a feeling) to see what happens?
- thinking creatively, making discoveries and solving problems?
- expressing ideas, including fears and anxieties?
- taking risks?
- interacting and cooperating with others?

In Units SC2, CYP3.2, CYP3.7 and EYMP4, we explored the ideas involved in a setting being inclusive so children's rights to play and learn are available to all children — whatever their gender, ethnicity, social or family background, or disability.

Understand how to provide play and other activities for children in home-based settings that will support equality and inclusion

Inclusive play

Healthy children play from their earliest days, and children of all ages should have daily opportunities to play. If a child does not or cannot play, there is cause for concern. In Unit EYMP2 (page 225) you learned about the importance of play for children's learning and development.

Play should come spontaneously from the child's own interests and motivations. It does not always have a tangible end-product — it is the *doing* and *being* that matter and which enable the learning to happen.

Reflect

How do you ensure that the play environment you provide is accessible and welcoming to all children?

Do the play experiences and activities you offer avoid stereotyping and give each individual child an equal chance to participate and learn?

Is any prejudice or discriminatory behaviour that arises promptly and firmly challenged?

Play in a home-based setting

In your home-based setting, you may have space for a specific play room or area, or you may provide play activities in the family living space. In either case, you need to provide:

- storage for toys and equipment which is accessible to the children so they can choose for themselves, and help with putting away

- clear floor space

- table-top space (with a wipe-clean surface or plastic cover)

- access to play out of doors, either in the garden or a park or playground.

You should not feel that you have to provide a mini-pre-school or nursery — it is important to maintain the home atmosphere as that is why many parents choose to use childminders for their children rather than a nursery.

You do not have to spend large sums of money on elaborate toys. Stick to basic play equipment and materials, and use your imagination to improvise play things from household objects. Cardboard boxes, wooden spoons and old saucepans have great play potential, as does a tablecloth draped over a clothes-horse.

Children enjoy being involved in 'grown up' tasks, and there are many opportunities for children's development and learning in everyday activities in the home setting.

- Laying the table involves counting and sorting, and so does hanging out and bringing in washing.

Everyday objects have play potential

Reflect

In your home-based setting, how can you provide most of these play activities and opportunities? What equipment and materials can you use? When and how can you lay them out and give children access to them?

- Make believe or imaginative play with dressing up clothes and 'props' (tea set, pots and pans, iron and ironing board), 'small world' toys like a garage, farm or doll's house, dolls and puppets.

- Puzzles.

- Construction materials like wooden blocks or Lego.

- Drawing and painting – large sheets of paper with crayons, pencils and felt-tip pens, paint and brushes.

- Junk modelling – scissors and glue to make things from cardboard boxes, tubes and other

recycled materials like fabric and pictures cut from catalogues – and a bit of glitter for special occasions!

- Books – from card books for babies to reference books for school age-children.

- Shape sorters and threading toys.

- Playdough.

- Board games – from simple picture lotto for pre-schoolers to more complicated games for school-age children

- Water or sand play, perhaps out of doors.

- Physical play.

- Treasure baskets for babies.

- Helping to prepare food can develop hand—eye coordination and weighing ingredients for cooking is early maths.

- Watering plants and watching them grow is early science.

- Helping with the washing-up (non-breakable and non-sharp things) is a form of water play.

Observing children's play

In Unit CYP3.2 you learned about observing children (see Unit CYP3.2 page 84). Observation is a valuable aspect of practice. However well you know a child, it is worth setting aside specific times to spend quietly watching and listening, taking time to focus specifically on the individual child, to reassess what they can do and how they are behaving.

The EYFS expects practitioners to base the activities and experiences they provide to support children's development and learning on their observation of each child. Home-based practitioners sometimes feel daunted at the idea of carrying out observations, but, in fact, childminders and nannies observe children closely, often without being consciously aware that they are doing so, and know each child well as an individual.

Learning from everyday activities

Case study: Karen's observations

When she first became a childminder, Karen just watched children in a general way to check on their safety and well-being but she discovered this informal approach led her to focus on an aspect of development which was of particular interest at the time and to miss other things. When Edward was just learning to walk, Karen was concentrating on helping him take his first steps, and she found she was distracted from supporting his development of early speech. She explained to other childminders in her network why she had started more careful and consistent active observations.

'Just watching children is very enjoyable, but you may not get all the information you need to help a particular child because you miss important things.

If you observe a child carefully, you get to know what they can do and what they're trying to do, and what they're interested in. That helps to plan play that will help them to learn and progress. You pick up the sort of health concerns or delays in a child's development that might flag up something that needs attention. If you observe unexpected changes in behaviour, there may be problems in the child's life that you need to be aware of.'

Have there been occasions when you have used your observations of a child to help you identify either an aspect of their development which might give rise to concern, or to indicate suitable play which would support their progress?

As children play, you observe them by watching and listening to them. Consciously watching and listening to children, really paying attention to them, can show you:

- what each child is capable of doing and when they develop new skills

- how they behave and any changes in their behaviour

- what particularly interests them

- their reactions to new situations and opportunities.

Home-based practitioners observe the children they work with all the time, but are less likely to make extensive observation records since they do not have colleagues to pass on information to. You might choose to write some more detailed observations to share with parents from time to time, or to create some examples to demonstrate to an inspector how you make use of your observations. But don't get too obsessed with keeping masses of observation records — taking your time away from the children. That is not the purpose of observation! You can meet the inspection requirements of the EYFS by talking about the observations you make and showing that you know how to record them to share with parents and other professionals when necessary.

Getting ready for assessment

Prepare a policy on equality and inclusion in your home-based setting. Include statements about your intentions to:

- welcome all children and families

- meet the needs of each individual child whatever their ethnicity, cultural or social and family background, gender or disability

- treat all children fairly and equally so each child has an equal chance to develop and learn

- help children to learn about people who are different from themselves, and to respect and enjoy the differences between people

- guide children away from prejudice and discriminatory behaviour.

Equality

In Units SC2, CYP3.7 and EYMP4, you learned about children's rights to equality of opportunity and inclusion, according to their individual requirements. Look again at these units now. As a home-based childcare worker, you need to be equally aware of your responsibilities in this regard.

Other resources

You can extend and enhance the opportunities for play you provide in your home-based setting by making use of resources in your neighbourhood.

Case study: Using local facilities

These childminders and nannies make use of local facilities.

Bushra has found that her local library has special arrangements for home-based practitioners to borrow more than the usual number of books.

Andy uses the toy library to try out play equipment to see whether it's worth buying.

Kirsty has found the childminding network's equipment loan scheme invaluable for getting equipment like a play gym that babies only use for a few months.

Mel makes trips to the scrap store to get paper, paint and junk materials for reasonable prices.

Penny takes the children to the childminding group's drop-in sessions so they have opportunities to play in a group with other children.

There isn't room in Sarah's garden for vigorous ball games or a climbing frame, slide and swing, so she takes the children to the local play park several times in a week.

1. What use do you make of facilities like these in your area?

2. Find out about other local resources that could support your work.

Understand how home-based childcarers can support the safeguarding of children in their care

Safeguarding and the duty of care

Like all early years professionals, it is very important that home-based practitioners are well-informed about child abuse since you might find yourself in contact with an abused child. Don't think that it could never happen to you because you work with 'nice families'. Child abuse happens in all social and cultural groups in our society, and children of all ages from tiny babies to teenagers, including disabled children, are abused. It is estimated that 150 to 200 children die in England and Wales every year as the result of abuse or neglect. Abuse can have long-lasting traumatic effects which may damage children's development — physical and emotional.

Besides being aware of some of the signs of abuse, you must know what to do if you are concerned. Children, especially young children, are very vulnerable and cannot seek help for themselves. They have to rely on adults to protect them from pain and distress. In Unit CYP3.3, we saw that all practitioners have a **duty of care** to **safeguard** children. Before reading the following section, you should read again Unit CYP3.3 pages 110–15.

Key terms

Duty of care: a requirement to exercise a 'reasonable' degree of attention and caution to avoid negligence which would lead to harm to other people

Safeguard: promote children's welfare and put measures in place to improve children's safety and prevent abuse

To safeguard children, you need knowledge of signs that might indicate that a child is experiencing abuse or bullying, and you should know what action to take to protect them.

Signs of possible abuse

The possible signs, symptoms, indicators and behaviour which might indicate that a child is being abused were outlined earlier — see Unit CYP3.3 page 123.

Reflect

Which of these physical indicators might make you suspect that a child was being abused? Which might have other explanations?

- bruises on a child's buttocks
- cuts on a child's knees
- small round burns
- loss of appetite and weight
- dirty and/or smelly child
- irritation in the genital area.

Which of these behavioural indicators might be cause for concern about abuse or have other causes?

- sexually explicit behaviour
- reverting to younger behaviour
- child is fearful of adults
- changes in behaviour such as the child suddenly becoming very quiet or becoming aggressive.

You should not rush into making an assumption that a child has been abused but, if you observe several signs, or if they are persistent or extreme, alarm bells should be set off for you.

Regulations

The requirements which regulate your registration include a section on safeguarding. It is your responsibility to become familiar with what this says and understand what action you might have to take if you became concerned that a child needed your intervention to safeguard them. It is essential that you identify the relevant section of the regulations and become familiar with them.

EYFS in action

The Statutory Framework of EYFS requires you to have 'an effective safeguarding children policy and procedure', and also to inform both Ofsted and your local child protection agency if allegations are made that a child is harmed or abused in your home-based setting.

Read the following example:

Julie, a childminder, was deeply shocked when the father of one of the children she looks after accused her teenage son, Aaron, who has learning difficulties, of causing the bruises on his daughter's back.

Aaron was away staying with respite carers for two days before the allegation was made, and Julie had noticed the bruises earlier in the day and made a note about them in her accident and incident book.

Julie knew she had to comply with the EYFS requirements and informed both the local social services department and Ofsted about the allegation, but she also contacted NCMA for help and support in dealing with the situation.

What actions could you take which would help to protect you and members of your family from the effects of such allegations?

Procedures for lone workers

If a child tells you about someone who is harming them, or signs of possible abuse give you cause for concern, you must not ignore the situation. You must take action to protect the child. You could prevent pain or suffering for a child — or even save a life. Having policies and procedures set out clearly will guide you about the action you need to take.

In group settings, practitioners can discuss their concerns with a manager or other senior colleague. However, most home-based childcarers are lone workers and have no one at hand to explore how seriously to take a possible situation, and the appropriate actions. If you feel unsure about whether to report a situation to social services, you can contact the NSPCC on 0808 800 5000 to get advice and help with thinking through what to do. You do not have to name children or families, but can explore the situation in confidence. NCMA, SCMA or NICMA may also be able to offer advice and information.

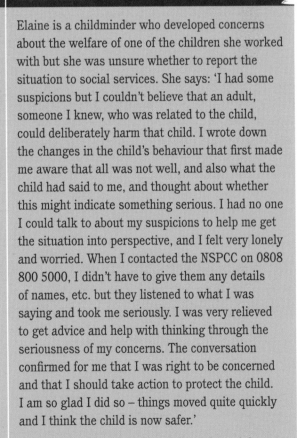

Case study: Elaine's concerns

Elaine is a childminder who developed concerns about the welfare of one of the children she worked with but she was unsure whether to report the situation to social services. She says: 'I had some suspicions but I couldn't believe that an adult, someone I knew, who was related to the child, could deliberately harm that child. I wrote down the changes in the child's behaviour that first made me aware that all was not well, and also what the child had said to me, and thought about whether this might indicate something serious. I had no one I could talk to about my suspicions to help me get the situation into perspective, and I felt very lonely and worried. When I contacted the NSPCC on 0808 800 5000, I didn't have to give them any details of names, etc. but they listened to what I was saying and took me seriously. I was very relieved to get advice and help with thinking through the seriousness of my concerns. The conversation confirmed for me that I was right to be concerned and that I should take action to protect the child. I am so glad I did so – things moved quite quickly and I think the child is now safer.'

1. If you were in Elaine's position, what might you have done?

2. How do you think you might feel?

Getting ready for assessment

Prepare a policy setting out your intentions if you become aware that a child is being harmed or abused. Make it clear that:

- if you have reason to suspect that a child is being harmed or abused, you will take action to protect the child, putting their interests and welfare first, and that the law requires you to do so

- if a child starts to tell you about harm they are experiencing, you will listen carefully to what they tell you, but will allow them to communicate in their own way and at their own pace, explaining to them that you have to share the information with other people to try to help them

- in certain circumstances, you might take action without informing parents (if a child has told you that it is a parent who is harming them).

You should share this policy with parents when their child joins your home-based setting, so they are fully aware of what you would do if you suspected abuse.

Prepare procedures to follow in the event of suspicions of harm or abuse. Include:

- details of who should be informed about suspected abuse (social services department/police)

- how you would record your concerns, writing down factual information about what you have seen and observed, with dates and times

- how you would maintain confidentiality

- details of how you would inform your regulating body

- how you would keep your focus on the care of the child, giving warm, calm comfort and reassurance

- the actions you must take if allegations are made about harm or abuse occurring in your setting.

Understand the principles of supporting positive behaviour in home-based childcare settings

Children's behaviour

In earlier units, we looked at children's behaviour. See Units CYP3.2 and EYMP1. The way children behave is linked mainly to:

- the stage of their development

- events in their lives.

At times, their behaviour may cause concern or be challenging to adults.

Stage of development

Not all children will behave in the same way at the same age, but some patterns of age-related behaviour are quite common. Although not exhaustive, the following list includes some age-related behaviours.

- As we saw earlier in this unit:

  ○ babies are likely to develop stranger anxiety towards the end of their first year

  ○ under-threes often develop separation anxiety.

- Babies and under-twos are naturally curious and want to explore their environment.

- Around the age of 2 years, many children have not yet developed the communication skills they need to express their strong emotions, and this may lead to what are sometimes called 'tantrums', when they resort to crying uncontrollably.

- Through their early years, young children are learning to understand that some situations are risky and sometimes they want to do things that could be dangerous for them because they have not yet learned, for example, how to climb safely.

- Young children are sometimes confused by the way adults behave and they may copy what they *think* others are doing (for example, an adult pulling up plants in the garden).

- Most children take time to acquire the ability to share and take turns, as they gradually emerge from the **egocentricity** of the early years and acquire **empathy** for the feelings and rights of others.

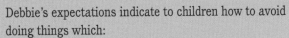

Key terms

Egocentricity: the self-centredness of very young children who do not comprehend anyone or anything beyond themselves and their own feelings

Empathy: the ability to understand situations from another person's viewpoint

Life events

As might be expected, it is not uncommon for children to react strongly to changes in their lives, such as:

- the birth of a sibling
- the illness of a family member
- stress or tension in the family

- changes such as moving house or starting to attend a new setting (transition).

Events like this often lead to a child appearing to go backwards (regress) in their development, so perhaps a child who is potty trained may start to wet themselves again. They can also lead to changes in patterns of behaviour, and a child may either become aggressive or withdrawn.

Rules and expectations

The overall purpose of supporting children's behaviour should be to help them develop self-discipline. As they grow, children need to learn how to control their behaviour for themselves and should not always have an adult controlling it for them.

Setting expectations

Children benefit from having a framework set for their behaviour which clarifies the sort of behaviour which is and is not acceptable in your home-based setting (your 'house rules'). Making clear to children what the boundaries or limits are for the way they behave can be very reassuring to them. Discussing this framework with

Case study: Debbie's house rules

Debbie's expectations indicate to children how to avoid doing things which:

- are dangerous, hurtful or offensive to others
- are a danger to the children themselves
- will make the child unwelcome or unacceptable to other people
- damage other people's belongings.

She and the children have drawn up a list:

'We try to be kind to one another, so we don't fight or hit, bite or scratch one another, or call each other names.

We share.

Everyone helps at clearing up time.

We hold hands when we're out, and don't run into the road.

We don't touch dangerous things like electric sockets.

We sit at the table to eat a meal.

We don't swear or use rude words.

We don't run about indoors or climb on furniture.

We take care of toys and books.'

1. What 'rules' do you use in your setting?
2. Have the children helped to set expectations that everybody can agree to?

parents before you start caring for their child will help you to agree a shared approach.

'Rules' are often expressed in a negative way, so children feel that adults are always telling them what they should not or must not do, but they may not be clear about what adults actually *do* want them to do. 'Expectations' describe how you do want them to behave – in a positive way – and this provides children with something to aim for.

Best practice checklist: Setting expectations

When you are setting expectations, make sure that you:

✓ avoid expectations which a child can't really understand yet – they will not be able to live up to them.

✓ are fair – for example, set similar expectations of behaviour for both boys and girls: do not allow boys to be rough, but not girls

✓ remember that children from some social and cultural groupings may have learned different rules about what is and is not acceptable behaviour. For example:

  ✓ in some traditions it is not considered polite for a child to look an adult straight in the eyes

  ✓ in some social groups, it is not 'the done thing' to express strong emotions

  ✓ in some cultures, saying 'please' and 'thank you' is less important than in others

✓ if you are a childminder, think whether you have the same expectations and rules for your own children.

Positive encouragement

On the whole, children want to please the adults who are important to them and they will respond well to encouragement to behave in positive ways.

Best practice checklist: Giving positive encouragement

You can help children to live up to your expectations:

✓ When they behave well, show your approval with rewards like:

  ✓ hugs and smiles

  ✓ approving words and praise

  ✓ your attention and time to talk and play (children become 'attention seeking' when they are not given attention).

✓ Make sure you tell their parents and other people when they have behaved well.

✓ Explain why certain kinds of behaviour are expected. ('It's dangerous, it will hurt.')

✓ Don't create confrontations. Don't over-react or make a big deal over minor matters – avoid battles.

✓ Be firm – make it clear you won't surrender to whining or tantrums.

✓ Be consistent: apply the same expectations from one day to the next.

✓ Set a good example: be kind and gentle, considerate and polite; don't shout. Children learn how to behave by copying adults.

Give praise and attention for 'good' behaviour

Responding to unwanted behaviour

There will be times when children's behaviour falls short of your expectations, and you need to respond to behaviour which you do not find acceptable, according to the child's stage of development and understanding.

One response to unwanted behaviour may be to use 'sanctions' like withholding a treat. This will only work if the sanction follows the behaviour immediately and the child understands what behaviour the action is related to. The sanction on its own will not make it clear to the child how you want them to behave in future.

Case study: Unwanted behaviour

Read the strategies these four childminders have developed for dealing with unwanted behaviour.

Tanya says: I find the best way with young children is distraction, I just offer them something more attractive and interesting to do. If they're holding something breakable or dangerous, I replace it with a safe object. If there's danger, I simply grab the child and say 'no' very firmly.

Maria says: One of my main methods is to remove the child from the situation – perhaps to somewhere less interesting for a short while. But I never humiliate or belittle the child by using a 'naughty chair' or shutting them away – I just give them a bit of 'time out' to calm down.

Dave says: I think it's important not to reward unacceptable behaviour by giving attention to the child. I turn away and get busy with other children. I try never to argue with the child – I just say a short, sharp 'That's enough' with a serious expression on my face.

Kathy says: My approach to tantrums is to restrain the child gently but firmly until the tantrum subsides. If we're in a public place, I try to remove them to somewhere out of view and wait for them to calm down. When they're coming out of it, I give cuddles to soothe and reassure them.

1. Which of these strategies have you found to be useful?

2. Do you have other ways of responding to unwanted behaviour?

Best practice checklist: A consistent approach

Handling challenging behaviour requires a firm and consistent approach:

✓ Make it clear that *you* are in charge. Say no and mean no – and make sure you give the same message by your facial expression and tone of voice.

✓ Show disapproval and make it clear that the behaviour is not acceptable. But if you say something like 'I still love you, but I didn't like what you did', the child will understand that it is the behaviour you are rejecting, not them.

✓ Explain that what they have done is dangerous, hurtful or unpleasant.

✓ If they have hurt someone else, you may want to insist they say sorry – but remember this depends on how far they understand that being really sorry means 'I wish I hadn't done it, and I won't do it again'.

✓ When an incident is over, always go back to your normal affectionate relationship – show you care about the child – give plenty of cuddles.

End each incident with a hug

Working with parents

You need to work closely with parents to achieve continuity and consistency in handling children's behaviour. You may find that some parents expect rules which are different from the ones you usually work with, or have attitudes to punishment that are different from yours. If children face totally different expectations from their parents and from you, it can be very confusing and difficult for them to measure up to what's expected, so you may need to negotiate a compromise with parents. The best situation for the child is one in which you have shared rules and shared strategies.

If concerns or difficulties arise about children's behaviour, it is essential for you and parents to discuss the matter thoroughly. They may be able to identify something in the child's life which is unsettling them. If you and they feel that efforts need to be made to change the behaviour, you should plan together what to do, and keep each other well informed about how your plans are going.

For childminders, one potential flash point for children to let their behaviour slip is at the beginning and end of the day — when children move from the care of their parents to you and back again. It is most necessary for you and parents to have a united front about what is and is not expected — otherwise the children will play you and their parents off against one another.

Getting ready for assessment

Prepare a policy on supporting children's behaviour so parents are aware of how you intend to work. Include how you:

- set expectations for children's behaviour, involving children and parents
- encourage positive behaviour
- respond to unwanted behaviour
- work in partnership with parents.

Check your knowledge

1. (a) What is a policy?

   (b) What are procedures?

2. Under what circumstances should you share confidential information without the permission of parents?

3. What are the main expenses encountered by childminders in running their business?

4. Where can you get advice on running your childminding business?

5. List five hygiene precautions you should take if there are pets in your setting.

6. What procedures should you follow in administering medication?

7. What are stranger anxiety and separation anxiety?

8. Give two examples of how children can learn from being involved in everyday domestic activities.

9. Give two examples of what you can learn by observing children.

10. Give two examples of events in a child's life that might have a negative effect on their behaviour.

CYPOP6

Support disabled children & young people & those with specific requirements

In order to work effectively with disabled children, young people and those with specific requirements, it is helpful to understand some key perspectives and also to gain some practical skills. This unit looks at the principles of working with this group of children and young people and their parents as well as ways in which we might support them.

Learning outcomes

By the end of this unit you will:

1. Understand the principles of working inclusively with disabled children and young people and those with specific requirements

2. Be able to work in partnership with families with disabled children or young people and those with specific requirements

3. Be able to support age and developmentally appropriate learning, play or leisure opportunities for disabled children or young people and those with specific requirements

4. Be able to evaluate, support and develop existing practice with disabled children and young people and those with specific requirements

5. Understand how to work in partnership with other agencies and professionals to support provision for disabled children and young people and those with specific requirements.

Understand the principles of working inclusively with disabled children and young people and those with specific requirements

The legal entitlements of disabled children and young people

Over the past thirty years, there have been many pieces of legislation that have gradually given disabled children and those with specific requirements more legal rights. It is important that everyone working with children understands these legal entitlements.

The right to be educated alongside others

Children and young people now have the right to be educated alongside others. Settings are expected to find ways of adapting their premises and ways of working that include all children and young people. In some cases, parents may not choose this option for their children, but it is there as a legal entitlement.

The right to be treated no less favourably than others

All disabled people – including children and adults – have the right to be treated as well as any other citizen when it comes to services and education. This right is covered by the Disability Discrimination Act 1995 and 2005 and the Special Education Needs and Disability Act 2001. See also Unit SC2 (Promote equality, diversity and inclusion) page 19. This means that a restaurant cannot tell parents that their learning disabled children are not welcome because they may upset other customers. Likewise, schools have to make adjustments so that disabled children and those with **specific needs** can join in.

The right to have their needs assessed and met

Under various different pieces of legislation, children and young people have a right to have their needs assessed and provided for. In practical terms, local authorities have to ensure that disabled children and their families are identified and given support, while in schools parents can ask for their children to be assessed. In addition to this, for settings working with young children in England, the EYFS Statutory Framework also requires early years settings to meet children's needs. The legal requirement states that 'Providers must plan and organise their systems to ensure that every child receives an enjoyable and challenging learning and development experience that is tailored to meet their individual needs' (page 37 EYFS Statutory Framework).

The right to be involved in decisions that will affect them

Under the United Nations Convention on the Rights of the Child, all children and young people have rights. For children and young people with a **disability** or **impairment**, and those with special requirements, these rights have been integrated into various pieces of legislation. Schools and other educational settings, for example, have to involve children when drawing up educational plans for them. It is worth noting that while children and young people have the right to be involved and to express views, it does not mean that their opinions are overriding.

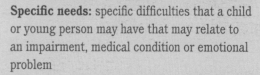

Key terms

Specific needs: specific difficulties that a child or young person may have that may relate to an impairment, medical condition or emotional problem

Disability: 'a physical or mental impairment which has a substantial and long-term adverse effect on a person's ability to perform normal day-to-day activities' (Disability Discrimination Act 1995)

Impairment: describes a condition which is different from what is usually expected in a child at a particular age or stage of development

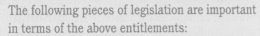

Over to you

The following pieces of legislation are important in terms of the above entitlements:

United Nations Convention on the Rights of the Child

Disability Discrimination Act 1995 and 2005

Special Education Needs Code of Practice 2001

Find out more about this legislation by visiting the following websites:

www.unicef.org/crc

www.equalityhumanrights.com

www.teachernet.gov.uk

The child/young person at the centre

It is important when working with children or young people that we see each of them as a whole person rather than children with problems. It is also important that everything we do is linked to their needs, strengths and interests rather than our own organisational needs. This approach to working with children is what is meant by the term '**child-centred**'. In addition there are some key principles that should underpin our work with all children, but which are essential when working with children with disabilities or those with **learning difficulties** or **special needs**.

Key terms

Child-centred: a way of working that focuses on the needs and interests of the child

Learning difficulty: a problem in processing information in the same way or at the same speed as others

Special needs: an umbrella term for children whose needs are different from those of other children

Respect

It is essential that we show respect to children and young people. This means listening to them, talking *to* them — not over them — and also valuing them unconditionally. It is important that we respect their families as well.

Interest

It is important that children feel we are interested in them as people rather than as children who may have a medical condition or disability. Being interested means finding out about their hobbies, tastes, interests and also dislikes.

Empathy

Empathy is about trying to understand another person's point of view. It is not about sympathy or pity. Being empathetic will help you to think about what it might be like for a child or young person and can help you to improve your practice.

Empowerment

All children and young people benefit from being with adults who aim to empower them. Disabled children and young people will need us to work in ways that are empowering, as often they find themselves in situations where they are expected to be passive and 'recipients' of care and education rather than active. Empowering children and young people is about finding ways to involve them in decision making, listening to them and giving them as many opportunities as possible to take on responsibility or have control.

Service-led and child- and young person-led models of provision

There are broadly two types of provision when it comes to providing support and education for disabled children and young people: a service-led model and a child- or young person-led model.

A service-led model of provision is one where outcomes and strategies for their delivery are created without consultation with children or young people. In some cases, there may be good reason for this, for example the government might dictate which subjects should be taught in schools or as part of the curriculum for early years. The danger with a service-led model of support

Case study: Creating a website

Michael and Jed attend a local FE college; both have cerebral palsy. They both enjoy using computers and decided to set up a website so that young people with cerebral palsy could 'meet'. They approached their IT tutor for advice who in turn suggested that they seek some funding from the local authority. Their IT tutor helped them with the application and they were given a small grant. The grant required that the project was monitored. During the first meeting with the person acting as monitor, Michael and Jed noticed that suddenly the project was not being referred to as 'theirs', but instead had become 'ours'. Decisions started to be made about the content of the website based on a list of set criteria and Michael and

Jed's ideas no longer seemed to matter. After a few meetings, Michael and Jed decided to leave the project. When asked by the IT tutor about the project, Michael replied that the whole point of the website was that it was meant to be run *by* young people with cerebral palsy *for* young people with cerebral palsy and that there were already plenty of other sites written by 'do-gooders'.

1. At what point did the project change from being young person led to being service led?

2. How did the monitor disempower Michael and Jed?

3. How might this experience colour Michael and Jed's future attempts at being independent?

for children, young people and their families is that other people are making decisions about services without necessarily involving them. This can mean that the support offered may not actually be useful or effective. It also means that children, young people and their families can feel dependent on others and passive in the process.

A child or young person-led model of provision is one where the support or service is designed or heavily influenced by those who will be using it. Young people

may decide they would like a youth group and decide what type of activities, equipment and resources it should have. In a young person-led model, they would be leading its development and be supported in turn by others. The child- or young person-led model of provision has many benefits. It gives children and young people a say in what happens to them and the type of support that they receive and so it is empowering. Children and young people can gain skills and also learn about taking responsibility.

Social and medical models of disability

There is more information on the social model of disability and the **medical model of disability** in Unit CYP3.7 and how they help us to understand the effect of disability on individuals. See Unit CYP3.7 page 200.

A child-led service empowers children

Key term

Medical model of disability: this treats the person as a sick patient and tends to focus on 'How can we make this person more normal?'

Medical model of disability

The medical model of disability is in many ways the traditional way of thinking about disability. It reflects society's faith in doctors and perhaps has come about because of the advances in medical knowledge. The medical model views disability as something that must whenever possible be cured. Where that is not possible, a feeling of failure results unless the person can be made to look or act 'normally'. The medical model of disability therefore treats people with impairments as victims and patients — words such as 'handicapped', 'incurable', 'suffering' and 'wheelchair bound' are associated with this attitude. The medical model of disability puts the emphasis more on the condition rather than on the person, resulting in a tendency to label people according to their impairments, for example 'the boy who's wheelchair bound' rather than 'James, who uses a wheelchair'. If a setting veers towards the medical model of disability, children and young people are not seen in a holistic way as having strengths, interests and competencies; instead the focus of the setting will be on the child's or young person's disability.

Social model of disability

The **social model of disability** reflects a very different attitude towards people with impairments. It considers that first and foremost they are people with rights and feelings. The social model of disability has been a very empowering one for many disabled people, as it emphasises their rights to make choices, question values and asks whether it is society with the real problem. The social model of disability has meant that terms such as 'mentally handicapped' and 'wheelchair bound' are now considered unhelpful. Settings that take a social model of disability will try to find ways of involving children and young people in their care and education. Settings will also focus on the child or young person rather than just on their medical condition. Settings are also likely to provide more diverse opportunities for children and young people.

Key term

Social model of disability: recognises that discrimination against disabled people is created by society, not by disabled people's impairments

Reflect

To what extent does your setting reflect a social model of disability?

In what ways are children and young people involved in their own care and education?

How do staff show that their focus is on the 'whole child' rather than on children's needs and impairments?

Are there any areas where your setting could change its focus?

Advocacy and facilitated advocacy

We have already seen in this unit the importance of empowering children and young people. Some children and young people who are potentially vulnerable (because, for example, they have learning difficulties or significant communication difficulties) may need an adult to represent their point of view; this person is an **advocate**. Advocates are often volunteers, but can be paid and appointed by courts to represent children and young people so that their views can be heard. It is important that advocates only represent children or young people's views rather than their own. In some situations children will not be present when advocates are working on their behalf, for example at a case conference, but at other times advocates will work alongside children and young people and facilitate for them.

Key term

Advocate: someone who puts forward ideas, views or suggestions on the behalf of someone else

The personal assistant role

Some children and young people will have a personal assistant who will support their care, but will also help them achieve things that otherwise would be difficult for them. Adults in this role should work in ways that empower the child or young person as the case study below shows.

Case study: Sophie's personal assistant

Sophie is 17 years old. She has significant learning difficulties that affect her communication and cognition skills. This does not stop her knowing her own mind and having clear preferences about where she wants to go, who and what she wants to see and what she would like to wear. Clare, her personal assistant, works with Sophie to help her to be as independent as possible. In consultation with Sophie's parents and, most importantly with Sophie herself, Clare accompanies Sophie on outings to the shops, cinema and restaurants. Through the use of **Makaton**, photographs and body language, Sophie tells Clare what she wants to do during the day. Now Sophie has a personal assistant, she is much happier and far less frustrated than before.

1. Why is it important that Sophie chooses what she wants to do?
2. Why is Sophie less frustrated than before?
3. Why is it important that a personal assistant works in ways that are empowering?

Key term

Makaton: a system of signs to help children understand the meaning of words and phrases

Encouraging the participation of disabled children and young people

It is very easy for a model of working with children and young people to be created in which 'things' are done to and for them. This model of working is not in children's best interests as they miss out on opportunities to take responsibility for and have a say in their own lives. This often leads to frustration, aggressive behaviour or depression and withdrawal. That is why it is so important when we work with disabled children and young people to find genuine ways of involving them and, wherever possible, allowing them to take responsibility and make decisions. With children who have significant learning difficulties, opportunities for participation may revolve around immediate decisions such as which socks to put on or whether they would like to press the start button on the CD player.

Be able to work in partnership with families with disabled children or young people and those with specific requirements

Families are important to all children and young people and parents in particular often play an essential part in their care and education. This learning outcome looks at the importance of working with families and considers ways in which we might do this. In this unit, the term 'parents' is used in its broadest sense and includes those carers who may have parental responsibility, either permanently or temporarily, such as foster parents or grandparents.

Concepts and principles of partnership with parents/carers

In earlier units we looked at the role of parents and the importance of working effectively with them (see Unit SC2 page 25 and Unit CYP3.5 pages 164–5). For disabled children, and those with specific requirements, it is especially important that we build a partnership with them as parents will play a central role in their care and education. The SEN Code of Practice 2001 outlines seven principles that you should adopt when working with parents. They emphasise the vested interest that parents have in the lives of children and young people and also the knowledge and contribution that parents provide. The seven principles are outlined overleaf.

1. *Acknowledge and draw on parental knowledge and expertise in relation to their child*

Parents will often have spent many years learning about the needs of their child, and working out how best to communicate and care for them. This expertise needs to be recognised and more importantly *used*.

2. *Focus on the children's strength as well as areas of additional need*

Parents do not see their children as having 'conditions' or 'learning difficulties'; they know their child as 'Josh' or 'Ayse' who may have a lovely smile, dislike cabbage or be excited when there is football on the television. This means that our interactions with them must always recognise the 'whole' child.

3. *Recognise the personal and emotional investment of parents and be aware of their feelings*

The journey for parents who have disabled children or children with additional needs is not always easy. We have to understand this and be empathetic to their situation. We also have to realise that they are long-term carers of their children and have a strong emotional attachment.

4. *Ensure that parents understand the procedures, are aware of how to access support in preparing their contributions and are given documents well before the meetings*

If parents are to be equal partners, it is essential that they are given the information they need in order to make decisions and also understand the implications of our suggestions.

5. *Respect the validity of differing perspectives and seek constructive ways of reconciling different viewpoints*

Parents will sometimes have different ideas and priorities from practitioners. This is because they are with their children long term and see other sides to their child. This means they may have a different outlook, for example they may prefer that steps are taken to help their child gain control over the bladder rather than learn to make a sandwich.

6. *Respect the differing needs that parents themselves may have, such as disability or communication and linguistic barriers*

We can only work in partnership effectively if we can understand that parents may have their own needs (see page 391 for ways of supporting parents).

7. *Recognise the need for flexibility and structure of meetings*

Parents of disabled children and those with additional needs will usually need to be more involved and attend more meetings than other parents. In some cases, parents may be attending meetings with several different services, such as social services, respite care, or physiotherapy. It is worth remembering this when organising meetings and also remembering that parents may have other children as well. This might mean checking with parents about what is the most convenient time and place to arrange meetings. It is important to create a friendly tone to meetings, but also to avoid situations where parents feel that time has been wasted because documents are missing or too much time has been spent talking about non-related matters.

In addition, as we saw in Unit SC1 on communication it is important to remember that much of the information that we exchange and gain from parents will be confidential (see Unit SC1 page 15).

Best practice checklist: Talking to parents

✓ Consider whether you need to talk to parents in a quiet place where you will be undisturbed.

✓ Remember that you are talking to parents about a child, not a 'syndrome' or a condition. Reflect this in your tone of voice.

✓ Listen to and acknowledge any differing perspectives that parents may have.

✓ Remember that parents want the best for their child and want to protect him or her.

✓ Do not show embarrassment or surprise if a parent openly cries; have tissues to hand and make sure that the parent does not feel rushed.

Types of support and information that parents/carers may require

All parents find that family life can be demanding and stressful at times. For parents and carers who have a child or young person with a disability or specific need, these feelings can be amplified. Practitioners need to be supportive of these parents – both emotionally and also in practical ways. The spider diagram below shows examples of the support and information that parents and carers may require.

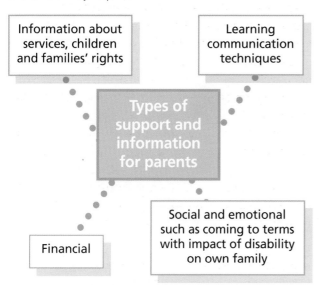

Parents and carers need different types of information and support

Learning to use communication techniques

Where children have communication needs, either because of a hearing impairment or learning difficulty, it may be suggested that they will benefit from a communication technique such as Makaton, Picture Exchange Communication System or to use a language such as British Sign Language. For parents this may mean that they need to learn how to use these techniques. Some settings invite parents in to show them how to use the picture exchange system or lend out DVDs which show Makaton signing. Where children are to learn British Sign language, the sensory impairment team should be contacted to see how they can support parents.

Social and emotional support

Many families with children often experience times of stress, but families who have disabled children or young people can feel under additional pressure. Many parents of children with special needs find that so much of their time and energy is used in caring for the child that it is hard to find the extra time for each other or for themselves, especially where there are other children in the family. This may result in some couples splitting up. In addition, parents have to come to terms with having a child who is different from other children — and from the child who they were expecting to have.

Some parents find it very isolating to have a child with learning difficulties or emotional and behavioural difficulties. Public places can be nightmares to negotiate and finding friends who can cope with the behaviour of the child can be difficult.

Siblings in families can also be affected, as more attention and time might have to be given to the disabled child or young person. Outcomes for siblings are variable and quite complex. Some siblings learn to care for their brother or sister and 'grow up' very quickly; others at times may feel great resentment as they do not get the same level of attention.

Financial issues

Money can be a source of worry for families as in many cases one parent has to give up work in order to care for the child or young person. This can lead to a significant drop in the family income and many families, especially lone parents, find themselves reliant on state benefits. There is a range of benefits and bursaries for families, some of which go unclaimed. To help parents find out about these, it is worth putting out information on organisations such as the Citizens Advice Bureau that can provide advice or help.

Information about services, children and families' rights

Parents need to have access to information about the services that are on offer. Although there are some national services, many services and organisations are provided locally. Before the age of the Internet, finding out about what was available both locally and nationally was very difficult; but the World Wide Web has helped to make information gathering easier today. It can be helpful for parents without Internet access to have times when they can use a laptop in the setting.

Many parents report that they also find out about services to help their children through word of mouth. Helping parents to find out about services might involve organising occasions when parents can meet each other, for example holding coffee mornings or creating a group web page. It is also good practice for settings to put out leaflets, posters and other information that can help parents find out about what is on offer. Some settings create opportunities for local organisations to come in and talk to parents as part of their drop-in services (for example a benefits adviser or voluntary organisations).

Your own practice in partnership working with families

For this assessment criterion, you need to show that you can work in partnership with parents. This will mean showing how you find ways of communicating with parents, making joint decisions and also how you support parents who may need your help. The Reflect feature below may help you think about the way you work in partnership with families.

Children and young people are entitled to have opportunities to play and learn regardless of any disability or specific requirement

Reflect

How do you communicate with those parents who may not come into the setting frequently, e.g. email, home-setting diary?

What information do you provide for parents about other services, for example voluntary organisations, local services and benefits?

How do you use the information that parents give you about their child?

How do your exchanges with parents recognise them as 'people' as well as just parents?

How do you gain feedback about your work from parents?

Be able to support age and developmentally appropriate learning, play or leisure opportunities for disabled children or young people and those with specific requirements

Children and young people are entitled to have opportunities to play and learn regardless of any disability or specific requirement. Play is particularly important as it supports learning and helps children and young people to gain self-esteem and confidence while doing something that is pleasurable. This learning outcome looks at ways in which we may support children and young people's play and learning.

Engaging with disabled children or young people

It is essential that children or young people do not become passive recipients of play and learning. Engaging with children means finding ways that allow them to be active and to feel part of what is happening in the setting and their own learning. A common mistake when working with disabled children or young people is to believe that by understanding the medical condition or implications of the disability, we have understood the child. This is rarely the case as all children are individuals — even if they have the same disability. Although having some background knowledge may help us to some extent, engaging with children is about getting to know the child. To help us engage with the child, it is important to work closely with parents as they usually 'know' their child better than anyone. They may tell us about toys, films or sounds that their child responds to or objects to. Engaging with children is also about spending sufficient time with them so as to learn more about their interests, needs and how to interpret these. This is why the **key person** role is considered to be so important.

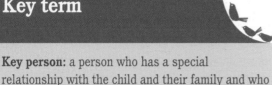

Key term

Key person: a person who has a special relationship with the child and their family and who acts as a surrogate attachment figure when the child is separated from parents and carers

The role of the key person

As we saw in earlier units (see Units CYP3.1 page 70 and EYMP3 page 258) all EYFS settings in England have to use a key person system. With disabled children and young people, this approach is essential as it allows us to build a close relationship with our allocated children and their families – and getting to know them does require time. The Reflect feature below will help you to consider how well you know the children who you work closely with.

Reflect

How well can you engage with your key child?

What is likely to upset your key child?

What is your key child's favourite activity?

How does your key child show pleasure?

How does your key child show distress?

What foods does your key child enjoy?

Does your key child have siblings?

Consistent quality of engagement

If we want children to engage with us, it is important that the quality of our work remains consistent. Children need to know that we are there for them, will try to communicate with them and that this is a constant. If children learn that sometimes people are keen to be with

them and play with them, but at other times their needs are ignored or they are left alone, they can 'tune' out as a way of protecting themselves.

Encourage children or young people to express their preferences and aspirations

For children and young people to be active in their play and learning, it is important that we encourage them to express themselves. If children are to learn that we genuinely want them to be involved, we must not rush them and must take time to learn about how they are trying to communicate. The following points are also important.

Posture

Do not stand over children when talking to them, but get down to their level. It is also essential that we show – through our posture and body language – our patience and support for the child.

Proximity

Make sure our proximity to children is appropriate. For some children, close proximity is essential, but for others this can be distressing.

Quick response

It is essential that we respond to children's attempts at communication immediately otherwise some children learn to withdraw. This means getting the toys or equipment straightaway or acknowledging the child's attempt to communicate.

Adapting our language

Our language has to be adapted to suit the communication level of the child we are working with. However, it is important to avoid sounding patronising as some children have good levels of language even though they may have difficulties in communicating.

Tone

Think about how we might sound when working with children. Tone of voice can convey our underlying feelings about a child.

Time

Some children need extra time to respond. This is because they need to process the information and work out its meaning before they are able to formulate words or respond. To support children with communication needs, it is important that we allow sufficient time for them to respond.

Body language, gesture and facial expression

As with tone, our body language, the way that we gesture and our facial expressions are also conveying underlying messages. It is important that we show patience, warmth and empathy in all these methods of expression.

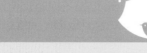

Over to you

Record yourself taking to a child or young person who you work with.

How do you sound?

What does your voice 'say'?

Do you allow sufficient time for a child to give a response?

There are several ways in which children may communicate with us.

Touch

Some children might use touch as a way of signalling their preferences. This may mean that we need to put our hand on theirs before asking a question, or show them something so that they can squeeze it. For some children with low vision, we may need to pass them toys and objects while describing them and allow the children to handle and feel them at the same time.

Pointing

Some children may try to point at things that are of interest to them. It will be important to get down to the child's level so that we can see what they have noticed.

Using pictures and signs

Some children can use pictures or Makaton signs to show us what they need or want.

Body language

Some children communicate using their body or head. They may indicate that they have seen something that is of interest to them by shaking or making whole limb movements.

Gesture

Some children use gestures to show their preferences.

Assessing a child or young person's learning, play or leisure needs

In order to work effectively with children it is important that we understand and assess their needs and then consider solutions. This is a process which will eventually culminate in the drawing up of a plan (see page 395). In order to assess a child's needs, we will need to get information from a range of sources.

Observations

Observations are one of the key starting points when assessing all children's needs. This is a requirement of the EYFS, but is good practice in all areas. Observation should help us to focus on what children enjoy doing, what difficulties they may have and also what their developmental needs are. It is important to observe children in a range of situations as they may show different interests and strengths. It is also necessary to observe very carefully as children may show very small steps of progress in certain developmental areas and these can be easily missed. (See also Unit CYP3.1 page 50.)

Information from others

While we gain a certain amount of information from observations, this is not sufficient in itself. Others involved with the child need to contribute so that we can gain an overall picture of the child's needs, interests and strengths. Other people such as parents and health professionals may also have ideas about how best to work with the child. (See pages 399–401 for examples of such agencies.)

Preferences of the child or young person

At the start of the chapter, we saw that children and young people are entitled to express their views and be involved in decision making. This means that we need to establish ways of finding out directly from the child or their advocate what they would like to do and areas of need they would like to address.

Barriers and obstacles

Through observation, from talking to others and from the child, we are likely to identify potential barriers. It may be that a piece of equipment is not available or that someone who can support the child is on sick leave. It is important to identify possible barriers in order to plan effectively, but it is also essential to look for ways of overcoming these obstacles. Again, this process can be helped by the involvement of others who may have previous experience of similar situations, or may have specialist contacts or knowledge.

Over to you

How does your setting work to assess the learning or play needs of disabled children or those with specific requirements?

How are parents involved in this process?

Which other professionals contribute to the process?

Develop a plan with an individual child or young person to support learning, play or leisure needs

It is a requirement of the SEN Code of Practice 2001 for children and young people in education settings to have plans drawn up that show how settings are working to support them. In addition, the EYFS in England requires settings to plan in ways that meet children's individual needs and interests.

Individual Education Plan

There are many different ways of planning, but it is likely that if you are in an educational setting (including pre-schools and nurseries), your setting will use Individual Education Plans, which are often known as IEPs. Individual Education Plans are drawn up using the information gained from the range of sources that

---

Name: Daniel

Early Years Action

Area/s of concern: Fine motor skills/concentration

Review Date: 14 March 2010

Early years practitioner: Miss Fletcher

Start date: Jan 2010

DOB: 4–12–06

IEP No. 1

Proposed Support:

Support began: Jan 2010

Targets to be achieved	Achievement Criteria	Possible resources/ techniques	Possible class strategies	Ideas for support/ assistant	Outcome
1. To grasp a small object between finger(s) and thumb **2.** To maintain attention in a small group activity and participate appropriately.	**1.** Pick up 5 beads and transfer to a pot in under 3 minutes. **2.** To participate fully in a sensory activity for 10 minutes.	**1.** Sorting activities e.g. beads, using spoons in sand tray Play-doh. **2.** Building sand castles. Sorting objects that float and sink.	**1.** Provide a variety of small objects within Daniel's reach. Encourage him to pick them up with fingers. **2.** Provide opportunity for Daniel to participate and take turns at an appropriate level with 1:1 support.	**1.** Demonstrate how to pick up objects with a pincer grip. Praise success. **2.** Encourage Daniel to participate and take turns. Praise him.	

Parents/practitioner contribution Work with Daniel on related activities at home. Practise taking turns at home. Playing games.

Parents's signature _____

Practitioner's signature _____

An Individual Education Plan

we have already looked at in the previous assessment criterion. IEPs should have parent involvement, and are normally drawn up by the child's key person alongside parents, the child and with support of the setting's Special Educational Needs Coordinator (or SENCO, see page 399). The aim of an IEP is to provide a short-term or medium-term plan that focuses on the areas of need identified. Targets are set and strategies to meet these targets are suggested along with ways of measuring them.

Although there is no set format for an IEP, the following information is usually noted:

- child's name and date of birth
- date of the IEP
- number of the IEP (where there has been more than one)
- date and level of support
- a brief summary of the child's difficulties and needs
- child's strengths and interests
- targets that the plan is to cover
- criteria for success
- teaching methods and strategies
- staff to be involved
- date for review
- signatures of parent, staff and child.

Learning journeys

In addition to IEPs, many early years settings will also observe and plan for children using a 'learning journey' style of planning. This style is used with all children in a setting. A learning journey style is based on a single observation of a child followed by some ideas as to how their play and interests might be developed. In England, settings using this format will link the learning journeys to the EYFS curriculum.

Implementing the plan

There is no point in planning for children and young people if no one aims to implement the plan. It is important when implementing the plan to be flexible. Children's interests can change, new stimuli such as the arrival of snow may make the plan feel irrelevant,

or you may realise that the plan is not realistic or enjoyable. When this happens, it is important to consider making changes, although these may need to take place in consultation with parents, the child and other professionals. For this assessment criterion, you will need to show that you can implement a plan and evaluate its effectiveness. You will also need to think about the next steps for the child, as planning for children should be ongoing.

Evaluating a plan

The following points might help you to evaluate a plan.

- How did the child react to the activities and strategies used?
- Was the child passive or active in terms of their responses?
- What were the positive outcomes of this plan?
- How could these be developed further?
- Were there any negative outcomes?
- Were there any difficulties in implementing the plan and how could these have been avoided?
- What are the views and responses of parents and other professionals?

Be able to evaluate, support and develop existing practice with disabled children and young people and those with specific requirements

Overcoming barriers

For this assessment criterion, you will need to show how in your setting and as a result of your practice, you are able to minimise or overcome barriers which could prevent children and young people from having the same opportunity as others. In many ways overcoming barriers is about determination and being creative. A sand tray that is too high for a child might be placed onto a lower table, a jigsaw puzzle that slides off a table is put onto a rubber mat to hold it steady. It is often these small adjustments that can make big differences for children – enabling them to join in with everyone else.

Below are examples of common barriers and ways in which they might be overcome in early years settings.

Food

Some children have specific requirements that relate to food and drink. Others may have a specific diet or may have particular needs when it comes to eating the food. In some settings, children may sit alongside other children at meal times, but are supported by staff (for example, ahead of time cutting up foods that would be difficult for the child to manage or giving them cutlery that will help them).

Choosing play opportunities

Some children may find it hard to communicate which activities and toys they would like to access. Some settings take photographs of the toys and resources they have and also photographs of children engaged in activities. These are then put in a book so that the children can point or use body language to show what they want.

Dressing up

Some children who have difficulties with fine or gross motor movements may be supported by providing dressing-up props that have easy fastenings or can be easily slipped over the head.

Toy libraries

Sometimes children will need specific toys to meet their play needs. To overcome this, many settings will join their local toy library so that they can borrow toys and equipment that will be enjoyed by individual children.

In addition, there are often quite small changes to the environment that will support children with specific needs – as the examples below show.

Supporting children with visual needs

- Think about the lighting in the environment – is it bright enough?

- Use textured resources to help children identify them more easily, for example spoons might have ridges on them, but forks are smooth.

- Use fluorescent strips to help children see pathways on floor.

- Do not change the physical layout so the child can learn and find their way around.

- Teach other children to pick up objects from the floor to prevent obstacles that might cause a fall.

- Look for toys and objects that can make sounds, for example a ball with a bell in it.

Supporting children with mobility needs

- Think about layout – check that the child can move around easily.

- Put floor activities onto boards on tables.

- Think about the height of tables and furniture.

- Find out from the child's physiotherapist how to include them in physical play, for example what type of equipment to use.

Challenging existing practice and becoming an agent of change

Inclusion means ensuring that all children, regardless of any disability or specific need, are given the same opportunities as other children. In practice this means thinking hard about how our setting works – the routine, equipment and activities – and ensuring that they are meeting the needs of individual children. The EYFS in England also states that the learning environment should be enjoyable and challenging. This requires careful consideration, as it is possible for children's needs to be met but for them not really to be part of the provision or find it enjoyable. Reflecting on our practice is therefore essential; we should then consider how we can change it in order to benefit children. A good starting point is to observe children and think about how well our provision is serving them. Ask yourself the following question: what is it like to be this child in our provision? The following case study shows how a member of staff in a pre-school did this.

Case study: Challenging and changing practice

Jasmine works at the Little Gems Pre-school. She has recently taken on the role of SENCO and is keen to think about the needs of the children who are on the special educational needs register. For the first time, she started to question some of the setting's traditional practices, such as having a whole group snack time, as a result of carrying out observations on specific children. Because of her observations, she became aware that some children with communication difficulties did not have much time to interact with staff and other children during these and other times. At a staff meeting, she showed members of the team her observations. Staff were also surprised, as they had not been aware that these children were missing out. At first they were quite defensive, but then after seeing the observations they began to consider ways in

which they could change their practice. They decided to re-visit the key person system so that children had more time with their key person and also to work in ways that helped children to play and communicate with each other. A few weeks later, Jasmine carried out further observations, again looking at the experience of individual children. She then reported back to the team.

1. Why is it important to carry out observations that focus on the experience of individual children?

2. Why might some staff become defensive about changing their practice?

3. Why is it useful to observe children again after making changes to practice?

Policies and procedures to challenge discriminatory, abusive or oppressive behaviour

Children with special needs and their families can sometimes be discriminated against. Assumptions are sometimes made about them which can affect the way others react. A child might not be given the opportunity to look at books because a practitioner thinks he is not capable. All practitioners have a duty towards children and so need to challenge **discrimination**. As part of their

anti-discriminatory policy, settings should have in place a procedure to follow where a practitioner has concerns. This means you should ensure that you understand the policy and procedures in your setting to deal with discriminatory behaviour. In addition, you should also be aware of your setting's policy in relation to protecting children from abuse. In early years settings, this policy may be termed a 'safeguarding policy'. See also Unit CYP3.3 page 111.

Culturally sensitive practice

Views towards disability and therefore its impact are not universal. In some cultures, disability is seen in terms of the medical model described on page 387 and disabled children, young people and their families may face high levels of discrimination. This can mean that when parents realise or are told that their child has a disability or specific need, they may be quite resistant or upset and may therefore need reassurance and support.

As with other areas of working with children, it is important to respect cultural practices (see Unit SC2 page 19), such as how children and young people are dressed and the type of food that is offered.

Key term

Discrimination: treating someone less or more favourably than other people, because they or their family are seen as belonging to a particular group in society

Systems to monitor, review and evaluate services for disabled children and young people

In order to ensure that children and young people's needs are being met, settings should have a system in place to monitor, review and evaluate their services. This may be part of their SEN policy. Reviewing and evaluating what we do with children is important as approaches to working with children can change over time and also because what has worked well in the past may no longer be working with the current cohort of children. Evaluating our work also means that we must continually focus on the needs of children and their families. Some settings review their effectiveness by gaining feedback from parents, children and other professionals who come into the setting. Other settings audit their provision, by checking that the systems they have for planning and implementing activities are working; there are also quality assurance schemes produced by many local authorities and voluntary organisations to assist with this.

Understand how to work in partnership with other agencies and professionals to support provision for disabled children and young people and those with specific requirements

Many of the children and young people who we work with will need support from a range of professionals. This learning outcome looks at the range of people we may work alongside and the principles of multi-agency working. This learning outcome links to Unit CYP3.7.

Roles and responsibilities of partners

Many disabled children and young people and those with specific requirements will need the support of a range

of professionals. Below is a list of professionals who are likely to work with children, young people and their families.

Special Educational Needs Coordinators (SENCO)

Every setting working with children will have a person who is designated as being the coordinator for SEN. This person liaises with staff, parents and other agencies to ensure that children in the setting have their needs met.

Educational psychologists

Educational psychologists consider how children learn and so are used to helping identify learning difficulties in children. They visit schools and settings regularly and work alongside parents and professionals in the setting. They may review and support staff in settings when drawing up IEPs and give guidance to staff as to how they can be implemented. Where a child requires a **statement** of **special educational need** or has a statement, they will be involved in the assessments and drawing up of the statements.

> ## Key terms
>
> **Special educational need:** the need of a child or young person for additional support or facilities in order to access education
>
> **Statement:** statutory assessment which outlines individual needs of a child and the specific provision required

Physiotherapists

Physiotherapists help to identify a child's main physical problems, working alongside other professionals and parents. They often devise a programme of exercises or treatments which they either administer themselves or help parents and others learn how to administer.

Speech and language therapists

Speech and language therapists work with children who have some difficulties with their language. They identify the causes of the problems as well as devising speech and language programmes. These may include exercises, advice for parents, early years teachers and other professionals. The range of children they work with can be quite wide and includes children with a cleft palate or lisp, as well as children who have autism.

Health visitors

Health visitors are important members of the community health team. In some areas health visitors have a mixed client list and work with many ages and needs of people in the community. In other areas, some health visitors will be specifically assigned to work with families with children under five and families who have children with special needs. Health visitors are able to give families support, advice and information in their own homes.

Paediatricians

Paediatricians are mainly based in hospitals and clinics. They have specialised training in children's medicine and children are referred to them via their family doctor for diagnosis. They make regular assessments of children's progress and medical needs. They are able to refer children to other health services, such as the speech and language therapists or dieticians.

Family doctors (general practitioners or GPs)

The family doctor has general training in medicine. GPs form part of the community health team and act as a base for a child's ongoing medical treatment and notes. The family doctor will often have been the person who referred the child to the paediatrician when an impairment was first suspected.

Child psychologists and psychotherapists

These professionals are often used when children show emotional and behavioural difficulties. They work with other professionals to determine the root cause of the unwanted or disturbed behaviour. Play therapy or family counselling is often used as a way of helping children and their families. Child psychiatrists may be called upon to give guidance to other professionals in some cases.

Special needs support teachers

These teachers travel between schools or visit children in their home or in pre-school settings. They are able to help a wide range of children and are often seen as useful sources of support and guidance. Special needs support teachers tend to build up a good relationship with

A counsellor working with a teenager

the child and may even work with children when they are admitted to hospitals.

Special needs assistants/learning support assistants

There are many variations on the title used for special needs assistants. Their main purpose is to support an individual child or group of children within a classroom, under the direction of the classroom teacher. They may also be responsible for carrying out the activities listed in the Individual Education Plan as well as recording the child's progress. Most classroom teachers, SENCOs and special needs assistants work closely together and collaborate on drawing up the Individual Education Plan.

Social workers

The majority of social workers are employed by the local authority, although some are employed by voluntary organisations. They are generally deployed in teams according to specialist areas, for example some social workers are involved in caring for older clients, others for adoption and fostering work. Children with special needs often have an assigned social worker as they are seen as potentially vulnerable. Social workers are often able to provide guidance and advice as well as practical support for families and as such are often welcome visitors.

Portage workers

Portage is a system that was developed in the United States and which has been adopted, although often modified, in the UK. It concentrates on helping children under five by working with parents in their home. It is based on the idea that early stimulation can help children with special needs. A portage worker will visit the home (in some areas this is a volunteer, whereas in others this is a trained teacher) and will carry out some assessments on the child. The parents and the portage worker together decide which skill or area of learning should be worked on. A step-by-step approach is agreed, with the parents being largely responsible for carrying out the programme. To support the programme, families are visited at least once a week by the portage worker and the child's progress is discussed. Portage workers take on the role of being a 'support' rather than a professional and parents are very much seen as equal partners.

Multi-agency and partnership working in your own practice

It is essential that we work effectively with others who are supporting children, young people and their families. It is very frustrating for parents, for example, to have to repeat the same information at each meeting or to find that something they thought had been arranged is not known about by another professional. This means that systems have to be put in place whereby everyone involved with the child or young person is regularly in contact. This is particularly important when the child or young person is not able to communicate. For children whose setting, is following the EYFS, the child's key

person should be the one to liaise with both parents and other agencies in situations when the child is spending significant amounts of time with them. In addition, some settings, with the consent of the parents, create a 'passport' which goes everywhere with the child. This 'passport' has the contact details of those currently working with the child so that a new professional knows who is working with the child and family.

For this assessment criterion you will need to show how you work with other agencies and that you understand the principles of doing so. Before completing this assessment criterion, you should re-visit Unit CYP3.6 pages 166–83.

Getting ready for assessment

Produce an information pack that could be given to someone new to your setting. The information pack should include:

- information about the roles and responsibilities of other professionals who are involved with children in your setting
- the principles of effective multi-agency working.

Check your knowledge

1. Identify two legal entitlements that children and young people have.

2. Explain how the medical model of disability can be limiting for children and their families.

3. What is meant by the term 'empowerment'?

4. How can participation benefit children and young people?

5. Why is it important to assess children using a range of sources?

6. What is meant by the term 'IEP'?

7. Why is it important that plans are flexible?

8. Outline three types of support that families may require.

9. Outline the roles of three different professionals who may work with children and young people.

10. Why is it essential for professionals who are working with a child or young person to exchange information?

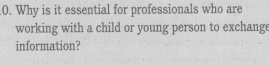

Promote creativity & creative learning in young children

It is recognised that creativity in its broadest sense should be developed in young children. This unit looks at the importance of creativity and creative learning. It also considers ways in which we may foster it in young children.

Learning outcomes

By the end of this unit you will:

1. Understand the concepts of creativity and creative learning and how these affect all aspects of young children's learning and development

2. Be able to provide opportunities for young children to develop their creativity and creative learning

3. Be able to develop the environment to support young children's creativity and creative learning

4. Be able to support the development of practice in promoting young children's creativity and creative learning within the setting.

Understand the concepts of creativity and creative learning and how these affect all aspects of young children's learning and development

The terms 'creativity' and 'creative learning' are frequently used in a variety of contexts. This learning outcome looks at the differences between them and also why each is important in children's overall development.

The differences between creative learning and creativity

Although most of us feel we know what creativity means, in educational forums creative learning and creativity can have a variety of meanings. For the purpose of this unit, creativity will be linked to the traditional creative arts and the development of imagination and imaginative play, while creative learning will be linked to the wider context in which children can show skills in problem solving, exploration and imaginative thinking. The spider diagrams below illustrate this.

Creativity

Creativity in this context is about helping children to find ways to express themselves through the arts. It is about exploring emotions and self-expression. Therefore, the focus of creativity in this sense is only partly about producing an end product and is more about enjoying and learning from the process. Later in this unit, we will see that, for us to support children's creativity, it will be important to provide a context where children not only learn skills but also have opportunities to explore different media. Creativity in this context links to the Creative Development area of learning both in the EYFS in England and the Foundation Phase in Wales.

Creative learning

Creative learning is about helping children develop problem-solving skills and imaginative thinking. It is about giving children opportunities to make connections between different areas and to apply them. A good example of a creative learning activity for a toddler might be **heuristic play**. In heuristic play, the child is given a

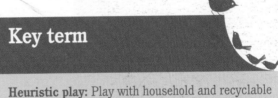

Key term

Heuristic play: Play with household and recyclable objects that encourage toddlers to explore

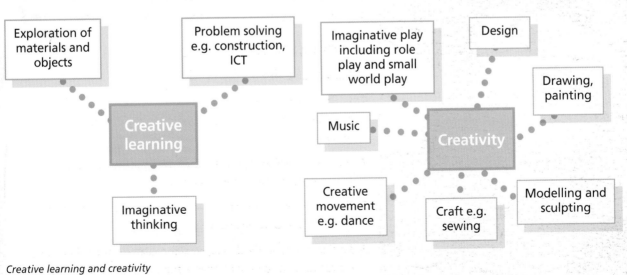

Creative learning and creativity

collection of random objects for them to explore. The child picks them up and explores them and sees what they can do with them.

Some creative learning activities may be goal orientated, such as making a den. The den is the goal but children will also be exploring different materials to use for a roof or working out how to support the roof, thus practising their problem-solving skills. Interestingly, while this is a key difference between creative learning and creativity, there will be times when a child will need to use the skills involved in creative learning to overcome a problem that they are having in creating, say, a sculpture.

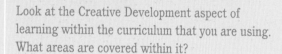

Over to you

Look at the Creative Development aspect of learning within the curriculum that you are using. What areas are covered within it?

Theoretical approaches

There are currently several different theoretical approaches that aim to explain creativity and creative learning. It is a complex area because being creative involves many processes. Below are some key approaches to creativity and creative learning.

Nature or nurture

As with many areas of psychology, there is a nature versus nurture debate in terms of children's creativity. Are some children naturally creative, for example having a gift for music or having a creative personality; or is creativity something that can be nurtured?

Cognitive theories

Cognitive theories involve the way in which children make associations and connections between things. These theories focus on the way in which the brain processes information. A child may look at a tube and, while concentrating on its shape, make a connection between it and a rocket. Some theorists, such as Robert Sternberg and Howard Gardner, argue that being able to make new connections and draw something new from them is a type of intelligence. In terms of our practice with children, cognitive theories suggest that we need to provide plenty

of first-hand experiences for children in order that they can develop pockets of knowledge and draw on their own experience.

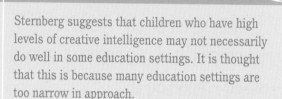

Over to you

Sternberg suggests that children who have high levels of creative intelligence may not necessarily do well in some education settings. It is thought that this is because many education settings are too narrow in approach.

How does your setting cope with children who 'explore' materials unconventionally and potentially creatively? For example, putting Lego into the loo…

Social models

Social models focus on the environment that children are in and the role of adults within it: meaning it is the environment and the experiences that children are given which allow them to be creative. Social models include those linked to cultural approaches and also role modelling.

Cultural approaches

These approaches suggest that all children can be creative, but that this can be suppressed or enhanced depending on how supportive the environment is. There is therefore the idea that sometimes society has to be ready for and receptive to new ideas and innovations. In terms of working with children, this would mean ensuring that we provide an environment where children can be creative and exploratory.

Role modelling

These approaches look at the way that children learn from watching and being with adults who are being creative. In terms of our work with children, this would mean showing in the way we work and think that we can be creative – being flexible, problem solving and also letting children see us draw, paint and so on. See also Unit CYP3.1.

Creativity as a process

Some theories focus on creativity as a process. These models look at how new ideas emerge. One of the earliest theories was put forward by Graham Wallas, who proposed a five-stage model. Interestingly, there is a focus on the importance of the unconscious mind:

- *preparation* – initial thoughts about a problem
- *incubation* – time spent thinking unconsciously about the problem
- *intimation* – an awareness that an answer is within grasp
- *insight* – conscious awareness of the answer
- *verification* – the solution is then worked upon.

In support of Wallas's model, there is some recent research by psychologists with adults showing that sleep is an important component in solving problems. An experiment was done in which one group was given a problem to solve immediately, while another group was told about the problem before going to sleep. Those in the group that had 'slept' on the probem were quicker to find a solution.

Lateral thinking

Edward De Bono proposes that creative thinking needs to be planned and organised and has written several books about this, including ones for children which help them to problem solve using a process model. This style has been criticised as being too 'pragmatic' by others including Robert Sternberg.

EYFS in action

Look at the creative development area of learning within the practice guidance of the EYFS.

How does the 'effective practice' section convey a 'social model' of creativity?

How creativity and creative learning can support other areas of development

Both creativity and creative learning are essential to foster in young children as they support other curriculum and developmental areas.

Creativity is important because it gives children a way of expressing their feelings and a route for self-exploration and expression.

Imaginative play seems to help young children explore a variety of roles that they have seen among adults and other children as well as in their own family. We may, for example, spot a young child who is pretending to be a parent or another child who is pretending to be a baby. It also can make children feel powerful and this is one explanation for why so many children enjoy being superheroes. Imaginative play also helps children's language and communication skills as they often play together or use their language to direct small world characters.

Art

The term 'art' is used here to include mark making, drawing and painting. Finding ways to represent either words or images is another way in which children can express themselves. They can express emotions and feelings through the physical way in which they make marks as well as the colours and size of shapes and lines they use. Mark making, drawing and painting also help children's gross and fine motor skills to develop, which is important for later handwriting development. Creating marks or pictures also helps children's cognitive development as they are using symbols to make representations.

Creative movement

Moving to music, including dance, or simply moving creatively allows for self-expression, but can be an enjoyable social activity. Children are also gaining in terms of gross motor skills, balance and co-ordination.

Design including modelling and sculpting

Design helps children's cognitive development as they learn about the properties of materials. As with other areas of creativity, design and modelling help children to express themselves and they can gain confidence as well as competence. Children's fine motor skills are also helped by, for example, cutting and handling materials.

Music

Singing and playing instruments is a fun way in which children can learn to communicate. Singing also helps

Singing and playing instruments is a way in which children can communicate

children's speech production and it helps their auditory discrimination, which is a skill required for reading. Music in all its forms can also help children to gain in confidence and learn to work together. Children's gross and fine motor skills are also developed through the use of instruments. In addition, there seems to be a correlation between early musical experiences and mathematical ability. This is linked to hearing rhythms, beats and patterns in music.

Creative learning

Creative learning is beneficial for children as it is about problem solving and applying knowledge. There are creative learning opportunities within most areas of the curriculum and so it can support children's development easily; for example children can design an obstacle course for a programmable toy, which helps them to learn about direction, size, shape and objects.

Problem solving

Problem solving can help children's confidence if they succeed. They also gain other skills including concentration and perseverance. Some problem-solving situations may involve being with other children and learning to listen to each other's ideas and working in a team. These are good communication and social skills. Problem solving is also at the heart of some later curriculum subjects such as science, design and technology and mathematics.

Making connections and applying knowledge

Making connections and applying knowledge are skills that support children's cognitive development. Learning to apply knowledge and use it in a variety of contexts is an example of **metacognition skills** and is a key part of creative learning.

Key term

Metacognition skills: a set of skills which allow the user to make the best use of their cognitive abilities and to gain control over some of their thinking

Exploration

Creative learning may often involve exploration. One example is when a range of objects is put out on a table and the children are able to see what the objects can do and what they can make them do. This exploration gives children confidence and is motivating. Children also benefit from the cognitive aspect of exploration as they learn to categorise and sort as a result of their exploration.

Children benefit from the cognitive aspect of exploration

Making decisions

Creative learning is good for children as it should involve making decisions and having choices: deciding where to play and what to use. This is good for children's confidence, but also for their cognitive development as they have to think about the advantages and disadvantages of the choices they are making.

Be able to provide opportunities for young children to develop their creativity and creative learning

We have seen the importance of creativity and creative learning. In this learning outcome, we look at how in practice we can promote it and the importance of giving children sufficient time to develop their creativity.

Promote creativity and creative learning

There are many ways that we can promote children's creativity and creative learning. The spider diagram shows some of the key ways.

Time

Children need to have sufficient time in order to explore fully their ideas and sometimes also to gain the skills that they need (see also page 410).

Ownership

Being creative is not a 'second hand' skill. Children need to find their own ways of working and thinking. While we might need to support and facilitate this, it is important that they retain ownership of their projects and ideas.

Choice and options

Creative activities — either in the traditional arts or as creative learning — must have a strong element of choice or options. This might mean providing a good choice of resources (see page 411) or several options as to how to approach a problem-solving activity.

Language

It is useful if we can help children to express themselves as this is important for imaginative play, as well as for developing their cognitive skills. It is therefore important that we look for ways of helping children to learn specific vocabulary that is associated with what they are doing. This can be done in context, when we are taking an interest in what children are doing or working alongside them or supporting them.

Role modelling

One way in which children can pick up some of the skills they will need later is by watching us as we are being creative. Children may hear us make up our own tunes or watch us as we paint alongside them. Role modelling should be seen as informal learning rather than instruction whereby children are 'told' to watch and learn.

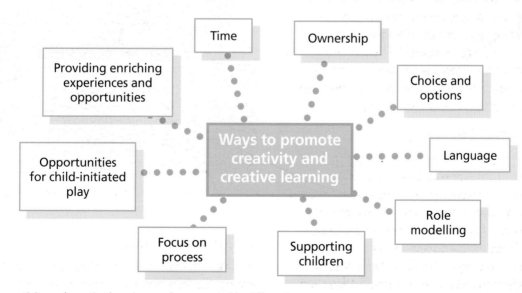

Children's creativity and creative learning can be promoted in different ways

Supporting children

Sometimes children will need us to support them in achieving their goals. They may not have the experience, skill level or knowledge about the tools they need. There will be times when we might hold something to assist a child, ask them if they would like to use a stapler or ask if they would like us to show them how to mix a colour. When supporting children, it is important that we do not take over ownership of what they are trying to achieve.

Focus on process

While some creative learning activities may be about problem solving, and therefore will be goal orientated, our focus when working with children should still be about ensuring that they find the process enjoyable. In some cases children may not arrive at a solution. In the same way, children need to enjoy the process when it comes to traditional creative arts such as painting and making music.

Opportunities for child-initiated play

Children can be very creative when engaged in child-initiated play. This is because it is an opportunity for them to follow their own ideas without adult structure or intentions. This is why it is considered to be an important part of an early years curriculum. Children can also draw upon what they have seen, done and experienced and weave it into their play. For example, children who have visited a fire station may choose to create a fire engine or be focused on trying to make a siren.

Reflect

Consider the following questions relating to the provision of enriching experiences and opportunities.

- Do children in your setting hear a range of styles of music?
- Do your children have experience of watching live performances such as pantomime or puppet shows?
- Do you invite local artists, including parents, into your setting to work alongside the children?
- Do you take children on outings to museums, art galleries etc?

Providing enriching experiences and opportunities

For both creativity and creative learning, children need plenty of first-hand experiences in order that they can be inspired by them but also for creative learning – so that they can make connections between them. This means looking for ways of enriching children's experience by, for example, taking children on outings, inviting artists into settings, playing different types of music and giving children opportunities to visit museums, art galleries or the theatre.

Promoting creativity

For the purpose of this unit, creativity is linked to the creative development aspect of learning found in the EYFS and Foundation Stage curricula.

Developing imagination and imaginative play

We can support imagination and imaginative play by giving children plenty of different experiences so that they can draw upon these in their own play. We also must make sure that children have props that are of interest to them. When children are engaged in imaginative play, it is important that any interventions we make are sensitive. This means that it can be a good idea to observe children first in order to understand what they are doing so that, if they would like us to join in, we can slot into a role without changing the direction of their play. (See also environment pages 411–414.)

Traditional creative arts

Painting, drawing and modelling are examples of creative arts that children often enjoy. Our role with children is to give them plenty of opportunities to see creative arts and also to explore a range of materials and resources. Role modelling can play an effective part in helping children to learn some of the skills that will support their development; for example if an adult picks up a sponge and dabs it, a child who is interested may try the same technique later.

Colouring sheets

It is thought that colouring sheets, templates or other pre-given images are not always helpful in supporting young children's development. This is because children may become dissatisfied with their own representations and, while colouring in, they are not exploring ways of making their own marks.

Reflect

Are there any children in your setting who prefer to colour in rather than attempting to draw? What could you do to encourage them to make their own marks?

can also help children by showing them film clips of dancers or, better still, taking children to a local dance school for them to see older children performing.

Working with babies and toddlers

When babies are not mobile, we can help them to experience dance and movement by holding them as we dance or move to music. For mobile babies and toddlers, simply putting on music that has a strong beat can help them to move rhythmically.

Working with babies and toddlers

Babies and toddlers need time to enjoy making their own marks, which may be in yoghurt on a tray or with a paintbrush and water. It is important to let them make these marks in their own way rather than 'guiding' their hands. Babies and toddlers can also enjoy early building activities, such as making and knocking down towers of bricks.

Music

Most children enjoy music. We can help children develop in this area by having regular opportunities when we sing together and where children are encouraged to put new words to songs or create their own. Children need to hear different musical styles and also experience using a range of different instruments that make sounds. Many children will also find ways of making their own sounds.

Working with babies and toddlers

Most babies and toddlers are very receptive to music. To support their development, we need to sing to them, preferably when we are holding them. They can experience music by being rocked or swung gently to the beat. We can also help babies and toddlers experience making a range of sounds by looking out for rattles, shakers and simple music instruments that they can use. Home-made instruments from everyday or household objects can also be very popular with toddlers.

Dance and movement

Dance and movement are both linked to children's physical development. This means that few 3-year-olds can skip to music, but they may enjoy running to it! Children can also enjoy movement by having scarves, ribbons or masks provided. As with other areas, children may also copy our movements and so role modelling is a good way of helping children to gain new ideas. We

Creative learning

Creative learning should be embedded in all areas of learning and within our everyday routines. We should regularly look for opportunities for children to explore and problem solve. This means that we might work with children to design an obstacle course as part of promoting their physical development or ask children to find a system of keeping the coats from falling onto the floor. The table below shows some of the ways in which creative learning can be embedded into EYFS and Foundation Stage areas of learning.

Table 1: Links between creative learning and other areas of learning

Area of learning	Example of activity
Personal, social and emotional development	Experiment — which is the best way to wash our hands?
Communication, language and literacy	How can we organise our book corner?
Knowledge and understanding of the world	Here's a box of odds and ends — what can you find? Here's a box of toys that need mending — what do we need to do?
ICT	Can you make an obstacle course for the programmable toy?
Problem solving, reasoning and numeracy (mathematical development)	How old do you think Teddy is? Why?
Physical development	Which ball will travel the furthest when it is thrown?
Creative development	Colour mixing — what happens when...?

Working with babies and toddlers

Babies and toddlers, like older children, need plenty of direct experiences and opportunities to handle and explore new objects. Treasure basket and heuristic play are helpful in this (see Unit CYPOP2 page 321). Babies and toddlers also need to have opportunities to develop language as this is linked to cognition. It is therefore helpful if we name things accurately and involve them in a running commentary when we are out and about with them.

Taking time to develop their creativity

In order that children can enjoy being creative, both in terms of creativity and creative learning, we need to think about how much time is available. In settings that value children's creativity, time is abundant, but where a setting places less value on it, it tends to be timetabled or restricted. The advantages of providing time for children to be creative are shown by the spider diagram below. Interestingly, some of the skills that adults value, such as concentration or perseverance, are essential for being creative. This is because children need time to properly think, explore and also to imagine. Some theoretical approaches also suggest that time is required as our subconscious plays a part in problem solving and the creation of new ideas.

We are likely to find that children will respond differently to the opportunities that are provided. Some children will quickly know what they would like to do or achieve, while others will take their time. It is also common for children, like adults, to explore one idea or theme for a while before deciding to disregard it and wanting to start afresh. It is unfair for children to be given only short periods of time or limited materials, as this can make them feel under pressure and may lead to a lack of confidence.

It is also helpful for children to be given opportunities to re-visit what they have done before — to look again at a model that they have created or to collage on top of a painting. Where time is short, children tend to let adults take over or simply copy what adults or other children are doing rather than genuinely exploring what they would like to do.

Ideally, we should try to make sure that opportunities for creativity and creative learning are ongoing during a session rather than giving them a 'slot' or finite time; for example saying 'we do craft on Wednesdays after lunch'. Where this is not possible, perhaps because indoor space is limited for moving to music, it will be important to find ways of allowing children to revisit what they were doing as soon as possible afterwards. It can also be useful to film or photograph what children were doing so they can pick up the threads of their thinking later on.

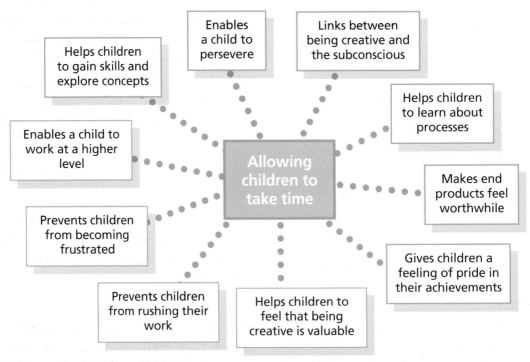

Children need time to develop their creativity

need to make connections between different materials. In the same way, members of staff who become anxious because children are making a mess – or are not using just the materials that have been put out – will not make children feel that they can do anything new or experiment.

It is also important for children to see good role models. When we join with children in being creative, or they see us being creative on our own account, children develop positive attitudes towards creativity. This is perhaps why certain families are often 'creative' – no doubt children learn the value of creativity from being with their parents and siblings. It is therefore not helpful for children to hear statements such as 'I'm no good at drawing', as this can lead children to believe it is a skill that you are born good at rather than one that can be developed. You may like to use the Reflect box below to consider what the underlying messages are for children in your setting about being creative.

Be able to develop the environment to support young children's creativity and creative learning

If creativity and creative learning are to take place, the environment must be conducive. This learning outcome looks at the features of a supportive environment and ways in which the environment might be monitored.

Features of a supportive environment

Before looking at the features of the physical environment, it is worth focusing on the emotional environment that children are experiencing. This is because children need to feel that adults are giving them permission to explore, try out new things and master skills. The attitudes of the staff and our work patterns are therefore important in helping an environment to have a creative atmosphere.

Staff who are over zealous in keeping areas neat and tidy are not fostering creative learning as quite often children

Physical environment to support creativity

What is available for children will hugely affect their potential to be imaginative and enjoy the creative arts. This means we need to think about what we provide for each of the areas in the setting.

Collage

Many children enjoy sticking and putting things onto paper and card. For it to be a truly creative experience, children need a choice of interesting textures, colours

and shapes. Look out for a variety of different resources such as lace, buttons, string, feathers, metal springs, magazines, birthday cards, tissue paper and so on. Note that some children will simply enjoy choosing and exploring materials rather than sticking them!

Paint

Young children need large areas where they can paint. A traditional easel can be quite limiting and many children leave a painting activity because they have run out of paper. Look out for ways of creating large spaces for painting by, for example, putting rolls of paper onto tables or better still creating a painting wall as shown in the photograph below. Children also need to be able to mix colours, so consider using a palette – a small plastic tray with a few blobs of primary coloured paint. Children also need opportunities to see how to create different types of textures. This means creating a collection of objects such as sponges or bricks that can be used for printing.

Look out for ways of creating large spaces for painting

Mark making

From as early as 18 months, children can enjoy mark-making activities as long as they are provided with suitable resources. Children will need space to mark make and so large strips of paper can work well together with markers, soft pencils, pastels and charcoals. Children may also like to combine collage with mark making. Mark making can also take place using sensory materials such as sand, cornflour and water and salt.

This type of mark making is extremely pleasurable for young children.

Role play

Children from around the age of 3 years onwards usually enjoy role play. As many objects as possible in role play areas should be 'real', for example carrots, yams, metal saucepans, as these types of object are more sensory. Toy substitutes are usually plastic and rarely give children as much satisfaction. The same applies to dressing-up props which again should be taken from the 'real world', for example adult belts, handbags. Ready-made dressing up costumes can prevent children from exploring across gender roles – a strip of shiny fabric will have more possibilities than a 'fairy costume' as the shiny fabric can be used as a cape, a magic blanket or a skirt or can be tied around the body to make a pirate's costume. It is also important to choose furniture that is neutral so it can be used for different scenarios. For example, a small plain table can be turned into a shop counter, a conveyor belt, an ironing board or a cooker.

Small world play

Small world play includes toy cars, play people, dinosaurs and farm animals. To support children's creativity, it is helpful if small world resources are married up with sensory materials, for example farm animals in a tray of turf, rather than additional 'toys' such as a doll's house or a road mat. This is because the sensory materials allow children to explore and create their own worlds for their small world characters while the commercial 'extras' tend to be more limiting. One idea is to provide some shoe boxes and patches of small fabric to allow children to make their own 'home' for the play people.

Music

Children will need opportunities to use a range of different musical instruments so that they can explore a range of sounds. Some instruments can be made with children, such as a plastic bottle filled with rice, or bells. It is also helpful if children can have opportunities to record themselves and so a microphone attached to a recording device is often popular.

Creative movement

To allow for creative movement, children will need to have sufficient space and access to music. Props such as ribbons, scarves, masks and hats can also stimulate children to explore movement.

Modelling

Children need opportunities to create 3D shapes using malleable materials such as dough, clay and plasticine as well as from large materials such as boxes, cardboard tubes and string. It is important that sufficient choice and range of materials is provided so that children are able to vary what they do and make.

Physical environment to support creative learning

The environment to support creative learning has to allow opportunities for problem solving and exploration. It is therefore essential to think about what types of toys and resources are provided. Ideally, we are always looking for resources and toys that will provide open-ended possibilities for children. Toys that are very specific in purpose tend to be of less interest than those that can be used in a multitude of ways, such as Lego or large wooden blocks. It is well known that a large cardboard box and some cardboard tubes, costing nothing, provide more opportunities for creative learning than an expensive toy. This is because children can bring their own ideas and imagination to the cardboard box rather than being led by the design and purpose of a toy. An environment for creative learning should have a range of materials that do not have a designated purpose so that children can find and use them. Materials should be placed in and out of doors and might include car tyres, wooden planks or plastic crates.

Varying the environment

Children need variety in order to be stimulated. We should always look out for new materials and resources that we can bring into the setting. We may not know how or what the children will use them for, but children will often find their own use for them. They may, for example, use a piece of tubing from a vacuum cleaner to create a water run. Most local areas have a scrap store which, for an annual fee, may allow members to take materials that have been donated by local factories and businesses. Scrap stores are great places to find interesting materials for children which can be used to support their creative learning.

Anything can happen here!

For children to be creative learners, they do need to make connections between different types of materials. Children tend to 'mix' materials, for example taking the sand over to the water. To allow and encourage this type of play, some settings create specific areas where there is a range of materials which children can mix and play with in any way they choose. These are 'Anything can happen here' areas.

Babies and toddlers need variety

Babies and toddlers must have a varied environment and changing resources as this is a key way in which they can be stimulated. Objects for their treasure basket and heuristic play must be regularly changed and supplemented so they have new ways of making connections. It is also important that we provide them with items such as fabrics, containers and boxes rather than just toys; as with older children, these items can help them to explore.

Monitor and evaluate the environment

A key way in which we can monitor and evaluate our effectiveness in providing a creative environment is to observe children carefully in a range of situations. The following points may help us to monitor and evaluate the effectiveness of the environment.

Levels of engagement

When an environment is working well, we are likely to find that children quickly settle down and become engaged in either a creative activity or in creative learning. This can be checked by observing a few children during a session and considering how focused they seem.

Length of engagement

It is likely that children who are in a creative environment not only find things that they are interested in doing, but they also persevere and explore for long periods. Interestingly, babies will often spend 30 minutes or so exploring a quality treasure basket that has a good range of natural objects.

Over to you

Find out the contact details of your local scrap store and make arrangements to visit it.

Awe and excitement

When they are in a creative environment that is dynamic, children will often experience great excitement and awe. They may be thrilled to discover that they can blow a bubble using a coat hanger or that they can stretch a piece of elastic. It is important that we consider whether we are regularly providing an environment that provokes these reactions.

Be able to support the development of practice in promoting young children's creativity and creative learning within the setting

While we can create creative environments and plan some activities that will develop children's creativity, for children's creativity and creative learning to be developed, it is essential that we reflect on our own practice.

Evaluate and reflect on own practice

We looked above at ways in which we can monitor and evaluate the environment to ensure its effectiveness. We also saw that adults are very important in creating an environment in which children feel comfortable and can be creative. For this learning outcome, you will need to consider your own practice in promoting creativity and creative learning. The spider diagram shows some ways in which you might do this.

Recording practice

It can be useful to record yourself as you talk to children or to ask a colleague to film you when you work alongside children. This can help you to consider whether you are controlling children or allowing them to explore possibilities for themselves. It is also a way of understanding more about the needs of individual children.

Visiting other settings

It can be very helpful to visit settings that work with similar age children as it can give you ideas about new

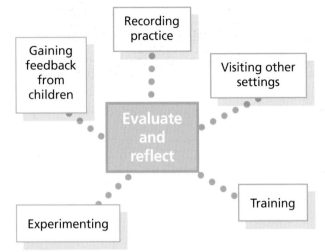

Evaluation and reflection is valuable to support children's creativity

ways to do things and may also help you to reflect on your own work. Other settings may be strong in areas that you feel are a weakness in your setting. They may, for example, be strong at encouraging creative learning outdoors or in a specific area of the creative arts.

Training

Training is a key way of updating your skills and also gaining competence and ideas in areas of creativity or creative learning where you feel less confident. Look out for training that your local authority or professional body organises (for example conferences or twilight training).

Experimenting

A key way to reflect on your practice is by experimenting a little with your approach, resources or activities. Look to see how the changes affect the children and whether they enhance their opportunities.

Gaining feedback from children

Children are able to provide valuable feedback about the opportunities that we have provided for them. Older children will tell us what they enjoy most, while younger children show us through their expressions, level of engagement and persistence.

Using the information

Once you have gained information from a range of sources, you will need to consider your personal strengths and weaknesses. The Reflect activity opposite might be helpful in this.

Reflect

Are there any areas within creativity where children have few opportunities?

Are there any areas within creativity in which you could benefit from further knowledge or training?

How focused are you on ensuring that children have 'end products', for example when painting, modelling or doing collage?

How easy do you find it to set up creative learning opportunities for children?

Do you work in ways that allow children to have choices and ownership of activities and opportunities?

Support others to develop their practice

Creativity and creative learning are often areas where people feel that unless they have personally achieved a high level, they cannot work effectively with children. While this might be true when working with much older children and young people, this is not the case when working with young children. What is important is that children are given opportunities to be creative and also that they see positive role models. This means that confidence and reassurance is often required when offering support to other adults in the setting. It is therefore often useful to look for areas where people are comfortable and aim to enhance these so that they can gain confidence. Below are some suggestions that can be used to help others develop their practice.

Show not tell

Some people find it hard to visualise what we mean by allowing children to be creative. It can therefore be helpful to show film clips taken either in your setting or from other sources that show situations where children are being creative.

Suggest and discuss

It is often worth making suggestions and discussing issues that are holding staff back from being creative with

children. Some staff need to take small steps towards a more creative approach rather than suddenly make sweeping changes. This might mean that a starting point for improving role play opportunities could be to include more real props and ask the staff member to note how children play differently with them. Staff can often gain confidence by seeing how children respond positively to such small changes.

Role model

It is important that you act as a role model if you want to foster a creative environment. This means letting staff see that you are ready to change your practice and 'have a go'.

Evaluation

Working with children is not always straightforward. Sometimes changing the way we work will have unforeseen consequences. This means, that after any changes, it is worth spending time with a member of staff to talk about what has been positive and also what has not worked. This avoids staff from 'giving up' if what they have tried has not had the effect they desired.

Understand people's limits

Everyone has some limits – they may be happy for children to mix paint on palettes, but not on the table or happy for children to use guttering to roll cars down, but not the books. It is important to discuss these limits as sometimes people fear that allowing children to be more creative will mean anarchy. If your setting is currently very structured, children and staff may need to take more gradual steps.

Develop a programme of change

For this assessment criterion, you will need to show that the reflection you have done, about how you might improve the environment to further enhance creativity and creative learning, has enabled you to create a plan of action. As with other plans that we have seen in this book, you will need to show that it is realistic and give reasons for the plan, together with expected outcomes for each area of change or development. There is no single format for such a plan, but overleaf is an example that may act as a starting point for your own.

Area for development	Reason for action	Action to be taken	Resources required	Person responsible	Date for completion	Date of completion
Painting area	Children do not have sufficient opportunities to paint using a variety of colours	Paint palettes to be provided rather than pots of paint so that children can colour mix and have more choice of colours	Palettes	Justine	End of September	

An example of a plan of action

Check your knowledge

1. Outline one theoretical approach to creativity and creative learning.

2. How do creativity and creative learning support children's overall development?

3. Why is it important for children to have rich first-hand experiences?

4. Why do adults need to act as role models to support children's creativity?

5. Give an example of a creative learning activity that links to an area of learning.

6. Explain why time is important to foster children's creativity and creative learning?

7. Outline three ways in which adults can provide an effective environment for children to be creative.

8. Describe how imaginative play may be supported in an early years setting.

9. Explain why it is essential to observe children in order to monitor the effectiveness of the provision.

10. Suggest one way in which you may gain feedback on your practice.

Glossary

A

Active participation: gives children and families a say in how provision is made for them

Activity: what will be happening at a particular time

Advocate: someone who puts forward ideas, views or suggestions on the behalf of someone else

Anaphylactic shock: a severe allergic reaction which can be fatal

Anoxia: a decrease in the level of oxygen

Anti-discriminatory (or anti-bias) practice: promoting equality of opportunity by —

- being positive about differences and similarities between people
- identifying and challenging prejudice
- taking positive action to counter discrimination

Axons: part of a neuron cell which carries electrical impulses

C

Caesarean section: a surgical procedure in which the baby is removed from the womb via the abdomen

Care status: where children deemed to be in need are the responsibility of the local authority because a care order has been granted by the courts

Child abuse: harm or the likelihood of harm from physical, emotional or sexual abuse, neglect and failure to thrive not based on illness, or bullying and harassment

Child-centred: a way of working that focuses on the needs and interests of the child

Child protection: part of the safeguarding process where it is necessary to take action when there is a reasonable belief that a child is at risk of significant harm

Communication: a way of sending signals to other people; includes body language, facial expression, gesture and language

Confidential information: that which should be shared only with people who have a right to have it, for example your lead practitioner, supervisor or manager

Confidentiality: not sharing with other people or passing on personal information about the families you are working with, except when it is in a child's best interests to do so

Continuous provision: resources, toys and equipment that are put out for children to play with throughout the session

Control measure: any activity or measures put in place to control or minimise identified risks

Culture: the attitudes and values underpinning patterns of tradition and custom which determine everyday aspects of life

D

Dendrites: part of a neuron cell to which other cells can link

Disability: 'a physical or mental impairment which has a substantial and long-term adverse effect on a person's ability to perform normal day-to-day activities' (Disability Discrimination Act 1995)

Disclosure of abuse: when a child tells or implies to you that he or she has been abused

Discrimination: treating someone less or more favourably than other people, because they or their family are seen as belonging to a particular group in society

Diversity: the differences between individuals and groups in society arising from gender, ethnic origins, social, cultural or religious background, family structure, disabilities, sexuality and appearance

Duty of care: a requirement to exercise a 'reasonable' degree of attention and caution to avoid negligence which would lead to harm to other people

E

Early Learning Goals: targets in the Early Years Foundation Stage curriculum that it is expected that children at the end of the reception year will meet

Early Years Profile: a record to show how children are progressing towards the Early Learning Goals that is completed by reception teachers in England

Echolalia: a baby's babble — meaningless and automatic repetition of vocalisations made by another person

Eczema: common skin condition characterised by intense itching and a rash

Egocentricity: the self-centredness of very young children who do not comprehend anyone or anything beyond themselves and their own feelings

Empathy: the ability to understand situations from another person's viewpoint

Equal concern: taking as much care to promote the opportunities and progress of one child as you do for any other child

Equality of opportunity: each individual in society experiences opportunities to achieve and flourish which are as good as the opportunities experienced by other people

Evaluate: identify the strength of your performance — how well you are doing, and how you could improve

Evidence-based practice: practice which is influenced by objective evidence derived from research

G

Genetics: the unique biological code that each person inherits

Gross motor skills: whole limb movements

H

Hazard: something that has the potential to cause harm

Heuristic play: play with household and recyclable objects that encourage toddlers to explore

Holistically: taken together as a whole

I

Impairment: describes a condition which is different from what is usually expected in a child at a particular age or stage of development

Inclusion: a process of identifying, understanding and breaking down barriers to participation and belonging

Individuality: the uniqueness of a child or young person

Integrated working: different services joining together to offer more effective care for young children

Interpreting: translating one language into another language while it is being spoken

K

Key person: a person who has a special relationship with the child and their family and who acts as a surrogate attachment figure when the child is separated from parents and carers

L

Language: structured communication with rules and a set of symbols that are spoken, written or signed

Learning difficulty: a problem in processing information in the same way or at the same speed as others

Locomotive: large movements that allow babies and children to gain mobility

Likelihood: the probability of any harm from the hazard actually happening

M

Makaton: a system of signs to help children understand the meaning of words and phrases

Marketing: promoting your business to potential customers

Medical model of disability: this treats the person as a sick patient and tends to focus on 'How can we make this person more normal?'

Metacognition skills: a set of skills which allow the user to make the best use of their cognitive abilities and to gain control over some of their thinking

Monitor: review the processes and outcomes of what you do; taking a hard look at the way you work and how you do it

Multi-agency working: different services working together to meet the needs of young children and their parents or carers

N

Neurons: cells in the brain which transmit electrical impulses to other cells

P

Participation: concerned with giving children and families a say in how provision is made for them

Picture Exchange Communication System (PECS): a resource that helps children communicate by exchanging pictures with adults

Policy: a written statement which guides how you work in one area of your practice

Portage: a system of supporting children with additional needs that is carried out in children's homes by portage workers who involve parents in the process

Positive images: visual and other representations showing people who are sometimes marginalised or discriminated against in roles and activities which go against stereotypes

Pre-eclampsia: a life threatening condition in late pregnancy that often requires babies to be born earlier

Prejudice: a judgment or opinion, often negative, of a person or group, made without careful consideration of accurate relevant information, which may lead to the view that some people are inferior to other human beings, and of less worth and significance

Procedures: step-by-step plans for dealing with a particular situation

Puberty: the process of sexual maturation

Public inquiry: an official review of events or actions ordered by the government. The report that is produced makes recommendations for improving practice

R

Rating: a value to show the seriousness and level of risk. The higher the numeric value, the more significant the risk

Reflective practitioner: someone who takes a questioning approach to their work, taking time to think critically and assess the effectiveness of what they do at work

Risk: the outcome or likely impact of the hazard associated with the activity to be undertaken

Risk assessment: process of assessing hazards and identifying control measures for all activities and outings

S

Safeguarding: promoting children's welfare and putting measures in place to improve children's safety and prevent abuse

Self-confidence: feeling able to do things and capable of achieving

Self-esteem: valuing ourselves, and seeing ourselves as being of value in other people's eyes

Sensory materials: materials that are usually tactile and will stimulate children's senses e.g. clay, cornflour, sand

Separation anxiety: the under-threes often find it difficult to cope with being separated from the familiar adults in their lives

Shadowing: following another practitioner in order to understand his or her way of working

Social inclusion policies: aim to enable all people to participate fully in society

Social model of disability: recognises that discrimination against disabled people is created by society, not by disabled people's impairments

Special educational need: a child or young person who needs additional support or facilities in order to access education

Specific legal requirement: requirements that have to be complied with in the way stated

Special needs: an umbrella term for children whose needs are different from those of other children

Specific needs: specific difficulties that a child or young person may have that may relate to an impairment, medical condition or emotional problem

Speech: vocalised language

Statement: statutory assessment which outlines individual needs of a child and the specific provision required

Statutory guidance: guidance that providers must follow when complying with the legal requirements

Stereotypes: generalisations about a person and assumptions (usually inaccurate) that because they are part of a particular group, that individual will have certain characteristics, the same needs as all other members of that group and will (or should) behave in a particular way

Stranger anxiety: from the age of about 8 months, it is usual for children to become wary of people they don't know

Sustained shared thinking: ways in which children are encouraged by adults to use language to explore a topic, object or concept

Synapses: network of connections which enable neurons to transmit electrical impulses, so passing information from one part of the brain to another

W

Weaning: the process of encouraging babies to move from a milk-only diet to taking in other foods

List of weblinks

SC1

www.ico.gov.uk

SC2

www.ncb.org.uk/dotpdf/open_access_2/earlyyears_inclusion_20080228.pdf

CYP3.2

www.bullying.co.uk
www.kidscape.co.uk
www.nspcc.org.uk
www.winstonswish.org.uk

CYP3.3

www.childpolicyinfo.childreninscotland.org.uk
www.cpinfo.org.uk
www.ci-ni.org.uk
www.childreninwales.org.uk
www.dcsf.gov.uk/everychildmatters/safeguardingandsocialcare
www.isa-gov.org.uk
www.nspcc.org.uk
www.childline.org.uk
www.kidscape.org.uk
www.bullying.co.uk
www.baspcan.org.uk
www.teachernet.gov.uk
www.kidscape.org.uk/childrenteens/keepsafe.shtml
www.dcsf.gov.uk/byronreview
www.plymouth.gov.uk/safeguarding_children_in_cyber_world.pdf

CYP3.4

www.hse.gov.uk
www.capt.org.uk
www.dcsf.gov.uk
www.deni.gov.uk
www.standards.dcsf.gov.uk/eyfs/site/requirements/index.htm

www.scotland.gov.uk/Publications/2005/04/12103332/33329
www.hse.gov.uk/services/education/index.htm
www.hse.gov.uk/services/education/schoolvisits.htm

CYP3.5

www.nationalstrategies.standards.dcsf.gov.uk/earlyyears
www.mumsnet.com
www.childrens-centres.org/default.aspx

CYP3.6

www.nspcc.org.uk
www.everychildmatters.org.uk

CYP3.7

www.gypsy-traveller.org
www.everychildmatters.org.uk
www.ncb.org.uk
www.crae.org.uk
www.byc.org.uk
www.nspcc.org.uk
www.coram.org.uk
www.ncvo-vol.org.uk
www.ncvys.org.uk
www.ukyouthparliament.co.uk
www.everychildmatters.org.uk
www.makaton.org
www.portage.org.uk
www.earlysupport.org.uk
www.poverty.org

EYMP1

www.dcsf.gov.uk
www.foundationphasewales.com
www.tls.gov.uk
www.nicurriculum.org

EYMP2

www.tls.gov.uk

www.foundationphasewales.com
www.nicurriculum.org
www.early-years.org

EYMP3

www.fsid.org.uk
www.eatwell.gov.uk
www.bhf.org.uk
www.food.gov.uk
www.diabetes.org.uk
www.coeliac.org.uk
www.vegsoc.org
www.vegansociety.com
www.weightconcern.org.uk
www.bhf.org.uk
www.nhs.uk/change4life
www.hse.gov.uk

EYMP4

http://nationalstrategies.standards.dcsf.gov.uk/
http://wales.gov.uk/topics/educationandskills/
www.ltscotland.org.uk/earlyyears/
http://eppe.ioe.ac.uk/

EYMP5

www.ican.org.uk
www.literacytrust.org.uk
http://eppe.ioe.ac.uk

CYPOP1

www.tlrp.org.uk

CYPOP2

www.sunsmart.org.uk/index.htm
www.rospa.com
www.capt.org.uk
www.food.gov.uk
www.eatwell.gov.uk
www.nice.org.uk
www.vegsoc.org

CYPOP5

www.ofsted.gov.uk
wales.gov.uk/cssiwsubsite/newcssiw
www.carecommission.com
www.ncma.org.uk
www.childminding.org
www.nicma.org
www.ico.gov.uk
www.hse.gov.uk

CYPOP6

www.unicef.org/crc
www.equalityhumanrights.com
www.teachernet.gov.uk

Index